Ethics for Journali

WITHDRAWN FROM STOCK

Ethics for Journalists tackles many of the issues which journalists face in their everyday lives – from the media's supposed obsession with sex, sleaze and sensationalism, to issues of regulation and censorship. Its accessible style and question and answer approach highlights the relevance of ethical issues for everyone involved in journalism, both trainees and professionals, whether working in print, broadcast or new media.

Ethics for Journalists provides a comprehensive overview of ethical dilemmas and features interviews with a number of journalists, including the celebrated investigative reporter Phillip Knightley. Presenting a range of imaginative strategies for improving media standards and supported by a thorough bibliography and a wide ranging list of websites, *Ethics for Journalists, Second Edition*, considers many problematic subjects including:

- representations of gender, race, sexual orientation, disability, mental health and suicide
- ethics online – 'citizen journalism' and its challenges to 'professionalism'
- controversial calls for a privacy law to restrain the power of the press
- journalistic techniques such as sourcing the news, doorstepping, death-knocks and the use of subterfuge
- the impact of competition, ownership and advertising on media standards
- the handling of confidential sources and the dilemmas of war and peace reporting.

A 'must read' for anyone studying journalism ethics or working in the field.

Richard Keeble is Professor of Journalism at Lincoln University. He is author of *The Newspapers Handbook* (4th edition, 2005), editor of *Print Journalism: A Critical Introduction* (2005) and co-editor of *The Journalistic Imagination: Literary Journalists from Defoe to Capote and Carter* (2007).

Media Skills

SERIES EDITOR: RICHARD KEEBLE, LINCOLN UNIVERSITY
SERIES ADVISERS: WYNFORD HICKS AND JENNY MCKAY

The *Media Skills* series provides a concise and thorough introduction to a rapidly changing media landscape. Each book is written by media and journalism lecturers or experienced professionals and is a key resource for a particular industry. Offering helpful advice and information and using practical examples from print, broadcast and digital media, as well as discussing ethical and regulatory issues, *Media Skills* books are essential guides for students and media professionals.

English for Journalists
3rd edition
Wynford Hicks

Writing for Journalists
2nd edition
*Wynford Hicks with Sally Adams,
Harriett Gilbert and Tim Holmes*

Interviewing for Radio
Jim Beaman

**Web Production for Writers and
Journalists**
2nd edition
Jason Whittaker

Ethics for Journalists
2nd edition
Richard Keeble

Scriptwriting for the Screen
2nd edition
Charlie Moritz

Interviewing for Journalists
*Sally Adams, with an introduction and
additional material by Wynford Hicks*

**Researching for Television
and Radio**
Ad le Emm

Reporting for Journalists
Chris Frost

Subediting for Journalists
Wynford Hicks and Tim Holmes

**Designing for Newspapers and
Magazines**
Chris Frost

**Writing for Broadcast
Journalists**
Rick Thompson

**Freelancing For Television
and Radio**
Leslie Mitchell

Programme Making for Radio
Jim Beaman

Magazine Production
Jason Whittaker

Find more details of current *Media Skills* books and forthcoming titles at
www.producing.routledge.com

Ethics
for
Journalists

Second Edition

Richard Keeble

Routledge
Taylor & Francis Group

LONDON AND NEW YORK

First published 2001
by Routledge
2 Park Square, Milton Park, Abingdon, Oxon OX14 4RN

Simultaneously published in the USA and Canada
by Routledge
711 Third Avenue, New York, NY 10017

Reprinted 2004, 2005

This edition published 2009

Routledge is an imprint of the Taylor & Francis Group, an informa business

© 2001, 2009 Richard Keeble

Typeset in Goudy and Scala Sans by
Florence Production Ltd, Stoodleigh, Devon

British Library Cataloguing in Publication Data
A catalogue record for this book is available from the British Library

Library of Congress Cataloging in Publication Data
Keeble, Richard, 1948–
    Ethics for journalists/Richard Keeble. – 2nd ed.
        p. cm.
    Includes bibliographical references and index.
    1. Journalistic ethics.   I. Title.
    PN4756.K37 2008
    070.4–dc22   2008022612

ISBN10: 0–415–43074–7 (hbk)
ISBN10: 0–415–43076–3 (pbk)
ISBN10: 0–203–69882–7 (ebk)

ISBN13: 978–0–415–43074–6 (hbk)
ISBN13: 978–0–415–43076–0 (pbk)
ISBN13: 978–0–203–69882–2 (ebk)

For Maryline
With all my love

Contents

Preface

A lot has happened since the first edition of *Ethics for Journalists* was published in 2001. On a personal level, in 2003 I moved (after 19 years) from City University to the University of Lincoln. Not only have I enjoyed myself thoroughly at Lincoln, but I have learned a lot from teaching journalism ethics and international human rights to the lively and always appreciative students. So sincere thanks to my students and colleagues who have been so supportive and challenging.

Since 2001, the journalism ethics debate in the UK has exploded – and this is reflected in the vast number of recent texts referenced throughout the book and listed in the substantial bibliography at the end. The Internet has also given birth to countless sites and blogs devoted to media ethics – and the most important of these are acknowledged here.

But the essential message of the text remains the same: the basic roles of the journalist are to promote peace and understanding, to work with honesty, clarity and compassion, to give voice to the voiceless, the desperately poor, the oppressed; to challenge stereotyping and expose corruption and lying – and to respect diversity and difference. The text is built around questions since the listening/questioning approach lies at the heart of ethics. My spin on the issues raised is usually clear (sometimes even through the kind of questions I ask). But at the same time I try to acknowledge the range of responses and constantly question my own.

I have also been the editor of *Ethical Space: The International Journal of Communication Ethics* since 2003 (and most recently joint editor with Donald Matheson, of Canterbury University, New Zealand) and that role has put me in touch with media ethicists from around the world and helped expand my knowledge of the field. *Ethical Space* is the quarterly journal of the Institute of Communication Ethics, which I helped launch, and I have benefited enormously from the contacts and friendships I have made there – with Robert Beckett, Jule de Varenne, David Houlton, Fiona Thompson, Anne Gregory, Paul Jackson, Ian Richards, Simon Rogerson, John Strain, Johanna Fawkes, Chris Atton, Cees Hamelink, Simon Cross, Will Barton, Gitte Meyer, Omar Swartz, Pratap Rughani, Chris Frost, Karen Sanders, Mike Jempson, Gavin Fairbairn, Valerie Alia, Simon Goldsworthy, David Finkelstein, Clifford Christians, Nick Winkfield, Marlis Prinzing and Stephan Russ-Mohl (of the European Journalism Observatory), Robin Williamson and Bernard Margueritte (of the International Communications Forum), Michael Foley, Antonia Carling, Thom Blair, Saviour Chircop, Nick Jones, James Winter, Richard Franklin (of Arima Publishing), Julian Petley, Jane Taylor, Sonia Ambrosio de Nelson, Milverton Wallace, Joseph Borg, Raphael Cohen-Almagor, Frank Davies and John Mair.

Special thanks to Tessa Mayes, Kristine Lowe, Phillip Knightley and Jon Grubb for spending the time (at short notice) to respond to my searching questions for the ethical profiles at the end of Chapter 1 – and for the support they have given in many different ways to the journalism programmes at Lincoln University. Thanks also to Don Hale, Dorothy Byrne, Bridget Kendall, Yvonne Ridley, Libby Purves, Ahmed Versi, Fareena Alam, David Woodfall, Yosri Fouda, Milica Pesic, John Pilger, Fuad Nahdi, Jake Lynch, Judith Vidal-Hall, Marc Wadsworth, Bob Franklin, Peter Cole, Jackie Harrison, Martin Conboy, Tony Harcup, Stuart Allan, Sarah Maltby (of the War and Media Network), David Edwards and David Cromwell (of Medialens) for helping keep me in touch with the many debates that rage in the rapidly changing media environment of today. Special thanks, too, to Aileen Storry and all at Routledge for their support over the years.

Sadly, three of my friends and colleagues, Peter McGregor, Claude-Jean Bertrand and Dennis Foy (all of them important though contrasting voices in the global debate over media standards) have died recently – and so this text is written in part in memory of them and their outstanding contributions.

Withcall,
Lincolnshire,
May 2008

1
The ethical challenge

Why ethical dilemmas are especially difficult today

Ethical inquiry is crucial for all media workers – and managers. It encourages journalists to examine their basic moral and political principles; their responsibilities and rights; their relationship to their employer and audience; their ultimate goals. Self-criticism and the reflective, questioning approach are always required. And journalists need to be eloquent about ethics and politics, confident in articulating and handling the issues – and imaginative in their promotion of standards, both individually and collectively.[1] But many factors in Britain are making ethical/political challenges particularly difficult today.

- The helter-skelter expansion of the media industry in Britain in recent years and its increasing globalisation may suggest it is impossible to apply general principles to all of them. For example, in 1980 only three television channels were available; by 2005 this figure had shot up to more than 400 (Kuhn 2007: 11). Between 1995 and 2005, the number of radio stations broadcasting in the UK increased by more than 100 to 325 (ibid.: 13). By December 2006 the figure had risen to 389. And thousands of radio stations broadcasting on the web were accessible with a simple click of a button. In 2007, an estimated five million people in Britain were regular users of the social networking site Facebook (then valued at $15 billion: £7.3 billion) while the two most frequently searched terms on Google were Bebo and MySpace, both social networking sites.

- Along with the plethora of media outlets go the many journalistic roles: reporters, designers, sub-editors, reviewers, photographers, editors, freelances, broadcast producers, camera (or camera phone) operators, web designers, researchers, HTML experts. As the various platforms (print, online, video, podcasting and so on) converge so the boundaries between journalists' different tasks merge. And the range of specific ethical dilemmas ends up being enormous. Is it possible to speak in general terms?

- The dominant journalistic culture stresses the importance of technical skills (this bias being intensified with the introduction of new technology, direct-input and multi-skilling) and 'on the job' experience. Accordingly, the reflective, analytical, ethical approach is downgraded. There is a general scepticism in the industry about 'political correctness' which is often linked with issues such as racism, sexism, militarism and this serves to constrain further ethical debate among mainstream journalists.

- At a time of hyper-competition and falling circulations among the media, the need for profits in an advertising/ratings-driven environment can be seen to outweigh all other considerations. As Colin Sparks (1999: 46) argues:

> Newspapers in Britain are first and foremost businesses. They do not exist to report news, to act as watchdogs for the public, to be a check on the doings of government, to defend the ordinary citizens against abuses of power, to unearth scandals or to do any of the other fine and noble things that are sometimes claimed for the press. They exist to make money, just as any other business does. To the extent that they discharge any of their public functions, they do so in order to succeed as businesses.

Similarly Edward Herman, in stressing the role of the mainstream, corporate media in propagandising dominant, capitalist 'values', argues (1996):

> The crucial structural factors derive from the fact that the dominant media are firmly imbedded in the market system. They are profit-seeking businesses, owned by wealthy people (or other companies); they are funded largely by advertisers who are also profit-seeking entities and who want their ads to appear in a supporting selling environment. The media are also dependent on government and major business firms as information sources, and both efficiency and political considerations,

and frequently overlapping interests cause a certain degree of solidarity to prevail among the government, major media and other corporate businesses.

Piers Morgan, the former editor of the *Daily Mirror*, articulated with admirable frankness the ethical vacuum at the heart of the mainstream media when he told a profiler in the *Observer Magazine* of 22 December 2002: 'Tabloid newspapers are a fast-moving torrent of contradictions, U-turns, self-serving policy changes and shocking hypocrisy. That's why I love them so much.' Of his earlier time in charge of the *News of the World*, Morgan commented:

> I was . . . lacking in any real humanity for the mayhem we were causing, which is probably the right way to be on the *News of the World*, because the humanity aspect just compromises you. There's no point in pretending what you're doing is good for the human spirit. Most of the time, the public interest defence was trumped up nonsense. The reason we were doing it was to sell papers and amuse and titillate people.
>
> (Hattenstone 2005 cited in Harcup 2007a: 42)

Even Andrew Marr, the highly respected former BBC political editor, reflected the cynicism so embedded in the profession when he suggested in *My Trade*, his brilliantly witty and idiosyncratic overview of the history and current state of journalism, that the term 'responsible journalism' should be shunned (2004: 5): 'Responsible to whom? The state? Never. To "the people"? But which people, and of what views? To the readers? It is vanity to think you know them. Responsible, then, to some general belief in truth and accuracy? Well, that would be nice.'

• Ethics implies freedom to choose. But journalists are constrained by so many factors – proprietors, fear, the law, time and space to name but a few (see Chapter 10). There is much talk about the freedom of the press but the freedom of the individual journalist (particularly of the young trainee) in any media operation is restricted by vested interests, routinised working practices and hierarchical, bureaucratic, organisational structures.

• Further questions complicate the issues: can, say, gender representations by journalists be considered without reference to the powerful stereotypes of male and female sexuality found in advertising, Hollywood films, computer games, millions of websites and TV soaps? Can journalistic ethics be separated from their broader cultural and political contexts?

- How credibly can we debate ethics in journalism when the financial structures of the media are so transparently unfair? On the one hand, editor-in-chief of Associated Newspapers (owners of the *Daily Mail*, London's *Evening Standard* and the *Metro* series of freesheets), Paul Dacre, received a 21 per cent pay increase in 2007 bringing his total remuneration to more than £1.4 million while chief executive of the regional newspaper publisher, Johnston Press, Tim Bowdler, earned more than £1 million. At the other end of the scale graduate trainees are earning around £11,000 (when the average graduate salary is £20,000) while an NUJ survey in 2007 found that journalists' pay is so poor 80 per cent cannot afford the average mortgage. An investigation by the *Guardian* in September 2007 (Lawrence 2007) into the exploitation of a million agency workers (many of them migrants desperate for work) showed that Trinity Mirror, publishers of the *Daily Mirror*, were employing African and East European agency staff as printers 'on lower rates of pay'. Trinity Mirror denied the allegations. And right at the bottom of the career heap, journalism students often do many months on grinding work attachments for no money at all, as an NUJ survey revealed in April 2008 (Smith and Gallagher 2008). Perhaps the corruption at the heart of Fleet Street is best epitomised in the career of Conrad Black, one time proprietor of the *Telegraphs*. A firm friend of former Prime Minister Margaret Thatcher and prominent Freemason, he was convicted in July 2006 (along with other company executives) of defrauding his own company Hollinger International of $6.1 million (£3 million) and sentenced to six and a half years in prison. At the height of his career he owned more than 200 titles including the *Jerusalem Post* and the *Chicago Sun-Times*, and had a fortune estimated at $136 million.

- Moreover, while the Internet makes even the hyper-local media accessible to an international audience and globalisation trends in media monopoly ownership increase (along with the global ambitions of US/UK militarism), is it relevant and even possible to study media ethics in relation to one country, Britain, as here? Is it possible to discuss the relative cultural and political freedoms in the West without detailed reference to the suppression of such freedoms and the financial impoverishment in Second and Third World countries on which they are based?

How will you respond?

In the face of the vastness and complexities of the ethical dilemmas thrown up by the modern media, how is the journalist to react? What precisely is good journalism? What are the models for 'good' practice? How can the bad, the ugly and the unacceptable be eliminated? Journalists often focus on skills when describing a 'good journalist'. Thus, 'having a nose for a story', being able to take a reliable note and handle the computer technology confidently, writing accurately and colourfully are among the attributes commonly stressed. However, most journalists, if pressed to identify the strictly ethical aspects of 'good journalism', are likely to display ambivalent, contradictory and confused attitudes. To clarify the issue, it might be useful to identify a few prominent positions.

The cynical approach

You may be tempted to adopt the cynical, amoral approach. This was summed up by a national newspaper editor, invited to a London journalism school to give a talk on ethics. 'Efficks – wot's that?' he asked, bemused. And so he simply proceeded to tell the gathered throng of students about his life and (highly successful) times in the industry. It is an attitude based on the conviction that ethical issues have little relevance for journalists. There is not enough time for them, and journalists have little power to influence them anyway. Profits are at the root of all journalism, so why bother with such idealistic fancies as ethics? 'Don't let the facts get in the way of a good story' is an instruction often heard in newsroom (Frost 2007: 11). As Raphael Cohen-Almagor (2001: xvii) comments:

> The concept of media ethics is conceived to be an oxymoron. Sadly many segments of the modern media are stripped of almost all ethical concerns. In a reality of competition, ratings, and economic considerations, ethics becomes a secondary,

> sometimes irritating issue ... Many people in the industry
> portray their work as a hack, a trade and not as a profession,
> in order to legitimise their moral-free conduct.

Such cynicism may be linked to a philosophical, existential position (propounded by the nineteenth century German, Max Stirner) which regards all human experience as essentially amoral. Ethical egotism takes a cynical view of the altruism behind moral conduct, suggesting that all actions (however much they are clothed in the rhetoric of morality) are essentially motivated by self interest (see Paterson 1971). A variant on this appeared in the thinking of Friedrich Nietzsche (1844–1900) who described himself as an 'immoralist', arguing in *Beyond Good and Evil* (1886) that there were no moral facts and that evil made no sense (see Sanders 2003: 23).

Often accompanying this stance, paradoxically, is a belief in the market. In other words, people get what they want and deserve. If the masses want trashy TV, then why should middle-class, snooty journalists with their highfalutin' ethical concerns, deny them that? The cynical approach has been evident in widespread criticisms by mainstream journalists of media training courses which are increasingly incorporating courses on ethics. Consequently, media studies have, in the national media, acquired the demonised status held by sociology in the 1960s and peace studies in the 1980s. A leader in the *Independent* of 31 October 1996 summed up this view bluntly saying 'this paper regards a degree in media studies as a disqualification for a career of journalism'.

The stress on individual conscience

Some journalists prefer to adopt *ad hoc* responses to specific ethical challenges rather than follow some broadly defined ethical system. Such an approach can be accompanied by an ethical relativism according to which moral judgments are viewed as varying across historical periods and cultures. Thus all moral systems can be considered equally good, even if they are antithetical. But, as Sanders (somewhat critical of the relativist position) argues:

> If we are a relativist, faced with someone who believes in the
> rightness of child sacrifice, we would have no way of advancing

an argument in our favour. We would have to maintain that they have as much right to believe that child sacrifice was acceptable as I to say that it was wrong. In a certain sense, relativism extinguishes ethics because it maintains that neither right nor wrong exist apart from the opinions we adopt about them. No opinion has any authority apart from the point of view of the person who adopts it.

(2003: 23)

Formal codes of ethics are viewed with scepticism. As American media theorist John C. Merrill argues: 'Journalists must seek ethical guidance from within themselves not from codes of organisations, commissions or councils.' Bob Norris, former *Times* correspondent, says on codes (2000: 325): 'they all have one thing in common: they are not worth the paper they are written on.' He continues: 'Every story is different and every reporter is driven by the compulsion to get the story and get it first. To imagine that he or she is going to consult the union's code of ethics while struggling to meet a deadline is to live in cloud-cuckoo land.' But he stresses he lives by his personal code of ethics (ibid.: 329); 'I will not wear a uniform, carry a gun or act as a spy for my own government or any other. Yet I have known reporters who will do any or all of these things and regard them as perfectly ethical.' He describes how, when working for *The Times*, he was asked to spy for his country by the Military Attaché at the British High Commission in Lagos. He turned down the offer. 'I later learned that his offer had been taken up by one of my colleagues on a rival paper.'

Former assistant editor of the *Observer* David Randall (1996: 93) takes a similar approach: 'So these journalistic ethics are either the codification of prevailing behaviour and culture or an irrelevant exhortation to standards of behaviour that are doomed to be unmet. Either way, there is not a great deal of point to them.' This emphasis on personal conscience is often linked by journalists with an idiosyncratic, maverick stance according to which it becomes the responsibility of the virtuous journalist to question authority and, where necessary, break rules. As Klaidman and Beauchamp argue (1987: 138): 'Persons seeking wholeness and maturity rise above the implicit utilitarianism of rule-keeping to develop the conscience of virtuous persons. To follow rules blindly is to surrender moral impulse.'

The stress on professionalism

As a journalist you may be inclined to claim a professional commitment to journalistic standards. Such an approach can be driven by a religious or humanistic value system. Sanders (2003: 32–9), for instance, draws on Aristotle (384–322 BC) and the Christian tradition of virtue ethics (which places practical wisdom at the heart of doing good) for a definition of professional ethics. Underlying this approach is a range of closely interlinked notions, listed below.

The free press

The free press is a central feature of the dominant value system of Western, capitalist democracy, distinguishing it clearly from, say, military or Islamic dictatorships where state-controlled propaganda enjoys total control. According to the theory, the free press, independent of the state and free from any direct funding by political parties, mediates between the rulers and the ruled, providing the necessary political, financial and social information to the electorate which they can use to form rational voting decisions. As John O'Neill says (1992: 15): 'A free market brings with it a free press that supplies the diversity of opinion and access to information that a citizenry requires in order to act in a democratic, responsible manner. The free market, journalism and democracy form an interdependent trinity of institutions in an open society.' Charles Moore (1997), then editor of the *Daily Telegraph*, summed up this view when he described the general election of 1997 as 'the sacred moment in a democracy'. He continued: 'The people's choice is what validates the whole process. Newspapers must try to give their readers all the material they need to make that choice.'

The free press notion essentially emerged from the Reformation's stress on the liberty of religious expression. This became part of a broader assertion and defence of freedom of expression in general. One of the most celebrated celebrations of the 'free press' principle came in John Stuart Mill's 1859 essay *On Liberty*. Here he argued that free expression was essential not only for the political health of the country but for humanity's ability to expand its knowledge and progress scientifically (see Hargreaves 2003: 45):

> The peculiar evil of silencing an expression of opinion is that
> it is robbing the human race; posterity as well as the existing

generation; those who dissent from the opinion, still more than those who hold it.

Accordingly, the media carry special responsibilities to guard the public's 'right to know' – such as later enshrined in Article 19 of the Universal Declaration of Human Rights (Bromley 2000: 113–14). According to Brian Winston (1998: 44) John Milton's assertion of '[T]he liberty to know, to utter and to argue freely according to conscience, above all' marked the beginnings of a powerful dissenting tradition in our political life. Yet until the 1998 legislation incorporating the European Convention on Human Rights into British law, there were no legal guarantees of freedom of expression or of the press such as that contained in the First Amendment to the American constitution. The concept of the free individual is also critical here. Emerging during the Renaissance and achieving maturity in the Enlightenment, this concept was developed by the French philosopher Jean-Jacques Rousseau (1712–78) who promoted the notion of the self-determination of the personality as the highest good (Klaidman and Beauchamp op. cit.: 59). Thus, you may wish to argue, journalists, operating freely, are able to pursue the highest professional standards. Or they can serve as agenda setters, alerting their audience to the significance of an issue, and encouraging them to place it on their personal agendas of important issues (McNair 1996: 18).

The press/media as Fourth Estate

The notion of the press/media as the Fourth Estate is closely linked to the free press concept. First propounded by the historian Thomas Babington Macaulay (1800–59), for whom the first three estates of the realm were the Lords temporal, Lords spiritual and the Commons, it stresses the watchdog role of the media in providing checks on abuses of power by both government and professionals. In this spirit, mainstream journalists often say: 'The best stories are those that afflict the comfortable and comfort the afflicted, the ones that the people of power do not want told,' as, indeed, Peter Beaumont and John Sweeney (2000) wrote in their *Observer* tribute to two colleagues, killed covering the fighting in Sierra Leone. Accordingly, journalists assume the role of the 'public's guardians' protecting them against the moral failures of the authorities. This role is perhaps best reflected in the many campaigns local and national media run (complete with appropriate logos) bringing authorities to account. Details of the hundreds of campaigns run each year by local newspapers are listed at www.holdthefrontpage.co.uk. For instance:

- In September 1997, the *Independent on Sunday* launched a campaign to decriminalise cannabis, inspiring 16,000 people to march in support in March 1998.
- In May 1998, the *Guardian* joined the Jubilee 2000 campaign and launched its own 'The new slavery' campaign aiming to relieve the poorest countries of their debt burden.
- In November 1998, the *Evening Chronicle*, Newcastle, forced the local council to think again about charging for Sunday parking in the city centre.
- Early in 1999, the *Lancashire Evening Post* launched a campaign to persuade the Queen to make Preston a city.
- During the NATO attacks on Yugoslavia in 1999, many newspapers raised money for Kosovo refugees (though did any collect for the Chechen refugees when the Russians began attacking them soon afterwards?).
- In February 2000, a campaign by the *Oxford Mail* to create an offence of corporate killing, following the Paddington rail disaster of October 1999, was backed by an all-party group of MPs.
- In March 2000, the *Manchester Evening News* celebrated victory in its 'Metrolink for the Millennium' campaign after Deputy Prime Minister John Prescott announced plans to spend nearly £300m extending the city's tram system.
- In April 2000, the *Huddersfield Daily Examiner* won a victory in its campaign to save a local maternity unit after 10,000 people signed a petition.
- In September 2003, the *Eastern Daily Press* finally won the right to bid for lottery funding for its 'We care' campaign to support unpaid carers in Norfolk.
- In December 2003, Liverpool's *Daily Post* was able to celebrate victory in its 'Fight for a Flight' campaign to restore the city's air link to London.
- In August 2004, the *News and Star*, Carlisle, and *Dundee Courier* campaigned to save local regiments after defence secretary Geoff Hoon announced cuts of 20,000 local army jobs.

- A campaign by the Exeter *Express and Echo* to reduce the use of plastic bags and to cut excess packaging in November 2007 won the official seal of approval from Prime Minister Gordon Brown (shown smiling and signing outside No. 10).
- In January 2008, the *Independent* launched a petition to save an Afghan student from being sentenced to death for blasphemy. Sayed Pervez Kambaksh simply downloaded an Internet report on women's rights – but was then tried and convicted by a religious court in a secret session.

Interestingly, such ideals of campaigning/muckraking journalism can coexist in an often ambiguous relationship with the ideology of objective journalism. Similarly, the Fourth Estate concept is often linked to support for a liberal model of adversarial state-media relations. This model appears particularly prominent during wars. As Derrik Mercer commented in a major study of the Falklands War coverage (1987: 3): 'The clash of interests between media and government has always been fundamental and frequently acrimonious. In a democracy this is inevitable and many would say desirable.'

The Watergate investigation by the two *Washington Post* journalists, Bob Woodward and Carl Bernstein (immortalised in Alan J. Pakula's 1976 film, *All the President's Men* starring Robert Redford and Dustin Hoffman as the intrepid hacks), is seen as the most famous example of this 'adversarialism' since their reports ultimately led to the resignation of US President Richard Nixon in 1974 (see Burgh 2000: 78–9; and www.washingtonpost.com/wp-srv/politics/special/watergate/index.html for the *Post*'s full coverage analysis, interactive features and multimedia content). Yet Watergate perhaps most significantly highlights the limits of the adversarial model since Woodward's celebrated confidential source, Deep Throat, kept secret for 30 years, finally revealed himself to be W. Mark Felt, a disgruntled former FBI Associate Director and not a political activist outside the dominant elite. Moreover, Schudson (1992) argued that the role of the *Washington Post* duo in bringing down the president had been exaggerated; other government agencies, politicians and lawyers had 'forced disclosure that kept the Watergate story in the public eye'. And Herman and Chomsky (1988) pointed out that while the break-in at the Democratic Party's HQ had received massive coverage, little attention had been given to equally illegal acts by the FBI against progressive parties of the Left.

Objectivity, neutrality, impartiality and balance

These concepts were first used by journalists in the latter part of the nineteenth century in the United States and Britain, alongside notions of professionalism (McNair 1998: 64–77). As newspapers gradually lost their party affiliations, journalists worked to establish their independence as searchers after objective truth. And news became a commodity which acquired its market value on account of its accuracy (see Chalaby 1998). Over time, these concepts were modified to mean not so much the quest for absolute truth, rather more an assertion of the need to strive for truth in the face of subjective anarchy and propagandist bias. Accordingly, sources are balanced, fact is separated from fiction, value judgments are avoided in reporting news. Matthew Kieran (1998: 23) argues that 'it has become increasingly fashionable, within cultural, media and even journalistic studies, to dismiss claims concerning objectivity'. Bad journalism, he says, is 'truth-indifferent and fails to respect truth-promoting practices'. And he concludes (ibid.: 35): 'Honesty, discipline and impartiality are required to be a good journalist.' Similarly, John Wilson, former editorial policy controller for the BBC, comments (1996: 44):

> For the normal run of programme making and newspaper reporting, balanced treatment means being even-handed, not giving one side of an argument unreasonable attention to its advantage or disadvantage. It means exploring issues in an uncommitted way so that viewers, listeners and readers appreciate all the important arguments, including the weight of support they enjoy.

Veteran Scots journalist Sinclair Dunnett (1996: 38) said the good journalist should be 'interested in everything, cultivate an accurate memory and be able to detach himself from his prejudices and his passions'. Robert Thomson, then editor of *The Times*, put it this way in an interview with Roy Greenslade, in the *Guardian* of 10 March 2003: 'Our reporting is objective and our news agenda is never skewed to match the views we take in our leader columns' (Greenslade 2003a). Moreover, as Denis McQuail points out (1987: 130) the rise of television has helped promote the concept of objectivity: 'Most European public broadcasting systems either legally require or expect news and information to be neutral (non-evaluative and factual) or balanced, according to various criteria, depending on the particular society.' Ofcom, the Office of Communications set up in 2003 to regulate broadcasting, stresses in its literature the responsibilities of the terrestrial channels – the BBC, ITV, Channels 4 and 5 – to carry news that is reliable and impartial.

Significantly in 2007 the BBC highlighted its commitment to these values: 'Impartiality is and should remain the hallmark of the BBC as the leading provider of information and entertainment in the United Kingdom and as a pre-eminent broadcaster internationally. It is a legal requirement, but it should also be a source of pride' (BBC 2007: 6). And in the following year, TalkSport late-night show host James Whale lost his job after encouraging listeners to vote for the Conservative candidate, Boris Johnson, in the campaign for Mayor of London. This clearly breached Ofcom rules on political impartiality. Linked to the notions of objectivity and impartiality is the belief that journalists should remain detached from the events they cover. As Gill Swain comments (2000): 'It is one of the fundamental rules of journalism: don't get emotionally involved.' Textbooks on interviewing skills tend to stress the need for the reporter to remain detached, listening carefully and simply asking pertinent questions.

Accuracy and truthfulness

The American journalist and publisher, Joseph Pulitzer (1847–1911) famously said there were three rules for reporters: 'Accuracy, accuracy and accuracy.' Indeed, there is a strong ethical commitment among many journalists towards accuracy and truthfulness in their reporting. These values are stressed in codes of conduct throughout the world. Despite all the pressures facing the media (from proprietors, advertisers, politicians), the special freedoms allowed by the market economy are said to make these values attainable. According to Kovach and Rosenstiel, in their influential text *The Elements of Journalism* (2003: 37), journalism's first obligation is to the truth. They challenge the epistemological scepticism associated with postmodernism which, they claim, has pervaded every aspect of intellectual life: the belief, summed up by the Columbia University historian Simon Schama, that 'the certainty of an ultimately observable, empirically verifiable truth' is dead. Thus, accuracy is the foundation on which everything else builds: context, interpretation, debate and all of public communication.

Australian journalist and academic Ian Richards (2005: 19) also challenges the postmodernist critique rather more bluntly this way:

For example, to assert that there is no truth is to assert as a truth the view that there is no truth, a position that is logically indefensible. Similarly, if every view is 'socially constructed', the view that everything is socially constructed is itself socially constructed and we gain no insights.

In its place, Richards promotes the notion of a specific 'journalistic truth': 'notwithstanding philosophical differences over the nature of facts, we need to assume there is an external world "out there". Similarly journalists share some commonsense theories about the world and in a day-to-day sense they, too, "just get on with things". The result is the "journalistic truth" of an event' (ibid.: 21).

Significantly, Carl Bernstein (1992) said of the Watergate investigation: 'We relied more on shoe leather and common sense and respect for the truth than for anything else'. And Nick Davies, author of the damning critique of contemporary British journalism, *Flat Earth News* (2008a), comments (Gopsill 2008): 'I'm afraid to say there are some cynical liars in our profession but most journalists are not. Most journalists want to tell the truth. There is still a lot of seriously good journalists working in British media.'

Social responsibility and the public interest

You may be attracted to the notion that journalists have a social responsibility to work ultimately in the interests of the public. While it is usually acknowledged that the media operate according to the demands of a profit-oriented economy, it is still stressed that the market can function benignly, not just in the interests of shareholders but of all the people (Whale 1972). This notion is particularly applied to the public service operations of the terrestrial television channels, though this is seen as coming under threat from mounting commercial pressures and privately-owned channels. Yet there remains a strong belief that the public service responsibility of the BBC has tended to protect it from the worst excesses of commercialisation (see Bell 1998: 17).

In recent years in the United States, many journalists have updated the social responsibility theory by promoting the concept of civic journalism. In the face of mass voter apathy in the States, journalists have opted to drop their detachment and intervene in the political process deliberately to increase knowledge and encourage participation. As Davis Merritt

(1995: 6), one of the leading advocates of public journalism, put it: 'We can help revitalize public life and restore the core importance to our profession by becoming fair-minded participants in public life rather than detached observers,' but, as Michael Bromley stresses, this concept has, intriguingly, found few promoters in Britain (2000: 114). The social responsibility theory was famously highlighted in the report of the 1947 Commission on the Freedom of the Press, chaired by Robert M. Hutchins, of the University of Chicago (Jaehnig 1998). Denis McQuail sums it up this way (1987: 116–17):

> It can be seen that social responsibility theory has to try to reconcile three somewhat divergent principles: of individual freedom and choice, of media freedom and of media obligation to society. There can be no single way of resolving the potential inconsistencies but the theory has favoured two main kinds of solution. One is the development of public, but independent institutions for the management of broadcasting. The second is the further development of professionalism as a means of achieving higher standards of performance.

The promotion of pluralism: media as the mirror of society

You may consider that the media are crucial in promoting political and cultural pluralism. Along with this attitude generally goes the view that the media bear the responsibility of reflecting society in all its complexity: with as many (legal) viewpoints as possible covered; and the different perspectives – of the old and young, working class and middle class, black and white, women and men, gay and heterosexual and so on – acknowledged.

Codes of conduct/practice

Professionalism is usually linked to deontology, namely the promotion of codes of conduct. Accordingly, individual journalists unite with others to acknowledge common standards of behaviour with various practices recognised as being the best to which they should all aspire. Ethical codes, in effect, stressing the public interest, the public's right to know and freedom of expression, serve to create a collective conscience of a profession. That's the theory at least. Some even argue that journalists, given their social and political responsibilities, should be considered on a par with doctors and lawyers and thus those who violated its professional code would suffer the penalty of being removed from the 'professional register' (see Chapter 3).

The need for training

Linked to notions of professionalism comes the emphasis on the need for training to impart standards. Not surprisingly, journalism textbooks tend to promote professionalism unproblematically (e.g. Dick 1998: 139–45). And in his seminal work on broadcasting training, Ivor Yorke reproduced dominant notions of neutrality and objective truth. He wrote (1987: ii): 'Our job is to present fact and truth with clarity, dispassion and neutrality however inconvenient or dismaying much of that information is.'

Critical responses

There are a number of critical responses to the dominant professional perspective. A liberal critique would challenge one or a few of these basic 'pillars' of the professional stance. Accordingly, you may choose to reject the notion of objectivity or argue that training is useless compared to learning through 'on-the-job' experience. But the other central 'pillars' remain untouched. A radical critique would tend to adopt most, if not all, of the following attitudes.

The political perspective

The more radical response to the ethical dilemmas facing journalists comes largely from the political left, being based on a politically-rooted value system. Thus, you may be inclined to stress journalism's function as one of social reproduction in the interests not of the whole of society but of dominant groups and classes. Accordingly, all the central concepts highlighted above (the free press, democracy, the public interest, objectivity, neutrality) are exposed as myths. Strict Marxists go further and argue that the media are best viewed as 'tools of the ruling class' (Coxall and Robins: 1998: 194).

The myths of objectivity and impartiality and the importance of empathy

On the myth of objectivity, Brian McNair comments: (1996: 33): 'News is never a mere recording or reporting of the world "out there" but a synthetic, value-laden account which carries within it dominant assumptions and ideas of the society within which it is produced.' Accordingly, objectivity becomes part of a strategic ritual for journalists to legitimise their activities which are, at root, serving the interests of the economic and political elite. Chris Frost (2000: 40) even argues that the very act of attempting to be impartial carries dangers, leading 'some journalists to limit independent thinking for fear that using unusual sources or contacts would be seen as abandoning impartiality'.

How can a journalist use creative intellect to advance a story, make unusual connections or talk to different people to widen their reader's view of a topic and still remain objective? According to freelance environment journalist Hugh Warwick: 'Journalism should be about making people aware of what is going on and encouraging them to take action. When you've got issues as big and all-encompassing as the environment or war, any debate about impartiality is simply hindering the opportunities for positive change' (Walsey 2000). Similarly, Merritt (1995: 18–19) argued that the objectivity tradition meant that journalists were expected to separate their professional identity from their personal identity while truth-telling was separated from the consequences of truth-telling. 'How, citizens properly wonder, can people who profess to not care what happens be trusted to inform us? Why should the public value the perspectives on the importance of events offered by people who insist they have no stake in those events?'

Critics of objectivity also point to the many great writers/journalists (such as William Cobbett, William Hazlitt, George Sand, Albert Camus, Jean-Paul Sartre, Simone de Beauvoir, Nawal El Saadawi, George Orwell, Rebecca West, Martha Gellhorn, James Cameron, Jessica Mitford, John Pilger, Paul Foot, Seymour Hersh, Robert Fisk) who have been outspoken and far from impartial on the great issues of their day. And many reporters, inevitably as sensitive human beings, become emotionally involved with the people they meet. John Langdon-Davies (1897–1971) was an eminent pacifist writer and journalist who covered for the *News Chronicle* the Spanish civil war in 1936 (the subject of his extraordinary piece of reportage *Behind the Spanish Barricades*). He was deeply shocked by the plight of refugees and with his friend, Eric Muggeridge, devised a 'Foster Parents Scheme' whereby families in Britain and the US would foster a named child. This became the basis for the Plan organisation which today works with 11 million children in 60 countries (see Langdon-Davies 2007/1936).

Photojournalist Nick Ut took the iconic photograph of the napalmed child Kim Phuc running naked and terrified down a road in Vietnam following a US attack on her village. Later he took the child to hospital, visited her during her time there and kept in touch with her regularly in the following years – when she became a representative of the communist Vietnamese government and then, after defecting to Canada, a campaigner for peace and reconciliation. During the 1990s ITN reporter Mike Nicholson discovered young Natasha Mihaljcic caught up in the Balkans war in Sarajevo and ended up taking her to live with his family. Bronwen Jones, a freelance, met the appallingly scarred young Dorah Mokoena in South Africa. She ended up bringing Dorah back to England with her mother for operations and launching the charity, Children of Fire, for burns victims. In 2004, Luis Sinco's photograph of a bleeding, smoking marine during the US assault on Fallujah, Iraq, rapidly became iconic as the 'Marlboro man'. And when Miller afterwards suffered from post-traumatic stress disorder, Sinco kept in close touch with him. All these acts by concerned journalists rightly challenge dominant notions about 'neutrality', 'detachment' and 'professionalism'. In other words, compassion and humanity are essential attributes of the journalist. For Joseph B. Atkins and Bernard Nezmah the Polish journalist Ryszard Kapuscinski (author of such classics as *The Soccer War*, *The Emperor*, *The Shah of Shahs* and *Imperium*) represents the ideal correspondent: one who identifies strongly with the defeated, downtrodden and colonised of the world. As Kapuscinski stresses: 'Empathy is perhaps the most important quality for a foreign correspondent. If you have it, other deficiencies are forgiveable; if you don't nothing much can help' (Atkins and Nezmah 2002: 219).

Some journalists are even outspoken advocates of 'subjectivity'. James Cameron, the first Western journalist to visit Hanoi during the Vietnam War, dared to show the North Vietnamese as human rather than communist monsters. He commented: 'It never occurred to me, in such a situation to be other than subjective. I have always tended to argue that objectivity was of less importance than the truth' (1967/2006). Former BBC war correspondent Martin Bell (1998: 15–22) also famously challenged the corporation's commitment to impartiality, stressing instead 'the journalism of attachment'. He defined this as 'a journalism that cares as well as knows . . . that will not stand neutrally between good and evil, right and wrong, the victim and the oppressor' (ibid.: 16). The BBC's guidelines required reporters to be objective and dispassionate. 'I am no longer sure what "objective" means: I see nothing object-like in the relationship between the reporter and the event, but rather a human and dynamic interaction between them. As for "dispassionate", it is not only impossible but inappropriate to be thus neutralized – I would say even *neutered* – at the scene of an atrocity or massacre, or most man-made calamities' (ibid.: 18; see also Sanders 2003: 43). Myra Macdonald has added further important problematics to the objectivity/ subjectivity debate, highlighting both the positives and negatives in broadcasters' subjectivity (2003: 75):

> Subjectivity can take very different forms, however, and some of these may aid knowledge formation. Self-reflexivity on the part of reporters and presenters enables better understanding of the discursive constitution of their account and dispels the myth of objectivity whereas a more egotistical presentation of the investigating self encourages an absorption in personality that is more akin to celebrity adulation.

Moreover, according to Alan Rusbridger, editor of the *Guardian*, the 24/7 news flow, the Internet and the blurring of the distinctions between publisher and recipient have transformed journalists' conventional notions of truth (2007). Thus,

> it's not about delivering the truth, the whole truth and nothing but the truth. It's not an infallible way of ascertaining what is going on around us. It's not defined by an arbitrary moment in the 24-hour clock to suit the historic schedules of print plants, distribution chains and wholesale delivery. It's rarely something to which we, as journalists, have exclusive know-ledge of, or access. It is something more fluid . . . a much more interactive thing than the tablet of stone.

The myth of professionalism

Similarly, the promotion of professionalism is seen as a sophisticated rhetorical strategy aiming to hide journalism's inherent pro-systemic bias. Ivan Illich (1973) famously described the professions as 'a form of imperialism' operating in modern societies as repressive mechanisms undermining democracy and turning active citizens into passive consumers. Daniel Hallin commented (1986: 10):

> The 'profession' of journalism has not one but many sets of standards and procedures, each applied in different kinds of political situations. In situations where political consensus seems to prevail journalists tend to act as 'responsible' members of the political establishment, upholding the dominant political perspective and passing on more or less at face value the views of authorities assumed to represent the nation as a whole. In situations of political conflict, they become more detached or even adversarial though this normally will stay well within the bounds of debate going on within the political 'establishment'.

According to Jeff Schmidt (2000: 204) the notion that experts should confine themselves to their 'legitimate professional concerns' and not 'politicise' their work helps keep professionals in line by encouraging them to view their narrow technical orientation as a virtue, a sign of objectivity rather than of subordination. 'This doesn't mean that experts are forbidden to let independent political thoughts cross their minds. They can do so as citizens, of course, and they can even do so as experts, but then only in the "proper" places and in the "proper" way.' Edwards and Cromwell argue (2006: 11) that the dangers of the mainstream media's reliance on elite sources were particularly evident in the run-up to the 2003 invasion of Iraq when government and intelligence lies about Weapons of Mass Destruction were peddled uncritically. They report ITV News political editor Nick Robinson as typifying this approach when in July 2004 he wrote in *The Times*:

> In the run-up to the conflict, I and many of my colleagues, were bombarded with complaints that we were acting as mouthpieces for Mr Blair. Why, the complainants demanded to know, did we report without question his warning that Saddam was a threat? Hadn't we read what Scott Ritter had said or Hans Blix? [two voices critical of WMD claims]. I always replied in the same way. It was my job to report what those in power were doing or thinking . . . That is all someone in my sort of job can do.

Moreover, many dissenting journalists prefer to see journalism, not as a profession but as a trade. One such was James Cameron who wrote in his 1967 autobiography about the insecurity journalists felt about their status. He continued (op. cit.): 'It is fatuous, however, to compensate for our insecurity by calling ourselves members of a profession; it is both pretentious and disabling; we are at best craftsmen [sic], and that is by no means an ignoble thing to be.'

Critique of the notion that fact and opinion are separate

Opinion and fact are so closely interlinked, you may consider it is impossible to separate them. Notions of objectivity and balance, moreover, become highly problematised when it is seen that a subjective process of selectivity governs the reporting of 'facts'. As mainstream media commentator Roy Greenslade (2000) argues: 'The concept of the separation of facts and opinion does not exist and never has in most of Britain's press. It is partisan and it does not hide that fact except, of course, from readers.'

Critique of BBC claims to 'impartiality'

Even the BBC's claims to impartiality, supposedly enshrined in law, have come under attack from critical media sociologists. The Glasgow University Media Group (1976; 1980; 1982; 1985; 1993), in studying coverage of industrial disputes and the peace movement of the early 1980s, argued controversially how even television news reflected the interests of the British establishment against those of organised labour and the peace movement. For instance, in its 1976 study, *Bad News*, the group found that while employers were given studio interviews and asked deferential questions, trade unionists were either ignored or made to appear unreasonable, being interviewed in the street and asked intimidating questions. Formed in 1922, the BBC, it is argued, has been an integral part of the British state at least since 1926 when it refused striking miners or representatives of the Labour opposition access to the airwaves. Significantly, from 1948 to 1985 all BBC applications were vetted by MI5. As investigative journalist John Pilger argued (1998: 489):

Perhaps in no other country does broadcasting hold such a privileged position as opinion leader as in Britain. When 'information' is conveyed on the BBC with such professional gravitas, it is more likely to be believed. Possessing highly professional talent, the illusion of impartiality and an essentially liberal ethos, Britain's 'public service broadcasting' has become a finely crafted and infinitely adaptable instrument of state propaganda and censorship.

Propaganda and the critique of the notion of pluralism

Contrary to the notion of pluralism, some journalists highlight the consensual news value system operating throughout the mainstream media, with only a limited range of opinions permitted, particularly at times of crisis. This view stresses the collusion between propagandist dominant media and the national security state in the manufacture of consent to the status quo. Traditional theorists see propaganda as being a useful conceptual tool to apply to media products of totalitarian dictatorships while applicable to the media of Western democracies only in exceptional periods – such as during overt wars.

In their classic study, *Four Theories of the Press*, Siebert, Peterson and Schramm (1963) apply the libertarian and social responsibility systems to the Western free press and relate notions of propaganda and indoctrination to the Soviet communist and authoritarian systems. Herman and Chomsky (1988: xi), in contrast, argue that the propaganda function is a permanent feature of Western media systems with the powerful elite 'able to fix the premises of discourse, to decide what the general populace is allowed to see, hear and think about and to manage public opinion by regular propaganda campaigns'.

In a modified form, Douglas Kellner draws on the theories of Antonio Gramsci (1971) in stressing that the dominant ideology is not all-powerful but can be contested. News organisations, accordingly, can be seen to play a crucial role in the hegemonic struggle for ideological domination. There is a consensus but it can be shifted by dissenting voices. This position, Kellner argues (1990: 73), more aptly portrays the formidable antagonisms of a social order governed by class divisions and often contradictory imperatives of capitalism and democracy. With reference to radio, Peter Wilby and Andy Conroy take issue with the notion of the media reflecting reality. They comment (1994: 183): 'The codes through which listeners interpret radio's portrayal of the "real" world are journalistic. The audio text overall purports to reflect the world but in fact applies codes to construct a representation of the world within the terms of the radio experience.' And according to John Pilger (op. cit.: 488):

'Far from the independent "Fourth Estate" envisaged by Lord Macaulay, much of serious journalism in Britain, dominated by television, serves as a parallel arm of government, testing or "floating" establishment planning, restricting political debate to the "main centres of power"' and 'promoting Western power in the wider world'.

The economic roots of media practice – and ethics

Critics of the dominant media myths often focus on the economic roots of journalistic practices and bureaucratic structures. As the media consensus has narrowed, so the monopoly ownership structures have intensified. Critics who highlight the monopoly structures in media industries often refocus the ethical debate away from the individual journalist to the employer. As media commentator and journalism lecturer Michael Foley argues (2000: 49–50):

> For too long it has been assumed that unethical behaviour is the prerogative of the individual journalist . . . Much that passes for unethical behaviour takes place because too few journalists are taking too many decisions quickly and without time to reflect. This is because proprietors have not invested in journalism. It is difficult for journalists to refuse to write particular stories or take certain decisions when a proprietor sees increased circulation or readership potential. Journalists have to know that if tickets or freebies are refused that the employer will pay for it.

The democratic façade

Some critics even challenge the very notion of democracy which under-pins all the activities and ethical claims of the mainstream media, arguing it is a myth serving to legitimise the rule of the few over the many.

Daniel Hellinger and Dennis Judd (1991: 9–10) suggest there are three major arenas used by the elites for creating a popular sense of legitimacy: the educational institutions which inculcate in each new generation a political ideology that legitimates the state; the mass media which are 'pivotal for socialising mass publics into accepting sanctioned versions of political and economic reality'; and, finally, the electoral process which 'provides ritualised opportunities for people to participate, as individuals and as members of a collective citizenry, in the political process. When people vote, they reaffirm their belief that the political system listens to their voice'.

With specific reference to radio, Wilby and Conroy (op. cit.: 33) highlight its capacity to 'propagate an illusion of public participation and create a mythologised listening "community"'. They continue: 'Presenters frequently play the role of devil's advocate when conducting interviews or hosting phone-in discussions, reinforcing radio's cultural role of stimulating discussion, providing a forum of debate and maintaining a neutral position within "consensual" and ideological boundaries of acceptability and non-deviance'.

Critique of campaigning journalism

Critics argue that even journalists' exalted claims to be working as the noble Fourth Estate, safeguarding the interests of the public, are mere rhetoric. In essence, media practices do not reflect a genuine public spiritness but rather a concern to boost sales or improve ratings. As Magnus Linklater (2000) said of the *Daily Record*'s campaign against the repeal of Section 28 (which forbids the promotion of homosexuality in schools): 'They have detected a populist issue on which to build much-needed circulation and demonstrate their credentials as a red-blooded, red top paper – a combination of the *Mail* and *Sun*, though, without the charm of either. In pursuit of that, anything goes.'

The need for political action

The increasing media emphasis on infotainment has accompanied (and even helped promote) the depoliticising of civil society. In contrast to this trend, dissenting journalists are more likely to focus on the need for political action (through trade unions/political parties/campaigning groups) to improve ethical standards in the media. Such journalists may choose to work critically within mainstream media or for alternative media (trade union, political, human rights, environmental campaigning, gay or feminist). Tony Harcup, in a series of crucial texts, has stressed the importance of journalists' *collective* intervention in defence of standards. He acknowledges the individual's responsibilities: he cites, for instance, the eminent anti-war journalist James Cameron resigning in 1950 from the *Express* over its coverage of a spy scandal and Katy Weitz, who quit her job as *Sun* features writer over its gung-ho reporting of the Iraq invasion in March 2003 (2007a: 124). But at the same time he is keen to highlight the protests by the *Express* NUJ branch over the newspaper's coverage of Gypsies in 2004 – and the spontaneous protests by thousands of BBC staff in the same year following the sacking of director general Greg Dyke (in the wake of the damning criticisms of the corporation in the Hutton Report into the death of Dr David Kelly). Another important and brave protest was made by journalists at the *Lancet*, the highly respected medical journal, in 2005, when an editorial criticised its publisher, Reed Elsevier, for promoting the arms trade (Fixter 2005). Similarly, Des Freedman (2003) is keen to highlight the actions of the millions of people globally who took to the streets on 15 February 2003 in protest against the looming invasion of Iraq. These, he says, were 'more likely to create a space and a need for passionate, critical and contextualised reporting than a naïve belief in the power and professionalism of the traditional reporter'.

A critical response is possible, of course, based on religious principles: the journalist may decide to work critically within mainstream media or within religious alternative media. These dissident responses to the ethical challenges are becoming all the more difficult to adopt given the growth of a globalised infotainment media, the increasing power of proprietors, the decline in alternative media and power of trade unions. But is not the challenge worth taking up?

Dealing with the dilemmas: four journalists under the spotlight

Phillip Knightley was an investigative journalist with the *Sunday Times* for 20 years where he won many awards. His books include *The Second*

Oldest Profession: The Spy as Patriot, Bureaucrat, Fantasist and Whore and
The First Casualty, a seminal study of war reporting.

*What do you think are the three most important ethical issues facing journalists
today in Britain?*

1   Finding the courage to resist executive pressure to push stories
     further than the facts justify, often by the use of anonymous
     quotes.
2   Finding the determination to distinguish what is important and
     what is froth.
3   Finding the energy to return journalism to its public service function.

*You have written and spoken about the 'death' of war reporting, given the
government and military controls over the media. What can journalists do to
reverse these trends?*

They could put aside their commercial and professional rivalry to form
a united front against the military and the government.

*Given the control of the embeds during the Iraq invasion of 2003, do you
think there is a case for journalists refusing to participate in such arrangements?*

Yes, but see 2. Their ambition and rivalry probably means that there
will always be enough willing to accept pools.

*Some journalists have promoted the notion of a more responsible 'peace
journalism' (see Chapter 9). How viable is this for mainstream journalists?
Will commitment be inevitably tokenistic?*

I'm afraid that both the public and journalists themselves think that
peace journalism is not sexy. Unfortunately war sells papers.

*Which is the most impressive individual example of war reporting that young
journalists could look to as providing models of good practice?*

Nick Tomalin in Vietnam (*The General Goes Zapping Charlie Cong*).
Robert Fisk in Kosovo. And in Iraq, Patrick Cockburn's reports. On the
fifth anniversary of the invasion, Robert Fisk, of the *Independent*, wrote
that the war had been one of the most disastrous ever fought by Britain.
'All governments lie in wartime but American and British propaganda
in Iraq over the last five years has been more untruthful than in any
conflict since the First World War.' I agree with that wholeheartedly.

Noam Chomsky accuses the mainstream media of being the propaganda arm of the state – in periods of both peace and war. How would you respond?

Certainly in wartime, frequently in peace time. The commercial interests of newspapers are usually best served by supporting the government of the day (maybe the realm is a better word), especially in times of national crisis. Sure, they appear to be attacking the government at every opportunity but a lot of that is froth. They quickly fall in line when the national interest appears to demand it.

How do you rate the performance of alternative, leftist journals (such as Socialist Worker, Living Marxism/deceased, New Left Review, Morning Star) in the coverage of wars?

A frequently valuable alternative view of what is happening as long as you keep in mind that they have agendas of their own. Certainly a corrective to the official view put out by most of the media.

War correspondents are likely to be approached at some time by the security services and asked to provide assistance. In your experience, how do journalists respond? What do you feel is the correct response?

More likely by intelligence services rather than by security services, but both apply. How do they respond? Depends on the approach. A friend who was a *Newsweek* war correspondent says he was approached by the Saigon CIA chief with the suggestion that they collaborate. 'You've been up on the Plain of Jars. I haven't. I've been in town. You tell me what's going on up there and I'll give you my slant on what's been happening here.' My friend thought it over and agreed. But he made the mental reservation that he would tell the CIA guy nothing more than what he planned to write for *Newsweek* that week. True, he was telling him two days before it appeared in the magazine. The collaboration worked very well. My friend got the CIA slant on what was happening in Vietnam. The CIA guy got herograms from Langley on the lines of 'Great report on Plain of Jars situation. It's now confirmed by *Newsweek*'s current issue. Well done.' This is the only case I know of where it has worked. There is, of course, still the risk that if the opposition discovers that one journalist is (or has) helped an intelligence service, then it is entitled to assume that all journalists are doing the same thing and treat the lot of them as spies (as frequently happens).

If during a war you were leaked information which, if released, could seriously damage the country's war effort and morale at home would you still publish?

Depends on the war. In a war of national survival I would probably not publish, although even here it is a tricky decision. Someone published an article about British shell shortages in WWI. Certainly damaging to the war effort. But it led to reforms that ended the shortage. But in a war that was not one of national survival (the Gulf, Falklands, Kosovo, Iraq) I would publish.

There is a lot of talk about the 'dumbing down' of the media. Can this notion be applied in any way to the coverage of wars?

Yes. There were lots of stories from Kosovo about mass graves, rape camps, bombing missions, missile strikes, but not a lot of analysis, historical back-ground, reflection and stories expressing honest doubt. Understandable when the chief propagandist for NATO says he ran the NATO infor-mation campaign on the lines of a soap opera because that is what the public wanted.

What are the major ethical issues thrown up for war reporting by the Internet?

The temptation that in the absence of solid, reliable reporting you will be tempted to accept information from the Internet at face value. You have an ethical duty to inform your readers/viewers of your source and give them your honest opinion of its reliability.

Tessa Mayes is an investigative journalist and author. Her investigative reports have been show on BBC's *Panorama*, ITV's *The Cook Report*, Channel 4 and Carlton TV's *The Investigators* and published at www. spiked-online, *The Sunday Times* and the *Spectator* magazine.

What do you consider are the most important ethical challenges facing journalists in Britain today?

In news reporting one of the most difficult challenges is to avoid filling news reports with too many opinions (the reporter's own and/or those of others) at the expense of scrutinising and reporting new facts. Sometimes the content of the news story *is* the exchange of opinions (such as a political row or debate). However I'm talking about the *approach* to covering the content (opinions and/or facts) of the story which can sometimes become opinion-heavy and new facts-lite. This is a problem.

An example of this is on the issue of climate change. News reporters are in danger of approaching the news content (whether it be a political exchange of opinions such as a debate about solutions to climate change or a new report by a group of scientists) by offering mainly their and/or the opinions of others on this content. At a recent International Journalism Programme (IJP) debate I spoke at in Bonn, Germany, on the reporting of green issues, news reporters told me how their editors encourage them to include two experts to disagree with each other in their reports as normal practice leaving the reporters with no time to scrutinise the facts of new scientific studies or evaluate the importance of a scientific report by putting it in the context of other studies.

What should be happening is that news reporters scrutinise the truth of the content with less emphasis on an opinion-heavy approach to the story. Are those offering political debate about the solutions to climate change representing their opponents accurately? Does a new policy initiative really have no critics or points worthy of criticism? Is a new scientific report described truthfully, clearly and fairly? How do the facts of the report compare to the findings of other key works on the science of climate change? Worse still, some campaigning reports masquerade as objective news reports (such as uncritical news reports on local council litter campaigns and the deployment of name-and-shame-and-fine CCTV methods to target individuals) as if it's clear what the human and political response to the science should be. It's what I term 'green journalism'. This is a new and worrying trend in news journalism.

What special ethical dilemmas does the Internet throw up for you?

For me as an investigative reporter, the Internet offers great opportunities for research and asking those online for help. Yet there are limits as to what you can publicise about a story as it is being researched and before publication/broadcast. For instance, if you publicise details of the story you need help with online, perhaps the person or company you are investigating may sue you for libel before publication/broadcast which may kill the story. Your online users may want confidentiality if they help you so you may need to offer that facility on your website. Any investigative journalist has to weigh up constantly the benefits of how much you publicise about a story before it's finished.

Can you identify a couple of assignments where you faced particularly difficult ethical decisions?

I reported undercover recently on the Church of Scientology for the *Spectator* magazine. The idea was to investigate the new way the church promoted their London celebrity centre to aspiring creatives such as actresses, musicians and designers. The church had recently opened a new centre in the City of London and they were receiving more press attention for all kinds of community works. Scientologists were also receiving press attention (some negative) about their giving gifts to the police, the promotion of their celebrity members in London and their works in schools and with trauma victims. I wanted to see if any of the allegations such as Scientologists pressurising people were true and if Scientologists were in any way as scary as some suggest. It was an interesting assignment.

Along the way I faced an editorial dilemma – should I secretly film inside their celebrity centre? In this case, I decided not to since I did not have firm evidence of major harm or wrong-doing to justify such an intrusion which would identify their members and broadcast their private feelings and acts. It would have made sensational Internet television but viewers would have quite rightly questioned the editorial judgment I made. It's easy to go in with secret cameras to any situation – including a very private one – but was there a story to justify this method? Although the Scientology celebrity centre is open to the public I was also taken to private rooms with members as part of a course I went on. In the private rooms very intimate exchanges took place between myself and various Scientologists but nothing of concern. They were the kind of normal discussions you have with anyone interested in explaining their beliefs. In other words, it was all culturally interesting but there was no crime or secret, disturbing practice to reveal that I came across. If I had discovered something of significant public interest during my research, I may have changed my mind about secretly filming as with any subject. In this case, however, after three months of visiting the Scientology celebrity centre undercover, I found nothing to justify secret filming.

The article was published as a front cover *Spectator* magazine investigation. I discovered that contrary to other stories about pressurised sales, the church members I encountered were no more or less enthusiastic to sell you something than a salesman from a high street electronics shop. I also found out about Scientologists' new approach to creatives and their plans for expanding this area of their work in London. To read the article, click on: www.spectator.co.uk/the-magazine/features/32548/stars-in-their-eyes.thtml.

As an investigative journalist you used subterfuge to gain a story. Did any broadcasting guideline/code help you resolve the ethical issues involved? If not, what special considerations came into play?

As an independent journalist I am not bound by any guidelines apart from my own and that is to report the truth. However, when working with other media companies and outlets, you have to work within the currently regulatory framework that they are bound by. My approach is to get the story first and then decide – with editors and their lawyers – what can be published/broadcast according to relevant rules, guidelines and laws. And there are a lot of them to consider. There is some discussion before and during the research process, too, but most decisions happen during the editing process.

What lessons should journalists draw from the killings of Veronica Guerin and Martin O'Hagan (see Chapter 10)?

Journalism can be a dangerous pursuit especially when covering serious crime or wars. My main advice is always trust your own judgment about safety risks. Get advice but make your own independent assessment. If you don't feel happy about a situation, you are allowed to decline the work. Some stories are worth backing off from. Some journalists have taken their employers to court for insisting they cover a dangerous story. In the end it's not about the company's needs, you have to decide whether any of these situations are worth the risk to you. Sometimes they are.

Journalists are accused of relying too much on elite sources. How have you managed to expand the range (ethnic, gender, age, etc.) of your sources?

What's wrong with elite sources? Are we to ignore those with political power, those who have shown expertise in a subject such as science or art? The point is that elites should have their views challenged by a range of opinions but sometimes journalists seem to want to ignore elite views altogether. The fact that the elites may not be offering anything inspirational or interesting is a different matter and needs challenging rather than ignoring. It is useful to include a diversity of opinion but not all opinions are equal: some are more incisive and true than others. I don't judge my sources according to their ethnic background or sexuality but according to their expertise, depth of opinion, closeness to a story, experience and relevance to an issue.

The issues I tackle often focus on those in society who are subject to the rules and legislation enforced by elites including women, immigrants or young men. But the reason I am interested in their stories is because I wish to explore the nature of power and the effects of policy on people's lives. I do not wish to be answerable to some kind of official, politically correct quota system concerning sources. Stories should be judged on the merits of the content, whether it's true or not, and not whether the stories fulfil a quota system.

Insofar as some social groups don't get much of a hearing in the media, this is a different issue. Their stories – if important – should be covered but again, not because of a quota system. Theirs must be a story that is worth reporting on. News reporting, for example, is not a charity or bound by equality quotas. It should be judged according to its key role in society – to report the truth about something that is new.

You have written a lot about the move away from factual reporting to an over–emphasis on subjectivity (which you call 'therapy news'). Which is the most recent manifestation of the 'therapy news' syndrome? And how can it be eliminated?

In the UK, the rise of 'therapy news' – the rise of emotions (the reporter's own and/or the reporting of other's emotions) in news reports compared to the balance of facts and an objective approach to stories – has been going on for some time. Now this phenomena has gone global unfortunately. A recent example of 'therapy news' is on Al-Jazeera, the satellite, Arabic news channel. Al-Jazeera has been called 'the CNN of the Arab World', a fitting description for a station that concentrated on images of injured Iraqis during the war, just like the emotionally-centred news reporting values of its Western counterparts. As Al-Jazeera's website states: 'Al-Jazeera's correspondents opened a window for the world on the millennium's first two wars in Afghanistan and Iraq. Our expanded coverage competed with and sometimes out-performed our competitors, bringing into the spotlight the war's devastating impact on the lives of ordinary people.'

It is one thing to report the facts of the human cost of war and the feelings of those who have suffered. I can understand why Al-Jazeera felt the need to balance global news given the censorship of such images by other channels. It is another issue to dwell repeatedly on the emotional side of those who are suffering as if this in itself is news. It is not. There are other places for this kind of approach to journalism such as documentary, feature-writing, interview-led articles/broadcasts and debate shows. 'Therapy news' can be corrected if news reporters adhere to their essential role as reporting the truth as they find it, investigating and interrogating the facts (including but not dominated by opinion and feelings) and offering a summary based on this.

Kristine Lowe is a journalist specialising in the media who writes for a number of British, Norwegian and American publications. *Journalisten* is the trade journal for Norway's journalists and is one of her clients.

What are the major new ethical dilemmas thrown up by the Internet?

People often think that reporting from virtual life and real life is tremendously different. I think not. I see the web (blogs, social networks etc) a bit like a virtual pub or coffee bar. Just as you do not go home and write up a story on the basis of a chat with a random stranger over a few pints in the pub, you do not use online sources you don't know or trust or verify. However, to expand on that metaphor, you might go home and write up that story from the pub if you met with a CEO you know well and know has the authority to say what he or she said.

However, one important ethical issue to be aware of online, and one that can be difficult for a journalist to handle, is getting the distinction between public and private right. People, especially teenagers, may choose to make a lot of very private information publicly available on blogs and in social networks such as Facebook and MySpace and still consider it private. Is it ethical for journalists to still use this information? One example is how (in March 2008) reporters latched on to and republished lots of pictures and information placed on her MySpace profile by the prostitute New York governor Elliot Spitzer was first caught cajoling with. Closely related is the issue of digital door-stepping, so dubbed by blogger-journalist Adam Tinworth. What rules of engagement apply when journalists approach eyewitnesses to traumatic events via their blogs of social networking profiles, such as, for instance, after the Virginia Tech Massacre on 16 April 2007?

What relevance, if any, do the professional codes of conduct have to the work of bloggers?

There is no formal code of conduct for bloggers, but there is an informal one which is so central to web culture that it is changing the rules of engagement – over time also for mainstream media (MSM). Most influential and serious bloggers adhere to certain basic unwritten 'rules' such as always disclosing their interests and ties, always linking back to their sources and engaging with readers in a civil manner. Blogging is very conversational: you can not behave like an institution without being punished for it, partly, I think, because blogging is so democratic. You need to apply a more human, relaxed tone – basically good manners will take you far, but reporters, especially for big prestigious media organisations, are often found lacking in this and struggle in this new online environment.

Is 'citizen journalism' leading to better journalism?

Citizen journalism is a much abused term, but if we use it to describe eyewitness reports and blogs, I think it serves to broaden the picture and debate. This can be especially true in conflicts and under totalitarian regimes where it is difficult for MSM to gain access. Reporters Without Borders say that in the field of human rights, it is citizen journalists and not professional journalists who have been responsible for the most reliable reports and information – the information that has most upset governments. I think both blogs and eyewitness reports can and will supplement, transform and serve as a healthy correction to journalism, but not supplant it.

There are other ways in which it may broaden MSM coverage and the public discourse. For instance, to help me stay on top of my beat as a media journalist I track the blog buzz around the media companies and issues I follow using blogsearch engines such as Technorati. This means that I'm often able to pick up on blog discussions around media acquistions, mergers and other controversial issues – which can be an excellent starting point for more informed reporting. The way I see it, blogs enable me to tap into people's conversations things they are passionate about in distant corners of the world without leaving my armchair. Of course, the old rules about verifying the credibility of your sources, standing up the information and so on still apply, but this means the source pool gets bigger, it prevents me from falling into the trap of talking to the same heads all the time.

Is blogging anything more than the ramblings of insignificant folk on the margins of the public sphere?

Of course there are lots of what some people may see as 'insignificant folk on the margins of the public sphere blogging', but the marvellous thing about it is that blogs enable everyone to be his or her own publisher: they do not have to curry favours with editors, the powers that be, or be privileged enough to have their own printing presses. Now many people may not choose to exercise their newfound voices in ways which do not resemble journalism, or to talk about issues you and I do not care too much about, but the great thing is that they have that voice in the first place. People may choose to blog about stamps, parenting, fishing, their political concerns or their academic research, and, for whichever niche it is that interests me, it gives me an opportunity to tap into their thoughts and conversations. In this way, blogging is very democratic: it does not really matter which title, age, race the blogger is, what matters is the soundness of his or her ideas. And because permalinks make all blog content searchable, I'm able to find this person, who may be too young or too old, or live in a too distant place for me to normally talk to.

Who do you consider are the best bloggers in the UK – and why?

My answer above is precisely why I think this question is simply the wrong one. This question is seeing a new medium through the lens of the old. Blogging is a niche medium and lists of the xx best blogs in whichever country, or even worldwide, always puzzle me. Very often I find I do not read any blogs on those lists. In general, a good blog has a strong voice and/or covers its niche expertly, but looking at audience figures could be misleading: a blog read by 50 opinion leaders or experts in a certain field could be much more influential than one read by 500,000 random readers. I could name my favourite UK media bloggers here, and the UK has some really excellent ones, but people with other passions, say for stamps or politics, would wildly disagree. If you have to do 'top ten' lists, looking at the best within a niche makes more sense. Having said that, it is interesting to see how certain blogs have managed to set the MSM agenda, such as Drudge Report and Huffington Post in the US, and political bloggers like Iain Dale, Guido Fawks, Tom Watson and Recess Monkey in the UK.

Which UK websites are setting new standards for journalism?

In general, I think too many news sites approach online media as it is just digitalised old media, just another place to shovel content, and fail to exploit all the opportunities the social web offers. On the positive side, I like how the *Guardian* is using *Comment is Free* and blogs both to bring in new and more voices, and to cover issues more in-depth. I also like how the BBC have many of their high-profile correspondents and editors blogging, which helps make their journalism more transparent and more personal; the way the website uses links and deep-links to add more context to their reporting, and how they use eyewitness reports to broaden their coverage during conflicts where journalists struggle to get access, like the crackdown on protesters in Burma. I'm also a big fan of how Reed Business Information (RBI) uses blogs and forums to better serve and inform their readers, such as how reporters at their title *Farmer's Weekly* liveblogs from livestock fairs and posted information into online forums during outbreaks of foot and mouth disease.

Do you agree that the UK mainstream media are 'dumbing down'? Can the same be said of the media in Norway?

Maybe, but the audience is smartening up. I certainly see online newspapers in Norway and the UK becoming more 'tabloid' in the rush to get as much traffic and as high click-rates as possible. But to some extent, it stopped concerning me too much. Now that I get most of my news via my self-chosen RSS-feeds in my newsreader, I rarely go to a news site's front pages anymore and only subscribe to feeds on issues I care about. As a result I'm rarely exposed to all the 'click-friendly' stories on celebrities, boobs, sex and the like.

Of course, RSS is not very mainstream, but I think we are seeing that people, especially younger people, get their news from so many different sources today, including via their friends' online recommendations and social networking sites, that the fact that MSM is dumbing down becomes largely irrelevant to the reader. If it is the right strategy for MSM in view of the intensified competition in today's fragmented media landscape is of course a different matter. In fact, since the threshold for becoming your own publisher has been so radically lowered, I think MSM need to work harder to show that they do cover each niche to a level that can compete with all the excellent niche coverage out there. If they can't do that, they should at least aggregate and link to all the niche expertise available in order to provide something of value to their readers.

Jon Grubb has been editor of the award-winning *Lincolnshire Echo* for two and a half years. He secured his first editor's chair at the *Scunthorpe Telegraph*, where he worked for three years. Previously, he was deputy editor and head of content at the *Nottingham Evening Post*, worked on the newsdesk at the *Gloucester Citizen* and started his career as a trainee on the weekly *Buckinghamshire Advertiser*.

What do you consider are the major issues confronting journalists in Britain today?

The problem is where to start? We've already seen editorial departments downsized in the last few years and it's hard to see a reversal of that in the future. Couple this with the expectations upon journalists to deliver their stories across a number of different mediums – video, web, print and audio – and it presents some real challenges to the industry and, in turn, the journalists that work within it. Along with those challenges come opportunities. Journalists will be expected to be skilled across a number of different disciplines from audio and video to traditional print and on-line reporting. Those who multi-skill will excel and the chance to switch jobs from TV to newspapers and from radio to web will be greater. Yet despite the media industry's obsession with the method and channel of delivery at its very core one key element has not changed for journalists and hopefully never will. What is important for the audience is not how but what is delivered. The story is still the central most important part of the journalist's job. Without the right stories the way it is delivered is immaterial.

So the key skills of maintaining a contacts book, having good interview skills, a keen news sense, the creativity to find your own stories, the tenacity to chase them down and the ability to tell a good, accurate, ethically sound story will all remain central to a journalist's job. What we must ensure is that we do not lose focus on those key skills whilst grappling with new and complex models of delivery.

What special ethical dilemmas has the Internet thrown up for you?

I suppose the dilemma we are grappling with the most at the moment is balancing the increasing demands from our audience for 'instant' interactivity against a need to ensure that we maintain the same standards of legal, taste and moral judgments we make with our printed products. Our online audience now expects to be able to react to a story and see their comment instantly yet we need to ensure that those comments – whilst enabling the important freedom of expression – fall within the bounds of decency and the law. Monitoring comments on a constant basis provides a practical challenge. The dilemma is: do we allow that instant expression or do we insist that only registered users whose details we can verify are allowed to comment?

What effect has 'citizen journalism' had on journalism standards?

Firstly there are one or two important facts to establish about the idea of citizen journalism. Firstly, I think it's important to make the distinction between 'citizen journalism' and 'user generated content' – very often it seems people don't make the distinction. Citizen journalism in its true sense should be people from the community gathering evidence from different sources and writing a balanced and fair interpretation of that research. In short, the true citizen journalist should only be defined by the fact they are not employed by a media organisation or paid to carry out the role. In reality, of course, citizen journalism is some form has existed for decades. They used to take the form of an army of volunteer village correspondents writing for their local newspaper or people who contributed articles for their parish magazines and church newsletters. We think of citizen journalism as a child of the Internet but it has long existed.

However, bloggers and 'user generated content' often gets put under the umbrella of citizen journalism and is a very different animal. Both of these tend to be blatantly and openly opinionated and don't pretend to be based upon any research. Valuable and interesting in their own way they don't belong anywhere near the label of journalism. Of course, a quick glance at letters pages and newspaper columnists from local newspapers of 10 or 20 years ago will quite quickly prove that neither of these apparently modern inventions are new either. Once you make that distinction then actually the range and extent of proper citizen journalism appears to be fairly small anyway – and certainly no greater in number than the village correspondents of yesteryear and in my opinion has had no greater effect either.

As far as the audience becoming news 'producers' rather than news 'consumers' then I think the effect is more fundamental on a number of fronts. Firstly, the tastes and opinions of a modern media company's audience are more often expressed, quicker to materialise and easier to measure since the dawn of new media. Media companies are certainly more attuned to them than ever before and more likely to adapt their own style and products to meet those opinions.

Secondly readers are less likely to accept the 'tablets of stone' passed down by their local paper. Newspapers are becoming more of a conversation than a lecture and stories evolve and change more rapidly and in different ways than they used to.

Thirdly, newspapers, national or local, do not enjoy the dominance over the news agenda they once did. The cycle of a news story – from breaking to analysis to follow-up to finish – can play out much quicker through the Internet, radio and 24-hour news channels before newspapers can even publish the first sentence.

To survive newspapers and their journalists will have to find an answer to this problem.

Do you think local papers can be accused of dumbing down?

I'm not sure dumbing down is a fair reflection of what has happened to local newspapers. In the vast majority of cases I think modern local newspapers are considerably better than they were ten years ago. They've had to improve to maintain their readers in the face of so much competition. I think many local papers are more creative, passionate, entertaining and diverse in coverage than ever before.

What is true is that society and communities have become more fragmented. Communities of interest have emerged where communities of geography have waned. People's lives, their choices and their responsibilities to families, work and leisure have become more complex.

It is increasingly difficult to find issues, stories and information that have the mass appeal it once commanded. As an example, when I was at school it was almost impossible to find someone who didn't watch the *Morecambe and Wise Xmas Special* (I'm showing my age now!). It united the playground, the workplace, the staff room and the shop floor. Now you'd struggle to find more than a handful of people that even watched the same TV channel let alone the same programme. With limited space and limited resource newspapers are chasing the stories that can interest a very wide spectrum of people from all ages, all walks of life and all parts of their circulation area. It's little wonder in these circumstances that newspapers sometimes fall into the trap of appealing to a common denominator.

But I don't think that can necessarily be described as dumbing down. When you look at the level and depth of stories, the fact files, expert opinions, readers' comments, links to to other websites and the rest of the myriad of alternative views and perspectives that newspapers and their websites provide now I'm not sure that people have ever been so well informed.

What efforts have you made at the Lincolnshire Echo *to relate to the many different ethnic groups in the county?*

Once again this issue is about balance. How do we embrace and meet the needs of new populations whilst retaining and not alienating our existing readers? In Lincolnshire we've found this difficult. My own opinion is that we need to treat the issue with sensitivity and understand the resistance to change that exists in many communities. If the newspaper – or any authority – pushes that change too far too quickly then disharmony, distrust and resentment soon follow.

In the case of the *Echo* we try to help readers understand more about the new residents through articles on food, culture and the economy. We haven't gone down the route of columns written in Polish or pages devoted to these communities because I'm not sure our existing readers would react positively – at least not yet. But the change in Lincolnshire is still relatively new and I think we must do our best to ease people through that change with understanding, education and empathy on all sides.

Sports reporting is often accused of marginalising women's achievements. How do you deal with women's sports at the Lincolnshire Echo?

My colleague John Pakey, the sports editor, has provided an answer for me on this one. He says: 'I think there has been great change in the reporting of women's sport over the last few years. It is recognised that in athletics our greatest performers in the Great Britain vest have been Dame Kelly Holmes and Paula Radcliffe and they have received plenty of coverage and plaudits for their achievements. At the *Lincolnshire Echo* we take great pride in all our sports, men and women. While this might seem a cliché line, it is a point that we take the merits of people's achievements and weigh them up regardless of gender.

'The proof in this has been the coverage we have afforded Lincoln City Ladies FC this season. The Lady Imps have reached the semi-final of the Women's FA Cup and almost clinched promotion to the Women's Premier League. We gave them the coverage this warranted with back page splashes and double page previews on the occasion they played Arsenal Ladies in the Women's FA Cup semi-final. Lincolnshire's best medal hopes at this year's Beijing Olympics are women. In shooting we have Lesley Goddard and in the pool we have Lizzie Simmonds, Kate Haywood and Mel Marshall. Lizzie Simmonds has already commanded back page splashes with her silver medal success in the World Short Course Championships in Manchester in April. There is no marginal-isation of sport because of gender. We give coverage based on interest and the quality of the story.'

What story did your newspaper carry recently that involved special ethical dilemmas?

The one that sticks in my mind is from a year ago when we ran a two-page spread of an interview we conducted with the leader of the BNP. At the time the BNP had announced it would field several candidates in the local elections and we interviewed the leader when he visited the city. The publication of his views – done in the paper via a straight Q and A – attracted some criticism. We agonised long and hard about the ethical issues surrounding the decision of whether to print.

In essence they fell on two sides. First there are many people, we knew, who would find the views expressed as abhorrent. There was the argument that the interview would inflame opinions and further divide opinion around sensitive issues, particularly but not exclusively, of immigration. We were also conscious that giving the BNP what some would describe as the 'oxygen of publicity' so close to an election might affect the outcome. On the other side was the argument about the freedom of speech and the freedom of expression. As long as those views published fell within the bounds of the law then to not publish them would be a form of censorship that we were uncomfortable with.

In the end we decided to publish the story. There were several reasons but the over-riding one was the freedom of speech. Let me be clear that there were opinions expressed by that party that I object to very deeply indeed. But it was my deep dislike of the politics of the BNP that eventually swayed my opinion. The freedom of speech is an absolute cornerstone of both democracy and a free media. Censorship is the enemy of a free press. It is also, in my opinion, the seed from which understanding and harmony grow. Once the state and the press begins deciding what its people can hear and be told – and withhold opinions which differ from their own – then it will only breed distrust, resentment and eventually disharmony. The freedom of speech is worthless if we only use it to defend the right to express views we agree with. It only really becomes tested when we find those opinions we give space to are opposed to our own. I'm not pretending it was an easy decision but in the end, I believe, the freedom of expression was worth defending above many other factors.

How important is it for local newspapers to adopt campaigns?

It's important for newspapers to keep their readers' interest, sell newspapers to secure their future and remain a trusted brand. If a campaign meets those criteria then newspapers should run them. Unfortunately, all too often newspapers run campaigns without a clear aim and without hope of an end. All too often they are worthy but dull. Too often they simply peter out because both the staff and the readers have lost interest in something they didn't really care about in the first place. A good campaign should have a definable end, a good chance of victory and stir the passions of its readers. Newspapers should adopt good campaigns – not campaigns for the sake of it.

Note

1   I would like to thank John Tulloch for stressing the importance of 'eloquence' to me during our many discussions on media ethics and other matters . . . Kovach and Rosenstiel (2003: 181) make the same point: 'Every journalist – from newsroom to boardroom – must have a personal sense of ethics and responsibility – a moral compass. What's more, they have a responsibility to voice their personal conscience out loud and allow others around them to do so as well.'

2

Ethical controversies today

An overview

The moral panic over the media: is it justified?

Significantly, ethical considerations have become a major preoccupation in dominant political circles since the end of the Cold War between the West and East (the North/South conflict, it is argued, continues). President Bush proclaimed the moral defence of the 'new world order' against 'evil monster' Saddam Hussein in 1991. Tory Premier John Major talked of going 'back to basics', Labour PM Tony Blair preached a 'moral crusade' and boasted for a while of pursuing an 'ethical' foreign policy. The Nato bombing of Serbia in 1999 was, according to the rhetoric, 'humanitarian' while the 2003 ultimately disastrous invasion of Iraq by US/UK forces was justified at the time as being in defence of the human rights of the oppressed Iraqi people.

Even Hollywood joined in. Michael Mann's 2000 blockbuster, *The Insider*, a *60-Minute* exposé of the tobacco industry (pulled when CBS detected a conflict with its commercial interests) was described in the *Big Issue* (6–12 March 2000) as 'that rarest of things: a story about ethical journalism'. And George Clooney's 2005 film *Good Night, and Good Luck* presented the American broadcaster, Edward R. Murrow, as a highly principled and outspoken critic of the communist-baiting Senator Joseph McCarthy in the 1950s.

While ethics dominates political discourse, a moral panic has emerged over the 'dumbing down' and 'tabloidisation' of the media – in both Britain, the United States and France (where celebrity scandal journals are often dismissed as 'presse people'). A typical view is expressed by Andrew Belsey and Ruth Chadwick (1992: 4): 'In the light of the problems the world faces, the typical daily content of an American television

channel or a British tabloid newspaper is not just a shame but a crime.'
John Lloyd, former editor of the *New Statesman, Financial Times* journalist
and more recently director of the Reuters Institute at the University of
Oxford, expressed similar anxieties about the media's power to defile the
public sphere in his widely-covered *What the media are doing to our politics*
(2004). In a typical broadside, Lloyd wrote (ibid.: 156): 'One reason why
journalism is unpopular, especially with publically accountable people
like politicians, scientists, medical workers and public officials, is that
the reporters and the commentators keep popping up to slam them from
both the right and left of them – and they're the same people. Many
public figures thus conclude that journalists don't believe in anything
but slamming people.'

Most surveys of public opinion place journalists at the bottom of 15
groups in terms of public credibility – even below politicians and estate
agents. British journalists are consistently placed at the bottom of the
league for truth telling. In 1983 some 19 per cent of respondents to a
Mori poll expected journalists to be generally truthful. In 2003 the figure
was roughly the same (18 per cent) but it had dipped to as low as 10
per cent in 1993. In contrast 91 per cent said they trusted doctors, 87
per cent teachers. By 2008, Google had become the most trusted source
of news – even though it gathered no news (Monck 2008). As Davis
Merritt (1995: xv) commented: 'In a time of declining trust in virtually
all institutions, journalism's decline is by far the steepest.' Phil Hall
(2000), former editor of the *News of the World*, commented: 'One of the
most frustrating parts of working on the *NoW* was the lack of trust the
public has in journalists.' In an intriguing attempt to help rebuild viewers'
trust, Channel Five news editor David Kermode introduced a ban on a
number of television techniques. They included 'noddies' (reconstructed
images of the interviewer nodding in response to the interviewee's
comments), 'contrived cutaways' and 'contrived walking shots'. According
to Vian Bakir and David Barlow (2007: 210) the public's lack of trust
is hardly surprising. They rightly suggest the public should distrust power
holders even more:

> Given that in the contemporary public sphere, there is minimal
> interest in forming a public . . . but every intention to inform
> and indoctrinate one for political and economic gains; given
> that government and business have professionalised their
> communications; and given that this strategic communication

non-transparently subsidises and co-opts media, the public are right to withhold their trust from both the power holders and the media.

Yet a survey conducted by YouGov for the journalists' trade weekly, *Press Gazette*, in 2005 came up (perhaps not surprisingly) with somewhat different results about trust and the media. More than half those surveyed (52 per cent) agreed with the statement: 'Journalism makes a positive contribution to life in Britain.' Some 32 per cent did not agree while 16 per cent were 'don't knows' (Ponsford 2005). Certainly this confirms how important it is to be sceptical about all poll results: so often their results differ according to the questions posed and the polling organisations involved.

According to Postman (1985: 4), entertainment has become the supra-ideology; the natural format for the representation of all experience. 'Our politics, religion, news, athletics, education and commerce have been transformed into congenial adjuncts of show business, largely without protest or even much popular notice. The result is that we are a people amusing ourselves to death.' Significantly Richard Desmond, owner of the *Daily Star*, *Daily Express* and *OK!* magazine, commented on his media empire: 'We're a branch of showbiz, aren't we?' (cited in Greenslade 2004). Bob Franklin (1997) bewails the spread of trashy 'newzak'. Ian Jack (1999) condemns the media's 'fickle, orgasmic sensationalism. Every branch is infected'. And for Dario Fo, the Italian anarchist and 1997 Nobel Prize winner, 'making people ignorant has become an art. Journalism is the science of not informing people' (see McNab 2007).

During the 1990s and early 'noughties', major controversies emerged over invasions of privacy by the media, particularly of celebrities, male MPs, a certain US President and various randy royals. And calls grew, supported by some prominent journalists, for the introduction of privacy laws such as in Germany where politicians' private lives (marriage problems, sexual inclinations and so on) are protected. The media in general, and not just the red-top tabloids, were accused of promoting 'bonk journalism', being obsessed with sex, sleaze and 'human interest'. Interestingly, Tessa Hilton, then editor of the *Sunday Mirror*, when asked what her perfect story was, replied: 'A cabinet minister who is married and having an illicit affair with some very big name actress who is very glamorous . . . and we have got pictures' (*Guardian*, 11 March 1996). Kelvin MacKenzie, former editor of the *Sun*, made clear his own priorities: 'I wish there was more sex in the *News of the World*. I look to it for a good dollop of shagging and if I don't get it I feel robbed' (*The Times*, 17 March 2000). On the typical *Sun* reader, he had no doubts:

> He's the bloke you see in the pub – a right old fascist, wants to send the wogs back, buy his poxy council house; he's afraid of the unions, afraid of the Russians, hates the queers and weirdos and drug dealers.
> (Chippendale and Horrie 1999: 176–7)

Right-wing commentators such as Mark Steyn (1998) blame the human interest obsessions of the media on the 'sentimentalisation' of the broader culture. Even a central theme of 1999 Booker prize-winning novel, *Amsterdam* (London: Vintage), by Ian McEwan, had as its central theme the growth of chequebook journalism according to which news and information becomes a commodity to sell to the highest bidder. Serious political analysis and coverage is said to be giving way to 'attack journalism' with politicians (within a corrupted civil society) trading good-sounding but essentially simplistic 'sound-bites' at each other. In 1996, the publication in the US of James Fallows' *Breaking the News: How the Media Undermine American Democracy* drew claims that a similar process was at work in Britain. For instance, Steve Barnett (op. cit.: 406) argued:

> I believe there is growing evidence that in Britain, as in the US, we have now entered an age when journalists are intent on going beyond the bounds of informed scepticism to unthinking ridicule – a coarsening of political reporting which is in danger of undermining respect for democratic institutions and actors and therefore democracy itself. We have entered the age of contempt.

Alongside these criticisms go concerns over a decline in straight reporting and the arrival on the media scene of a New Punditocracy with their often under-researched comment pieces (the new 'me journalism') mixing extremist views, speculation, gossip, innuendo and abuse (Glover 1999; Heller 1999). As Nick Cohen argued (1999: 125): 'Those who believe in the information revolution should measure the space in newspapers filled with consumer and show-business journalism, trite features and opinion from the same pundits who – the best fat can be chewed for ever – will be back on television later in the day to read out their columns.' Political coverage is said to be coming under the growing dominance of 'spin-doctors' – a clique of unelected, though immensely powerful officials, typified by Alastair Campbell, Tony Blair's often demonised press officer (Oborne 1999). As publicists such as Max Clifford came to outnumber journalists, PR-manufactured pseudo-events won increasing media space (Boorstin 1962).

The depoliticisation of the media and their obsessions with sport, lifestyles, sex, health and single events (such as the O.J. Simpson trial of 1995, the Gulf Wars of 1991 and 2003, the death of Princess Diana on 31 August 1997, the abduction of Madeleine McCann in May 2007) are said to be transforming citizens into indifferent consumers. Some critics even argue that media saturation of the cultural space is leading to political apathy (Bourdieu 1998). Critics have also focused on the rundown of foreign news coverage (with the media becoming paradoxically more parochial while communications systems are increasingly globalised) and the narrowing of range of debate permitted. Journalists are also accused of being too close to the political establishment. As Franklin (2004: 18) argues: 'Journalists and politicians may sometimes pursue different goals but this occurs within an agreed framework which offer potential benefits to both groups. Each group requires the other, no matter how reluctantly, to prosecute its own interests and purposes. Mutuality of interests drives and sustains the relationship.' At the same time, the dissenting voices of feminists, peace campaigners, environmental activists, anarchists, lesbians and gays, it is claimed, have been marginalised or even demonised – in ways so acutely dissected in Heinrich Böll's *The Lost Honour of Katarina Blum* (Harmondsworth: Penguin 1978). Journalists themselves have highlighted failures of management ethics with the increasing stresses of the job, particularly with the launch of 24-hour news services and the information overload accompanying the spread of the Internet. Multi-skilling is seen as threatening the very future of journalistic professionalism. As Michael Bromley has argued (Bromley and O'Malley 1997: 350):

> Multi-skilling contains the potential for the final fragmentation of journalism, enskilling some as 'entrepreneurial editors' but deskilling others to the status of machine hands and extensions of the computer. In between there may develop several levels of employment as mediatechnicians-with-words (and pictures). None, however, will be journalists, as such.

Alongside the growth of union de-recognition and the decentralisation of collective bargaining came management assaults on journalists' jobs, wages and conditions leading to fear, obsequiousness and conformism within newsrooms (Foot 1991). As American media theorist John C. Merrill argues (1996): 'The journalist finds that he has less and less incentive, encouragement or chance to exert his own creativity; he knows that his organisation demands more and more of his time and effort. He conforms or he suffers. So generally he conforms.'

But not always. As important research by Gregor Gall (2005a and 2005b) and Tony Harcup (2002a and 2004) highlighted, there have been instances when unionised journalists have acted collectively to promote higher standards. Examples include action by journalists at the *Mirror* and the *South Wales Argus* in 1991, at the Express Group in 2001, the *Scotsman* in 2002 (when the editorial director, Andrew Neil, was accused of damaging the reputation of the paper) and at the Telegraph Group in early 2004 (when concerns were expressed that pornographer and *Express* owner Richard Desmond would take over the paper after the collapse of Conrad Black). As Harcup concluded: '[A]ny critique of the ethics of journalism that fails to address the role of journalists as workers can only be partial' (2004: 112).

Internet: new media, new dilemmas?

By 2007, many doomsters were claiming that the emergence of the Internet was threatening the very existence of traditional (old) media in Britain. According to a *Western Mail and Echo* internal document dated 17 November 2006, quoted by Williams and Franklin (2007: 63):

> All branches of the traditional media – print, radio, and TV – are converging on the digital space. Radio stations are broadcasting moving pictures over the web, the BBC are trialling an ultra-local TV service with the aim of spreading it across the UK, ITV are developing local classified web sites. Digital newcomers – search engines such as Google and Yahoo, and online classified sites like Craigslist – are invading the territory that for decades has been at the heart of local and regional newspapers.

Certainly the official figures for the online readership of the national press were showing sensational surges by March 2008. The Mail Online's unique number users soared 165 per cent year on year to 17,903,172, the site's emphasis on entertainment-led stories and celebrity photographs (so competing with showbiz blogs such as PerezHilton.com and TMZ.com) appearing to account for much of the growth. Over the same period Telegraph.co.uk increased 65 per cent, Sun Online 40 per cent while the Guardian.co.uk remained the highest traffic website with 19,708711, a rise of 26 per cent (Kiss 2008). The *News of the World* site recorded a massive 201 per cent year-on-year increase – with soft-porn videos accounting for much of the traffic. One 90-second video showing Formula One president Max Mosley in a role play with five prostitutes was watched 2,000 times a minute in April 2008 after a High Court judge refused to grant an injunction preventing its posting. But concerns remained that, while a report from the regulatory body Ofcom in 2007 recorded more than half UK households had broadband access, many elderly and poorer families were excluded. As the *Observer* of 6 January 2008 reported, there was a danger of the digital world creating a 'new underclass'. The organisation, the Campaign for Press and Broadcasting Freedom (www.cpbf.org.uk), urged the government to ensure universal access to broadband Internet – and digital broadcasting – for all people in the UK. Do you agree with this strategy?

In a speech which is now often seen as marking a watershed in traditional news providers' attitudes to the Internet, News Corporation chief Rupert Murdoch told the American Society of Newspaper Editors in April 2005: 'A new generation of media consumers has risen demanding content delivered . . . very much as they want it. The emphasis online is shifting from text only to text with video' (Murdoch 2005). For Mark Deuze, also, traditional journalism is coming to an end (2007: 141). 'The boundaries between journalism and other forms of public communication – ranging from public relations or advertorials to weblogs and podcast – are vanishing,' he says. 'Commercialisation and cross-media mergers have gradually eroded the distinct professional identity of newsrooms and their publications (whether in print or broadcast).'

A number of seminal events appeared to seal the democratisation of the media with the rise and rise of citizen web journalism and the use by professional journalists of user-generated material. These were the:

- blogs of 11 September 2001 US 'terrorist' outrages;
- the reports of Salam Pax, the 'Baghdad blogger' during the US/UK invasion of Iraq in 2003, which secured him international fame;
- the success of the US bloggers in 2004 who forced Fox News anchor Dan Rather to resign after they discredited one of his reports (and the global online population reached an estimated 934 million);
- the camcorder images of the 2004 Asian Boxing Day tsunami;
- the mobile phone images of 7 July 2005 'terrorist' attacks in London: according to Julia Day (2005), 'newsrooms around the capital were being deluged with pictures and video clips sent directly from the scene. The long predicted democratisation of the media had become a reality as ordinary members of the public turned photographers and reporters';
- the video images of the arrest of the two suspects in the failed attempt to bomb London on 21 July 2005. The shots of them walking out of their flat bare-chested and with their hands held high, surrounded by scores of armed police, were beamed across the world – and netted amateur 'snaparazzi' Nick Sophocleous £60,000 in a deal with ITN and the *Daily Mail*;
- the Facebook[1] pages and the cellphone video clips (globally distributed by CNN) taken by graduate student Jamal Albarghouti of the Virginia Tech massacre, when 30 people were killed in a shooting spree at the US campus on 16 April 2007.

According to media analyst, blogger and freelance journalist Kristine Lowe, *all* journalists today (whether they realise it or not) are working at the intersection of the mainstream media (increasing dubbed MSM) and the web, which she calls the 'social media'. 'The revolutionary force of the web is not the technology in itself but the fact that it enables us to talk together without intermediaries – and this fosters a powerful global conversation' (Lowe 2008). But with up to 4 million bloggers at work in the UK alone by 2008, concerns were mounting that the younger generation was losing all sense of the right to privacy. Marina Hyde commented (2007):

> Gradually the older generations are having to adjust to the notion that not only do younger people not really care about privacy, they often don't even comprehend the idea of it. Watch the audition rounds of any television talent show and it seems as if an entire generation now believes fame to be a

basic human right. Maybe one of the other rights had to give. Maybe it was privacy.

In 2000, just 25 per cent of UK homes had Internet access. By 2007, more than half of UK homes had broadband with connection speeds having risen almost eight times over the previous four years (White 2007). Meanwhile, online advertising spending surged past the £2 billion mark (with one company, Google, grabbing 40 per cent of the market) while Internet consumers spent more than £50 billion in 2006. Many of the mainstream newspaper companies have been busy gobbling up online advertising agencies: in 2004 Daily Mail and General Trust paid £14 million for a property sales website while in the following year its competitor, Trinity Mirror, bought the online recruitment agency Hot Group for around £50 million and GAAPweb.com for £10.45 million (Wachman 2005). By 2009, more money would be spent advertising on the Internet than on television, according to the Internet Advertising Bureau. Though the average time spent watching television dropped 4 per cent in 2006, average daily Internet use more than doubled. A report from Ofcom, the independent regulator and competition authority for the communication industries in the UK, in December 2006 showed a massive increase in the use of mobile phones. The number of mobile connections reached 67.7 million compared with just 33.6 million landline connects. Some 41 per cent of mobile phone users regularly used their phone as a digital camera, 10 per cent listened to radio broadcasts while 21 per cent used it for games. But just 13 per cent used their mobiles for web access (ibid.).

At the global level the rapid emergence of the Internet (since its origins in the 1960s when the US Department of Defense began to sponsor research into new modes of communication under severe military conditions) has been phenomenal. It took radio 38 years to have an audience of 50 million people. It took television 13 years to reach the same audience. The Internet, once it was opened up to the public, reached the 50m mark in just four years. According to the Internet Innovation Alliance (www.internetinnovation.org), it took two centuries to fill the shelves of the Library of Congress with more than 57 million mansuscripts, 29 million books and periodicals, 12 million photographs and more. Now, the world generates an equivalent amount of digital information almost 100 times every day (Smith 2008). By 2007, users were estimated at more than 1 billion while the Internet Society estimated 80 per cent of the planet would have Internet access by 2010 (Abdullah 2007: 29–30).

By the following year, China had overtaken the US at the top of the Internet league with more than 210 million users – and 200,000 new netizens every day, according to the China Internet Network Information Centre (Watts 2008). In contrast, only 4 per cent of people in the Arab world had broadband access (Leadbetter 2008a). In Britain, media companies such as AOL UK were even outsourcing some editorial activities to developing countries such as India, while publications as diverse as the *Daily Mail*, *Vogue*, *GQ*, *Glamour*, *Vanity Fair*, the *Economist* and the *Independent* were planning to raid the potentially massive Indian market (Joseph 2007).

Since its launch in February 2005, the video sharing site YouTube has proved a sensational success, being snatched up by Google for £1.6 billion and hosting 76 million videos by March 2008. And while YouTube was beginning to offer its own live television channels, traditional news operators such as the *Daily Telegraph*, *thelondonpaper*, *Daily Mirror*, *News of the World*, Al-Jazeera, BBC World News, Sky News and ITN were moving on to the site with their own specialist video channels. According to the regulatory body Ofcom, 4 in 10 UK adults said they regularly visited social networking sites and spent on average 5.3 hours each month on them (while figures from the Office for National Statistics suggest that 25 per cent of Britons never read a book). As convergence continued across so many media platforms, blurring the distinctions between the various sectors, in November 2007, Bebo, the UK's biggest social networking site, announced partnerships with broadcasters including the BBC, Channel 4, Sky, ITN and CBS. Clearly the traditional providers were aiming to connect with the so-called 'lost generation' of 13 to 24-year-olds who make up the core of Bebo's 10.7 million users (Gibson 2007a). And as the web's constant invention of new platforms brought radical changes to work and sourcing routines, increasingly journalists and bloggers used the microblogging platform, Twitter which enables people to publish 140 character-long messages via the Internet and mobile phones. Mainstream companies were also setting up stations in Second Life, the Matrix-like, virtual world on the world wide web: global news agency Reuters had its own 'in-world' correspondent while Sky News had purchased an island where presenter Adam Boulter had even interviewed Foreign Secretary David Miliband (D. Smith 2008b).

Mainstream moral concerns over the Internet have tended to focus on the easy access it allows to extremist political views and weird cults. On 30 May 2004, for instance, the *Sunday Times* reported on a series of bizarre murders by Internet addicts (Woods and Nathan 2004). Many Internet Service Providers (ISPs) say the network's main use is providing access to porn. Concerns over children's vulnerability to paedophiles on the Internet have also mounted in the media. In 2004, the children's charity, NCH, blamed the Internet for the massive 1,500 per cent rise in child pornography crimes since 1988 (BBC 2004). Critics argue that Internet usage for many is leading to information overload with users spending, on average, three hours a day e-mailing. On a national scale, such addiction is leading to a decline in social involvement and a rise in aggressive, selfish capitalism. According to top US psychiatrist Dr Jerald Block, Internet addiction, involving excessive gaming, emailing, text messaging and online pornography should be officially recognised as a clinical mental disorder (D. Smith 2008c).

The Internet, it is claimed, will also accentuate moves towards the commodification and superficiality of the media's soundbite culture while the spread of anonymous and aggressive 'flaming' calls is said to be debasing the public sphere. There are also concerns that the Internet is reinforcing global structures of economic control rather than opening up new democratic possibilities. Some 85 per cent of the revenue from Internet businesses goes to American firms which hold 95 per cent of the stock market value of Internet properties. By 2008, the market value of Google, which accounted for three quarters of all searches on the Internet, was a staggering $160 billion, with its profits soaring 40 per cent to $4.2 billion in 2007 after it swallowed up the video-sharing website YouTube (Clark 2008). But concerns persisted over Google's links with US intelligence. In April 2008, the *San Francisco Chronicle* reported that Google had been recruited by US intelligence agencies to help them process and share information they gathered about suspects. Agencies such as the National Security Agency had bought servers on which Google-supplied search technology was being used to process information gathered by networks of spies around the world. Google was also providing the search features for a Wikipedia-style site, called Intellipedia, on which agents post information about their targets that can be accessed and appended by colleagues (see Richards 2008).

Concerns are also mounting that journalism standards are falling because of the increasing, multi-skilling demands on reporters. *Guardian* blogger and Professor of Journalism at City University, London, Roy Greenslade (2008) decribes a reporter handling a running story in the new, seven-day business division of the *Daily Telegraph*:

Stage one: a quick text story on the website to break the news. Stage two: updates as and when necessary on the site. Stage three: if a video or audio clip seems appropriate then he/she will go into the studio, located on the same floor. Stage four: as the day progresses the writer gets both extra background and reaction, some of it from contributions to the site. This will help in the writing of a more analytical and contextual piece for the paper.

A report from the National Union of Journalists in December 2007 suggested that reporters were being made to work longer hours and taking on more responsibilities for no extra pay. Some 52 per cent of respondents to a survey considered the standards of online journalism merely 'adequate'. The most serious threat to online standards was the publishing of copy without it first being checked by a qualified journalist (Stabe, Smith and McNally 2007).

Since now anyone with Internet access can, in theory, set up their own media operation there are widespread fears that this new 'citizen journalism' will lead to a 'deprofessionalisation' of the industry (Richstad 1999: 41). When a video sharing website such as www.liveleak.com is able to show uncensored footage of frontline action of US soldiers, what special role can professional war correspondents such as Kate Adie, John Simpson and Robert Fisk play? According to John Sutherland, soldiers' use of the web was transforming the reporting of war:

> Milblogging and combat blogging have re-pictured war as drastically as William Howard Russell's telegraphed despatches from the Crimean front did in 1855. It was the millblogs, intermilitary email rings and mobile phones – not war journalism – that leaked the Abu Ghraib pictures [showing US soldiers torturing and humiliating Iraqi prisoners] into general circulation. And the enemy also have their blogs, gleefully circulating images of carnage.
>
> (Sutherland 2007)

A study by online ticket-seller Goldstar Events found in 2008 that arts enthusiasts were already deserting the traditional media in droves – with 60 per cent saying they would seek out a website review compared to just 25 per cent who preferred to look at a newspaper or magazine review. Indeed, theorists such as Charles Leadbeater (2008) and Clay Shirky (2008) are keen to celebrate the new, democratic potentials of reader-edited wikis and other web-based social tools which, they argue, encourage a redefinition of the public sphere with their extreme openness, decentralisation and collaborative publishing ventures.

Similarly, anyone with a camera can take shots and submit them to the media. In September 2005, Scoopt, a syndication agency for 'citizen journalists', sold its first photograph – to the Bristol *Evening Post* for a 'two-figure sum' of an allegedly stolen car that crashed following a police chase – and by 2008 it was able to claim it had transformed the routines of picture editors around the country. On its website (www.scoopt.org) it was able to report the *Independent* saying: 'Many images we see nowadays are not taken by professionals but by members of the public.' Outrage accompanied the paparazzi hounding of Britney Spears (allegedly worth around £120 million – £60 million – per year to the US economy) during her mental breakdown in 2008 with allegations that many of the photographers pursuing her were 'renegades'. As Gary Morgan, co-founder of the Splash News photo agency, told *Press Gazette* (Ponsford 2008): 'The situation is out of control. The problem is there are so many renegade shooters out there – not even photographers. People who used to be waiters and tipsters can now just pick up a digital camera and shoot.' Nick Stern, who worked for Splash in Los Angeles, quit his job in protest at the treatment of Spears by the 'paps' while even the Holy Moly celebrity gossip website (visited by 1 million people every month in addition to its 180,000 regular subscribers) in February 2008 adopted a new policy ruling out images taken while 'pursuing people in cars and on bikes', 'celebrities with their kids', 'people in distress at being photographed' and celebrities who are not 'on duty' (Byrne 2008). In the UK, pressure mounted to introduce some form of registering of photographers to curb the hounding of celebrities. How viable are such suggestions?

And while many Internet activists argued that the web was enabling an expansion of media freedoms, providing a public space for a wide variety of views, a survey by Privacy International (2003) found that Internet censorship was widespread in most regions of the world. In February 2003, the magazine *Index on Censorship* reported on a British government survey which indicated that big business was increasingly using libel laws to close websites set up by disgruntled customers and protest groups. The law, it said, put ISPs under considerable pressure to remove sites as soon as they were told of material which might be defamatory, regardless of whether it was in the public interest or true. In 2007, Amnesty International launched a campaign called irrepressible.info to draw attention to the growing attacks by governments on websites and blogs alongside the moves by IT companies (such as Yahoo!, Microsoft and Google) to build systems enabling surveillance and censorship to take place (Lezard 2007). And on 12 March 2008, Reporters Without Borders launched the first 'Online Free Expression Day' to highlight the plight of bloggers in the many countries where the government controls the media – such as Burma, China, Cuba, Egypt, North Korea, Tunisia and Turkmenistan. 'At least 62 cyber-dissidents are currently imprisoned worldwide, while more than 2,600 websites, blogs or discussions forums were closed or made inaccessible in 2007,' it was reported on www.rsf.org (see also www.fromthefrontline.co.uk). In 2007, the founder of the Internet company Yahoo! had to apologise to the family of reporter Shi Tao for passing on information to the Chinese government which led to his being jailed for ten years.

Print: streets of shame?

In Britain, Fleet Street is now commonly known as the Street of Shame. Polly Toynbee, award-winning *Guardian* columnist, summed up a popular sentiment when she pronounced (2007): 'The British press, the worst in the West, demoralises the national psyche. It makes people miserable. It raises false fears. It proclaims that nothing works, everything gets worse and it urges distrust of any public official or politician.' Yet 80 per cent of adults read at least one national newspaper while 75 per cent read a Sunday (McNair 1996: 15). A Family Spending Survey in January 2008 found that British households spent £76 million on newspapers and magazines every week – the equivalent of £1.37 per person.

The national mainstream press comprises 10 morning dailies and 10 Sundays. The 'qualities' (*Daily Telegraph, Financial Times, Guardian, Independent, The Times*) sell around 2.6 million copies daily, the mid-market tabloids (*Daily Mail, Daily Express*) 3 million and red top tabloids (*Daily Star, Daily Mirror, Sun*) 5.3 million. On Sundays, the 'qualities' (*Observer, Independent on Sunday, Sunday Telegraph* and *Sunday Times*) sell 2.56 million copies; the *Mail on Sunday* and *Sunday Express* 3.03 million while the *News of the World, Sunday Mirror, Sunday People* and *Daily Star Sunday* sell 5.79 million. At the local level, 36 million regional dailies are sold or given away every week while around six million local paid-for weeklies and 24 million free weeklies are distributed.

Yet newspaper circulations have been in severe decline since 1945. To take just one example, in the two years since Johnston Press purchased the Edinburgh-based *Scotsman* and its sister titles, sales slumped 17 per cent (Neil 2008). This trend has been blamed on rivalry first from television and more recently the web. But as media professor Julian Petley comments (2007):

> The idea that falling readership might be explained by the fact that many erstwhile readers simply couldn't stand the journalism on offer is rarely considered. If online newspapers simply replicate the kind of journalism which has alienated readers of the printed versions, it will hardly be a recipe for success. Furthermore, if newspaper proprietors fail to invest in good journalism then the future for the whole journalistic enterprise, online as well as print looks bleak.

Similar trends were evident in the United States. There the combined market value of independent, publicly traded newspaper publishers had fallen by 42 per cent between 2005 and 2008; spending on print advertisements fell 9 per cent in the 2007–8 fiscal year; the time Americans spent reading newspapers had fallen to just 15 hours a month and newspapers were receiving a declining share of Internet advertising as well (Alterman 2008).

Despite falling circulations, the political, cultural and social roles of the mass-selling press remain crucial in the UK – all the more so because they (and not television) are the primary agenda setters. In addition, there is a vast range of alternative peace movement, ethnic minority, gay and lesbian, religious and leftist newspapers (all with their associated websites). While their ethical standards are far higher than those in the mainstream press, their lack of financial muscle means their political and cultural influence is limited.

Moral concerns over recent years have focused on the spread of 'junk journalism' (Baistow 1985) epitomised with the emergence of the 'tits and bums'-obsessed *Daily Sport*. Launched on 17 August 1988, it was published originally only on three days a week but later became a six-day paper. Like *Sunday Sport* (launched in September 1986) it is owned by David Sullivan, his fortune based on the production of pornographic magazines, films and sex aids (Killick 1994). Both publications publish plainly invented stories – such as sightings of Elvis Presley and children conceived by aliens.

In the face of the Internet onslaught, the magazine industry in the UK appears to be surviving, with research suggesting that 20 million magazines are sold every week and the majority of people saying the Web had had no impact on the number of titles they had bought (Robinson 2007a). But mags such as *Loaded, FHM* and *Stuff* – and more recently *Nuts* and *Zoo* (with their associated websites and, in the case of *Nuts*, television channel) have been blamed for spawning a male chauvinist, laddish culture while glossy women's monthlies have become increasingly dominated by one subject: sex (O'Sullivan 1999). In 1997, the right-wing Social Affairs Unit criticised them for portraying women as 'selfish, superficial and obsessed by sex'. GQ editor James Brown came under fire in February 1999 after his magazine named the Nazis among 'the smartest men of the 20th century'. Even teenage girls' magazines came under fire in 1996 from Peter Luff MP who proposed a private member's bill aiming to limit what he viewed as the over-use of sexual material in the publications.

Press obsessions with sleaze have led to growing calls by politicians – supported by the public in opinion polls – for privacy legislation to 'restrain' the prying press. Many argue that the hyper-competition among the national press, with the over-emphasis on scoop journalism, is the most serious factor behind the decline in standards. Concerns have also been expressed over the decline of investigative, fact-based reporting (Foot 1999). For Tessa Mayes (2000: 30): 'Instead of news reporter's starting point being facts and analysis about the outside world, people's inner lives and emotional reactions to events including the reporter's own dominate how events are perceived. Emotional indulgence and sentimentalism are replacing informative, facts-based reporting. Today reporters are providing Therapy News.'

The cynical politics of the Fleet Street consensus – formerly largely pro-Tory now (bar three dailies and four Sundays) pro-Labour – has drawn criticisms just as its propaganda consensus in support of US/UK military adventurism – such as over Iraq in 1991, Serbia in 1999 and Afghanistan in 2001 – is said to have marginalised calls for diplomatic restraint and constructive dialogue. The pro-war consensus significantly broke down over the 2003 invasion of Iraq – but opposing newspapers (the *Independents*, the *Guardian* and *Mirrors*) still remained a minority. And even the *Mirrors* wobbled in their opposition in the face of protest from readers, according to the then-editor Piers Morgan.

The growing influence of the PR industry and spin-doctors on media content is reducing newspapers to being nothing more than publicity sheets for government and big business, so critics allege, while the growth of 'advertorials' (advertising copy written by journalists and flagged as such) is said to provide evidence of the power advertisers now wield over newspaper and magazine content. According to investigative journalist Nick Davies, newspaper reporters are increasingly reduced to being 'churnalists', simply recycling agency and PR material (Davies 2008a: 69–70). Some 80 per cent of reports about the UK in Fleet Street's 'qualities' are based to some degree on copy from the Press Association (PA), the country's leading agency. David Miller and William Dinan also suggest PR is bringing about the death of genuine news (2008): 'The aim is to undermine or marginalise independent journalism, control decision-making and, lastly, mystify and misinform the public.' In a similar vein, media academic Bob Franklin applies the term 'McJournalism' to define the standardised, predictable 'mush' of local journalism (2005a: 148):

> While market theorists claim diversity and quality as essential products of competition, the reality is McJournalism and McPapers with similar stories and even pictures reflecting a growing reliance on agency copy. The reduced numbers of journalists, the influence of local advertisers, the increasing reliance on information, subsidies from local government and other organisations with active public relations staffs means that, from Land's End to John O'Groats, McJournalism delivers the same flavourless mush.

The narrowing of the political debate in newspapers has been accompanied by a growing monopoly ownership of Fleet Street with the top four companies owning 90 per cent of the total in circulation terms. Anti-monopoly legislation has actually been in existence for more than 30 years but has had little impact. As James Curran points out (2000: 45): 'Between 1965 and 1993, 151 transfers of newspaper ownership gained approval and only four (all relatively minor) were stopped.' Every major acquisition, such as Murdoch's purchase of *The Times* and *Sunday Times*, and the *Guardian*'s purchase of the *Observer* were waved through by the government. Yet such trends towards monopolisation are global trends affecting not just media industries. As Peter Morgan stresses (2000), the top 200 companies now control a quarter of the world's economy. Also the growing control of the publishing industry by giant, multi-national companies (e.g. Rupert Murdoch's News International Corporation, Bertelsmann AG and the Dutch companies VNU and Elsevier) has led to calls for laws to prevent cross media ownership and such concentrations of power.

At the local level the newspaper industry is dominated by a small clique of companies – Trinity Mirror, the Daily Mail and General Trust's Associated Newspapers and Northcliffe division, Johnston Press, Newsquest Media Group, the Guardian Media Group, Archant, the Midlands News Association, DC Thomson and Tindle Newspapers. The UK's magazine industry – with more than 3,000 mainstream periodical titles – is also dominated by just a few companies. IPC (with 71 titles) was sold by Reed Elsevier to Cinven, an investment company, in January 1998 for £860 million. Then in July 2001, IPC (publishers of *Marie Claire*, *Loaded* and *Country* Life) was sold to AOL Time Warner for £1.1 billion. EMAP (with 90 consumer magazines) was valued in 2000 at £1.8 billion. But by January 2008 the company had broken up with its consumer magazine and radio businesses being sold to German publisher H. Bauer for £1.14 billion while its Business to Business (B2B) portfolio was sold to the Guardian Media Group and private equity group Apax. Also in the magazine sector, recent years have seen an explosion of free customer titles where the stress is on publicity, not journalism.

Journalists have focused particularly on the slump in management standards, highlighting the scandal of low salaries in the provincial press. Despite the vast economic power of the mainstream press, a lively alternative print industry (ethnic minority/left-wing/peace movement/ feminist/single-issue campaigning) survives against the odds – yet it tends to be ignored by both Fleet Street and academe. Critics allege this sector is too inward looking, concerned with esoteric, marginal issues and this is ultimately reflected in low circulations. Significantly, the left-wing *News on Sunday*, launched on 26 April 1987, lasted only six weeks (Chippendale and Horrie 1988) with blame directed at poor management, marketing and inadequate investment – the £6 million raised proving totally inadequate.

Broadcasting: public service ethos under threat?

Most people claim TV is their main source of national and international news. Every UK household has at least one radio and research undertaken by the Henley Centre for Forecasting suggests radio's popularity will grow still further in the future, particularly with the increase in car usage. Radio reaches 91 per cent of the population at some point during the week – with almost 25.8 million adults listening to a local station every week (Allen 2007). And figures from the Broadcasters' Audience Research Board (www.barb.org) for December 2007 indicated that people watched television on average for more than 28 hours a week. But the style of viewing is changing rapidly. Tiscali, the Internet broadband provider, was joining BT vision in offering television channels over phonelines. Another 19 channels such as UKTVGold, Living TV, Paramount Comedy and MTV were offering Top Up TV on Freeview, downloading previously ordered programmes to hard-disc-based digital recorders (Armstrong 2008).

Given this enormous output, broadcasting's political, cultural and educational roles are, then, hugely significant. And ethical issues assume paramount importance. Concerns have recently focused on a wide range of issues. According to the critics, the preference for polemic over argument and superficiality instead of depth has created a superficial 'soundbite culture'. Over-confrontational, gladiatorial, entertainment-oriented interviewing techniques (by Jeremy Paxman and John Humphrys, for instance) are said to have led to 'hyperadversarialism' with the radio and TV interviewer becoming more important than the interviewed. Focusing on television's coverage of disasters, Tamar Liebes (1998: 75) argues that the new conditions make responsible journalism 'all but impossible . . . The decision to go to live coverage means scrapping all of the accepted norms. There is no time for investigative reporting which entails a lengthy process of interviewing sources, checking reliability, searching data, editing and so on'.

Commercial pressures are blamed for the spate of faked programmes (one of the most notorious being *The Connection* in which journalists concocted a story about heroin smuggling into Britain). Talk shows have been shown to have hired actors from talent agencies to pose as guests while controversies have exploded over a long and embarrassing list of phone-in scandals in which viewers to such programmes as *The X-Factor*, *Richard and Judy*, *Blue Peter* and *Ant and Dec* were conned out of millions of pounds. Other BBC programmes to have duped their audiences included *Film Café* (Asian Network), the *Clare McDonnell Show* (6 Music) and *Tom Robinson* (6 Music). GMTV, which is 75 per cent owned by ITV, was fined £2 million by Ofcom in 2007 after admitting that millions of viewers taking part in phone-in competitions entered after lines had closed. Later in the same year Channel 4 was fined £1.5 million for misconduct over telephone lines in *Richard and Judy*'s 'You Say We Pay' competition and the *Deal or No Deal* programme. And in May 2008, ITV was fined a record £5.67 million for a yet another series of phone rip-offs. Do such scandals place public trust in broadcasters almost beyond repair?

Trash TV, it is claimed, has taken over from 'public service' programming particularly since television deregulation following the 1990 Broadcasting Act. Steven Barnett traces the start of the recent decline in broadcast standards to 1993 when the regime that insisted on a minimum level of current affairs on commercial channels was abandoned and Channel 4 was forced to compete for advertising revenue with ITV (2002: 401):

> Over the last ten years, therefore, competition for commercial revenue has first increased between ITV and Channel 4, then been exacerbated by the arrival of Channel 5 and all the while is becoming more vulnerable to the progressive encroachment of cable and satellite channels. The result has been more peak-time emphasis on high-profile, big-rating programmes and the end of those current affairs series of the seventies and eighties – *This Week* and *World in Action* on ITV, *First Tuesday* on Channel 4 – which carried precisely the kind of well-researched and critical programmes which define the press's watchdog role.

Critics also allege that television channels are now competing over the supply of soft porn, with philosopher Roger Scruton and the National Viewers and Listeners Association (founded by Mary Whitehouse as the 'Clean-up TV' campaign in 1963) claiming this amounts to a deliberate attack on 'family values'. Not surprisingly, Channel 5 head Dawn Airey walked straight into controversy when she claimed it was essentially about 'the three fs: football, films and fucking'.

A seemingly endless glut of voyeuristic 'fly-on-the-wall'/'camera on the body' 'reality' documentaries and docu-soaps (satirised in the Hollywood blockbusters, *The Truman Show* and *Being John Malkovich*) such as

Castaway 2000, Survivor, Big Brother, Wife Swap, I'm a Celebrity . . . Get me out of Here!, The Osbournes, Star Academy, Pop Idol have raised serious issues relating to privacy and the lust for celebrity status (Hill 2005). Stuart Jeffries bewailed the 'pornography of intrusion' of the endless reality television series (1997). Significantly, a report in January 2006 by England's Learning and Skills Council suggested that one in ten youngsters would drop out of school to be on television while one in six believed they would win fame on a reality television show – even though their odds were around one in 300 million (Williams 2007: 211). According to Jessica Williams, a slowing down in social mobility over the last two decades and the growth of critically deprived social underclass meant it was harder for working class people to escape their origins. 'No wonder so many kids want a comparatively easy route to fame and fortune' (ibid.: 213).

The domestication of the dreaded Big Brother in reality television (where the many watch the few) has serious implications for the growth of the 'surveillance society', according to a number of theorists. Interactive television, currently represented by companies such as PiVo and Replay, circumvents all timing inconveniences of traditional TV. Yet while it appears to provide for audience empowerment and the personalisation of televisual worlds, for Serra Tinic (2006) and David Lyon (2007: 157) it has serious surveillance dimensions. According to novelist Salman Rushdie (2001), reality television represents the dearth of talent and the death of morality. 'Add the contestants' exhibitionism to the viewers' voyeurism and you get a picture of a society sickly in thrall to what Saul Bellow [the American novelist] called "event glamour".' Moreover, concerns were expressed over people's vulnerability before the seductive power of the media, with voyeur TV fuelling the creation of a superficial, vanity-pandering culture. As novelist David Lodge (2000) pointed out:

> The readiness of people to let programme makers into their homes, to answer the most intimate questions about their lives and to allow themselves to be filmed in the most undignified and unflattering situations never ceases to amaze and is some measure of the contemporary lust for celebrity. Very often the subjects complain after the transmission of the programmes in which they figure so disadvantageously that they were deceived by the producers.

Film-maker Roger Graef (2000) also argued that 'reality television' was increasingly failing to protect people's rights to privacy and dignity: 'These days, people put themselves in unbearable positions and simply do not realise they are doing it.' Changes to the running of the BBC brought in by director-general John Birt (1992–2000) were denounced as threatening the editorial integrity of the World Service, downgrading domestic radio services and unnecessarily boosting bureaucracy. As the BBC was transformed into an increasingly commercial enterprise, critics claimed it had been privatised 'by the back door' with over-emphasis on ratings and a major shift away from its public service ethos. According to media expert Professor Michael Tracey (2000), public service broadcasting was under threat not only in Britain but globally because of 'the rise of competitive new media and the ideological dominance of the market in almost every facet of life'. Small increases in the BBC licence fee announced by the Culture Secretary Tessa Jowell in 2007 heightened fears of further job cuts and falling standards in public service programming. Barry White, of the Campaign for Press and Broadcasting Freedom, reported (2007):

> The BBC has also to finance the move of some departments to a £190m media centre in Salford and on top of all this is expected to make so-called future 'efficiency' savings of 3 per cent. All this will weaken the BBC (step forward a smiling Rupert Murdoch [owner of the rival Sky TV]) and lead to more repeats and further dumbing down – which viewers resent.

While many BBC employees face job uncertainty, a few Big Names receive outrageously high salaries, according to critics. Comedian Jonathan Ross reportedly earns £6 million a year and proudly told the audience at the British Comedy Awards in 2007: 'I'm worth 1,000 BBC journalists.' From the political right have come allegations that the BBC (with an annual £2.2 billion from the licence fee and 260 radio stations around the country) is run by a bunch of left-wingers. Before the 1997 general election, Brian Mawhinney, chairman of the Conservative Party, protested that the corporation's journalists were displaying 'eager anticipation' at the prospect of a Labour victory. Paul Dacre, editor of the *Daily Mail*, went further in January 2007, accusing the BBC of 'a kind of cultural Marxism' that was damaging political debate, feeding political apathy and failing to represent the views of millions of licence fee payers (Gibson 2007b). From the political left have come criticisms that the BBC is state propagandist, its board of governors a 'safe' collection of the Great and Good; its routine news values reflecting conventional racist, sexist and militarist assumptions.

But governments have also routinely attacked broadcasters as the 'enemy within'. For instance, the controversial ban on Irish 'terrorist' organisations (the IRA, INLA, Sinn Fein, UDA) launched in October 1988 and finally dropped in 1994, denying 'terrorists' the 'oxygen of publicity' in Margaret Thatcher's celebrated words, followed TV news coverage of the killing of two British soldiers at the funeral of the IRA unit killed by the SAS in Gibraltar in March 1988 (Devenport 2000: 58–62).

Concerns are also growing that the concentration of ownership in the independent television sector is leading to a dull uniformity of coverage. After the 1990 Broadcasting Act, the ITV network fell into the hands of just a few media empires such as Michael Green's Carlton Communications and Lord Hollick's United News and Media and Granada. Legislation assisted these trends towards monopoly and cross-media ownership. From November 1996 newspapers with no more than 20 per cent of national circulation have been able to increase their holding in ITV companies while broadcasters have been allowed to expand up to 15 per cent of the total television audience.

By 2000, the big newspaper and television companies were lobbying for all ownership constraints to be removed. Many saw Granada's purchase of the Meridian, Anglia and HTV franchises from United News and Media for £175 billion in July 2000 as a major step on the road towards a single owner for ITV with its £1.8 billion in annual advertising revenues. In 2003, the merger of Carlton with Granada (which together controlled 52 per cent of the television advertising market) finally brought into being ITV plc. Concerns grew that ITV's centre of gravity would also shift south, and with it, advertising revenue and jobs, while the NUJ feared regional news would be the final casualty. Elsewhere the trend was similarly towards the 'convergence' of media companies: in June 2000, Seagram, Vivendi (formerly a utility company) and the French pay-TV channel Canal-Plus merged to form the world's second largest media company (valued at $100 billion) after Time Warner–AOL.

The Broadcasting Acts of 1990 and 1996 established a host of commercial local radio stations, and licences were granted to three new national stations: Talk Radio, Virgin Radio and Classic FM. But, as Williams argues (op. cit.: 247):

On the surface the de-regulation of British radio would seem to offer diversity of programming. However, diversity is in reality limited by a number of factors. Most of Britain's local stations are owned by a small number of larger companies. Companies such as Radio Clyde, which controls virtually every radio station in Scotland, dominate large areas of the British Isles and commercial considerations make such companies play safe in the content of their stations. Output is dominated by talk and music.

Bob Franklin similarly complains (2004: 14): 'Commercial local radio has little local identity and reports only a scattering of local news. Whether in Blackpool, Bristol or Basingstoke, ILR offers an unrelentingly tedious and uniform output.'

Note

1   For Facebook's links with the American conservative neocons and the CIA see 'With friends like these', by Tom Hodgkinson, *Guardian*, 14 January 2008.

3
Regulating the mainstream media

Dawdling in the last chance saloon?

Why bother with ethical codes?

At the heart of British journalism lies the principle of self regulation and the celebration of the 'free press'. Our democracy is supposedly the fruit of centuries of struggle for freedom of oppression (Winston 2005) with the mass selling press which emerged in the second half of the nineteenth century free from direct government and political controls seen as the culmination of this process. Interestingly, Prime Minister Tony Blair suggested just before standing down in 2007 that, in the light of media convergence, newspapers should face the same regulation as broadcasters who are subject to statutory regulation (Rose 2007). Such a move would have completely upset long-held principles of media freedom: not surprisingly, one of the first statements of the new Gordon Brown government was to reject the Blair suggestion.

Media self regulation is built around the promotion of ethical codes. Yet these provoke a range of responses from journalists (see Nordenstreng 1997). Some regard them as vehicles of professionalisation, as a means of professional education, as instruments of consciousness-raising and as deliberate attempts by journalists to regulate the media and ward off legislation restricting their activities. Significantly, the first codes emerged in the first decade of the last century in Poland and the United States as part of the more general moves towards professionalisation. In Europe such codes were adopted gradually – after World War One (in Sweden, France and the UK), immediately after World War Two (Italy, Belgium) and around the late 1960s and 1970s (Spain, Portugal). A database of more than 400 codes from around the world is maintained by the Missouri

School of Journalism at www.media-accountability.org. In America, many newspapers have their own customised codes, watched over by an ombudsman (they usually are men). And US research suggests that journalists on newspapers with ombudsmen are more likely to exercise 'ethical caution' in their work (see Wilkins and Coleman 2005: 112).

A contrasting response stresses the role of codes as mere rhetorical devices to preserve special privileges such as access to the powerful and camouflage hypocrisy. Codes can also fulfil important public relations functions for professionals. As Frost suggests (2007: 248): 'They are often introduced to reassure the public that a profession has standards of practice and to imply, at least, that professionals who transgress those standards will be disciplined. Many professions and trades have raced to introduce codes of practice over the past few years in the light of rising consumer consciousness.' Some even argue that codes inherently restrict press freedom by encouraging certain patterns of behaviour and condemning others, while some suggest the media are more effectively regulated by the market, anyway.

Critics claim that few journalists are aware of the content of codes, particularly when they are constantly being changed: the original Press Complaints Commission's code of 1991, for instance, had been amended almost thirty times by 2006.[1] Guy Black, former PCC director, however, claimed the code's flexibility was its strength. 'Codes are meant to change from time to time. They need to be flexible documents especially in an industry like this.' Some journalists claim codes are there simply to be broken. Wilkins and Coleman see value in this journalistic scepticism (ibid.): 'Genuine moral development can occur only when people go beyond a stage of being other-directed by rules to an inner-directed stage of internalised rules . . . Perhaps the rejection of written codes of ethics is a reflection of this growth.'

Debate has arisen in recent years over how offensive and abusive comments can be filtered from the Internet – and whether such filtering is needed anyway. Certainly when Tim O'Reilly (inventor of the phrase Web 2.0) and Jimmy Wales (founder of the communal encyclopaedia Wikipedia) proposed such a 'bloggers' code of conduct' in April 2007 they were met by a torrent of offensive and abusive responses (Pilkington 2007). Any blogger signing up to their code would commit themselves to a 'civility enforced' standard to cut unacceptable comments. 'Unacceptable' is defined as:

- content that is used to abuse, harass, stalk or threaten others;
- libellous or misrepresentative;
- infringes copyright or privacy rights.

Anonymous postings are also unacceptable with all comments requiring a recognised email address, even if made under a pseudonym. Dan Gillmor, of the Centre for Citizen Media, linked to Berkeley's Graduate School of Journalism, said the code was unnecessary. Bloggers needed one simple rule: be civil. Do you agree?

What are the principal underlying values you can identify in the codes?

Some values are evident in codes throughout the world (Grevisse 1999; Laitila 1995):

- fairness;
- the separation of fact and opinion;
- the need for accuracy linked with the responsibility to correct errors;
- the deliberate distortion and suppression of information are condemned;
- maintaining confidentiality of sources;
- upholding journalists' responsibility to guard citizens' right to freedom of expression;
- recognising a duty to defend the dignity and independence of the profession;
- protecting people's right to privacy;
- respecting and seeking after truth;
- struggling against censorship;
- avoiding discrimination on grounds of race, sexual orientation, gender, language, religion or political opinions;
- avoiding conflicts of interests (particularly with respect to political and financial journalists/editors holding shares in companies they report on).

What are the major differences between the NUJ and the other industry codes?

The National Union of Journalists' Code, first adopted in 1936, now incorporates 13 general principles (accessible at www.nuj.org.uk). Other codes tend to contain detailed specifications of what is deemed either ethical or unethical. But as Harris (1992: 67) points out:

> One of the consequences of bringing out detailed sets of regulations is that it fosters a loophole seeking attitude of mind. The result could be that journalists will come to treat as permissible anything that does not fit the precise specifications of unethical behaviour. Furthermore, short codes consisting of broad principles can often be applied to new types of situation which could not have been envisaged by those drawing them up.

And Chris Frost (2000: 98) argues: 'A short code has the advantage of being easier for journalists to remember and use. They are able to measure directly their performance against the principles contained in the code and quickly realise when they are straying from the straight and narrow.' In 1979, the NUJ set up an Ethics Council to promote higher ethical standards and hear complaints against members alleged to have breached the Code of Conduct. But after a number of extremely controversial attempts to discipline its own members, important changes were made in the early 1990s. Now only members can complain about another member: complaints from members of the public are no longer permitted (Frost 2007: 276). The Code is seen more as a 'positive thing, a beacon for journalists to aim for rather than a means to punish', according to Tim Gopsill, the union's press officer. There have been few changes to the Code since its introduction. In 1998, the annual conference backed a call for a clause on the digital manipulation of images; in 2001, the privacy clause was slightly amended and in 2004 the clause relating to children was altered.

In contrast, the Institute of Journalists (www.ioj.co.uk) does discipline its members who breach its code. The PCC can force editors to publish adjudications. But it has no powers to fine a publication for breaching the code. In February 1998, the Lord Chancellor, Lord Irvine, demanded that the PCC should exact fines for breaches of the code, but this was simply ignored. National newspapers such as the *Guardian*, *Observer*, the *Independent* and *Daily Express* have in the past supported calls for the introduction of fines but this has been strongly opposed by regional newspapers.

What success did the Press Council have in regulating standards?

Since World War Two, press standards have attracted constant concern from governments and politicians. A General Council of the Press was proposed by the first Royal Commission (1947–9) to safeguard press freedoms and encourage the development of a sense of public responsibility among journalists. Launched on 21 July 1953, its first ruling was that a *Daily Mirror* poll on whether Princess Margaret should marry Group Captain Townsend was 'contrary to the best traditions of British journalism' (how royal reporting has changed!).

A second Royal Commission, set up in 1961, followed continuing concerns over monopolies. It stressed the importance of including a lay element on the General Council but when the Press Council came into being in July 1963 it did so with 20 industry representatives and just five lay members. A third Royal Commission (1974–7) was particularly critical of the performance of the Press Council, making 12 recommendations to transform its operating procedures. These were largely rejected and the council remained a weak body, lacking the confidence of both managers and the NUJ and accused of being over-long in its adjudications on complaints (see O'Malley and Soley 2000).

Then in 1989, following a spate of controversies over press intrusions into private grief, the Thatcher government authorised a committee to investigate the possible introduction of a privacy law. Chaired by David Calcutt, master of Magdalene College, Cambridge, the committee in the end backed making physical intrusion an offence but opposed a privacy law. It also proposed the creation of a Statutory Press Complaints Tribunal, to be chaired by a judicial figure appointed by the Lord Chancellor, with powers to draw up a code of practice and investigate alleged breaches as well as stop publication of offending material, take evidence on oath and impose fines.

Quickly, to ward off such legislation and marginalise the NUJ (which had been represented on the Press Council but which was not invited on to the new body) the industry formed the Press Complaints Commission in the place of the Press Council to administer a code of practice. Based largely on the former Press Council's code and on the existing Newspaper Publishers' Association code, it covers such issues as accuracy, opportunity to reply, privacy, harassment, children in sex cases, misrepresentation, the coverage of victims of sexual assault, financial journalism, confidential sources and payment for articles (and is accessible at www.pcc.org.uk). Since 1990 many newspapers have incorporated the code into contracts of employment (a policy which should become the norm, according to the Commons media committee in July 2007) and express a commitment to it in their pages, though knowledge of its clauses remains low among journalists. So let's end this section with a series of questions:

- Surveys suggest that the media (in particular the press) are held in low esteem by the public. Does this mean that the codes of ethics have failed?
- How important are codes in the formation of the notion of 'professionalism'?
- Are journalists today primarily supplying infotainment? Does this not change the nature of the industry and further problematise the notion of professionalism?
- Can journalism be compared to the legal, medicine and teaching professions?
- Do codes provide a framework around which debate can develop? Do not journalists need to be able to articulate ethical decisions in being accountable to their readers?
- Should journalists have to agree to follow a code of practice in their contracts and thus face dismissal if they transgress the code?

How can the performance of the PCC be rated?

You may argue that the PCC has responded well to the rapidly evolving media environment of recent years. For instance, in December 1997, following the death of Princess Diana, the PCC responded to mounting concerns over invasions of privacy, harassment by reporters and paparazzi and cheque-book journalism by introducing major changes to its code. Lord Wakeham, its then chairman, was moved to claim that the new code was 'the toughest in Europe'. New provisions included a tightening of areas considered 'private' and rules on the sensitive handling of news stories involving grief or shock. Payments to children for stories were also banned and the clauses on accuracy were expanded to include photographs. Rules on the investigation of stories were tightened with reporters banned from being involved in the 'persistent pursuit' of sources. In many cases, the former use of the words 'should' and 'may' were changed to 'must'. Stuart Higgins, the then editor of the *Sun*, commented on the new code: 'I and all *Sun* journalists are committed to implement it.'

In its 1997 annual report the PCC said it had 'extended its jurisdiction to certain publications on the Internet' and in 2006 it began adjudicating on complaints about the content of video and audio material on newspaper websites (though user-generated content such as blogs and chatrooms continued to be excluded). Its many supporters claim that its interventions are crucial in maintaining standards in the industry. Witnesses' payments were outlawed in 2004; a Charter Compliance Panel was set up to oversee the work of the PCC and produce a report and recommendations each year; transgendered people were added to the list of vulnerable people in the following year. In 2006, it added a new clause advising newspapers to take particular care in the reporting on suicide (see Chapter 8). And in the same year its chair, Sir Christopher Meyer, former Ambassador to the United States, confirmed that complaints from third parties would be considered. In 2007, it strongly criticised the magazine, *Chat*, for publishing a staged photograph of a female body wrapped in bin liners to illustrate how a murder victim was found. In using the image near the first anniversary of the death, the magazine had shown total disregard for the family of the dead woman. Again, following a complaint to the PCC, celebrity gossip magazine *Heat* apologised to model and television presenter Katie Price (aka Jordan) after putting a set of stickers in an edition including one which ridiculed her disabled son Harvey.

Provincial and national editors are some of the PCC's most vocal supporters. Even David Yelland, then editor of the *Sun*, said: 'Anybody who thinks the PCC doesn't have teeth is wrong because I can tell you it's the most horrible thing.' He was particularly impressed by its success in reducing the use of intrusive pictures by the paparazzi. 'I can turn down pictures in the full knowledge that none of my competitors can use them either. The way the two princes are pretty much left alone by the British press is an amazing achievement.' Supporters of the PCC also stress that it conducts business swiftly, resolving most complaints within three months. And the cost of any complaint is just the price of a first class stamp. Given the millions of words written and photographs published every year, very few people choose to complain, reflecting, it is claimed, the success of self regulation (see Shannon 2001). Journalism professor and chair of the NUJ's ethics council Chris Frost (2007: 233) also has these positive words on the PCC and the performance of its most recent chair, Sir Christopher Meyer: 'the PCC's calm behind-the-scenes approach to self-regulation and Meyer's subtle improvements and more careful pressure on editors has meant that it has been able to rein in the worst excesses over the past ten years, making it easier for governments to resist public pressure to bring in statutory regulation.'

PCC supporters say it regularly provides useful advice to editors before publication, organises effective open days around the country and its helplines deal with hundreds of calls from members of the public – often requesting journalists to desist from asking questions, following or photographing people (ibid.: 261). Its annual reports also offer intriguing insights into public perceptions of the press. For instance, in 2006, as in previous years, the majority of complaints were about accuracy (72.6 per cent, compared to 67.4 per cent in 2005) while only 10.8 per cent (12.5 per cent in 2005) were related to privacy. Of the 231 privacy cases, 38.4 concerned national newspapers, 46 per cent regional, 8.9 per cent Scottish, 1.3 Irish and just 5.4 per cent magazines. The PCC is also keen to stress its role as a conciliator. As the 2006 report commented:

> There has been a clear culture change over the last decade. Editors now routinely offer meaningful resolutions to breaches of the code – and on occasion offer to resolve matters that may not in fact breach the code. This is one of the advantages of a system of conciliation which brings parties together rather than having to make a judgment on who was right on each occasion. Since 1996, the number of resolved complaints has increased by around 400 per cent when overall complaints numbers have increased by about 20 per cent.

The PCC also claims to have defended the freedom of the press in the face of government pressures: for instance, in 1998 when the Data Protection Act incorporated the EU Data Protection Directive into UK legislation. As Robert Pinker, who served as the PCC's privacy commissioner from 1994 to 2004 and its acting chair from 2002 to 2003, comments (2006: 122): 'In its original form, the Act would have classified as private information large amounts of data that were not intrinsically private in nature. As such, the Act would have posed a substantial threat to press freedom.' After some months of negotiation with ministers and civil servants, the government agreed to an amendment which reconciled the rights and obligations of the press to report on matters of public interest with the privacy rights of individuals since it allowed editors a 'public interest' defence when faced with an action by the Data Protection Commissioner. Following PCC pressure in 2000, the government agreed to exclude financial journalists from the provisions of the Financial Services and Markets Act since they were subject to the requirements of the Code of Practice.

But you may choose to join the many critics who are equally vehement in their condemnation of the PCC as a toothless watchdog. According to Geoffrey Robertson (1993: 111): 'The PCC is a confidence trick which has failed to inspire confidence and 40 years' experience of "press regulation" demonstrates only that the very concept is an oxymoron.' Julian Petley (1999: 155) has these harsh words: 'To read its code's high-flown rhetoric about "accuracy", "opportunity to reply", "privacy", "harassment", "intrusion into grief or shock", "discrimination" and so on, and then to immerse oneself in the daily, debased reality of much of the British press, which quite clearly cares not a jot for such self-deluding nonsense, is all that is needed to understand why the PCC cannot be seriously regarded as a regulatory body.' Media sociologist James Curran is equally damning (2000: 41):

> All that the Press Council did, other than to adjudicate public complaints, was to develop from the 1960s onwards a low-key corporate role that included occasional pronouncements on ethical and freedom issues. Even this was largely abandoned when the Press Council was reincarnated as the PCC in 1991. It became simply a customer complaints' service, a far cry from the professionalising vocation to which it had been called with such wide-eyed hope by the first Royal Commission on the Press.

The MP Clive Soley has constantly criticised the PCC over its failure to take a proactive role and accept complaints from third parties. In 2003, the commission unusually decided to launch its own investigation into the Guardian's payment for an account of Lord Archer's imprisonment by a fellow prisoner, even though there had been no complaint. The PCC ruled that the newspaper had breached Article 17 of the Code banning 'payment or offers of payment for stories, pictures or information . . . to convicted or confessed criminals or their associates'. Yet, as Mike Jempson, director of PressWise, the media ethics campaigning body, argued (2003), the PCC significantly chose not to investigate newspapers' more obvious breaches – such as in their inaccurate and discriminatory coverage of refugees and asylum seekers.

Some of the media's worst excesses were shown in their massive, wall-to-wall coverage of Kate and Gerry McCann after their daughter Madeleine ('Maddy' to the tabloids) was seized while on holiday in Portugal in 2007. Suspicions fell on the couple (who deliberately exploited their sudden elevation into the ranks of media celebrities to publicise their cause) after the Portuguese police named them as official *arguidos* (suspects) on 7 September. But many newspapers and broadcast stations turned to rumours and lies to feed an apparently insatiable desire among the public for news of the saga. In March 2008, the harsh reckoning came when Express Newspapers (owned by pornographer Richard Desmond and comprising the *Daily Express*, *Star* and their Sunday equivalents) was forced to pay £550,000 in damages and issue a grovelling apology for more than 100 'seriously defamatory' articles alleging the McCanns had killed their daughter. The Express group were not alone, and questions arose over the abject failure of the Press Complaints Commission to restrain the media dogs.

What other forms of regulation are in place in Britain?

In December 2003, the Office of Communications (Ofcom) took over the regulatory responsibilities of five bodies:

- the Broadcasting Standards Commission,
- the Independent Television Commission,
- the Office of Telecommunications (Oftel),
- the Radio Authority, and
- the Radiocommunications Agency.

The Broadcasting Standards Commission (BSC)

This had two codes – on privacy and fairness – to administer (covering such issues as the use of hidden microphones and cameras, doorstepping, the handling of people suffering a personal tragedy and reporting on children) though its main priority had been to monitor that programmes shown before 9 p.m. were suitable for children. Introduced in June 1998, interestingly they were the first journalists' codes in Britain demanded by statute – Section 107 of the Broadcasting Act 1996, to be precise. The Act also created the BSC by merging the Broadcasting Standards Council – formed by the Broadcasting Act of 1990 and dealing with alleged offences against taste and decency in the areas of sex, violence, bad language and treatment of disasters – with the Broadcasting Complaints Commission. This had been set up following the Labour government's Annan committee in 1981 and dealt with complaints over lack of factual accuracy, unfairness in presentation and intrusions into privacy. The Act also relaxed the rules on cross-media ownership, much to the delight of the big media groups.

The BSC regulated all radio and television – both BBC and commercial – as well as text, cable, satellite and digital services. It could call a hearing at which the complainant, a representative of the broadcaster and other witnesses were able to give their version of events while its verdicts were published in a monthly bulletin. The broadcaster could also be ordered to publish the verdict on-air at the same time as the original programme.

The Independent Television Commission (ITC)

The role of the ITC, which replaced the Independent Broadcasting Authority in 1990, was to license and regulate all commercial television in the UK, including teletext, terrestrial, cable, digital and satellite services. It had its own code and, unlike the PCC and BSC, could fine offending companies up to 3 per cent of their annual revenue for serious breaches of their licences. Moreover, it had powers to issue reprimands for minor breaches or genuine mistakes over its code terms; to give formal warnings, ask for on-screen corrections or apologies, disallow repeats, impose fines for more serious matters; and to shorten a company's licence or withdraw it altogether. This it did controversially on 22 March 1999 when it closed down the Kurdish satellite station, Med-TV, for 21 days for allegedly supporting terrorist acts against Turkey. The station denied it was a direct supporter of the Marxist-oriented Kurdish Workers Party (PKK).

Its annual performance review was taken seriously by the industry. In May 1998, for instance, it commended ITN for its 'high-quality news coverage of foreign and domestic stories'. But it complained that foreign news was concentrated in *News at Ten*. 'The *Early Evening News* gave greater prominence to crime, show business and royal stories. In the ITC's view this bulletin requires a much more balanced agenda.' On regional news programmes, the ITC criticised Central News for an 'unwelcome move' away from hard news towards more lifestyle coverage, while Yorkshire Television's *Summer Special* editions were 'unoriginal and contrived' though popular with audiences. In May 2000, the ITC criticised the decision to cut *News at Ten* and gave the network a short deadline to improve its news coverage. In its annual report, published in the same month, the watchdog criticised ITV for over-use of security camera footage and lightweight, human interest stories in current affairs programmes, singling out *Tonight with Trevor McDonald*. But it praised ITN for its coverage of the Balkans and Eastern Europe, Jonathan Dimbleby's US interview series and John Pilger's documentary from East Timor.

The Radio Authority (RA)

Set up in 1990 to replace the IBA's commercial radio responsibility, the RA was the watchdog for all national and local, cable, digital, satellite, hospital, community and student radio services. Though its main task was to organise frequencies so they did not overlap, it had several codes of practice covering news broadcasts, election campaigns, the portrayal of sex and violence, issues relating to taste and decency, religious programming, charity appeals, representations of royalty, privacy and accuracy in news and advice programmes. From June 2000, when a 'Memorandum of Understanding' was signed between the RA and BSC, privacy and fairness complaints were handled by the commission, while the RA continued to deal with licence-related standards matters.

There was also a code on advertising standards and programme sponsorship, as required by the 1990 Act. But it rejected calls in 2000 to draw up guidelines on how much local news should be aired by commercial radio stations. The RA had similar powers to the ITC, including sanctions such as on-air apologies and corrections, fines and the shortening or withdrawal of licences. For instance, it fined Huddersfield FM £5,000 for poor service including failure to broadcast a topical phone-in, not running educational features, inadequate sports coverage and no arts or entertainment features.

The Office of Communications (Ofcom)

Since Ofcom draws on the work of five regulatory bodies it is not surprising that its remit covers a wide range of areas such as licensing, the issuing of codes, conducting research, addressing complaints and overseeing competition issues. In total it has 263 duties (compared to the 128 specific duties of the previous regulators). Its code, introduced in July 2005, is a weighty document – its 10 sections have as many as 28 clauses in some cases (see www.ofcom.org.uk/tv/ifi/codes/bcode). Among the issues it covers are: commercial references, crime, elections and referenda, fairness, impartiality and accuracy, harm and offence, privacy, religion and sponsorship. Complaints about privacy or fairness can be brought by persons affected or someone they authorise to make the complaint. Other complaints can be brought by anyone and investigations can be launched by Ofcom itself. Overall, Ofcom has been dealing with around 20,000 complaints every year. If a breach of the code is found, Ofcom can, for instance, impose a fine (as it did on both GMTV and Channel 4 in 2007: see Chapter 2), revoke a licence or forbid a repeat of the programme.

Among its many rulings (all of which can be accessed on its website), in 2004, Ofcom ruled that a drugs company, Novartis, had been treated unfairly by a Channel 4 programme which had failed to give it adequate time to respond to allegations. In the following year, the satellite channel Bloomberg was found to have breached the code's provisions on impartiality by concentrating its general election coverage on the Labour Party while a complaint against BBC Radio Sheffield in 2006 was resolved after a caller to a football phone-in used highly offensive language. Ofcom acknowledged it had been very difficult for the station to have anticipated the incident and had taken steps to avoid a repeat. Also in 2006, following complaints about the filming of a minibus crash in Bangladesh which included shots of dead bodies and an interview with a distressed child, Ofcom found that the footage by satellite channel ATN Bangla of dead bodies, while disturbing, was 'not overly graphic in the context of a valid news report about such an horrific accident' (see Quinn 2007: 384–5).

In 2002, the Radio Authority licensed 15 stations as part of a community radio experiment. Since 2004, Ofcom has taken over licensing of community media projects (including, Internet, audio and video) – and by 2008 115 stations had been granted the five-year awards. As the website www.commedia.org stresses:

Community Media is providing media and information communication technology access, training and employment and
is an exciting source of social innovation and practical 'joined
up' outcomes. Combining social enterprise, creative content
production and skills for the digital economy, Community
Media has a vital role in reaching out to people and communities at risk of exclusion and disadvantage. Community-
based radio, television and Internet projects work by enabling
people to become media producers, to send as well as to receive,
and, by working together, to reinforce knowledge, dialogue
and cultural expression at neighbourhood and community level.
The freedom of expression underpins all other human rights.
It is the means by which other human rights are defended and
extended. In the Information Age the freedom of expression
takes on additional importance, as the ability to send and
receive information, regardless of frontiers, comes increasingly
to dominate our economic, social and cultural life. A new
grassroots agenda is emerging to articulate the right to communicate an agenda in which access to new media and
communication technologies is seen as an essential part of
public life and a democratic culture.

As an example of community media, Awaz FM, one of the first licensed,
full-time community radio stations, serves the Asian population in
Glasgow, broadcasting in Urdu, Punjabi and English delivering entertainment, local, national and community information in a bi-lingual format.
And as an example of a cross-media project, Tees Valley Community
Media involves many communities within the Tees Valley with a little
overspill into Durham and North Yorkshire. The project has a broad
range of community media activities from simple web pages to online
community newspapers and on demand audio and video streaming.

The Communications Act 2003 identified two distinct categories of
audience for broadcasters: citizens and consumers. As Frost explains (2007:
269): 'These two have very different requirements, although they may
well often be the same people. The term "citizen" is used to mean those
who access broadcasting in its public service role, whilst "consumers" is
used to mean customers who make choices about their communication
needs on the basis of payment for services used.' Most critics of Ofcom
argue that it has prioritised the interests of 'consumers' above those of

the 'citizen'. For instance, Sylvia Harvey, Professor of Broadcasting Policy at the University of Lincoln, and Carole Tongue, a former Member of the European Parliament (1984–99) commented in 2004:[2] 'Ofcom may have given too much weight to market expansion arguments and too little weight to public interest arguments. In particular, Ofcom appears to be downgrading the central role that public service broadcasting plays as part of the infrastructure of citizenship in a modern democracy.' Similarly, John Pilger, in the *New Statesman* of 5 March 2001, argued: 'Ofcom will be entirely undemocratic. It will be responsible for everything from mobile phones to commercial television and its main function will be to make broadcasting a commodity to be bought and sold.'

And in another stinging criticism of Ofcom's cowardly 'authoritarianism', Sandy Starr, who has written on Internet regulation for the Organisation for Security and Cooperation in Europe, commented (2004):

> If the regulators' interest in diversity were motivated by a genuine desire to bring us greater choice and variety of media content, then they would be happy to leave the Internet – where anyone with a computer and a connection is free to publish their views – unregulated. But the need for diversity and plurality to be imposed by the authorities is asserted just as strongly in relation to new media, where it would appear to be superflous, as in relation to traditional media.

The BBC Producers' Guidelines

The BBC also regulates its own performance through issuing detailed guidelines to producers (accessible at www.bbc.co.uk/guidelines/editorial guidelines/). Regularly revised, these cover a broad range of issues including accuracy and fairness, taste and decency, privacy, the reporting of crime, political coverage, war, terror and emergencies, interacting with audiences, Northern Ireland, religion and commercial relationships. Described by Chris Frost as the BBC's ethical 'bible' (2007: 273), they also incorporate a specific code on impartiality and accuracy and take account of the legal and statutory requirements on broadcasters, such as laws on defamation, national security and copyright and rules on advertising and sponsorship. Serious breach of the guidelines could lead to dismissal for a BBC employee.

The BBC governors (appointed by the Queen on the recommendation of ministers with the overall responsibility of monitoring the Corporation's performance) were replaced by the BBC Trust in January 2007 in the wake of the Hutton Report into the events surrounding the suicide of Dr David Kelly. In its first months of operations, the trust launched a series of reviews into areas such as impartiality, regional news coverage and a survey of talent costs following the furore over the pay packets of celebrities such as Jonathan Ross. The guidelines stress the key BBC values as:

- impartiality,
- fairness,
- giving a full and fair view of people and cultures,
- editorial integrity and independence,
- respect for privacy,
- respect for standards of taste and decency,
- avoiding the imitation of anti-social and criminal behaviour,
- safeguarding the welfare of children,
- fairness to interviewees,
- respect for diverse audiences in the UK,
- independence from commercial interests.

Significantly, in 2003, the BBC's director-general controversially banned senior news staff from joining the anti-war march on February 15, reminding staff they should remember their responsibilities to be 'independent, impartial and honest' ahead of the looming war with Iraq. But did this not infringe the staffs' right to protest and their freedom of expression?

Every year the BBC governors published a report (now taken over by the Trust) on the Corporation's performance. In recent years the report has been particularly critical, saying BBC1 was failing to win public support and lacking in quality. The 2006/7 report carried research which suggested that viewers considered new and innovative programming was being crowded out by entertainment formats and ratings chasers (see www.bbc. co.uk/annualreport/pdfs/bbctrust_eng.pdf). Viewers also appeared paralysed by choice with the explosion of multi-channel television over the previous 15 years. Certainly, the BBC's reputation was seriously damaged by the 'Queengate' controversy in July 2007 (when an upcoming documentary series about the Queen was doctored to show her apparently leaving a photo-shoot in a huff) and by the revelations of viewer deception in shows such as Children in Need, Comic Relief and Sport Relief.

Teenage Magazine Advisory Panel (TMAP)

The TMAP was set up by the Periodical Publishers Association (www.ppa. co.uk) after MPs expressed concern over the allegedly explicit sexual content of teenage magazines in 1996. TMAP guidelines to editors comprise (McGowan 2000: 27):

1   encouraging readers to take a responsible attitude to sex and contraception;
2   promoting safer sex in relevant articles;
3   stressing that under-age sex or sexual abuse is illegal;
4   giving the names of relevant professional organisations and using their guidance in advice pages;
5   encouraging readers to seek support from parents and other responsible adults;
6   explaining the emotional consequences of sexual activity.

In May 2000, the panel rejected complaints against an issue of *Bliss* which included articles such as 'Lewd quizzes' and 'Help, he wants oral sex'. Significantly, a survey in *Bliss* found that 75 per cent of readers considered teen magazines the best source of sex education, while only 28 per cent felt comfortable talking about sex with their parents. In May 2004, the PPA, which represents the publishers of magazines such as *Cosmo Girl, Bliss* and *Sugar*, and the government rejected moves to make them carry age-stamped restrictions on their front covers. A high-profile campaign to secure the changes had been led by the Association of Teachers and Lecturers after *Sugar* had carried a 12-page 'sex special' (Smithers 2004). And in 2005, the TMAP upheld a complaint over an article in *Sugar* about a young woman in Zambia forced into prostitution to feed her family. The panel ruled that the story had not made clear that underage sex was illegal in the UK (though prostitution in Zambia was not illegal).

In its 2006 report, the panel noted that its remit had been extended to include magazines where 25 per cent or more of the readers were boys under 16. Its guidelines, therefore, had been amended to read 'young people' rather than 'young women'. Three magazines' campaigns over sex education were described as 'impressive': *Cosmogirl* launched its campaign with an article on young people's rights to a comprehensive sex and relationship programme in the curriculum; *Bliss*'s 'Be Sexy, Be

Sussed' campaign stressed factual knowledge as the route to safe sex, while *Sugar*'s SAFE campaign highlighted the need to be sure of the facts.

The Internet Watch Foundation (IWF)

In January 2000, Internet Service Providers set up the IWF (see www.iwf.org.uk) as an industry-funded, self-regulatory body aiming to remove child pornography from UK administered web servers. But soon afterwards, the government asked the foundation to expand its remit. Its 2007 report, published in April 2008, said:

> Less than 1 per cent of child sexual abuse content has been hosted in the UK since 2003 as a result of the IWF's universal 'notice and take-down' arrangements with host companies and internet service providers in this country. In response to such content hosted around the world, the IWF's provision of a list of child sexual abuse websites hosted abroad to online companies enables blocking measures to be deployed to protect UK Internet users from accidental exposure. The IWF model relies on self-regulation and such success has been achieved through a partnership approach with funding and support from the online industry.[3]

Fewer than 3,000 English-language websites (mostly in the United States and Russia) produced the bulk of child pornography images, according to the IWF report. And contradicting many media scare stories, the numbers of web pages depicting child sexual abuse were falling. But Internet Freedom founder Chris Ellison criticised the body for promoting a form of 'silent censorship'.

And are there still more?

Well, yes. This is not the end of media regulation! There is a host of other bodies and industrial practices which impact on journalists' behaviour. The Brussels-based International Federation of Journalists has its own succinct Declaration of Principles on the Conduct of Journalists. Its first clause stresses: 'Respect for truth and for the right of the public to truth is the first duty of the journalist.' The NUJ issues guidelines on such issues as covering race, disability and dealing with freelances. Strict guidelines are in force covering the broadcasting of Parliament (Jones 1996: 17). Newspapers and magazines usually have their own style books which principally outline policies on such fundamental issues as the use of italics, capital or lower case letters for titles, spellings of words (jail or gaol?) but they can also cover ethical issues ranging from the avoidance of sexist and racist language and stereotyping, the coverage of children and disabled people, to the importance of maintaining the confidentiality of sources.

The readers' representative

Newspapers claim to represent their readers but are often slow to respond to their complaints. At least that was the view of Alan Rusbridger, editor of the *Guardian*. He commented: 'Newspapers generally are hopeless in customer relations. You would get a much better service at the gas board and Dixon's than you would from newspapers.' So he decided in 1997 to appoint Ian Mayes as a readers' representative who, virtually every week, commented on the issues raised and supervised a daily 'Corrections and Clarifications' column. The system had been pioneered in the United States where, for many decades, the top newspapers had appointed internal ombudsmen (the *Washington Post*, for instance, since 1970). Retiring in 2007, Mayes was succeeded by Siobhain Butterworth. In addition, at the *Guardian/Observer*, an external ombudsman looks after the serious complaints involving the integrity of the newspaper's staff – such as followed the then deputy foreign editor, Victoria Brittain's brush with MI5 and the use of her bank account to channel funds for a libel action against the *Independent* (see Machon 2005: 147–63). Significantly, in July 2007, a poll by University of Maryland researchers into media transparency (based on factors such as willingness to correct mistakes, receptivity to reader criticisms and openness about ownership) placed the *Guardian* at the top, followed by the *New York Times*, BBC News, CBS News and the *Christian Science Monitor* (Shepard 2007).

In 2001, the *Mirror* set up a similar post while in March 2004, Stephen Pritchard, of the *Observer*, became the first readers' editor to be appointed by a Sunday (followed by Simon O'Hagan on the *Independent on Sunday*).

Pritchard's column ('Putting on the style') on 18 November 2007 was typical. It covered the revision of the newspaper's style guide acknowledging the many suggestions from readers. One from reader Ellin Stein, for instance, on the use of the word 'pensioner' was to be included verbatim. Part of it read:

> The problem is it defines older people by their non-participation in the work-force and immediately typifies them as drains on the public purse, inviting attitudes of either pity or condescension . . . I would describe people as a retired or former whatever [including homemaker]. Surely this is more informative than lumping in former bricklayers with former bankers under the all-purpose label 'pensioner'.

Media campaigning bodies

In addition, there is a range of campaigning bodies seeking to improve media standards. They include MediaWise, the Campaign for Press and Broadcasting Freedom (publisher of *Free Press*), Article 19, the World Association for Christian Communication (*Media Education*), Women in Publishing (see Reading 1999: 170–83) and think-tanks such as the International Broadcasting Trust, set up in 1989 by groups including Oxfam, Action Aid, WWF, Save the Children, Voluntary Service Overseas and Christian Aid to promote more ethical foreign coverage.

What can Britain learn from the experience of media councils in other countries?

Many critics argue that, in Britain, management and editorial functions have become too closely intertwined. In some other countries steps have been taken to prevent such developments. In Holland, for instance, newspaper companies have introduced statutes into their collective labour agreements separating the interests of the editor and management. Thus, if journalists object to any particular assignment they can raise the issue with an editorial council which also has a say in any merger or sale plans and on advertising matters. In Germany, some newspapers have agreed understandings with staffers giving them a voice in editorial decisions and in the editor-in-chief's selection. Similarly, the code to which Norwegian Editors' Association and National Association of Norwegian

Newspapers are signatories (drafted in 1953 and revised in 1973), entitles editors to

> free and independent leadership of the editorial department and editorial work and full freedom to shape the opinions of the paper even if they in single matters are not shared by the publisher or board ... The editor must never allow himself/ herself to be influenced to advocate opinions that are not in accord with the editor's own conviction.
>
> (cited by Bromley 2000: 113)

Editorial staff are also given considerable powers to challenge interventions by proprietors. Publishers who have tampered with editorial decisions have found themselves without an editorial staff; in one case a paper went bankrupt when its staff quit following the publisher's order to remove an article about his family business. The strength of journalistic support for the code and for editorial autonomy has tended to reduce the potentially negative impacts of ownership concentration.

How can you act further to improve media standards?

There are a range of steps you can take to exploit what Claude-Jean Bertrand (1999) called 'media accountability systems':

- Letters to the editors.

- Boycotts: for instance, a major boycott was conducted in Liverpool over the *Sun*'s coverage of the Hillsborough football stadium disaster in April 1989 in which many fans were crushed to death. Under a report headed 'The truth' the tabloid alleged drunken Liverpool fans had harassed the police and abused the bodies of the victims. Sales of the *Sun* on Merseyside dropped by almost 40 per cent and editor Kelvin MacKenzie was forced to go on BBC Radio 4's *The World This Weekend* to apologise. 'I made a rather serious error,' he said (Pilger 1998: 448).

- Complain to relevant bodies.

- Join campaigning groups such as the Campaign for Press and Broadcasting Freedom (http://www.cpbf.org.uk/); the International Communications Forum (www.icforum.org); the Institute of Communication Ethics (www.communication-ethics.net), which publishes the quarterly journal, *Ethical Space*; the Media Standards

Trust (www.mediastandardstrust.org) and MediaWise (www.media wise.org.uk) (see Jempson 2007).

- Follow closely some of the many websites monitoring mainstream media coverage, such as www.medialens.org (I personally have a blog there!); www.spinwatch.org (which monitors PR and spin); the US-based Pew Research Centre at www.pewresearch.org; the excellent www.tomdispatch.com (run by historian Tom Engelhardt) and www.ukwatch.net (which often carries features analysing media coverage.

- Attend one of a series of public meeetings, organised by the BBC around the country (and occasionally by national and local newspapers) at which people are invited to comment on output.

- And, as a journalist, through constant self-evaluation and learning; study closely writers and broadcasters you admire. You may also choose to contribute to debates in the NUJ's magazine, the *Journalist*, in trade magazines such as *Press Gazette*, *Free Press* (of the Campaign for Press and Broadcasting Freedom), the *British Journalism Review* and *Broadcast* – or to broadsheet media sections. But investigative reporter John Pilger (1998: 480) is sceptical of their value:

> Media sections of broadsheet newspapers occasionally allow dissenting voices but that is not their purpose. Like the media itself, they are essentially marketing vehicles whose primary interest is not serious journalistic scrutiny of the industry but formulaic 'media village' tittle-tattle, something on circulation figures, something from the what I have had for breakfast school of journalism and perhaps a 'controversial' interview with a wily political 'spin doctor'. The reason why journalists are so malleable is rarely discussed.

Notes

1   The 65-page Editor's Codebook which describes and illustrates the workings of the code is available at www.editorscode.org.uk. It was first published in 2004 by the Newspaper Publishers Association, the Newspaper Society, the Periodical Publishers Association, the Scottish Daily Newspaper Society and the Scottish Newspaper Publishers Association.

2   See www.bftv.ac.uk/policy/ofcom040614.htm, accessed 17 April 2008.

3   See www.iwf.org.uk/media/news.229.htm, accessed 17 April 2008.

4
At the root of relationships

Sourcing dilemmas

How can journalists respond to the many ethical issues thrown up by interviewing?

As a source of information, despite its prominence in journalistic routines, the interview is problematic. The source may be lying, hiding crucial facts, uninformed, confused, intimidated and so not expressing true feelings – or speaking in a foreign language and so unable to speak their thoughts clearly. The reporter's bias, personality and body language, even their age and colour, can affect the kinds of responses solicited. The journalist needs to be aware of these problems. Extra pressures on reporters to produce 'exclusives' and brighten up copy is increasing the tendency of journalists to invent quotes and betray trust.

On- and off-the-record

Following conventional routines, journalists conduct three main types of interview: on-the-record, off-the-record and those for unattributed/background comments. Members of the public are often unaware of the distinctions and thus the journalist will sometimes have to clarify their position to the source. Most interviews are conducted on-the-record and on trust. The source trusts the journalist to report what is said fairly and accurately. Occasionally they will be reported verbatim; usually sections are used in either direct or indirect quotations. An off-the-record interview is completely different. Information is supplied but, because of its sensitive nature, the source asks for it not be reported. The off-the-record deal is normally fixed before the interview begins. Obviously, if the undertaking is broken, then trust (and the source) is lost. Occasionally, in a routine on-the-record interview or during a public meeting a source may say:

'By the way, that's off-the-record', but the reporter is not obliged to agree. Ideally they need to be told of the reporting conventions and persuaded to withdraw their request. An off-the-record agreement also leaves the journalist free to secure the same information from an alternative, on-the-record source or to return to the original source and try to persuade them to go on-the-record. Sometimes problems can arise when sources assume that asides or comments made outside the formal interview context are off-the-record and patience may well be needed in explaining the conventions.

Off-the-record interviews can benefit both journalist and source. For the source, the occasion provides the opportunity to impress their perspective on the reporter while the journalist can be briefed on complicated details about which they may not have any specialist knowledge. David Hencke, of the *Guardian*, points out (2000) that journalists often find it better to work with a network of moles. 'Then when they see the story, they can say truthfully that they have not leaked everything. It is amazing how much better that makes them feel, and how much more information they are then prepared to leak.'

But there are dangers: powerful institutions, groups and individuals have the power to organise such briefings and so influence the media's agenda. Weaker groups and individuals have no such opportunities (Tiffen 1989: 112). Campaigning journalist John Pilger (1996), following the tradition of the great American muckraker, I.F. Stone, advises: 'Beware all background briefings, especially from politicians. Indeed, try to avoid, where possible, all contact with politicians. That way you find out more about them.' Moreover, leaks accompanied by the use of anonymous quotes from compliant journalists can lead to institutionalised lying. Tiffen (op. cit.: 122) warns:

> The competitive rewards accompanying the publication of leaks makes journalists more open to manipulation. They may be seduced by the appearance of access and intimacy or the lure of an 'exclusive' and so not exploit others' perspectives. The wish to gain exclusives and maintain favoured access can induce selectivity, limited search and the possibility of manipulation.

He continues: 'Because the source remains covert, there is the possibility of them adopting different faces in public and private unbeknown to the public.' Moreover, secrecy can provide the cover for invention, and blur the boundaries between knowledge and surmise. Governments regularly issue leaks to test responses to controversial issues and then denounce the plans if an outcry emerges.

Journalists have to be particularly careful when covering confidential sources and not clumsily reveal all. In December 2007, the *Lancashire Telegraph* was criticised by the Press Complaints Commission for breaking Clause 14 of its code of practice which states journalists have a duty to protect confidentiality. A *Telegraph* report had described the confidential source as 'a worker at Burnley's mortuary' but because he was only one of two people who worked there (the other being his boss) his identity was easily established by his bosses. The source had subsequently been sacked for gross misconduct in talking to the newspaper.

Background/unattributed briefings: leaking in the public interest

Between off-the-record and on-the-record interviews lie those 'for background only' or unattributed and most confusion surrounds these. Reports can carry quotes from these interviews but attribution is vague to hide identities on particularly sensitive subjects. Journalism is, paradoxically, a secretive profession. Thus colleagues quoted on media personalities or issues are often described as 'a former associate editor on *The Times*', 'an insider at *Panorama*', or 'sources close to the editor of the *Mirror*'. 'Sources close to Prince Charles', a 'ministerial source' and 'diplomatic sources' are other constantly appearing phrases.

Ideally, if journalists are to carry unattributed quotes, then the source should be already known as reliable and they should be identified as clearly as possible without revealing their identities. Thus 'a city councillor' is preferred to 'an informed source'. The reason why the source wishes to remain anonymous should be explained and the information should be corroborated by at least one other source. *The Times* style book rules: 'Unattributed quotes are normally banned. Where they proliferate, for instance in the more pedestrian political reporting, they should be treated with caution.'

Unattributed pejorative quotes about someone need particular attention and should provide a sufficiently valuable insight to warrant the shield of anonymity. On 30 January 2004, following the publication of the Hutton Report, *Guardian* editor Alan Rusbridger issued new guidelines to staff on the use of anonymous sources. BBC *Today*'s Andrew Gilligan had sparked a massive controversy (and ultimately the Hutton inquiry) after using a secret source to back a claim the government had 'sexed up' WMD allegations against Iraq against the wishes of the intelligence services. Not surprisingly, Rusbridger advised staff to use anonymous sources sparingly and to avoid using unattributed pejorative quotes – unless in exceptional circumstances. Yet on that day alone in the *Guardian* there were 31 cases of the use of anonymous quotes!

Indeed, it could be argued that the practice of secret sourcing is now running out of control in Fleet Street – with national and international politics, 'human interest' gossip about celebrities and journalism being the main areas affected. Significantly these beats lie at the top of Fleet Street's priorities. The global media hype surrounding the disappearance of Madeleine McCann from her parents' holiday apartment at a Portuguese resort in May 2007 was a perfect example of the trend being largely fuelled by rumours, speculation and inventions from anonymous sources. As Mair (2008: 32) comments: 'The "Missing Madeleine" story provides us with a moral dipstick on the modern British media. Populist, concerned, knowing its audience but at the same time easily manipulated, gullible and prone to laziness and lying.'

Just take a look at any newspaper and see how dependent they are on secret sources. On Sunday 18 July 2004, the *Observer* led on the story 'Blair: no deal with Brown on No 10.' Not one named source was used. Instead, views came from 'one close associate of the Prime Minister', 'Cabinet allies of the Prime Minister', 'one friend of the Prime Minister', 'one Cabinet minister', 'friends of Brown', 'one senior MP close to Blair', 'one close ally of Blair', 'one Downing Street source', 'one aide'. Inside, a two-page special report by Gaby Hinsliff and Martin Bright, examining Blair's future in the wake of the by-election results and the Butler report on the handling of pre-invasion intelligence, again carried only two, on-the-record sources: Home Secretary David Blunkett and Culture Secretary Tessa Jowell.

Otherwise, it's simply 'one friend of Blair', 'one senior Downing Street source', 'one senior backbencher who knows Blair well', 'one firmly pro-war Cabinet minister', 'a second minister, equally convinced the war was right', 'one close ally', 'grumbling Blairites', 'a complaining friend', 'one senior Blair aide', 'friends of the Chancellor', 'one Cabinet minister', 'another Cabinet minister', 'one ally talking bluntly', 'one Tory frontbencher', 'one Downing Street aide', 'one Blair loyalist minister'. Could all this have been invented? The reader (already sceptical and distrustful of the media) can only wonder.

In a full-page *Observer* 'Comment special' on the same day, Andrew Rawnsley pondered Blair's predicament. Again the piece is drowned in anonymous quotes. This time there's 'one Cabinet member who has been through and just survived some terrific firestorms himself', 'one Cabinet ally', 'a different member of the Cabinet', 'one of Blair's closest allies' and so on. Shifting to the media, a report in the same edition on the investigation into allegations that Alan Yentob, the BBC arts chief, misused expenses, received the same treatment. Caroline Michel, 'managing director of HarperPress and a close friend' is the only named source. Otherwise it's all attributed to 'one BBC source', 'Yentob's supporters', 'one senior industry source', 'insiders' and 'one senior BBC journalist'.

The previous day, *The Times*' front page splash thundered: 'US sets sights on toppling Iran regime.' But Michael Binyon and Bronwen Maddox sourced this highly controversial report throughout simply to an unnamed 'senior official', described as being 'determined that there should be no let-up in the Administration's War on Terror'. Inside, the two reporters followed-up with a think-piece, again sourcing the threat to Iran to 'a senior US official'. But were not the journalists merely being used as conduits for blatant (and easily deniable) warmongering propaganda? At the beginning of June 2004, as Ahmad Chalabi's star among the American hawks began to dim, allegations from unnamed US intelligence sources alleging the then-leader of the Iraqi National Congress had spied for Iran were given prominent coverage by Fleet Street journalists. Did not the media, then, simply become the theatre in which competing factions of the intelligence agencies fought out their battles?

Virtually the whole of the over-hyped 'spat' between Prime Minister Tony Blair and Chancellor Gordon Brown (particularly during the final years of the Blair administration) was reported via unattributed sources. Thus, in the *Independent* of 29 April 2004, under a headline 'Ministers close ranks to shore up "isolated" Blair', reporters Andrew Grice and Colin Brown report 'a senior Labour backbencher', 'one minister', 'other ministers', 'Blair allies', 'some ministers', 'a senior Cabinet minister'. The practice extends beyond Fleet Street to the leftist *New Statesman*. For instance, John Kampfner, in a two-page analysis of Blair's plight on 17 May 2004, used no named sources. Instead readers were given the views of 'one of the Prime Minister's advisers', 'Labour MPs, ministers and officials loyal to Blair', 'one UK diplomat', 'one Cabinet minister', 'one MP close to Blair', 'one serving Cabinet minister', 'one minister', 'one senior MP, anything but a Brownite', 'some MPs sympathetic to the Chancellor', 'one veteran Labour MP who wishes Blair to stay'.

Similarly most of the tabloids' frenzied coverage of celebrities is fuelled by anonymous sources. Ben Todd, in a *Sunday Mirror* 'exclusive' on Posh and Becks and their 'marriage crisis', on 27 June 2004, was typical. Readers were offered detailed 'revelations' of 'behind-the-scenes bust-ups' but no-one dared attached their names to the accounts. So Todd had to rely on 'those close to the star', 'one associate of the England captain', 'one close friend of Victoria', 'a business associate of David', 'one who saw Victoria', 'a family member of one of the England team', 'another source close to the England squad', 'another friend', 'one bodyguard', 'one close associate', 'a guest at Elton John's ball', 'one friend of Victoria'.

The reasons for all this secret sourcing are clear. As newspaper sales dip, editors' demands for exclusives feed the process, blurring the distinctions between fact and fiction. So too is the growth of the secret state with intelligence moving to the centre of power in Blair's cabal. As the power of the intelligences services advances (both in Britain and the US) and Fleet Street hacks' links to the spooks deepen so the culture of anonymous sourcing will spread. Mainstream politics is now more about careerism than ideological controversy so rocking the boat over a principle is no longer an option. Keeping quiet (or keeping any disagreement with the leadership to safe, off-the-record briefings) is now the best option. Moreover, confidentiality agreements are becoming more widespread in the industry and beyond, forcing all sources (except the brave outspoken whistleblowers) either to shut up or hide behind the cloak of anonymity (Keeble 2004a).

One alarming use of anonymous sourcing emerged in 2002 when unsourced and unverifiable reports were submitted by the Attorney General as credible evidence to a hearing on the legality of the detention without charge or trial of Arabs in detention. As Nick Cohen commented (2002):

The PRs have set up a wonderfully self-justifying system. They talk to journalists on condition of anonymity. Hacks go along with this which cheats the reader because there is no other way of getting information from the security and intelligence services. MI5 then uses the reports of its own briefing as independent corroboration of the need for internment.

Yet *Guardian* journalist Dennis Barker argues there are worse tricks than using unattributed sources. He comments (2007): 'sometimes it may be a more chatty way of dramatising facts that might be thought dull if simply recounted abstractly: a quote, even from an un-named and composite or fictitious "friend" can have more life than a baldly reported fact. These may be justifiable tricks, especially if the object is to prevent the identification of a source.'

How should journalists handle confidential sources? Further dilemmas

A survey of journalists' attitudes by researchers at the London College of Printing in 1997 found a large majority agreeing that payments for confidential information can be justified, while more than 80 per cent were prepared to use confidential documents. Moreover, according to John Wilson (1996: 86), former editorial policy controller of the BBC, '[O]ne of the few accepted absolutes in journalism is that confidential sources must be protected.' Clearly, if promises over confidentiality are broken then the crucial trust between the source – and implicitly all other ones – and the journalist is lost. Such a stance is reaffirmed in media codes (such as Clause 7 of the NUJ's), though Britain is one of the few European countries not to enshrine the principle in law. Austria, Denmark, Finland, France, Germany, Italy and Sweden all provide explicit protection to journalists in maintaining confidentiality of sources. Campaigning groups such as Liberty and Article 19 argue that journalists should not be compelled to disclose sources unless under 'exceptional circumstances' where 'vital interests' are at stake (Liberty and Article 19 2000: 28).

Some journalists prefer the current state of affairs, arguing that the threat of imprisonment is merely an occupational hazard. Better this than facing a law which could potentially seek to define who was and was not a journalist – regardless of what journalists and their organisations felt. Under Section 10 of the Contempt of Court Act 1981, courts have the right to demand that journalists reveal sources if 'disclosure is necessary in the interests of justice or national security or for the prevention of disorder or crime'. Also, in line with the Police and Criminal Evidence Act of 1984, police investigating a 'serious offence' can obtain an order requiring the journalist to submit evidence considered useful to the court. This can include unpublished photographs, computer files and notes.

In a few celebrated cases journalists have risked fines and imprisonment to preserve confidential sources (and in the process, helping reaffirm the myth of the 'free press', some would argue). Occasionally they have succumbed to threats and revealed all.

- In 1963, Brendan Mulholland, of the *Daily Mail*, and Reginald Foster, of the *Daily Sketch*, were both jailed over their coverage of the Vassall spy tribunal.

- Eight years later Bernard Falk went to prison after he refused to tell the court whether one of two Provisional IRA men he interviewed for the BBC was a man subsequently charged with membership.

- In 1984 the *Guardian*, under pressure from the courts, handed over a document that helped reveal that civil servant Sarah Tisdall had leaked information about the delivery of cruise missiles to RAF Greenham Common. National security seemed hardly threatened but Tisdall was jailed. The lesson from this case is clear: when confidential sources supply journalists with documents they should be destroyed at the first opportunity; otherwise they can be seized in a police raid.

- In 1988, Jeremy Warner, of the *Independent*, was ordered to disclose the source of a story on insider dealing in the City, refused and was ordered to pay a £20,000 fine and £100,000 costs by the High Court.

- In 1990, Bill Goodwin, a trainee on the weekly trade magazine, the *Engineer*, refused to hand over notes of a telephone conversation revealing confidential details about a computer company's financial affairs. All the judges agreed it was in the interests of justice for a private company to be able to keep its business private. Goodwin was fined £5,000 for contempt of court. But, supported by the NUJ, he took his case to the European Court of Human Rights which ruled, in September 1993, in support of Goodwin and called on the government to negotiate a 'friendly settlement'. Three years later, the court summed up the law: 'Protection of journalistic sources is one of the basic conditions for press freedom . . . Without such protection, sources may be deterred from assisting the press in informing the public on matters of public interest' (see Rozenberg 2004: 154–6). But still the government refused to budge on the Contempt of Court Act.

- Following the poll tax riots of 31 March 1990, the police applied for possession of 'all transmitted, published and/or unpublished cine film, video tape, still photographs and negatives of the demonstration and subsequent disturbances' under PACE. Some national newspapers complied. But the NUJ moved fast, sending prints and negatives out of the country and so saving the other organisations from prosecution.

- In 1991, Channel 4 was fined £75,000 under the Prevention of Terrorism Act after refusing to reveal its source for a programme by the independent company, Box Productions, alleging collusion between Loyalist death squads and members of the security forces in Northern Ireland. A researcher on the programme, Ben Hamilton, was later charged with perjury by the Royal Ulster Constabulary, and though the charge was dropped in November 1992, the police retained all items seized from Mr Hamilton including his PC, disks, cuttings and notes of telephone calls and meetings with interested journalists. The programme later became the subject of an acrimonious libel action by the *Sunday Times* which, in May 1993, denounced the programme as a hoax (Lashmar 2000).

- In 1996 Dani Garavelli, then chief reporter for the *Journal*, Newcastle, won a 20-month battle in the High Court. She had refused to name a source after being subpoenaed to give evidence to a police disciplinary hearing.

- In March 1998, a judge's decision to throw out an application by Norfolk Police for the *Eastern Daily Press* and reporter Adrian Galvin to name a source was lauded as a 'landmark judgment' by editor Peter Franzen. Judge Michael Hyman ruled: 'There is undoubtedly a very formidable interest in a journalist being able to protect his sources.'

- In September 1999, Ed Moloney, northern editor of the Dublin-based *Sunday Tribune*, faced jail after refusing to hand over notes dating back 10 years of interviews with a Loyalist accused of murdering a Catholic solicitor. Moloney's ordeal ended the following month when the Belfast High Court overturned an order by Antrim Crown Court.

- In April 2000, the *Express* overturned a High Court ruling that it had to reveal the source from which financial reporter Rachel Baird obtained confidential documents about a High Court action involving Sir Elton John.

- Alex Thomson, chief correspondent of Channel 4 News, and Lena Ferguson, a former Channel 4 producer, were also prepared to face jail sentences for refusing to name British soldiers they interviewed anonymously about Bloody Sunday, the day in January 1972 when 13 people were shot dead by British troops after a civil rights march in Derry. The five soldiers challenged the outcome of the official inquiry into Bloody Sunday by Lord Widgery. First told they could be prosecuted for contempt in May 2002, Thomson and Ferguson had to wait until February 2004 to hear that Lord Saville's inquiry was no longer going to pursue them since it was 'unlikely to produce new information of any real value and, furthermore, would cause substantial delay in completing the inquiry'.

- And freelance journalist Robin Ackroyd had the shadow of a jail sentence looming over him for seven years until the Appeal Court finally ruled in July 2007 against the attempt by Mersey Care NHS Trust to force him to reveal his source who leaked confidential details about the medical treatment of Moors murderer Ian Brady (Stabe 2007). Sir Anthony Clarke, Master of the Rolls, said enforcing such a disclosure 'would not be proportionate to the pursuit of the hospital's legitimate aim to seek redress against the source, given the vital public interest in the protection of a journalist's source'.

But while journalists on many occasions will be concerned to guarantee anonymity to their sources on sensitive issues, there will be other times when it will be important to try to persuade the source to go public and thus give the report greater authority. As investigative broadcast journalist Paul Lashmar comments (2008a): 'When I was making a programme for Channel 4's *Dispatches* on a cervical screening scandal at Canterbury, a technician who had been acting as a confidential source finally agreed to be filmed. This gave the programme much greater authority with an insider on the record.'

Moreover, Andrew Gilligan said that the major lesson he had learned from the extraordinary David Kelly/Hutton saga 'was that anonymous sources, however accurate – and Kelly was accurate – are not enough because they can be pressured' (Burrell 2008a). So a major investigation he conducted into the London Development Agency in 2008 for the *Evening Standard* was largely based on Companies House records (showing budget and business data), leaked emails and testimony, mostly on the record, of whistleblowers. Significantly, on 4 March following the leak of an incriminating email to Gilligan, Lee Jasper, race adviser to Ken Livingstone, Mayor of London, was forced to resign.

Are there any occasions when confidentiality agreements can be broken?

In 2003, journalist Nick Martin-Clark appeared in a witness box giving evidence against a former confidential source who had admitted to him he had committed murder. Confidentiality was a promise he felt, 'after some agonising', he simply could not keep (2003). His decision provoked an enormous controversy among members of the National Union of Journalists, many of whom adopted the 'absolutist' position – that the journalist should *never* reveal confidential sources. As John Toner, of the NUJ, commented (Foley 2004: 18):

> Some have argued that Nick Martin-Clark was acting in the public interest by informing on a notorious killer. We must take a broader view of the public interest than this. Sources must believe that a promise of confidentiality is as binding on a journalist as it is on a doctor, a lawyer or a priest. Any weakening in that belief will result in sources drying up and countless issues of public interest may never see the light of day.

In response, Martin-Clark argued:

> An absolutist case on confidentiality is akin to total pacifism or to not telling a lie even to save a life. It is an eccentricity that has little to offer real-world journalism. What if someone told you about a murder he or she was going to commit? What if an egregious paedophile revealed all? Odd then to find absolutism championed in Northern Ireland where journalism is often as messy as the politics.

In support of this 'anti-absolutist' position, Michael Foley (2004: 19), journalist and academic, suggested that, while the NUJ ethics code also stressed the importance of preserving confidentiality, it was wrong to give an assurance of confidentiality whatever the outcome. 'If that outcome leads to a miscarriage of justice, for instance, is that going to instil confidence in another person whose information is of great public interest, but now fears giving it to a person who would rather see a guilty person go free rather than give a name to a court?'

Another controversy erupted in 2008 after Gerri Peev, the *Scotsman*'s political correspondent, interviewed Samantha Power, a senior aide to US Presidential hopeful Barack Obama, and carried her description of Democrat opponent Hillary Clinton as 'a monster', even though she had stressed that particular comment was off the record. Power was forced to resign. Peev commented (Brown and Martinson 2008):

> Our newspaper loyalties are to our readers, not our leaders. Most of my conversations with politicians are off the record but that is decided in advance of the discussion. The rules of engagement are clear about off the record, they are not made unilaterally through an interview. If someone in power says what they really think in an on the record interview, our readers have a right to know.

And lawyer Korieh Duodu confirmed that someone speaking off the record could rely on no more than the moral or ethical obligation of the journalist. Very occasionally the law on confidentiality could apply, but even that would be overridden if the information disclosed were sufficiently in the public interest to warrant publication (ibid.).

To what extent do the powers of authorities and social network sites to snoop on emails render journalists' assurances about confidentiality meaningless?

According to the government's information commissioner, Richard Thomas, Britain is sleepwalking into a 'surveillance society'.[1] Significantly, a YouGov poll released in September 2007 showed 60 per cent of Britons believed they lived in a surveillance state while only one in five trusted the government to keep personal details confidential (Porter 2007). David Lyon writes:

> the gaze is ubiquitous, constant, inescapable. What once was experienced only in specific contexts such as voter registration, tax files or medical records, in each of which personal records are held by an impersonal organisation, has spilled over into every dimension of daily life. Whether travelling, eating, shopping, telephoning, working, walking in the street or working out at the gym, some check occurs, some record is made or some image is captured.
>
> (2007: 25)

The Big Brother society George Orwell depicted in his dystopian novel, *Nineteen Eight-Four* (where record-keeping, monitoring, observation and serious restrictions on civil liberties have become routine), appears to have become a reality. British people are the most watched in the world. There are said to be 4.2 million CCTV cameras – one for every 14 people, while every person in a major city is watched by 300 cameras every day. One-fifth of CCTV cameras world-wide are in the UK (ibid.: 39; see also O'Hara and Shadbolt 2008).[2] Scary? And, according to all the research, these surveillance cameras (promoted by a massively expanding security industry) have little impact on reducing crime levels (Guha 2002): improved street lighting is far more effective.

In May 2001, a European Parliament report highlighted the existence of Echelon, a secret US-led worldwide electronic spying network.[3] The report claimed that Echelon was violating the fundamental right to privacy as defined in the European Convention on Human Rights and Article 7 of the Charter of Fundamental Rights of the EU – and called for the development and widespread use of encryption technology as a way of protecting privacy. According to a former member of the Canadian intelligence service, every day millions of emails, faxes and telephone conversations are intercepted (Miller, Norton-Taylor and Black 2001). And a survey conducted by Personnel Today found that a quarter of firms approached had dismissed workers for email abuse. In the first nine months of 2006, some 800 organisations including the police, HM Revenue and Customs and local and central government were able to demand 253,000 intrusions on citizen's privacy (Thain 2008). A European Union Data Detention Directive of October 2007 gave 795 bodies ranging from the police and Food Standards Agency to the Charity Commission the right to request journalists' telephone records going back a year. According to Simon Jenkins (2008a): 'The machine is out of control. Personal surveillance in Britain is so extensive that no democratic oversight is remotely plausible.' A report in 2007 from Privacy International (www.privacyinternational.org) ranked the UK as the worst country in the European Union for privacy protection.[4]

Journalists' investigative work and promises of confidentiality were, in particular, threatened by the Regulation of Investigatory Powers Act 2000. As Ian Reeves warned (2000), the contents and details of emails and telephone calls would potentially become accessible to a 'horrifying' variety of government agencies, police officers and even low-grade council officials. Authorities are able to monitor email and Internet traffic through 'black boxes' placed inside service providers' systems. Advances in technology also mean that the authorities can even keep tabs on you through tracking your mobile phone.

Concerns were also growing over the ways the social network site Facebook (with 55 million members by 2008) was marketing personal information. In a campaign spearheaded by the US based online democracy watchdog MoveOn, thousands called for the website to remove an advertising program called Facebook Beacon, able to track spending habits of Facebook users on external sites (Verkaik and Taylor 2007).

So how can a journalist best respond to these privacy invasions? Nick Rosen, editor of the Off-Grid website, recommends travelling to a town you have never visited before to an area with no CCTV cameras and asking a homeless person to buy a pay-as-you-go mobile phone for you. 'That way no shop will have your image on its CCTV. You will also have an anonymous mobile' (Rosen 2007). Moreover, if you use a web-based email service such as gmail your mail is being stored all the time to build up a picture of your contacts and interests. 'Instead, you can use a service called Hushmail to send encrypted emails. Or work out a private code with friends you want to communicate with.' Investigative journalist Paul Lashmar provides this further advice for keeping confidential sources secret (2008b): 'Try to avoid electronic communication with your sources, meet face to face; both you and your source should turn your phones off long before meeting, otherwise your phone can be used to approximate your location; try to meet away from CCTV cameras.' Other investigative journalists recommended using a voice-over-the Internet service such as Skype for making telephone calls to avoid the snoopers.

And remember that the 1998 Data Protection Act[5] in theory allows you to write to the data protection officer of organisations such as banks, Internet Service Providers and mobile phone providers to demand to see the information held on you. For instance, credit reporting agencies such as CallCredit, Experian and Equifax could hold vast details about your financial transactions. But, as journalist John Harris found, many such organisations will claim exemption from disclosure on spurious security, technical or confidentiality grounds (Harris 2008).

Should journalists support the Parliamentary lobby system?

One of the most famous, and controversial, manifestations of the background briefing is the Parliamentary lobby, providing privileged access to ministers, the PM and other politicians to a few journalists. Every day on which the House sits, Downing Street gives two briefings to around 175 accredited lobby correspondents (Hipwood 2008). Joe Haines, press secretary to Labour PM Harold Wilson, commented: 'They have privileged access which they are very jealous of and yet most are of low ability and totally precious.' The lobby was launched in 1884, five years before the first Official Secrets Act. As Michael Cockerell, Peter Hennessy and David Walker commented in their seminal study of the lobby (1984: 34):

> The paradox was that as Britain was moving towards becoming a democracy by extending the vote to men of all classes (women still had 40 years to wait) mechanisms were being created to frustrate popular participation in government and to control, channel and even manufacture the political news.

Until recently, the briefings were unattributable – and provoked enormous passions, both pro and anti. Bernard Ingham, Margaret Thatcher's press secretary, was alleged to use the system for blatant disinformation campaigns, even against Conservative colleagues, and in protest, the newly-launched *Independent*, as well as the *Guardian*, *Scotsman* and *Economist* withdrew from the lobby for a few years (Harris 1990). Since then, lobby rules have been continuously relaxed. Ingham's successor, Christopher Meyer, in 1995, allowed the briefings to be attributed directly to 'Downing Street'. Then Alastair Campbell, former *Daily Mirror* journalist and Tony Blair's director of communications and strategy from 1997–2003, on 13 March 2000, ruled that he could be named as the source of his briefings (rather than the 'Prime Minister's official spokesman').

Soon afterwards, Fleet Street printed verbatim versions of a lobby briefing. In the previous month the twice daily briefings for journalists were put on the Downing Street website. Why this remarkable openness? Some journalists welcomed the move, others argued it was an attempt by the government to bypass media 'spin' and communicate directly with the electorate. Those with Internet access could now find out what was said in the lobby just an hour after the meeting ended.

New Labour has been accused by some of seeking to downplay the role of the Commons and enhance the power of the Executive. Just as Alastair Campbell was seeking to bypass the lobby (Oborne 1999: 197–200) so Tony Blair rarely attended the Commons: his voting record was the lowest by far of any PM since the early eighteenth century, attending just 5 per cent of all votes. Even Margaret Thatcher (notoriously contemptuous of Parliament despite her rhetoric) voted six times more. Some commentators suggested it was only a matter of time before the Prime Minister's press secretary adopted the US system of nightly TV screenings of his comments. The lobby would then be transformed into showbiz, leaving the most important business to be conducted behind the scenes in informal, bilateral contacts between journalist and politician. As former lobby correspondent Andrew Pierce (2000) commented: 'Ministers, their special advisers and senior Labour Party workers are still being wined and dined by political journalists in fashionable restaurants within the shadow of Big Ben.' Similarly, John Hipwood, political editor of the *Express and Star* and *Shropshire Star*, and former chair of the Parliamentary Lobby, stresses (op. cit.): 'Nowadays it's more common for meetings to take place over lunch, in a quiet corridor or in Starners Bar, the MPs' favourite watering hole.'

Campbell's contempt for journalists boiled over in his amazing confrontation with the BBC's Andrew Gilligan following his infamous 'two-way' with presenter John Humphrys, early morning on the *Today* programme on 29 May 2003 (for a full transcript see: www.guardian.co.uk/media/2003/jul/09/Iraqandthemedia.bbc).

On the government's dossier which claimed the President of Iraq, Saddam Hussein, could launch WMDs within 45 minutes of an emergency, Gilligan said he had spoken to a 'British official':

> It was transformed in the week before it was published to make it sexier. The classic example was the claim that weapons of mass destruction were ready for use within 45 minutes. That information was not in the original draft. It was included in the dossier against our wishes, because it wasn't reliable. Most of the things in the dossier were double-sourced, but that was single sourced, and we believe that the source was wrong.

The 'British official' turned out to be arms inspector (and backer of military intervention against Iraq) Dr David Kelly who went on to die in suspicious circumstances after the government mercilessly outed him. The Hutton inquiry (see www.the-hutton-inquiry.org.uk/), set up to investigate Dr Kelly's death, was generally seen as a 'whitewash' since it somehow managed to exonerate the government from any blame. Campbell resigned in August 2003 and went on to make a profitable career mercilessly criticising the standards of British journalism. For instance, during the Hugh Cudlipp lecture at the London College of Communication in January 2008 he commented (A. Campbell 2008):

> When a prevailing wisdom takes hold that news is only news when it is bad for someone, and especially someone in power, then it narrows and distorts the view of the world . . . The pressures to get the story first, if wrong, are greater sometimes than the pressures to get the story right. Here the broadcasters are if anything more guilty than the print media.

But in response, Phil Harding (2008), a former chief political adviser at the BBC, accused Campbell of ruthlessly intimidating the media during his time as chief New Labour 'spin-master':

Individual journalists and presenters were picked out for attack, presumably on the grounds that their colleagues and bosses wouldn't come to their rescue. And when the phone calls didn't work, there was abuse and swearing. I remember one particularly unedifying spectacle when a senior BBC correspondent was chased and screamed at in the street by a Labour spinner. None of this seemed to me at the time to be the best way to build up a climate of trust.

And while Campbell accused the media of indulging in the 'language of extremes', Peter Wilby, media commentator on the *Guardian* (2008a) retorted:

> Campbell hugely extended the practice of trailing government announcements in advance, leaking them only partially so that they were reported in terms that suited his masters. And there have been few better examples of the 'language of extremes' than the notorious claim – almost universally accepted by the media at the time – that Saddam could blow us all off the planet within 45 minutes.

Many critics argue that the essential purpose of the lobby remains to protect the political elite from serious embarrassments. Former industrial correspondent of the *Daily Mirror* and founding editor of the *British Journalism Review*, Geoffrey Goodman (2008), tells how in 2004 the lobby knew of a scandal involving Prime Minister Tony Blair and his family 'which if it had become public could have led to his downfall' – and yet the lobby kept silent on it. For they (and their proprietors) were so closely linked to the success of the New Labour project. And that secrecy, amazingly, persists to this day.

Moreover, it is argued that the focus of political reporters on the minutiae of Parliamentary business means that they miss the 'big picture' – which is how business interests have colonised government and the public sector, turning most top politicians into their clients (Wilby 2008a). Investigative, campaigning journalist John Pilger is scathing in his critique of the lobby (1998: 503–4):

> Guardians of the faith, the clerics of the established order, are most commonly found in the 'lobby system'. This is periodically attacked as a 'cosy club', even 'pernicious', but it never changes. 'Lobby correspondents' have their own rules, 'officers'

and disciplinary procedures ... It shapes political news and commentary and it excludes genuine challengers – that is, those *outside* the collective responsibility of 'mainstream' journalists and politicians and their vested escorts. The influence of the parallel arm of government cannot be overestimated.

Should journalists reconsider boycotting the lobby?

To what extent do mainstream journalists, through their sourcing routines, reflect the full diversity of the society they report on?

Conventional sourcing routines divide sources into two categories: primary and secondary (Aitchison 1988). At a local level, primary sources include councils, MPs and Euro MPs, courts, police, fire brigade, ambulance service, hospitals, local industries and their representative bodies, the local football, cricket and rugby clubs. Schools and colleges, churches, army, naval and air force bases, local branches of national pressure groups and charities are secondary sources. In rural areas, other contacts in this category will include village post office workers, publicans and hotel keepers, agricultural merchants, livestock auctioneers, countryside rangers or wardens. In coastal areas they might include coastguards, harbourmasters and lifeboat stations.

Sources' details are held in contacts books/personal digital assistants, the journalist's most prized possession. But note: the ownership of the contacts list may not reside with the journalist but their employer. After journalist Junior Isles left PennWell Publishing in 2007 he took with him details of all his 1,650 contacts from his computer. PennWell applied for an injunction to stop Isles, who had moved to a competitor, from using the database – and the court found in its favour, ruling that ownership of the database always resided with the employer (Julyan 2008).

Reporters investigating sensitive issues (such as national security, the intelligence services, the arms or drugs trade, share dealings, prostitution) tend to keep details of important exclusive sources in their heads (Keeble 2005a: 51). Police have been known to raid the homes and computers of journalists involved in sensitive areas and thus every step should be taken to preserve the anonymity of such contacts. As Bruce Grundy advises (2007: 116–17);

> you must have a reliable 'contacts book' system. One that is not accessible to others is best. Some of your contacts at least

will expect that their existence, and certainly their addresses and phone numbers, will not be known to anyone else. Don't leave your contact book lying around or the file open on your computer screen.

A system of calls institutionalises reporters' sourcing routines. The police, ambulance station and fire brigade are rung at regular intervals for breaking news. Local reporters will habitually drop in for chats to help personalise the contact. Primary and secondary sources are often described as 'on-diary' since details of their activities are listed in diaries held by the news desk. 'Off-diary' sources are all those which fall outside these routines.

Many journalists argue that the media are like a mirror reflecting reality, presenting a credible first draft of history – and that their sourcing routines reflect the social and political realities (Frost 2000: 37). Accordingly, John Whale (1977: 85) argued that 'the media do more towards corroborating opinion than creating it'. He cited the *Morning Star* (a communist newspaper originally published as the *Daily Worker*) with its very low circulation as proof that the views it promoted were simply not popular. Jay Newman (1992: 213) argues that the national media have generally succeeded in 'balancing the interests' of minorities and majorities, 'which is no easy task'.

Yet others claim that mainstream journalists use a remarkably limited range of sources. Johan Galtung and Mari Ruge (1965; 1973), in their seminal analysis of news values, highlighted the bias in the Western media towards reporting elite, First World nations and elite people. The elements of the hierarchy were different within and across different media. Television soap stars and showbiz personalities feature far more in the tabloid media than in the broadsheets. Yet there exists a distinct consensus over sourcing routines in the mainstream media. Some sources are always prominent, others will be marginalised, eliminated or covered generally in a negative way.

Philip Schlesinger (1978) found that as much as 80 per cent of BBC news came from routine sources while Bob Franklin and David Murphy (1991), in a study of 865 stories in the local press, found local and regional government, voluntary organisations, the courts, police and business accounted for 67 per cent of the total. Inevitably journalists can become friends with their elite sources and that can subtly 'soften' coverage and cement loyalties. Some critics express concern over the failure of the mass media to represent working-class views. Newspapers such as the *Daily Herald*, *Daily Sketch* and *Sunday Graphic*, aimed specifically at the working class, failed through lack of sales. As James Curran and Jean Seaton comment (1991: 108): 'They all had predominantly working class readership and, in terms of mass marketing, relatively "small" circulations. They thus fell between two stools: they had neither the quantity nor the social "quality" of readership needed to attract sufficient advertising for them to survive.'

The Glasgow University Media Group also identified within the broadcasting institutions an underlying ideology critical of working-class institutions. Television coverage of strikes was 'clearly skewed against the interests of the working class and organised labour' and 'in favour of the managers of industry' (1980: 400). The spread of email/Internet journalism also seriously impacts on sourcing routines. Many journalists say that as much as 90 per cent of their work is now conducted at their desks, their job reduced to a form of glorified clerking, the links with their audience dramatically cut.

Web journalism is popular with proprietors and managers because it's cheaper – and provides quick access to information and sources. Investigative reporter Sylvia Jones commented (see Mayes 1998: 50):

> I was helping out doing a sleaze story for the *Mirror*. There was a contact of mine who had some information and I needed to go out and see him. When I suggested that I actually go out and see him the other journalists looked at me absolutely astounded and said: 'It's bottoms on seats these days luv. You don't go out on a story, you do it all from the office.'

Concerns have also mounted in recent years about the power of the PR industry to influence the news agenda. Nick Cohen (1999: 126–7) suggested there were 25,000 PRs in Britain and 50,000 journalists, and quoted a prominent City public relations consultant who estimated that 80 per cent of business news and 40 per cent of general news comes straight from the mouths of PRs. Research by Cardiff University's journalism department in 2008 also indicated that 80 per cent of news reports in 'quality' UK national newspapers were at least partly made up of PR or recycled newswire copy (Davies 2008a). Investigative reporter Nick Davies even coined (somewhat controversially) the term 'churnalism' to describe the new form of journalism in which reporters 'have become passive processors of second-hand material generated by the booming PR industry and a handful of wire agencies' (ibid.).

Notice how often the mainstream media celebrate the extraordinary, obscene wealth of business men (they usually are male), celebrities, sports stars and the like. A photo-feature in the *Sun*, of 8 May 2008 showed a glitzy line-up of celebs – and alongside each of them were the details of their private wealth: David Beckham £90 million, Giorgio Armani £2.2 billion, Beyonce £50 million, Kate Moss £40 million and so on. Certainly as a result of the media's obsession with elite sources and dependency on advertising the experiences of the poor are marginalised in news coverage. Two decades of Conservative rule left Britain with the worst poverty record in the developed world, according to figures produced by the Organisation for Economic Co-operation and Development and released on 11 January 2000. Poverty affected 20 per cent of the population on average between 1991 and 1996. During the six years of the study, 38 per cent of the population spent at least one year below the poverty line. By 2006, 12.7 million people were counted as living in relative poverty.

In 2007, the UK came bottom of a 'child well-being' league table of 21 industrialised countries which prompted the Children's Commissioner for England, Professor Sir Al Aynsley-Green, to say the current generation of young people were 'unhappy, unhealthy, engaging in risky behaviour, have poor relationships with their family and their peers, low expectations and don't feel safe' (Williams 2007: 213). The *Sunday Times* 2007 Rich List revealed that Britain's richest 1,000 people (worth an estimated £360 billion) had seen their wealth increase by 20 per cent over the previous 12 months. Yet by 2008, 2.8 million children were still living in poverty – despite the target of the Brown government to halve the figure by 2010 (Brown 2008). And more than 2 million people were being forced to endure 'intolerably poor working lives' and subjected to daily exploitation and abuse from employers, according to a TUC report in 2008 (Hill 2008). Yet the voices of the poor are rarely heard in the media. While the media remain obsessed about rich lists, there is no sustained effort to identify the historical, political and economic factors that lie behind these alarming statistics on nation-wide poverty. No mainstream media (constrained by the 'hidden hand' of the advertisers) campaigns for a radical redistribution of wealth to counter these injustices.

Should journalists allow their source access to the report before publication or broadcasting?

Most journalists place a blanket ban on allowing sources access to the report or script before it appears. Such promises can land the journalist in all kinds of problems. Sources sometimes allow the copy or script to go through untouched but invariably they will want minor if not major changes inserted. And the journalist can feel their professionalism and autonomy are being questioned. Chris Frost (2000: 76) argues strongly: 'Showing the copy to an interviewee is a tacit admission that the piece is Public Relations and not journalism.'

But a different approach may see the value in the journalist demystifying their role and adopting a collaborative attitude toward the source. The final piece then becomes the product of a joint exercise between journalist and source, each one learning from the other. Clearly, a political perspective may inspire action. Such collaboration would not be appropriate for conventional sources who are well equipped to deal with the media. But a member of a progressive group normally marginalised or demonised by the media may appreciate the involvement. And occasionally journalists will submit selected quotes and factual sections of pieces to sources for checking when particularly complex issues are being handled. Some argue that the conventional view, denying access to copy, is based on the myth of the journalist as the independent professional while, in reality, the media serve as sophisticated publicity for the status quo. In this context, there is a need for overtly partisan media (such as provided by campaigning, leftist, environmental groups) in which journalists identify more closely with their audience – and thus are likely to subvert the conventions of traditional news gathering.

American Janet Malcolm (1991: 1), in *The Journalist and the Murderer*, controversially argued that every relationship with a source was exploitative and 'morally indefensible'. 'Every journalist who is not too stupid or too full of himself [sic] to notice what is going on knows that what he does is morally indefensible. He is a kind of confidence man, preying on people's vanity, ignorance or loneliness gaining their trust and betraying them without remorse.' Need it always be so? Award-winning documentary maker Roger Graef challenges Malcolm, advocating a collaborative relationship with sources. His films for the BBC, such as *Breaking Point*, on the marriage guidance body, Relate, usually deal with extremely sensitive, controversial areas. He comments (1998):

The notion of any kind of collaboration evokes a kind of journalistic capitulation that would send shivers down the spine of many film-makers. But in our experience, the sense of collaboration allows the participants to keep their dignity not only during filming – when they could ask for the camera to be switched off, or us to leave – but crucially during and after transmission.

Yet the dilemmas persist. Say you are a radio journalist and the source says the interview is so good it should go out unedited: how do you respond?

Should journalists treat all sources the same?

Children: no small challenge

Adults thrown into the limelight are often unprepared for media attention, so don't children need even more protection? In Britain, certain laws are in place to protect children in courts: thus those under 18 who are alleged offenders or witnesses at youth courts cannot be identified under the Children and Young Persons Act 1933 and the Criminal Justice Act 1991. Similarly, the Children Act 1989 imposed restrictions on identifying children, as did the Criminal Evidence and Youth Justice Act 1999 whose Section 44 made it an offence for the media to reveal the identity of a person under 18 suspected of an offence. Media law expert Tom Welsh described the provision (which came into force in December 2000) as 'draconian'.

In 1993, the PCC advised journalists covering children who have been victims of a crime, accident or other event: 'Editors should consider carefully whether or not their pictures offer clues, albeit unwittingly, that will allow some readers to put a name to the individual concerned. Such clues may be found in unusual hairstyles or in distinctive clothing.' Following a complaint by Tory MP Roger Gale over a *Mirror* story outlining his son's suspension for firing a 'gun' on a bus, the PCC issued 'tough guidelines to protect the vulnerable position of children at school' in 1997. They suggested that, where possible, stories about public figures raising issues about or involving children should be published without detail, including name, which might lead to the identification of the child. And 'where the story about the parents of the child is justified in the public interest, the vulnerable position of a child must be taken into consideration – and the child only identified in exceptional circumstances'.

One of the changes to the PCC's code, introduced in January 2000, focused on the reporting of young children. A new Clause 10 directed editors to pay particular regard to children who are victims or witnesses to crime. The children of the royals and Prime Minister Tony Blair have also been the subject of rulings by the PCC. Significantly, after Euan Blair was found by police lying drunk and semi-conscious in Leicester Square at 11 p.m. one evening in July 2000, the press carefully followed the PCC guidelines, according to *Times* columnist Brian MacArthur. But such coverage would have been illegal under provisions of the Youth Justice and Criminal Evidence Act, due to be implemented a few months later.

Both the Ofcom and BBC *Guidelines* stress that children should not normally be interviewed without the consent of a parent, guardian or other person of 18 or over *in loco parentis*. Under-16s should not be asked their views on issues likely to be beyond their capacity to answer properly without such consent: an exception might be vox pops on non-controversial issues such as favourite pop stars and pocket money (Hudson and Rowlands 2007: 120). Al Tompkins, of the Poynter Institute, recommends journalists to leave a business card with the child so the parents have a way of making contact if they object to the interview being used. Radio reporter and lecturer Jim Beaman (2000: 38–9) suggests it can be easier and more profitable to interview children in groups. 'Ask open questions and show an interest in what they tell you.' And CNN has a specific policy on questioning children. Reporters should make sure they are safe and away from the news scene while 'a highly inquisitive or investigative style' of questioning should be avoided.

Significantly, the Broadcasting Standards Commission's report in June 2000 stressed that the inclusion of distressed children in both documentary and entertainment programmes had become a major issue over the previous year and it upheld a complaint against *Panorama* about an 'emotionally charged and intrusive' interview with a child. A clinical psychologist Oliver James also criticises the media's typical coverage of children's murders, usually by a paedophile stranger. Yet of the 80 children killed on average every year, just seven are by someone unknown to them. The vast majority are killed by their parents, usually those with low incomes. James comments (2000): 'The only reason why parents are worrying so much is because the tabloids, followed sheepishly by the broadcast media, have realised that playing on parents' fears sells newspapers.' These views appeared in the *Guardian* which, on the same day, ran a large, close-up picture of the family of a murdered child hugging each other in their grief. Was that a tasteless intrusion on their private grief?

Moreover, outrage greeted the *News of the World*'s decision to 'name and shame' 49 paedophiles on 23 July 2000, the first instalment of a proposed list of 110,000. Many argued the campaign was a blatant publicity stunt while a letter to *Private Eye* took a wry view on the controversy: 'Am I alone in thinking that there should be a register of *News of the World* readers? Surely we should be told if such people live in our midst.' A dossier compiled by the Association of Chief Officers of Probation listed 40 cases in which released sex offenders went underground or innocent people were attacked as a result of mistaken identity following newspaper 'pervert watch' campaigns. Earlier, after predatory paedophile Sidney Cooke was released and the government introduced a sex offenders register, the *Sunday Express* ran a similar campaign providing photographs, names and addresses of the 'evil men'. Does it serve the public interest to demonise these men as 'monsters'? *News of the World* editor Rebekah Wade was adamant: 'Our intention is not to provoke violence. The disturbing truth is that the authorities are failing to properly monitor the activities of paedophiles in the community.'

According to Andrew Marr (2004: 62–3), the number of stories about paedophilia has rocketed since the mid-1990s, particularly in the tabloid press. He continues:

> It is possible that the 'paedophile panic' is our way of setting limits on sexuality in an increasingly sexual age: perhaps the papers who whipped up enough hysteria to produce mobs on the streets are in the longer term helping society by warning it of a real and underestimated danger to children. On the other hand, much innocent voluntary work has been curtailed and many innocent men have been made miserable, while many children have been unnecessarily frightened.

In its guidance notes to editors on the coverage of paedophiles,[6] the PCC suggests it is wise to talk with representatives of the local probation service and police before publication. Relatives and friends have a right to privacy and should not be identified without their consent unless they are relevant to the case or there is a public interest in doing so. Moral panics over paedophiles fuelled by sensational media coverage partly accounted for the growing concerns of parents over media coverage of school events. Some 25 editors surveyed for the Newspaper Society's 2004 Press Freedom Survey said schools were either refusing to permit press photography of school events or, more commonly, allowing coverage but then claiming the Data Protection Act prevented them from supplying the names of children. Some schools were even reluctant to release examination results. As one editor commented: 'These restrictions are hampering local newspapers reporting on the many positive stories and preventing a whole generation of children from being proud to appear in their local newspaper' (see Quinn 2007: 281). In response, the Information Commissioner produced a Good Practice Note on the filming and photographing of school events stating that so long as the school agrees to the press coverage and parents are informed, then there is no breach of the Act.

Ofcom's broadcasting code, which came into force on 25 July 2005, has a special section on both the effect of broadcasting content on the under-18s and the treatment of this age group by broadcasters. It stresses that under-18s need to be protected from content which could seriously impair their emotional, physical or moral development – and thus the 9 p.m. 'watershed' must be strictly respected. Before this time, violence, dangerous behaviour, offensive language and sexual content should not be broadcast. When reporting sexual offences involving under-18s (whether as defendants, victims or witnesses in the criminal, civil or family courts) no information should be broadcast which might lead to identification (see Quinn 2007: 376).

And should children be used in investigative assignments? For instance, in August 2007 ITV's *Undercover Mum* showed children and their mothers probing the pub food industry and its effects on children. Earlier the BBC programme *Newsround* used a disabled child to go undercover to check disability access in banks and shops. But according to Tessa Mayes (2007: 13), such assignments are highly problematic:

> Children will only get the reaction of adult subjects of an investigation to their role as a child posing as somebody but still as a child nevertheless. They can only make conclusions based on their child's view of a situation as opposed to an adult's awareness of the broader context and other facts relating to an issue. Children have more limited abilities to

rationalise about the meaning of a situation which could be unfair to the adults under scrutiny. And, a child can also get things wrong.

The ambush interview

Certain sources accused of crimes or other wrong-doing are reluctant to meet reporters and require special treatment. Occasionally journalists, as a last resort, will decide to 'ambush' the source, suddenly confronting them with questions which they will find difficult then to avoid. This strategy is mainly used by television journalists when the drama of the spectacle provides extra news value. Journalists should also work in pairs at least on such assignments; sources can turn violent.

Doorstepping

This is a favourite device of reporters, waiting outside the homes or workplaces of people in the news, all set to interview them. When journalists wait in packs this can amount to intimidation and harassment, punishable by law. Very often the comments gained from the reluctant source are unsubstantial but the hype surrounding breaking big stories usually encourages reporters to doorstep. MediaWise, the media ethics watchdog, advises members of the public: 'If you would prefer not to get involved, simply tell them, politely but firmly. Don't be surprised if they persist – that is their job. However, if they refuse to leave your premises or stop pestering you on the telephone, you are entitled to call the police.' Journalists should also note that under the Criminal Justice and Police Act 2001, if an officer decides that alarm or distress may be caused to a household, they have the power to order anyone to leave the vicinity: refusal to leave when ordered constitutes a criminal offence (Stevens 2001).

Should journalists share their contacts and quotes with colleagues?

Journalism involves a fascinating mix of individual drive and co-operative action. For instance journalists, often for safety reasons, work in pairs (or even threesomes) on risky investigative assignments. Reporters and production staff can work together on the details and presentation of a graphic. There is intense competition between staff on different media outlets. But there are some occasions when journalists routinely share information. This can be formalised with the creation of pools: a few journalists are given access to a special source or event and their reports are distributed to other media. Sometimes at long-running conferences, reporters will 'pick up' details from colleagues of any items missed. Similarly, at press conferences journalists may work as a pack to ask a speaker a series of questions on a complex, controversial issue. Afterwards, they may confer if some of the quotes were unclear.

But what if a colleague on a rival media institution asks you for contacts in one of your specialist areas? Some journalists would impose a blanket ban on such requests. Some responses may be politically motivated: they may be prepared to share with a colleague on one outlet but not another because of its unacceptable political bias. Some journalists decide to share a few of their sources but not their main ones, acquired only after considerable effort. After all, a colleague you fail to help today will not be there to help you in the future.

Should it be possible for journalists to pay sources?

There is a rich tradition in Britain of cheque-book journalism. In November 1996, the then editor of the *News of the World* said, on average, subjects were paid in about 10 per cent of stories. Writers of works serialised in the Sundays can receive substantial payments just as prominent people in the news (often backed up by publicist Max Clifford) can receive large 'buy-outs' for their stories. In August 1996, a furore greeted a deal between the *News of the World* and prospective mother Mandy Allwood (at one time expected to give birth to eight children) but this payment was dependent on the number of babies born. Another row erupted when Rebekah Wade, editor of the *Sun*, admitted to a Commons select committee inquiry into privacy and media intrusion that payments had been made to the police (Bell and Alden 2003: 24). Sources are routinely paid to appear on the radio or television. The biggest ever cross media deal was thought to have been brokered by PR consultant Max Clifford in 2001 when the parents of conjoined twins Mary and Jodie were expected to earn £500,000 after two tabloid Sunday newspapers, a television company and a magazine purchased a package of exclusive interviews and photographs (Carter 2001). But does this not lead to the situation where information becomes the monopoly of the wealthy? Is there not a danger sources will exaggerate and lie to justify the payment?

Most of the critical attention in the mainstream media has fallen on the issue of payments to witnesses in criminal court cases, and to criminals or their associates, significantly outlawed in the PCC's first Code of Practice in 1991. Controversies had blown up over payments to witnesses in the Moors murders case (1966), in the trial of Jeremy Thorpe, former leader of the Liberal Party (1979) and in the Yorkshire Ripper trial (1981). But the controversy reached fever pitch after newspapers made deals with 19 witnesses in the trial of mass murderer Rosemary West in 1995, including daughter Anne Marie Davies, who was paid £3,000 by the *Daily Star* but promised up to £70,000 (Hanna and Epworth 1998).

A Green Paper published by the Lord Chancellor's department in October 1996 claimed the PCC's code had failed to prevent 'widespread and flagrant breaches' and recommended legislation to deal with the problem. The PCC adamantly opposed legislation, saying payments to witnesses and criminals occurred in any case only rarely. All the same, in the light of evidence from the Chief Constable of Gloucestershire, the commission revised its code in November 1996 to incorporate new clauses which placed a burden of justification on the editor to prove payment was in the public interest and had to be disclosed to the parties involved in the trial.

However, the all-party National Heritage Committee, chaired by Gerald Kaufman in January 1997, urged the government to bring in legislation to ban media payments for the stories of witnesses and called for the Contempt of Court Act 1981 to be strengthened so that the media could not escape punishment where pre-trial publicity caused a trial to collapse. In February 2000, the Lord Chancellor, Lord Irvine, announced the government was to review payments by the press to witnesses in criminal trials. Interestingly, a survey by Hanna and Epworth (op. cit.: 14) of journalists working in England and Wales showed 70 per cent saying that media payments to witnesses put justice at risk, though only 58.1 per cent agreed there should be a statutory ban on such payments. Then in September 2002, the government finally backed down on outlawing payments to witnesses relying on the self-regulatory regime to incorporate an absolute ban on paying potential witnesses for stories in active criminal proceedings while payments conditional on convictions would be unacceptable in all circumstances.

Over recent years, the PCC has clarified its position on payments in a series of much-publicised rulings. After nurses Deborah Parry and Lucille McLauchlan were released in May 1998 from a Saudi jail after sentencing for the murder of a colleague, their stories were 'bought' by the *Express* and the *Mirror*, respectively. But a PCC ruling in July did not condemn the payments. Controversies also emerged after *The Times* ran a serialisation of *Cries Unheard* (London: Macmillan 1998), Gitta Sereny's biography of 1960s child murderer, Mary Bell, and the *Daily Mail* paid £40,000 to the parents of nanny Louise Woodward, convicted of the manslaughter of baby Matthew Eapen in Boston. In both these cases the PCC ruled there was a clear public interest defence.

But the *Daily Telegraph* was censured in July 1999 for paying Victoria Aitken around £1,000 for writing about her father's plight. Her article was published a day after Jonathan Aitken was sentenced to 18 months in prison for lying about payment of his bill by a Saudi arms financier at the Ritz, Paris, when Minister for Defence Procurement in the Major government – and as revealed by the *Guardian*. This payment could not be defended in the public interest. In May 2000, the PCC ruled that the *Sunday Times* did not infringe its Code in agreeing to pay for the rights to serialise Aitken's memoirs. The *ST* maintained its payment would go directly to the trustee in bankruptcy for Aitken's creditors.

In December 1999, the *News of the World*'s £25,000 'conviction bonus' to the key witness, Allison Brown, against Gary Glitter (jailed for four months for child pornography offences) was condemned by the PCC and described as 'a clearly reprehensible state of affairs' by the judge. But *NoW*'s then editor Phil Hall said his conscience was clear. 'We acted in good faith and took her on when there was no suggestion the police would interview her. People say we should have dropped out of the contract then but I thought the best thing to do would be to leave it to the authorities to make a decision.'

In October 2003, the *Daily Mirror* was (surprisingly) cleared of breaching the Code after it paid Tony Martin £125,000 for his story on how he shot and killed a burglar trying to break into his isolated farmhouse in Norfolk. The PCC ruled that it was in 'the public interest' to expose Martin to public scrutiny while the articles in no way glorified the crime

(Rozenberg 2004: 161–4). Then in June 2004, the trial of five men charged with plotting to kidnap Victoria Beckham collapsed after a failed *News of the World* sting. One of the factors was the payment of £10,000 by the *NoW* to co-defendant Florim Gashi (P. Smith 2007).

Should journalists accept freebies from sources?

In Britain, bribery of journalists was commonplace in the seventeenth and eighteenth centuries and remains so in many countries around the world. But according to Karen Sanders (2003: 122): 'A modest contemporary descendant is the "freebie", that is any good or service received for which no charge is made, and the "junket", an all-expenses paid trip to promote a product.' So rare is the British journalist who has not enjoyed a free foreign trip, free hotel booking, a free book or seat at the theatre. Such perks are particularly prominent in travel journalism. As Kim Fletcher noted (2006): 'The world of travel journalism is one where journalism not just meets PR but walks off into the sun with it.' Many continental media ban such freebies; only a few do in Britain. The Lonely Planet tourist guides, for instance, have a rigid policy of always refusing corporate kickbacks, publicity trips or freebies (Berry 2008). Reviewers of new cars are sometimes given them on indefinite 'loans'. Virgin Airlines has even provided journalists with mobile phones and unlimited calls. Are freebies best seen as bribes? Clearly, the institution paying for it is gaining some publicity, whether good or bad. And many journalists object to news being bought in this way. There is an alternative view which stresses that journalists don't always lose their critical faculties when cash is thrown in their faces. As John Wilson says on the influence of the freebie culture (op. cit.: 168):

> Much of the time it is harmless. Some of the time it fails the public because editorial scrutiny is relaxed. The proper journalistic stance is that, whatever facilities are provided, they will be declared, no conditions will be accepted, no editorial favour granted and the nature of the coverage decided independently.

Significantly, the British Guild of Travel Writers promotes a code of conduct which incorporates a ban on paid and promotional work for travel companies. Members can accept freebies – but only on the understanding that this will not influence their judgement. Most journalists unite in their condemnation of financial journalists and editors who use insider knowledge for their own profit. Both the NUJ (Clause 12) and the PCC (Clause 14) codes condemn such practices. And the BBC's *Producer Guidelines* stress: 'Individuals must not accept personal benefits or benefits for family/close personal relations e.g. goods, discounts, services, cash, gratuities, or entertainment outside the normal scope of business hospitality, from organisations or people with whom they might have dealings with on the BBC's behalf.'

Piers Morgan, then-editor of the *Mirror*, and two of his colleagues on the *City Slickers* column were censured by the commission in May 2000 after they were found to have shares in companies they were reporting on. Some journalists argue they were simply unlucky. The practice is, in fact, more widespread than generally acknowledged. And some journalists are calling for a 'new transparency' in which journalists declare their financial interests. As investigative reporter Phillip Knightley commented in an interview with the author:

> Many journalists were indignant at the *Mirror* shares affair. But are their own deals, consultancies and commercial contracts above reproach? Should we not ask ourselves whether a craft that demands such high standards of transparency from others (MPs for example) should be prepared to conform to high standards itself? A 'Register of Journalists' Interests' in each editorial department, freely available to the public and placed on a company's website, would be a start. Who will lead the way?

Karen Sanders (op. cit.: 124), however, is more optimistic. She comments: 'As wages have improved in the national media, and media institutions have changed from personal fiefdoms to money-making machines in huge corporate empires, freebies, junkets and extravagant expenses seem to be going the same way as the print unions.'

When is it legitimate to conduct a confrontational interview?

Interviews for print are rarely confrontational. The journalist's main concern is to listen attentively and sensitively to the source. In broadcasting, where entertainment/spectacle priorities surface, different criteria apply. Interviewers such as John Humphrys and Jeremy Paxman have acquired the reputations of being the journalistic equivalents of 'Rottweilers' (though Paxman told a meeting at Coventry University in May 2008 that, in fact, 99 per cent of his interviews were 'non-confrontational'). Humphrys was even criticised by the BBC programme complaints unit in August 2000 over a 'confrontational' interview with Lord Robertson, NATO Secretary General.

Yet, in commenting on his technique, Humphrys stresses the democratic/ Fourth Estate function of the media: the interview with a politician, he says, constitutes 'an important bridge between the electorate and their political leaders. We have to try to distil the national argument, to represent voters' concerns'. Dr Grego Philo, of Glasgow University, however, argues that political interviews on television and radio remain deferential with 'very few people taking chances'. Certainly politicians are increasingly being trained to counter adversarial interviewing techniques (pioneered by Sir Robin Day and later Brian Walden) and thus it could be argued the 'confrontation' is in danger of becoming ritualised. Trevor McDonald, of ITN, was actually criticised by the Independent Television Commission for an over-sycophantic interview with John Major, on 18 July 1996, in which he praised his 'great courage' over Northern Ireland. Humphrys, for all his 'Rottweiler' reputation, was voted 'Political journalist of the year' by politicians in 2000.

Margaret Thatcher was, significantly, troubled only once – and this was by a member of the public during a discussion over the sinking of the *Belgrano* during the Falklands conflict of 1982. In 1987, David Dimbleby's *Nine O'Clock News* interview with Thatcher revealed her contempt for 'whingers' 'drooling and drivelling that they care', but this was cut from the bulletin and only shown 'at a late point in the campaign when it could make no significant difference to the outcome' (McNair 2000: 101).

Significantly Tony Blair was most rattled, not by any television interviewer, but by Carol, a nurse from Liverpool, who criticised him over interest rates and rising mortgages during the Nicky Campbell show on 15 July 1998. Leigh and Vulliamy (1997: 234) argue that inherently superficial television interviews are unable to delve into the complexities of modern politics. Others welcome the rise of confrontational interviews as representing the decline in deference among the electorate to authority figures.

Does the Internet throw up new ethical issues in this area?

Frankly, yes – and massively. But with the rapid explosion of the Internet in recent years, it is not surprising that media workers have found it difficult to identify its precise implications on their routines and ethics. The BBC's decision in May 2000 to allow content from its licence-payer-backed (and extremely popular) online operation to be distributed to the Yahoo! website raised concern that the corporation was sacrificing its journalistic independence by singling out one commercial service.

And certainly with so many people able to publish on the Web, journalistic 'professionalism' has come under increasing threat. How can journalists respond? Some argue that well-established brand names, already respected for their journalistic standards, will win out in the end over the brash new players in cyberspace. Others say such an approach is too complacent, with the new media environment demanding a radical rethink of media routines and of the relationship between journalists and their audience and sources. Certainly the interactivity of the Internet means journalists can have much closer contact with their audience and sources. A new 'participatory' or 'networked' journalism in which professional and amateur journalists work together is emerging. Journalism is now more a conversation than a lecture. As David Cohn comments (2007): 'Imagine a journalist who releases a story to the public. Then, using participatory or networked journalism, more reporting and information is added and the story is re-worked and republished. This method can produce amazing results.'

According to commentators such as Jon Katz (1997), the Internet is transforming the journalist–audience relationship: from being an unquestioned expert the journalist now becomes simply a facilitator of debate. Increasingly media are providing e-mail addresses of staffers encouraging feedback and input from consumers. Nora Paul (the *Guardian*, 28 February 2000, reprinted from www.poynter.org) argues that the 'us to them' model of television producers and viewers is dying. News consumers now expect to have control on many aspects of the newscast: when they watch it, from what angle, the depth of the coverage, the type of news they want to see. 'Time shifting, multi-casting, camera vantage point selection – all will provide the viewer with more power over the product. News consumers will have new means of communicating with you about news and will expect a response.'

The Internet certainly provides reporters with the chance to extend their range of sources, giving them easy access to so many formerly marginalised groups and to internationalising their sourcing strategies. But are journalists relying now too much on the Internet? Much of journalism's human dimension is being lost with reporters retreating into a virtual, lifeless world. And concerns are mounting that the temptations towards plagiarism will grow. Ian Mayes (2000), then readers' editor at the *Guardian*, pointed to the deadline pressures on reporters. 'Over-reliance on cuttings and now, even more to the point, the ease of electronically cutting and pasting from the Internet, may be not simply attractive options, but the only options open to hard-pressed journalists in certain circumstances.'

Does not the Internet provide remarkable opportunities to the media to internationalise their coverage? Well, research suggests that narrow nationalistic obsessions remain. Chris Paterson (2007: 57–66) found that in the online news world only four organisations were conducting extensive international reporting (Reuters, Associated Press, Agence France Presse, BBC), while a few others did some international reporting (CNN, MSN, the *New York Times*, the *Guardian* and a few other large newspapers and broadcasters). Most did no original international reporting. He concludes (ibid.: 63):

> discourse on international events of consequence within the global public sphere is substantially determined by the production practices and institutional priorities of two information services – Reuters and the Associated Press. The political economy of online news is not one of diversity but one of concentration, and the democratic potential of the medium remain that – potential.

Should journalists always identify themselves as such when joining an Internet discussion group – and how does the law of libel operate there?

When investigating sensitive and dangerous issues, journalists may be justified in seeking anonymity when gathering background information. But Randy Reddick and Elliott King argue (1997: 219):

> Journalists should always identify themselves as such if they plan to use information from discussion lists. In most cases,

journalists have the ethical obligation to allow people to choose to go on-the-record or not. To lurk in a discussion list, then quote people who did not know that what they wrote would be used in a different context is as deceptive as posing or going undercover to report a story.

The legal position on Internet content remains confused. In theory, online media discussion groups could face problems if they carried material considered defamatory, grossly indecent or offensive, with the website providers subject to a civil action for defamation or charged under the Telecommunications Act 1984. In November 1999, the Lord Chancellor's department had a website closed down because material posted on it criticised five judges. Anxieties mounted in March 2000, after Demon Internet paid Lawrence Godfrey, a university lecturer and physicist, £15,000 plus legal fees of around £250,000 in an out-of-court settlement after he was the subject of an allegedly libellous bulletin board posting. Within days British Internet Service Providers (ISPs) closed two websites – a gay one called *Outcast* and another devoted (fittingly) to opposing censorship.

Significantly, in the case of *Totalise plc v. Motley Food Ltd and Another*, the High Court ruled in 2001 that website operators must identify the source of defamatory views. Mr Justice Robert Owen ordered both websites to reveal the identity of 'Zeddust' as he was satisfied disclosure was necessary 'in the interests of justice'. A series of court cases has certainly made it very clear that journalists have to be very careful when leaving material on websites: for instance, in 2006 a businessman won second libel damages from the *Sunday Telegraph* after it accidentally left a libellous piece on its website archive. If a newspaper is accused of defamation over a posting on an electronic forum, bulletin board, chatroom and so on, media expert Tom Welsh has this advice:

> In these circumstances, the organisation may be able to rely on the 'innocent dissemination' protection provided by Section 1 of the Defamation Act 1996, which has enabled broadcasters to defend themselves if sued for defamatory comments blurted out by interviewees in unscripted programmes. The media organisation will have to show, among other things, it was not the 'author, editor or publisher' of the statement complained of and that it took reasonable care in

relation to its publication. To show that it will have to remove the statement, and do so promptly.

Should journalists join social networking sites such as Facebook?

Some reporters are concerned that revealing sources on social networking sites can endanger a journalist's credibility and lead to conflicts of interests. Others stress that journalists should never have politicians as Facebook friends; should decline from interviewing Facebook friends – and should not list their contacts as Facebook friends (Lowe 2007). Still others stress the value of such sites in making journalistic routines more transparent. Journalists are increasingly using networking sites to access information and photographs about people suddenly thrown into the news. And a lot of people, especially youngsters, are revealing often extraordinary personal details about themselves – probably not fully aware of the openness of the medium. Have journalists a responsibility to protect the privacy of such people?

Blogger and Internet expert Kristine Lowe advises journalists using Facebook to be 'intimately acquainted with the privacy settings': 'the default option on Facebook is to share as much as possible with as many as possible so make sure you set the privacy settings to a level you're comfortable with' (ibid.). And she adds: 'The inbuilt "newsfeed" and "minified" features will let everybody know just how much time you're spending on Facebook, so it might be an idea to turn it off altogether, or at least not use Facebook during office hours.'

To what extent should journalists involve themselves in abusive blogging threads?

Many online blogging debates can easily end up in vicious slanging matches. Comments on journalists' copy (whether in print or broadcast) can be mean-spirited, insulting, abusive or inaccurate – even despite website policies discouraging such responses. With online etiquette still at its formative stages, journalists are left wondering whether to become involved or not. Siobhain Butterworth (2008a), readers' editor of the *Guardian*, reported in March 2008 that journalists on her newspaper were divided on this issue. One blogger and columnist said he had a policy of 'killing the trolls with kindness'. Another commented: 'Isn't journalism provocative by nature?' What do you think?

Away on the *Sun* (and its sister sites of the *News of the World* and *thelondonnewspaper*), however, reader-generated copy was being moderated by a seven-member team to remove objectionable material within 15 minutes. According to News Corp Digital head of communities Danny Dagan, the policy was shaped not only by considering legal risks but also issues of taste and brand protection.

With the rise of the web, do not journalists need to be even more rigorous in their fact-checking?

Certainly the Internet is throwing up all manner of temptations to researchers to plagiarise. How often are journalists, facing ever tighter deadlines in the 24/7 environment, tempted to simply copy and paste material from a website? But journalists, while Googling and otherwise web-browsing, must always assess the relative merits of information from different sources. Wikipedia, the online encyclopaedia (www.wikipedia. org) with around 2,300,000 million entries in its English version in January 2008, is undoubtedly a remarkable resource with copy provided – and edited – by anonymous sources. But its content must always be regarded with some scepticism.

In October 2007, Ronald Hazlehurst, who composed many of the theme tunes for BBC comedies in the 1970s and 1980s, died but his obituaries throughout the media incorporated one strange 'fact': that he had also co-written a hit for the pop group S Club 7. It was all a hoax. Someone had inserted that 'information' into his Wikipedia entry – and most journalists, it appeared, failed to double check. Again, in March 2008, the *Guardian* ran a story (complete with photograph) that the Eiffel Tower was to have a temporary structure added to its top designed by the winners of a competition run by the tower's operating company. But it was all fictitious: the 'statement' from the company had appeared on a website and from there the journalist had gone to various architectural forums to fit the jigsaw together. 'I thought the story was genuine because I saw it in so many other places.' It was even later picked up by other newspapers, including the *New York Times* (Butterworth 2008b). As media academic and author of *The Ethical Journalist*, Tony Harcup, commented

(2007b): 'We should encourage student and trainee journalists to improve their information literacy by learning some of the skills of the librarian in the digital age, including effective Internet and database searching. But we must also nurture the natural scepticism of the journalist.'

Similarly, Robert Kiley (1999) advises Internet users to always check that the information is current. 'A well organised web page will state when it was first written and last updated.' See if there is a named author. If so, then search an appropriate database for their previous publications. 'If there is no identified author the information should be treated with caution.' Who is funding the site? The owner should be clearly displayed along with details of any sponsorship or advertising.

Yet errors will inevitably be made on websites. How, then, to correct them? In June 2007, the BBC News website wrongly reported that a defendant in a firearms case had been convicted. The error was quickly spotted and corrected. But the BBC Editorial Complaints Unit later required that the site post a link to its ruling at the foot of the corrected report.[7] Should not all sites similarly be expected to post links to corrections or adjudications in its archives?

Notes

1   See http://news.bbc.co.uk/1/hi/uk/6108496.stm, accessed 27 February 2008.

2   See www.surveillance-and-society.org, accessed 2 March 2008.

3   See http://home.hiwaay.net/~pspoole/echelon.html, and http://cryptome.org/echelon-ep-fin.htm accessed 27 February 2008.

4   See www.privacyinternational.org/article.shtml?cmd[347]=x-347-559597, accessed 27 February 2008.

5   See www.opsi.gov.uk/Acts/Acts1998/ukpga_19980029_en_1, accessed 12 April 2008.

6   See www.editorscode.org.uk/guidance_notes_10.html.

7   www.bbc.co.uk/complaints/news/2007/11/07/50533.shrml.

5
The ethics of sleaze coverage

Privacy, bugging, surveillance and subterfuge

How much were journalists to blame for making the 1990s the naughty decade of dirt and sleaze and the first years of the twenty-first century the naughties?

The 1990s seemed submerged in an endless series of scandals involving randy royals, MPs (always male and mostly Tory) and showbiz personalities. Screaming *News of the World* headlines such as 'Di found knickers in Charles' pocket', 'Charles bedded Camilla as Diana slept upstairs', 'I spied on Di and Hewitt making love in garden' and 'Royal sex orgy shame' became, as Matthew Engel commented, 'a Sunday morning routine' (1996: 304). Inevitably, issues surrounding invasions of privacy came to dominate media and political debate over the decade. But it is debatable how much the public was concerned. Relatively few complaints to regulatory bodies focused on privacy. People, after all, are ambivalent: often condemning invasions of privacy but lapping up the published results.

The 'dirty decade' may, in fact, be seen to have started on 23 July 1989, when the *Sunday People* carried a photograph of Prince William's 'sly pee' in a park under the headline 'The Royal Wee!'. Robert Maxwell, the proprietor and fervent royal supporter, promptly sacked the editor, Wendy Henry (see Greenslade 2003b: 516). But the tone for media coverage was set for the following decade. Hardly a month passed without some celebrity, Minister or MP being 'exposed': many lost their reputations, some their jobs (and Princess Diana her life). In the three years following John Major's election victory in 1992, there were 14 resignations on grounds of scandal; half the cases involved sexual activities;

about half financial irregularities. The *Independent on Sunday* (23 July 1995) claimed that between 1990 and 1995 there were 34 Conservative, one Liberal Democrat and four Labour scandals; of these around a quarter involved sex.

One theory accounting for this rash of sleaze stories stresses the impact of the end of the Cold War. Changes in the operation of the national security state mean the media become the theatre where inter-elite squabbles are fought out. Significantly, hardly any country has been unaffected by corruption scandals since 1989. Since the Cold War had a global reach it is not surprising that the consequences of its demise should be global. In the United States, for instance, President Clinton's affair with internee Monica Lewinsky dominated the headlines globally after Matt Drudge's maverick Internet site broke the story in February 1998. But President Kennedy's rampant sexuality and many affairs had not been covered in the media because national security in the Cold War would have been considered endangered by such revelations (Keeble 1998).

With the decline of ideology, critics claim there has been a breakdown in the old-fashioned divisions between the private and the public, and people's understanding of politics has to centre around personal narratives. At the same time it is argued 'human interest' stories can address deeper issues such as sexual harassment and the abuse of power. The Major Government's stress on 'Back to Basics' certainly put the spotlight on Conservative moral hypocrisy. While some criticised the media's descent into 'bonk journalism' and trivia, journalists argued that if a politician publicly promoted family values but in private was cavorting with prostitutes, then they had a duty to expose such hypocrisy in the public interest. According to Hywel Williams (2000):

> The cult of the personal and intimate dragged into the light of day is a powerful one here. The impulse is democratic, egalitarian and anti-heroic: leaders are shown to have feet of clay. It's a comforting conclusion that they are really just like ourselves. Politically, the result is that we've grown sceptical about leadership. Suspicion of politics has always been a powerful British trait. But television in particular and journalism in general have de-sacralised the tribalism of party politics. Daylight, let in on old mysteries, has revealed new banality.

Brian McNair (2000: 54) argues that sleaze journalism 'should be viewed as a welcome by-product of an era when journalistic deference toward political elites has been eroded and the normative watchdog function of the Fourth Estate is increasingly applied, in conditions of heightened competitiveness, to the secretive, insider networks which if left alone burrow away at and undermine the democratic process'. He also links sleaze journalism with the theories of Burke (1988) which focus on the feudal carnivalesque forms of popular culture when 'the world was turned upside down' (op. cit.: 58–9).

The explosion of sleaze journalism was also a product of the hyper-competition on Fleet Street. In the face of falling sales and the need for rising profits, the focus on sensationalism became inevitable. Yet, while stories tended to be exposed in the red-top, brasher tabloids, the rest of the media, operating similar news values, rapidly picked them up. It was the BBC's flagship investigative programme series, *Panorama*, which hosted Princess Diana's famous 1995 interview in which she described in detail her marriage breakdown and relations with the royal family. It was the highly-regarded *Channel 4 News* which paid Monica Lewinsky a reported £400,000 to be the first British broadcast institution to interview her. Dan Hogan complained (1998: 28): 'The major concern is that politicians are being let off the hook by an obsession with private lives. Other more crucial matters get less airtime and column centimetres.' Some media commentators suggested that the focus on sleaze in the run up to the 1997 election (with scandals surrounding Tory MPs such as Allan Stewart, Tim Smith, Piers Merchant and Neil Hamilton) meant that the BBC had lost its normal neutral stance.

Scandal, of course, continued unabated with the arrival of New Labour in power from 1997 – even though they were committed to being 'tough on sleaze and tough on the causes of sleaze'. Blair's government lurched from one embarrassing revelation to the next:

• Foreign Secretary Robin Cook's affairs;

• the £1 million donation to the party in 1997 by Formula One mogul Bernie Ecclestone (allegedly to help him escape a tobacco advertising ban);

• the two enforced resignations by minister Peter Mandelson (firstly over an undisclosed loan of £373,000 from fellow minister Geoffrey

Robinson to buy a house in London and then over a row concerning a passport application by an Indian billionaire);

- the Cheriegate Affair of December 2002, which involved the purchase by the Blairs of two flats in Bristol, a conman, leaked e-mails and Carole Caplin, Mrs Blair's friend and lifestyle adviser;

- David Blunkett was forced to resign from a second ministerial post in November 2005 following a row over his failure to consult a watchdog about several extra-parliamentary jobs. Sally Anderson, an estate agent, also claimed to have had a relationship with the MP. Blunkett had earlier been forced to resign as Home Secretary after admitting his office had helped speed the work permit application of the ex-nanny of his lover, Mrs Kimberly Quinn;

- the 'cash for honours' row in 2006 following a *Sunday Times* investigation (see Davies 2008a: 327–8). Tony Blair denied accusations of offering peerages for cash after four people he nominated for honours were found to have made substantial loans to the party ahead of the previous election without the knowledge of Labour's treasurer and other elected officials. In December 2006, Blair became the first serving prime minister to be questioned by police as part of a criminal investigation. He was interviewed again in late January and in June 2007. Downing Street stressed that he was not cautioned, which meant he was being treated as a witness rather than a suspect;

- revelations in 2007 that property developer David Abrahams had secretly donated £630,000 to the Labour Party over a four-year period. In April the following year, the police cleared him of any wrong-doing. No evidence had been produced to prove Abrahams had corruptly bought planning decisions in the north east.

And so on and so on . . .

What do the regulatory bodies have to say about privacy?

The NUJ Code of Conduct's Clause 6 states: A journalist shall do nothing which entails intrusion into anybody's private life, grief or distress, subject to justification by overriding considerations of the public interest.

The PCC Code says: Everyone is entitled to respect for his or her private and family life, home, health and correspondence, including digital communications. Editors will be expected to justify intrusions into any individual's private life without consent. The public interest includes, but it not confined to:

- Detecting or exposing crime or serious impropriety; protecting public health and safety; and preventing the public from being misled by an action or statement of an individual or organisation.
- There is a public interest in freedom of expression itself.
- Whenever the public interest is invoked, the PCC will require editors to demonstrate fully how the public interest was served.

A substantial section of the Ofcom broadcasting code, which came into force in July 2005, focuses on privacy issues. It says, for instance, that wherever broadcasters wish to justify an infringement of privacy they should be able to demonstrate why in the particular circumstances of the case it is in the public interest. Examples of public interest would include revealing or detecting crime, protecting public health or safety; exposing misleading claims made by individuals or organisations or disclosing incompetence that affects the public.

Material obtained surreptitiously should not be used except in the public interest. This includes material secured through using long lens or recording devices, by leaving a camera or recorder unattended on private property without the informed consent of the owner, by taping a telephone conversation without informing the other person or by continuing to record when the source believes you have stopped. Distressed people should not be pressurised to give interviews unless this is warranted (i.e. in the public interest). The location of a person's home or family should not be disclosed without their consent, unless warranted (see Quinn 2007: 381–2).

And finally the BBC's editorial guidelines state:

> The BBC seeks to balance the public interest in freedom of expression with the legitimate expectation of privacy by individuals . . . there is no single definition of public interest, it includes but is not confined to: exposing or detecting crime, exposing significantly anti-social behaviour . . . preventing people from being misled by some statement or action of an

individual or organisation . . . disclosing information that allows people to make a significantly more informed decision about matters of public importance.

Is a privacy law necessary to restrain the media?

One of the major problems about privacy is that it's extremely difficult for legislators to define. Lord Justice Sedley in the infamous *Douglas v Hello* case (see below) referred to privacy as a 'concept', a 'principle' and a 'qualified right'. The facets of privacy ranged from 'hard' information available to credit agencies – qualifications, credit status – through to aspects such as genetic identity, health issues, religion, personal and sexual habits, to 'soft' information such as future plans, personal space, personality, thoughts, dreams and emotions. Privacy, then, incorporates a wide range of issues not easily covered by a single formula. According to Matthew Kieran (2000: 163): 'Privacy concerns certain areas of our lives over which we exercise autonomous control and which it is not the business or right of others to concern themselves with unless we so choose.' Further complexities emerge if we consider how, in the age of reality television shows and confessional media which constantly feed our voyeuristic obsessions, so many people are happy to have their privacy invaded. Sanders (2003: 79–80) refers to Princess Diana's television 'confession' of adultery on the prestigious *Panorama* programme of 20 November 1995, which was watched by more than 21 million people, and comments: 'It was a haunting example of intimate self-betrayal and our prurient appetite for the private. When privacy is so easily surrendered, it becomes difficult to recognise its value.'

All the same, privacy is regarded as a fundamental human right – the essential bulwark against the state or social groups acquiring power over us to our disadvantage. It is a right enshrined in Article 12 of the Universal Declaration of Human Rights of 1948 (see www.un.org/Overview/rights.html). Polls suggest that the public places the protection of personal information as the second most important social issue – ahead of the environment and NHS.

Yet how can privacy be best protected? Since there will be on occasions justifiable invasions of privacy, how can criteria for these be identified? The French elite certainly believes in the importance of legislating to protect privacy. Its law helped keep the womanising and illegitimate daughter of President François Mitterrand (1981–95) away from media scrutiny. The constitutions of Italy and Belgium also protect citizen's rights to privacy. In the United States, Australia and Canada there are statutory defences to privacy. But in Britain, the political elite has remained consistently opposed to such legislation, concerned over the difficulties in precisely defining 'privacy' and the 'public interest', though the debate has raged for many years.

- The first Royal Commission on the Press (1947–9) decided against privacy legislation, leaving it to a newly-created General Council of the Press to condemn bad practice.

- The Younger Committee on Privacy which reported in 1972 also came down against legislating.

- Following a spate of controversies over invasions of privacy, backbench Tory MP John Browne introduced a Privacy Bill to the House of Commons in 1989 but it was voted down.

- On 13 February 1990, *Sunday Sport* journalists took unauthorised photographs of comedian Gordon Kaye when recovering from a serious head wound in hospital and interviewed him in a semi-conscious state. Ten days later the newspaper successfully appealed against an injunction obtained by the actor's agent preventing publication. The judge ruled there was no right to privacy in English common law, implying that Parliament should consider introducing legislation to prevent such intrusions.

- The Calcutt Committee of Inquiry into Privacy and Related Matters, set up by the Thatcher government, reported in 1990 and came down in favour of making physical intrusion an offence, but did not propose a privacy law. The government held back from following Calcutt's lead and the newly-formed PCC (which replaced the Press Council as recommended by Calcutt) largely concerned itself with issues of privacy in its Code of Practice. Separate clauses looked at privacy, inquiries at hospitals, harassment, intrusions into grief or shock, interviewing or photographing children and covering victims of crime. Invasions of privacy could be justified only when in the 'public interest'. This it defined as:

    i)   detecting or exposing crime or serious misdemeanour,
    ii)   detecting or exposing seriously anti-social behaviour,

     iii)   protecting public health and safety,
     iv)   preventing the public from being misled by some statement or action of that individual.

- On 7 June 1992 the *Sunday Times* began its serialisation of Andrew Morton's book on Princess Diana, revealing her unhappiness, suicide attempts and eating disorders. Though it later became known that the Princess had covertly assisted Morton, a huge row over the alleged unjustifiable invasion of privacy erupted. In July 1992, PCC chairman Lord MacGregor went so far as to describe reports of the royal marriage as 'an odious exhibition of journalists dabbling their fingers in the stuff of other people's souls'. In its defence the newspaper argued that the story raised important constitutional issues.

- David Mellor, the Heritage Minister (and Chelsea supporter), appointed Calcutt to head a new inquiry, warning the press they were drinking in the 'last chance saloon' in the face of the mounting threat of privacy legislation. But then, after Mellor's affair with an actress was revealed in the *People*, in July 1992, he was forced to resign in September.

- Privacy controversies continued after Prince Andrew's wife 'Fergie', the Duchess of York, was pictured in the *Daily Mirror* and *Observer* (clearly desperate for sales) frolicking topless with her 'financial adviser', and the *Sun* published the 'Squidgy' tapes of conversations supposedly between Princess Di and James Gilbey.

- Calcutt's second report, published in January 1993, recommended the replacement of the PCC with a statutory press tribunal. In addition, it proposed new offences carrying maximum fines of £5,000 for invasions of privacy and the use of surveillance and bugging devices in certain cases. In defence, journalists could claim the material was obtained for preventing, detecting or exposing crime or anti-social behaviour, or to prevent people being misled by some statement or action of the individual concerned. The Major government responded positively and, later in the year, proposed the introduction of a privacy law. Yet it was determined not to apply the restrictions to the security services.

- In March 1993 the Commons national heritage committee on privacy and media intrusion included in its 43 recommendations the suggestion that the government appoint a Press Ombudsman and a Protection of Privacy Bill, while in July the Lord Chancellor, Lord Mackay, published a consultation paper, *The Infringement of Privacy*, which proposed a new civil tort to protect privacy. In November the committee added an addendum to its March report calling for a new privacy tort.

- A new controversy erupted in November 1993 after the *Sunday Mirror* and *Daily Mirror* published 'peeping tom' photographs of Princess Di in L.A. Fitness Club, Isleworth, West London. Colin Myler, editor of the *Sunday Mirror*, defended publication on the grounds of the security issues it raised.

- The PCC introduced new clauses to the Code on bugging and the use of telephoto lenses and a lay majority (though only of the Great and the Good) was created among its members. In addition, Professor Robert Pinker, of the London School of Economics, was appointed special privacy commissioner in January 1994.

- In March 1994, the Association of British Editors, the Guild of British Editors and the International Press Institute issued 'an alternative white paper', *Media Freedom and Regulation*, which concluded that it was unnecessary to introduce a privacy law since it would 'risk seriously undermining legitimate public investigation by the media'.

- In October 1994, the *Guardian* began its own long campaign to expose MPs taking cash handouts from lobbyists in return for asking Parliamentary questions. After editor Peter Preston admitted his reporters had sent a 'cod fax' to the Ritz Hotel, Paris, and used a mock-up of the House of Commons notepaper to protect a source, all in search of financial information about cabinet minister Jonathan Aitken, the privacy debate hit fever pitch. Preston duly resigned from the PCC, though Premier John Major soon afterwards set up a committee, chaired by Lord Nolan, to investigate the ethical behaviour of MPs and lobbyists. Aitken was duly jailed for 18 months in July 1999 (though in the end he served only 30 weeks) after being discovered lying over the payment of a bill at the Ritz during a libel case against the *Guardian* (Leigh and Vulliamy 1997).

- The appointment in November 1994 of Lord Wakeham, former Tory Cabinet Minister, as PCC chairman was welcomed by many mainstream journalists as likely to smooth the relations between press and Parliament, particularly over privacy issues.

- In 1995, the PCC criticised the *News of the World* for publishing pictures, gained through the use of a long-lens camera, of yet another aristocrat, a frail-looking Countess Spencer, sister-in-law of the Princess of Wales, in the garden of a private health clinic. After her husband, Earl Spencer, complained, Professor Pinker contacted Rupert Murdoch, owner of the *News of the World*, who publicly reprimanded its editor, Piers Morgan. Murdoch described Morgan as 'a young man' who 'went over the top' in his coverage. Morgan duly apologised – and went on to even greater fame as editor of the *Mirror* (Browne 1996).

- In April 1995 the Commons privileges committee condemned the *Sunday Times* for 'falling substantially below the standards to be expected of legitimate journalism' over stories exposing Graham Riddick and David Tredinnick. The Tory MPs had accepted £1,000 from an undercover journalist to ask questions in Parliament. The newspaper was originally backed by the PCC but in March 1996, it reversed its decision, ruling that the newspaper did not gather enough information since an issue of serious public interest was involved.

- In July 1995, a new White Paper, presented by Heritage Minister Virginia Bottomley, called for the PCC to pay compensation to victims of privacy intrusion; for a clearer definition of privacy in its Code; and for a telephone line to be set up between the PCC and editors to head off breaches of Code. Tory backbenchers greeted the announcement with jeers; the Labour Party expressed disappointment.

- Much of the privacy controversy had focused around the media's coverage of Princess Diana. Her own attitude to the media was ambivalent: at times appearing to welcome and even encourage coverage; at other times frankly detesting it. In November 1995, nine days after her *Panorama* interview, she telephoned *News of the World* royal reporter Clive Goodman and gave him an exclusive interview. But then just months later in 1996 for instance, she won an injunction preventing a member of the paparazzi from approaching within 300 metres of her. After her death on 31 August 1997 in a Paris road crash, blame initially fell on the paparazzi who were allegedly pursuing the royal Mercedes at the time. New guidelines on the use of paparazzi photographs were introduced by the PCC and, in revising the Code, Lord Wakeham redefined 'a private place' as covering the interior of a church, a restaurant and other places 'where individuals might rightly be free from media attention'.

- In February 1998, the Lord Chancellor, Lord Irvine, caused enormous confusion after proposing a privacy law allowing for prior restraint by the PCC and the payment of compensation to victims of privacy invasions. He was promptly rebuked by Premier Tony Blair who remained committed to opposing privacy legislation.

- In June 1998, the Broadcasting Standards Commission introduced its code with a specific focus on the protection of privacy.

- Then in April 2000, the PCC condemned the *News of the World* in what Roy Greenslade, media commentator of the *Guardian*, called a 'landmark' judgment on privacy. A typical kiss 'n' tell story (headlined 'Street star's eight-month marathon of lust') by the former fiancé of *Coronation Street* actress, Jacqueline Pirie, was said to have breached Clause 3 of the Code: 'Everyone is entitled to his or her private and family life, home, health and correspondence.' As Greenslade concluded: 'In other words, the one-sided account by Pirie's ex-fiancé, even though its truth has not been disputed, was considered to have invaded her privacy.'

- While in opposition, the Labour Party had backed calls for privacy legislation as a way of curbing press excesses. When in office, its tune changed. Soon after its May 1997 landslide victory, New Labour made it clear it was not planning to introduce privacy laws unless newspapers behaved in an 'intolerable fashion'. Journalists disguising themselves as doctors was given as an example of such behaviour. Fears grew among prominent journalists that the 1950 European Convention on Human Rights, which the government was due to enshrine in the Human Rights Act, could introduce privacy legislation 'by the back door'. But on 11 February 1998, Tony Blair pledged in the Commons that the government had no such intention. Article 8 of the convention, incorporated into British law in October 2000, states: 'Everybody has the right to respect for his private and family life, his home and his correspondence.' Balancing this, Article 10 guarantees freedom of expression.

- Significantly, on 16 January 1998, the European Commission of Human Rights ruled that Earl Spencer and his former wife had insufficient grounds for starting a case under the European Convention of Human Rights over the government's failure to protect them against press intrusions. And in June 2000, after Lord Levy, a multi-millionaire fund-raiser for the Labour Party, was found by the *Sunday Times* to have paid just £5,000 tax for the previous year, his application for an injunction to prevent publication was rejected. Mr Justice Joulson ruled that there was an over-riding public interest in the information being published. Others objected to this invasion of privacy. The *Guardian* editorial of 26 June took the judge's ruling – 'He who actively involves himself in public life, as Lord Levy has, cannot altogether complain if he is caught by the heat' – as a major definition of the media's public interest defence.

- In July 2001, Anna Ford asked High Court judge for judicial review of a PCC decision to reject her claim that the *Daily Mail* and *OK!* Magazine had infringed her privacy by publishing secretly gained pictures of her in a bikini on a beach on holiday in Majorca. But Mr Justice Silber rejected her claim.

- November 2001, Mr Justice Jack banned the *Sunday People* from 'exposing a married Premiership footballer who has two secret mistresses'. The judge controversially declared that all sexual relations should remain private. Then in March 2002, Lord Chief Justice Woolf ruled that the judge was wrong to ban the *Sunday People* from publishing interviews with a lapdancer and teacher who had had affairs with a married Premiership footballer, Gary Flitcroft. As the *Guardian* editorialised on 16 March 2002, Lord Woolf came close to linking public interest with any story which interested the public. 'This was a dramatic break with all previous attempts by judges to find a definition of the public interest which involved some sort of benefit to the public.' Secondly he created a special category of public figure who had to 'expect or accept' their private and public actions to be examined by the media.

- In December 2001, publication of topless photographs of actress Amanda Holden taken while at a private holiday villa landed the *Daily Star* with £165,000 in an out-of-court settlement. She claimed her privacy had been invaded. In response, the *Star* claimed the photographs had not been taken with a long lens and that the garden was visible from a public track.

- In January 2002, the *Daily Telegraph* and *Daily Mail* were censured by the PCC for breaking the Code by publishing the fact that the Prime Minister's 17-year-old son, Euan Blair, had applied for a place at Trinity College, Oxford. Tony Blair and his wife, Cherie, complained the story breached clauses which protected children at school from intrusion and undue publicity because of their parents' fame.

- Vanessa Frisbee was paid £25,000 by the *News of the World* for revelations about her former employer, supermodel Naomi Campbell. But in March 2002 Mr Justice Lightman ruled that this was 'in flagrant breach of her express and implied duties of confidentiality'.

- The PCC ruled in February 2003 that the *People* had breached its Code when it used photographs, taken with a long-lens camera, of actor Julie Goodyear sitting in her back garden.

- In June 2003, DJ Sara Cox won a major our-of-court award after the *People* published pictures of her and husband nude while on honeymoon in the Seychelles. The newspaper was sued under Section 8 of the Human Rights Act. The case first went to the PCC and an apology was printed in the next week's issue of the paper in October 2001. According to the editor and photographer concerned, she had yielded her right to privacy because she had posed for candid pictures in the past and given supposedly intimate interviews (Greenslade 2004).

- In March 2002, Naomi Campbell's claim for breach of privacy, when the *Mirror* revealed she was attending Narcotics Anonymous meetings, crashed despite her success in persuading the judge she needed protection from intrusion. In October 2002 the Appeal Court overturned the decision to award her £3,500. The *Mirror* was cleared of breaching the Data Protection Act when it published 'sensitive personal details' about her. Finally, just to prove the absurdly confusing state of the privacy legislation (and the way it is able to feed the pockets of over-paid lawyers), in May 2004 the Law Lords ruled 3–2 in favour of Campbell. Piers Morgan, the editor, remarked that it was 'a good day for lying, drug-abusing prima donnas'. But Peter Hill, editor of the *Daily Express*, summed up the views of many: 'It's got nothing to do with freedom of the press or privacy. It's just a battle between two giant egos' (Morris 2004). The newspaper was afterwards sent a bill of £594,000 by Campbell's lawyers and it claimed the total bill for the appeal and two preceding trials had come to more than £1 million. The lawyers had virtually doubled their costs by charging a 'success fee' designed to reflect the risk involved in taking on cases on a 'no win no fee' basis. But in October 2005 five judges rejected the *Mirror*'s claims to challenge the bill, ruling that it was up to Parliament to introduce new legislation if considered necessary (see Gibson 2005a).

- In January 2003, a homeless man whose suicide attempt was captured by the CCTV cameras of his local council, Brentwood, Essex, and released to newspapers and TV companies won a landmark ruling from the European Court of Human Rights. The Strasbourg court ruled that Geoffrey Peck's right to respect for his private life was violated and that he had no remedy under the UK's existing privacy law. The court awarded him £7,800 in damages, and nearly £12,000 costs.

- Senior policeman Brian Paddick won a legal battle in December 2003 against the *Mail on Sunday* after claiming the newspaper invaded his privacy by revealing his gayness in two reports in March 2002. With the trial due to begin in February 2004, the newspaper agreed to apologise, contribute to the officer's legal costs and pay substantial damages. His lawyer, Tasmin Allen, claimed the case proved claimants had a right to privacy. But the newspaper claimed it had settled over libel – and not privacy.

- Also in 2003, the House of Commons Culture, Media and Sport Committee called for privacy legislation following hearings on privacy and media intrusion. In response, the Blair government rapidly reaffirmed its opposition to a privacy Act.

- In January 2004 Sebastian (later Lord) Coe failed in his attempt to prevent publication in two newspapers of the details of a 10-year affair with Vanessa Landers. Mr Justice Fulford decided that Coe's right to privacy was outweighed by Ms Lander's right to free speech and the *Sunday Mirror*'s right to tell its readers about the habits of those in the public eye. Thus it seemed that the courts (considering the possible harm involved) were not yet prepared to extend the right of privacy over medical treatment, as in Campbell, to the extramarital life of public figures.

- Catherine Zeta Jones and Michael Douglas objected to unauthorised photographs by Rupert Thorpe of their wedding in *Hello!* after formal publicity arrangements had been agreed with *OK!* Such spoilers have become a regular journalistic 'trick' – particularly since 1993 when the *Mirror* ruined the *Sunday Times*' serialisation of Margaret Thatcher's memoirs by publishing some of the most interesting extracts. The *Mirror* claimed public interest – and the court agreed. Moreover, there is no copyright in the news and a defence of fair dealing allows the reproduction of a few quotes – though not a substantial part of the publication. However, seemingly setting a new precedent, substantial damages of £1 million were paid in November 2003 for breach of commercial confidence to *OK!* which had lost huge sales as a result of the spoiler. The stars' claim for invasion of privacy was rejected. They received damages of only £14,600– 'hardly enough to make it worth the bother of jetting in to the High Court and asking for £50,000 for personal distress' (Lamont 2004). In May 2005, the Court of Appeal reversed the decision. By this time the case was focusing more on issues relating to commercial confidentiality than privacy. Then in May 2007, the Law Lords, by a 3–2 majority, reversed that decision concluding that *Hello!* was liable for breach of confidence between the Douglases and *OK!* when it published a 'spoiler' version of *OK!*'s exclusive spread on the couple's New York wedding in November 2000. The court roundly rejected *Hello!*'s claim to exemption from the Data Protection Act since there was no public interest reason for publishing the photographs. Mr Justice Lindsay said the fact that the public would be interested in the photographs was 'not to be confused with there being a public interest' (Quinn 2007: 277). But the court found that *Hello!* had not knowingly injured *OK!*'s business which meant that the estimated £8 million costs were expected to be shared by the two magazines.

As Simon Jenkins commented in the *Guardian* of 4 May 2007 ('Angry celebrities, come to Britain: our judges are suckers for a glamour trial'):

> Why the Law Lords felt obliged to act as judicial extras in a 'spoiler' row between two magazine picture desks is a mystery. The only plausible explanation is that British judges are suckers for a glamour trial and will sell their services anywhere to get their hands on one.

He continued:

> The Douglas case had nothing to do with the right to privacy, notoriously indefinable as it is. Nobody can stage a wedding, sell the publicity rights for £1 million and then claim that they were trying to remain private. Managed publicity is not privacy. As for the 'obligation of confidence' on newspapers not to scoop rivals who have paid for so-called exclusives, this is censorship born of madness.

- Then in June 2004, the European Court of Human Rights[1] ruled that photographs of Princess Caroline of Monaco and her children in a public place should not have been published since they invaded her privacy rights. The court overturned a German ruling in 1999 which said that as a public figure she had to accept being photographed in public. The rights of paparazzi photographers throughout Europe appeared threatened. Legal expert Dan Tench claimed the effects would be limited since many seemingly 'snatched' photographs of celebrities were taken with their permission while celebs would be reluctant to bring actions because of the relatively limited damages available (Ponsford and Slattery 2004). Then in May 2008, the Court of Appeal ruled that the law protected the children of celebrities from the publication of unauthorised photographs – unless their parents had exposed them to publicity. This Princess Caroline-style ruling came after author J.K. Rowling and her husband sought to ban publication of covert, long-lens photographs of their son taken when he was 19 months old. Lawyers argued it was a landmark decision as a fully developed law of privacy was being gradually constructed in the UK.

- Prince Charles featured in a prominent privacy case after his diaries were leaked by Sarah Goodall, a former secretary in his office, allegedly in breach of the duty of confidentiality written into her contract. The Prince's dispute with the *Mail on Sunday* over publication of his travel journals went to the Appeal Court in November 2006 where the panel of judges included the Lord Chief Justice and the Master of the Rolls. The High Court earlier held that the Prince was 'entitled to enjoy confidentiality for his private thoughts as an aspect of his own human autonomy and dignity'. On 21 May 2007, the High Court granted an injunction banning the publication of the remaining seven handwritten journals and upheld the Prince's right to confidentiality and privacy.

- On 14 December 2006, the Court of Appeal upheld a ruling by the High Court Judge Mr Justice Eady stopping publication of a book on the Canadian folk singer and songwriter Loreena McKennit by her former friend and confidante Neima Ash. Hugh Tomlinson QC, expert on privacy law at Matrix chambers commented: 'This judgment is a turning point in the development of English privacy law. It means the courts will not allow publication of "kiss and tell" stories after the breakdown of a friendship or a relationship. At the same time the Court of Appeal rejected the argument that a person who tells their own story to the press gives up their future privacy rights. The effects on the tabloids could be dramatic' (Dyer 2006). The appeal court also upheld Mr Justice Eady's ruling that even relatively trivial details about an individual's home would be protected. 'To describe a person's home, the décor, the layout, the state of cleanliness, or how the occupiers behave inside it . . . is almost as objectionable as spying into the home with a long distance lens and publishing the resultant photographs,' Mr Justice Eady said in his original judgment.

• Injunctions on the press and broadcasters to protect privacy were on the increase in 2006, according to Peter Preston, *Observer* media commentator (2006). He found through a trawl of a national newspaper's legal records over the previous two months that there had been 22 restrictions imposed to protect privacy – mostly that of celebrities. He commented: 'the battle for supremacy between Article 8 and Article 10 of the European Convention on Human Rights is being won inexorably at lower level courts by Privacy 8, not Right to Know 10.' Typically, in January 2008, the *Spectator* magazine reported that news about 'a famous broadcaster and his love child by another journalist' had been stopped by an injunction (Wade 2008). Again, on 16 March 2008, the *Sunday Times* carried a report on 'a member of the royal family said to have been the target of an alleged sex and drugs blackmail plot' – but a gagging order had prevented the royal identity being disclosed. At the same time, the newspaper said the royal had been 'widely named on Internet websites and American television' – so highlighting the difficulties in keeping sensitive information secret in the digital age.

• In an unusual case, England footballer Ashley Cole was not named in a libellous slur by the *News of the World* – but still received an apology and damages in June 2006. After the newspaper ran articles on 12 and 19 February 2006 alleging that an unnamed Premiership footballer and a DJ had used a mobile phone as a 'gay sex toy' (with the story accompanied by a partially obscured photograph) Internet rumours linked Cole and DJ Ian Thompson (otherwise known as 'Masterstepz') to the allegations. And this was enough to win the two men the apology and damages. Cole (married to Girls Aloud star Cheryl) was later the victim of a series of tabloid exposés over his 'wild, sex romps'. (White and Case 2008). But a new twist to the saga of 'kiss and tell' revelations later emerged with the Cole scandal when the *Sunday Mirror* claimed the Chelsea defender had given a woman £6,300 in cash for signing a declaration saying: 'I did not sleep with Ashley Cole and I will not go to the papers and say I did.' The newspaper also claimed New Zealander Coralie Robinson received £10,000 for signing, in the presence of a solicitor, a statement that said she 'had never at any time had a sexual relationship with him' and pledging to destroy all text messages, emails, notes and telephone recordings suggesting otherwise. Cole went on to sue Mirror Group Newspapers (and the *Sun*) for damages for invasion of privacy (citing Article 8 of the Human Rights Act). Concerns were growing over the use of 'no win, no fee' arrangements by wealthy claimants to take on the media: significantly Cole's solicitor, Graham Shear, had taken on the case with this agreement. As Bob Satchell, executive director of the Society of Editors, commented (Bousfield 2008): 'The idea that rich and famous people can get free use of the law with the media picking up exaggerated bills totally destroys the balance of the law and therefore undermines justice.'

- In February 2007, the PCC upheld a complaint from the supermodel Elle Macpherson that snatched beach photographs published in *Hello* magazine had infringed her privacy rights. Significantly, she was staying at a private house with a private beach. The PCC's verdict, then, appeared to be shifting the precedent set in 2000 when the complaint from Anna Ford was rejected since the private beach on which she was sunbathing was accessible to the public (Gibson 2007c).

- BP's chief executive Lord Browne was forced to resign in May 2007 after his attempts to keep his former relationship with his partner Jeff Chevalier a secret failed. The Law Lords lifted an injunction against Associated Newspapers, publishers of the *Mail on Sunday*, after they ruled Browne had lied over his relationship. Lord Browne attacked the invasion on his privacy: the *Mail on Sunday*, in reply, stressed that its main story focused on a business issue 'of great importance to shareholders and employees of BP' (*Media Lawyer* 2007a).

- Actor Sienna Miller received what was believed to be the largest payment of its kind for an invasion of privacy (£37,500) in December

2007 after the *News of the World* and *Sun* published nude pictures of her taken while filming *Hippie Hippie Shake*.

• Concerns over paparazzi hounding of celebrities came to a head in April 2008 following the verdict of the inquiry into the death of Princess Diana which cast considerable blame on the posse of photographers who were pursuing her on that fatal night in August 1997.

Is there a case for relaxing the libel laws in exchange for the introduction of a privacy law?

The public overwhelmingly supports the introduction of privacy law in Britain, at least according to Guardian/ICM poll in 2004 in the aftermath of media revelations about David Beckham's personal life (Travis 2004). Some 85 per cent of the public opposed disclosure of personal details while 69 per cent backed a law to protect the private lives of those in public life from media intrusion. The public appeared to support the introduction of a privacy law to protect popstars, footballers and members of the royal family but not MPs. Some 43 per cent said they didn't care about Beckham's private life. The *News of the World* added 100,000 sales to its circulation when it broke the Beckham story.

Even some journalists, such as Alan Rusbridger, editor of the *Guardian*, argue that a properly worded privacy law, which might reduce some of the media's excesses, could be exchanged for a new libel legislation that encouraged free expression on matters of public importance. The case stands on the US Supreme Court ruling in 1964 by Justice William J. Brennan. In the case of *New York Times v. Sullivan*, Brennan revolutionised American libel law by ruling: 'Debate on public issues should be uninhibited, robust and wide open and . . . it may well include vehement, caustic and sometimes unpleasantly sharp attacks on government and public officials.' He said that the fear of libel litigation dampened the vigour and limited the variety of public debate. Public officials would have to prove actual malice: in other words, the reporter would have to be shown to be reckless as to whether what they were writing was true or not.

In India, too, journalists have an established defence after defamatory claims have been made about the conduct of public officials, and in

Australia a special 'qualified privilege' has emerged for political discussion in a series of rulings culminating in a 1997 victory by ABC against David Lange, former New Zealand Premier. Concerns were raised in 2000 after ITN's successful libel action against the left-wing *LM*, over its coverage of the Bosnian prisoner-of-war camps, killed off the magazine. Under US libel laws, *LM* may well have survived. In a major 1997 survey conducted by researchers at the School of Media at the London College of Printing, more than a third of the journalists backed the introduction of a privacy law, while 41.3 per cent believed that in some circumstances such a law might be justified.

But Nicholas Jones, of the Campaign for Press and Broadcasting Freedom, argued (2008) that video sharing and social networking sites such as YouTube, MySpace and Facebook and the spread of mobile telephones able to take audio and video as well, had revolutionised public attitudes to privacy. 'So whoever we are and wherever we are we can find ourselves caught on camera, however much we may dislike it or hate the intrusion. Therefore, the thought that we can somehow legislate to enforce controls over who can and who cannot take pictures is just wishful thinking.' He suggested public figures had a much greater responsibility to think about their behaviour and set their own limits on the degree of access which they were prepared to offer both the media and the public.

Do you consider undercover 'sting' investigations unnecessarily invade people's privacy?

The codes (of Ofcom and the PCC) are unanimous in stressing that subterfuge is only legitimate in the public interest and when the material cannot be obtained by other means. In 2001, the PCC also made clear in a ruling that undercover 'fishing' expeditions (when there is no clear evidence at the start of an investigation of any wrong-doing – only the hope of discovering it) were unacceptable. An *Evening Standard* reporter, Alex Renton, had pretended for a week he was interested in becoming a teacher at a London primary school. The PCC said it required exceptional public interest justification in cases involving children. There was nothing to suggest that the journalist or newspaper knew in advance that anything was going on at the school that warranted an investigation.

There are many other problems linked to undercover reporting. For instance, when a journalist takes on a job in order to expose malpractice, they are, strictly speaking, obtaining money on false pretences. In one case, a *World in Action* reporter escaped prosecution after taking a job in an abattoir, though the programme returned the money earned. In 2000, Lesley Saunders, freelance for the *Reading Chronicle*, took a job at the town's legal aid office, where she was made to:

- invent a false name for a client;
- enter a false date of birth;
- over-ride computer warnings that cash limits were being exceeded;
- omit clients' National Insurance numbers;
- authorise a claim where the client's name differed from his signature.

The furore which followed her undercover investigation led to questions in Parliament and a promise by a government minister to look into the way solicitors' fee claims were being processed. Clearly the reporter's strategy was justified. In 1998, *Observer* reporter Gregory Palast claimed to represent an American company in his meetings with lobbyists at Westminster and was able to expose several boasting of the access to government information and ministers they could offer if the company became their client. In April 2000, Burhan Wazir, of the *Observer*, went undercover to show how a £350 bribe helped smuggle him into Britain in a truck with two Pakistanis and an Iranian. And in December 2001, Tessa Mayes daringly went undercover as a massage parlour receptionist to expose the plight of East European women who end up in prostitution (Mayes 2001).

Channel 4 News reporters went undercover in 2002 to reveal shocking levels of filth at four London area hospitals. They found pools of dried blood while used swabs and discarded surgical gloves were scattered throughout corridors. BBC reporter Mark Daly went undercover for months in 2003 as a police trainee and then officer to expose racism in the ranks. Daly wrote (2003):

> Racist abuse like 'Paki' and 'Nigger' were commonplace for these PCs. The idea that white and Asian members of the public should be treated differently because of their colour was not only acceptable for some, but preferable. I had become a friend to these men. They trusted me with their views. And they believed I was one of them. I operated under strict guidelines. I was not allowed to make racist comments or incite

anyone to do or say anything which they wouldn't have otherwise said or done. But I had to laugh at their jokes and behave like a dumb apprentice. I said I was eager to hear other people's views in order to form my own. And they didn't hold back.

A *Panorama* reporter went undercover as a prison officer at a private jail in 2007 to expose drugs-taking, staff shortages and the appalling treatment of a suicidal inmate (Allison 2007). In another celebrated piece of undercover reporting, BBC *Newsnight* journalist Simon Ostrovsky (2008) assumed the role of a cotton-company sales rep to highlight child labour in the former Soviet republic of Uzbekistan. Ricki Dewsbury, a student at the University of Central Lancashire, went undercover, joining a writers' group and getting paid for essays, to expose how a fellow student was selling custom-written essays.

One of the most famous undercover reporters is Donal MacIntyre, of *World in Action, MacIntyre Undercover, McIntyre Underworld* and *Street Crime Live* (see http:macintyre.com). Bravely adopting the roles of football hooligan, care worker, bodyguard and fashion photographer, MacIntyre gathered secret evidence of violence, corruption and exploitation which led to the suspension of four senior executives of an international model agency and the closure of the care home investigated. In addition, four other homes run by the same owners were also shut, leaving 42 mentally handicapped people homeless and 84 workers redundant. Questions were raised over MacIntyre's techniques after the police said they planned to sue the BBC for the £50,000 cost of an investigation into the 'misleading and distressing' claims made in November 1999 documentary on the Brompton Care Home for mentally handicapped patients in Gillingham. The BBC rejected the police claims – and criticisms from the *Sunday Telegraph* – as 'ludicrous'. MacIntyre went on to win a libel case against Kent police – and donated his five figure award to three charities in the sector. However, after MacIntyre's programme on the Elite model agency showed its president apparently offering an undercover model money for sex, the BBC settled out of court admitting that no sexual exploitation was proved.

MacIntyre stresses both that undercover work is 'a tool of absolute last resort' and the importance of the reporter deciding their principles before taking on an assignment. His own principles are (Spark op. cit.: 171):

1 Never make friends with anyone who isn't a criminal. Your friend might otherwise suffer retribution after you have gone.

2 Never break the law. You may buy drugs in certain limited circumstances but you must send them for analysis to check whether they are true narcotics. Give orders that they must be destroyed or given to the police.

3 Do not compromise your sources.

4 Simply be a witness of what you see. It's not your job to convict anyone.

5 Remember that anything written or recorded is a matter of record and may become evidence in a court case. Never be flippant in an inquiry.

In a BBC publication highlighting his investigative achievements, MacIntyre offered this further advice to prospective sleuths (1999: 8): 'The golden rule is this: as an undercover reporter you must never encourage anyone to do or say anything they would not otherwise do if you had not been there.' Some journalists have certainly been accused of failing to follow this golden rule and of acting as 'agents provocateurs' inciting victims to commit crimes. For instance, in March 1998, Freddie Shepherd and Douglas Hall, directors of Newcastle United Football Club, were taped by *News of the World* investigative reporter Mazher Mahmood (otherwise known as the 'fake sheik' because of his most famous disguise) mocking fans, Geordie women and (oh horror!) England football captain Alan Shearer. Mahmood had posed as a rich foreign businessman, taking them to a luxurious hotel suite and on a crawl around Marbella's nightspots. As Sparks comments (1999: 11), a touch of showmanship and cheek helped here. It was one of a series of 'exposés' by the red-top that raised concerns over journalistic entrapment of celebrities. Critics of the 'sting' strategy claimed that people's privacy was being invaded, being enticed into committing acts they would have avoided but for the presence or encouragement of the undercover reporter. Other celebrity victims of the *NoW*'s 'cocaine sting' strategy in the same year included Richard Bacon (fired from presenting *Blue Peter*), DJ Johnnie Walker (suspended from Radio 2) and England rugby captain Lawrence Dallaglio (fined £15,000 for bringing the game into disrepute).

Significantly, as concerns mounted, a judge in September 1999 passed a lenient sentence on the Earl of Hardwicke after he accepted that he had been entrapped into taking cocaine, and thus committing the offence, by the *News of the World*. The paper defended its position, claiming it was exposing 'one of the greatest social evils in Britain'. Earlier, John Alford, of TV's *London Burning*, was jailed after another *NoW* 'cocaine sting'. Also, following a *Sunday Times* investigation in July 2000 which revealed that Lord Levy, Tony Blair's special envoy to the Middle East, had paid just £5,000 in taxes for 1998–9 there were allegations that reporters had committed a crime to gather the information. Some journalists oppose the use of deception on principle. Benjamin C. Bradlee, executive editor of the *Washington Post*, criticised an operation by the *Chicago Sun-Times* in which undercover reporters had operated a bar for four months to expose bribery and fraud among building inspectors: 'In a day in which we are spending thousands of man-hours uncovering deception, we simply cannot deceive' (Meyer 1987: 79).

Mazher Mahmood's techniques came under particular scrutiny in March 2006 after his attempt to make controversial Respect MP George Galloway the target of one of his stings. But during a meeting in a London hotel, Mahmood failed abysmally to get the MP for Bethnal Green to make anti-semitic remarks and implicate himself in illegal party financing. Afterwards, Galloway, with the support of Roy Greenslade, *Guardian* media commentator and Professor of Journalism at City University, London, sought to display and publish a photograph of Mahmood. The *News of the World* obtained only a temporary injunction (supposedly needed to protect his privacy and the safety of his family); and a photograph of the reporter is now easily accessible on Wikipedia.[2] Later, in July 2006, still further questions were raised over Mahmood's dodgy investigative methods after three men were cleared at the Old Bailey on terrorism charges. In a September 2004 'exclusive', Mahmood had claimed the three were plotting to buy radioactive material for a terrorist 'dirty bomb'. Similarly, an exclusive about an alleged plot to kidnap Victoria Beckham collapsed after it emerged that Mahmood's main informant had been paid £10,000 and could not be considered a reliable witness. But Mahmood, who claims to have helped convict 231 criminals, denies the allegations and stresses there has not been one Press Complaints Commission ruling against him (Gallagher 2008).

Is bugging ever justified in the public interest?

News of the World reporter Clive Goodman paid the highest penalty for indulging in a botched 'fishing expedition' when he was jailed for four months on 26 January 2006 for intercepting phone messages of Prince William and two other royals. Goodman pleaded guilty to conspiracy to intercept communications without lawful authority, under the Criminal Law Act 1977. The scandal led to the resignation of editor Andy Coulson – who quickly moved on upwards to become communications chief of David Cameron's Conservative Party. Nor was Coulson called to answer to the PCC's inquiry into the affair. Instead Clive Myler who succeeded him as editor was. Strange.

The investigation found that targets for tapping may also have included David Blunkett, while he was Home Secretary, the government minister David Miliband, the England and Portsmouth defender Sol Campbell, and the *Sun* editor Rebekah Wade. Goodman's private investigator Glenn Mulcaire, a former Wimbledon footballer, also pleaded guilty to a further five counts of unlawful interception of communications under the Regulation of Investigatory Powers Act (RIPA) 2000, a law brought in to recognise technological advances in telephony and the Internet. Mulcaire had been paid £105,000 a year for 'information and research services' as well as more than £12,000 in cash by Goodman (Mayes and Hollingsworth 2007). Those counts related to Liberal Democrat MP Simon Hughes, supermodel Elle Macpherson, publicist Max Clifford, football agent Andrew Skylet, and Gordon Taylor, the chief executive of the Professional Footballers Association.

A PCC inquiry into the affair cleared the *News of the World* of any misbehaviour on the (somewhat surprising) grounds that no one at the paper knew of Goodman's activities. But when is the bugging of phones in the public interest? David Leigh, investigative reporter at the *Guardian*, has admitted he listened to company executives' phone messages while looking into corrupt arms deals. The *Sunday Times* used impersonation and secret tape recordings to kick-off the cash for honours story. Almost all newspapers have used private detectives to dig out confidential data. In 2006, Information Commissioner Richard Thomas claimed to have a list of 305 journalists who had obtained information using methods in possible breach of the Data Protection Act (see Davies 2008a: 259–86). And Mark Watts, author of a seminal study of Benji ('the binman') Pell who trawled the dustbins of the rich and famous for juicy information to sell to newspapers (2005), reported that many journalists were routinely breaking the law in their investigations. As investigative journalist David Leigh comments (2008): 'These newspapers know very well that what they are doing is disreputable and illegal. That is why they sub-contract the work to private detectives who in turn often subcontract it further down the food chain. The real villains hide behind minor criminals, who have to be willing to take the fall if necessary.'

Messages can generally be accessed remotely using a password code. These systems typically have default code settings, such as four zeros. A hacker can intercept such messages if the user has failed to change default settings or uses obvious passwords such as birth dates. Journalists on rival newspapers, and sometimes working for different departments on the same title, have even tapped into each other's voicemail messages. James Hipwell, a *Daily Mirror* journalist between 1998 and 2000, who was jailed for his part in the City Slickers share-tipping affair, said that voicemail hacking was widespread at tabloid newspapers, including his own title while he worked there (Watts 2007). But is not the rise of 'private detective-led journalism' in response to the growing powers of PR to controlling so much of what goes into newspapers? According to Mayes and Hollingsworth (ibid.), 'an insatiable appetite for celebrity and royal gossip has increased the commissioning of private detectives. Many journalists now act as managers of information uncovered by private detectives'.

Goodman was the first journalist to be jailed in the UK in 44 years. The NUJ (with membership in 2006 of more than 38,000: 15,280 women; 22,814 men) warned that journalists would end up being jailed with the passing of the RIPA Act. But no campaign in his defence was launched. Significantly, in May 2007, Lord Chancellor Charles Falconer said the government was pledged to passing legislation that would see journalists jailed if they paid private investigators to break the Data Protection Act to get information. Current penalties – a fine of up to £5,000 at a magistrates' court or unlimited fine at the crown court – were 'not enough of a deterrent'. But, then, following squeals from tabloid editors, the Lord Chancellor withdrew his threats.

Would you apply different criteria for covering the private lives of politicians and celebrities and 'ordinary people'?

Most journalists would reply immediately 'Yes'. Most politicians and celebrities expect constant public exposure as an inevitable part of their lifestyles. Most crave publicity, many are remarkably open (and even confessional) about the most intimate aspects of their private lives when interviewed. Thus, you may argue, they can hardly complain when they fall victim to 'bad publicity'. In January 2005, the *Sun* carried on its front page an exclusive photograph of Prince Harry dressed at a private fancy dress ball as a Nazi with a swastika on his arm. And in September 2005, the *Daily Mirror* ran an exclusive mobile phone photograph of supermodel Kate Moss (dubbed 'Cocaine Kate') snorting at a private party. Predictably, the newspaper claimed 'public interest'. Significantly both exclusives won top prizes in that year's British press awards.

But does this right to intrude on the privacy of people in the public eye mean that they, their friends and relatives are not entitled to compassionate reporting? Surely not. The PCC suggests in its guidance to editors that while celebrities may be expected to use the media for their own publicity purposes, this does not mean they should have no privacy rights and that the media can print anything about them. Thus, publishing details of a celebrity's home without their consent could infringe the code, especially because of security concerns and the threat of stalkers. Significantly, a complaint from singer Ms Dynamite was upheld after a local paper revealed she had moved into property near her mother, picturing the house and naming the street. Joseph Borg (2008) usefully distinguishes between the 'right to know' and the 'want to know' (or, in another word, 'curiosity'):

> Commercially owned media organizations constantly exalt the want to know and attempt to transform into a right or a 'need' to know. They do this in the belief that the satisfaction of the people's want to know will increase their audiences and, therefore, their profitability. This attitude can limit the terrain covered by privacy rights in a manner that is unjustified and unethical. Such invasions of the private sphere occur for commercial reasons but find no shelter in ethical reasoning.

Journalists often argue that intrusive exposés are justified to highlight hypocrisy. A celebrity may thrive on a squeaky clean image but, in private, may be found to be abusing children, say. But, what if a former male friend of a woman Labour MP approached the media with a 'kiss and tell' story of lust and betrayal, all of it happening ten years ago. Would this be legitimate? Could it be justified in the public interest? If the brother of a famous soccer personality was found to be an addicted gambler, would that be OK to carry?

In November 1996, Lord Wakeham (the then-PCC chairman who was forced to resign in January 2002 in the wake of the Enron financial scandal) outlined seven key public interest tests which he wanted editors to consider before publication:

1   Is there a genuine public interest involved in invading someone's privacy as defined by Clause 18 of the Code of Practice – detecting or exposing crime, protecting public health, preventing the public from being misled – or is this simply a story which interests the public?

2   If there is a genuine public interest, have you considered whether there are ways to disclose it which minimise invasion into the private life of the individual concerned?

3   If you are using photographs as part of the story, which will have to be (or have already been) obtained by clandestine means and therefore compound the invasion of privacy, does the public interest require their automatic publication or are they simply illustrative?

4   Is there a genuine public interest which cannot be exposed in any other way than intrusion; have you considered whether there is any other way to minimise the impact on the innocent and vulnerable relatives of the individual, in particular the children?

5   If you are intending to run a story about someone connected or related to a person in the public eye in order to illustrate a story about a public figure, are you satisfied the connection isn't too remote and there is a genuine public interest in mentioning the connection?

6   Where you are preparing to publish a story seeking to contrast what a public figure has said or done in the past with his current statements or behaviour, have you satisfied yourself it is fair to make such a comparison and that the original statement or behaviour was recent enough to justify publication in the public interest?

7   If you are intending to run a story about the private life of an individual where there used to be a public interest, have you applied each of these questions afresh in case a defence no longer exists?

On these criteria, both the story ideas fail. Red tops, however, are likely to publish in the hope of boosting sales – and then take the PCC flak.

The privacy issue becomes further confused when 'public office' comes to include everyone from vicars, council officers, teachers, lawyers, soldiers and police officers. Stories of randy vicars and teachers eloping with schoolchildren are part of the constant diet of red top Sundays. Can these be justified? In April 2008, Ken Livingstone, the Mayor of London, was forced by newspaper interest to admit that he had three more children than his *Who's Who* entry listed. But he made an interesting distinction in his own defence: there was an important difference between privacy (over such issues as numbers of offspring and sexual partners) to which he had a right and secrecy (such as over the concealment of illegal or suspect activities) which journalists had a right and duty to expose (Lawson 2008). At about the same time, Formula 1 boss Max Mosley was the subject of a series of *News of the World* exposés which showed him cavorting with prostitutes. Could Mosley be defined as a public figure? Hardly. So could he rightly claim his privacy had been invaded?

What criteria should you apply to the interviewing of relatives/friends after someone's death?

Such interviews (called 'deathknocks' in the jargon) can be particularly harassing for journalists. Mourners can be obviously acutely depressed with little interest in sharing their feelings with a stranger. Sometimes journalists simply decline to follow the news desk's lead and phone in with an excuse, though journalists have been known to be sacked over such refusals. In December 1999, Ian Bailey, a reporter on the *Stoke Sentinel*, who refused his editor's order to seek an interview with a football manager after his son's suicide, lost his claim for unfair dismissal (Morgan 1999). Sometimes people welcome the attention of the reporter and use the interview as an opportunity to celebrate the life of the deceased person. Clearly discretion is required. The PCC significantly ruled against one newspaper after its reporter broke news of death to relatives and carried out inquiries without 'sufficient discretion'.

One of the most celebrated examples of journalists respecting the privacy of individuals caught up in tragic circumstances came after Thomas Hamilton killed 16 children and a teacher in a primary school massacre at Dunblane in 1996. Immediately after the event, television broadcast shots of a mother breaking down as she heard her child had died and the *Sun* and *Daily Mail* used close-up pictures of the same woman in distress. But thereafter, the media showed restraint. As John Taylor comments (1998: 105):

> The response was also marked by a new, rare respect for privacy: the media voluntarily stopped invading the privacy of vulnerable people whose loved ones had died in the massacre. The anniversary of the massacre was marked by the continuing conspicuous absence of invasive 'doorstep' journalism from Dunblane, which in this case was regarded as unfitting or outlandish.

No images of dead bodies were seen in the media but the signs of youth, innocence and unity were reproduced by using an official school photograph of the class. But was this appropriate? Some parents were distressed by seeing the photograph of their smiling children, particularly alongside pictures of their killer.

Notes

1   See www.echr.coe.int/echr/.
2   See http://en.wikipedia.org/wiki/Mazher_Mahmood, accessed 27 February 2008.

6

Dumbing down or dumbing up?

The tabloidisation controversy

Are the media increasingly obsessed with sex and sensationalism in the hunt for profits, audiences and circulations?

Scandal has always been the staple ingredient of the mass media and few periods have escaped moral panics over alleged declining media standards. Journalists through the ages have tended to be asssociated with the 'street of shame'. Since their emergence in the early seventeenth century in Europe's cities, particularly London, the 'news media' (variously known as corantos, diurnals, gazettes, proceedings and mercuries) were associated with scandal, gossip and 'low' culture (see Keeble and Wheeler 2007: 3) As Samuel Johnson (1709–84) put it: 'If an ambassador is said to be a man of virtue sent abroad to tell lies for the advantage of his country, a newswriter is a man without virtue who writes lies for his own profit.' And Hugh Stephenson stressed (1998: 19): 'Sex, lies and the invasion of privacy of individuals have certainly been an important part of the staple diet of popular British newspapers since British newspapers have existed.' According to Larry Gross (2003: 98), the rhetoric of authenticity that permeates the discourse of celebrity reflects the view that sexuality is that aspect of human experience closest to the truth of character and motivation:

> In an age increasingly imbued with Freudian convictions about the importance of unconscious forces lurking out of sight, the truth about personality is to be discovered beneath the surface, behind the façade, and sexual secrets are assumed to be the most revealing.

The most recent panic over the alleged 'dumbing down' of the media (Mosley 2000) is generally seen as starting with Rupert Murdoch's purchase of the *News of the World* in 1968, serialising shortly afterwards the memoirs of Christine Keeler, so reviving memories of the Profumo affair. In the following year Rupert Murdoch purchased the tabloid *Sun* from the owners of the *Daily Mirror*, the International Publishing Corporation, and shortly afterwards the infamous topless 'Page Three girl' was introduced, allegedly institutionalising a new sexual 'permissiveness'. By 1978 the brash, 'soaraway' *Sun* had overtaken the *Mirror* and in June of that year sales passed the 4 million figure, while the 'downmarket' *Daily Star* was launched by Express Newspaper Group in 1978, targeted at northern male/chauvinist readers. According to the critics, this 'plague' of trivia, infotainment and tabloidisation shifted from the newspapers to the media in general. As Vincent Campbell (2004: 20) put it:

> For example, in British television where satellite and more recently digital television channels have begun to seriously fragment audiences, channels have been engaged in a widely criticised rescheduling of news and current affairs programming in order to try and maximise audiences, with entertainment programming replacing news and current affairs.

In his seminal analysis of media trends, *On Television and Journalism*, the French sociologist Pierre Bourdieu (1998) argued that the sensationalist media were distracting and entertaining their audience rather than informing them – leading to a profound depoliticisation of the public sphere. 'The journalistic evocation of the world does not serve to mobilise or politicise; on the contrary, it only increases xenophobic fears.' Nick Cohen (1999: 129–30) blames the dumbing down of the media on the rise in power of shareholders who have brought about the greatest change in Anglo-Saxon capitalism since the 1970s: 'Shareholders, encouraged by deregulatory governments, have broken out of the social democratic prison by becoming footloose. If a corporation does not produce short-term profits, they sell and the company faces takeover or closure.' He continues: 'Bad journalism is a consequence of an unregulated market in which would-be monopolists are free to treat the channels of democratic debate as their private property.' According to the writer and broadcaster David Cox (2002):

Increasingly news aims to shock, amuse or reassure rather than inform. Coverage of serious topics in the *Guardian* as much as the *Sun* is largely calculated to reinforce prejudice rather than enlighten. As a result, such news as we consume keeps us less and less abreast of the public agenda.

Even veteran war correspondent Kate Adie accused the BBC in 2001 of dumbing down its news, favouring 'cute faces and cute bottoms' of younger reporters over experience.

Lord Birt, former BBC director general, joined in using his keynote MacTaggart lecture at the Edinburgh international television festival in August 2005, to attack the 'tabloidisation' of British intellectual life, arguing that the media had become too reliant on 'easy cruelty' and the 'desire to humiliate' (Gibson 2005b). Bob Franklin (2004: 148), drawing on Ritzer's (1993; 1998) notion of McDonaldisation to characterise the bureaucratic, dehumanised aspects of social life, highlights the decline in local newspapers into a form of standardised, predictable 'McJournalism'. 'While market theorists claim diversity and quality as the essential products of competition, the reality is McJournalism and McPapers with similar stories and even pictures reflecting a growing reliance on agency copy.' In his detailed analysis of local newspaper coverage of the 2005 general election, Franklin (2005b) also found evidence of 'unprecedentedly dumbed down' coverage with editors 'preferring stories about garden gnomes and even fabricated scandals to any substantive discussion of policy issues'. 'Journalists acknowledge this trend, and argue that it reflects the shift to corporate ownership of the local press with incessant management requirements for editorial content which will deliver more readers, more advertisers and more profits: and all this with less journalists!'

But many question this approach. For instance, the Archbishop of Canterbury, in February 2000, said newspapers should delve into the private lives of politicians to expose extramarital affairs, sexual high jinx and homosexuality. Such exposés were a legitimate matter of public interest, he argued:

> I believe it is a self delusion for politicians and those at the centre of public life to think they can divest themselves of the responsibility to make and respect moral judgment. The

question has to be asked often enough whether in the Church's view, sexual sins have any relevance to standards in public life. I do not believe they can be disregarded. The question reasonably arises in the public mind why should we have confidence in someone in public life who cannot be trusted not to cheat in their private life?

Alan Rusbridger, editor of the *Guardian*, Will Hutton, former editor of the *Observer*, and Robert Thomson, former editor of *The Times*, have argued that recent years have witnessed a 'dumbing up' of the media. Hutton claimed the media were carrying more attractive writing, clearer 'hooks' and better narrative stories than in the past. An editorial in the *Independent* of 6 March 1999 highlighted this view, claiming that the increased emphasis on popular culture within the broadsheets was making cultural life more open and democratic. Thomson argued: '*The Times* is not a dumb newspaper but for many years has been adding layers of intelligent comment while eschewing the elitism that can be so personally satisfying for well-fed editors' (quoted in Preston 2002). He also claimed his newspaper's coverage of foreign news had never been better: They had 23 foreign correspondents, more than ever before – even five years earlier they had just 12.

Peregrine Worsthorne, former editor of the *Sunday Telegraph*, commented (1999: 122): 'Newspapers are far more sophisticated, far cleverer, far better written than they ever were before; incomparably more entertaining and readable.' In the same spirit, BBC executives consistently argue that, even in a period of hyper competition from the commercial sector, the Corporation has managed to maintain its public service commitment to high-quality broadcasting. Support for this view came from Steve Barnett, of the University of Westminster, who with other colleagues analysed changing trends in television news from 1975 to 1999. Their research, published in July 2000, disputed the 'dumbing down' thesis, claiming that journalists were 'working harder to make difficult stories more under-standable to people watching them'. At the same time, Barnett predicted a decline in news over the next ten years with the 'marginalisation of serious and foreign reporting', and a fall in the amount of political coverage. In a later quantitative analysis of broadcast output, Barnett (2005) found that soaps occupied just 1 per cent of the peak-time schedule in 1955 but 10 per cent in 2005. 'At the same time, current affairs programming has halved and is now at its lowest peak-time level at any

time since 1955. The level of peak-time news has remained fairly
consistent at 12 to 13 per cent throughout the past 50 years.' Other
academic defenders of the tabloids include John Fiske (1989) and Brian
McNair (2000) who argue that conventional, non-tabloid journalism is
too elitist: the tabloids have potentially 'democratising' consequences
since they incorporate previously marginalised topics and people. And
in their detailed quantitative survey of changes in British mainstream
newspaper content between 1952 and 1997, Shelley McLachlan and Peter
Golding (2000: 86–7) question the 'dumbing down' thesis, suggesting
that it is too simplistic to compare the worthwhile political discourse of
the campaigning *Daily Mirror* in the 30 years after 1945 to the 'dumbed-
down circus' of the Murdoch era. 'The very essence of tabloid provision
continues to be suffused with the political, or if you like, the ideological,
which makes the charge of tabloidisation inadequate as a capture of the
shift that has occurred.' Similarly journalist Neil Hogshire warns against
exaggerating the differences between the tabloid and non-tabloid media
(1997: 17 cited in Carter and Allan 2000; 144): 'The blurring of fact
and fiction is essential in both mainstream and tabloid press. The only
difference is the tabloids don't claim the Final Truth on anything.'

And Ian Hargreaves, author of *Journalism: Truth or Dare* (Oxford
University Press, 2003) also suggests that 'brilliant' tabloid journalism
in newspapers, magazines, television and radio 'brings issues alive and
broadens popular engagement' (ibid.: 135). He continues:

> Those who worry that once serious newspapers like the *New
> York Times*, the *Guardian* or *La Repubblica* have diminished
> themselves by including alongside news and analysis about
> politics and world events, features about restaurants and
> personal hygiene, should probably relax . . . What matters is
> whether people, faced with an apparently vast choice of sources
> of news and other topical information, know where and how
> to find information they need and that, one way or another,
> they are able to operate as informed citizens (ibid.).

Is there too much bad news in the media?

Switch on the box and you are most likely to hear terribly depressing
news: a murder, famine in Africa, a teacher jailed for sexual abuse, and

so on. How different from the news routines in the old Soviet Union where the stress was always on positive social phenomena. As Brian McNair (1994: 34) commented:

> The Soviet news media had no need to concern themselves with winning audience share or making profits, so they did not consistently have to outdo each other with exclusives and shock-horror headlines. Western news media, by contrast, are required to win audiences with entertainment as well as information. Entertainment is often about drama and drama is, more often than not, about conflict and negativity.

Significantly, Galtung and Ruge (1965) in their seminal analysis of news values identified 'negativity' as one of the leading factors while Harcup and O'Neill (2001), in a follow-up study, highlighted the importance of 'bad news'. Similarly, Harrison (2006), in her analysis of broadcast news values, stressed the 'negative' (such as violence, crime, confrontation, catastrophe). In 2005, a Department of Health study of national newspapers' coverage of the NHS over one month appeared to support these theories with just 14 per cent of stories being positive, 46 per cent negative and 40 per cent neutral (Ponsford and Farge 2005).

In 1993, the debate about good/bad news was highlighted by the broadcaster Martyn Lewis who used his prominent public position to call passionately for a complete rethink about news values. 'We are sitting on the outer circle of a whirlpool of negativity and in danger of being sucked into the vortex,' he said. Journalism award ceremonies leaned too heavily towards images of disasters. 'It has become locked in the journalistic lexicon that these are the kind of winning stories many talented reporters should aspire to. It is surely just as great a journalistic challenge to pursue positive stories – which don't present such dramatic pictures but are every bit as important to society as a whole – and turn them into TV news reports that people want to watch' (see Brighton and Foy 2007: 17). In February 1999, he maintained his crusade at a conference sponsored by the *Financial Times*, claiming that a BBC review of news policy stated that audiences were alienated by journalism which appeared fixated by problems. They wanted more of a sense of how issues could be resolved.

Reportedly warned by senior BBC executives against launching his campaign, Lewis received a generally hostile response from his national colleagues such as Jeremy Paxman, Peter Sissons, John Cole, John Humphrys and John Simpson. Perhaps he offended them because, at root, his views highlighted the bias and selectivity behind their supposedly 'objective' news values. But at the same time Lewis received much support from local journalists. Significantly, in 2000, three newspapers in the Courier group, the *Standish Courier*, *Shevington Courier* and *Wigan Courier*, put their success down to pursuing only positive news stories about the communities they covered. Publisher Mark Ashley commented: 'People tell us they can get depressing news if they want it from the national newspapers.' His stance went 'against all my years of training and work as a journalist but there is no doubt in my mind now that there is a market in the regions for a non-stop diet of good news'. Other newspapers followed the trend: for instance, in 2005, the *Coventry Telegraph* decided to concentrate more on positive news as part of a relaunch. Editor Alan Kirby commented (Lagan 2005): 'Some felt we were too negative and focused too much on "bad" news like crime. They wanted more fun. Every prominent story is now about real people and the way in which events affect their everyday lives. The new design gives the paper a more positive and upbeat feel.' A website at www.goodnewsnetwork.org is devoted entirely to good news. The *Guardian* described it as 'worthy and boring'.

During the 1990s the good news/bad news debate became enmeshed in controversies over the media's growing obsession with lifestyle and 'soft', infotainment features (such as on fashion, gardening, DIY, travel, wine, restaurants, shopping) at the expense of 'hard', serious news. As Michael Bromley comments (1994: 99):

> In the 1980s most journalists would have been extremely uncomfortable to find themselves relocated in show business. By the early 1990s many were already there, writing daily updates on the plots of television soap operas and paying enormous sums of money for anodyne interviews with celebrities. Some were becoming marketers of 'useful information' on the opening hours of chemist's shops and how to survive in a snow storm.

You may consider the local media's commitment to good news is driven by economic necessity: to survive they have to be actively involved in their local communities, praising their achievements (particularly in industry, the suppliers of the all-important advertising revenue), running campaigns, sponsoring events. Others claim Lewis's views over-simplified the complex issues surrounding news values (hence their popularity). Concepts of 'good' and 'bad' are always going to be subjective: the Glasgow University Media Group, for instance, during the 1970s and 1980s highlighted the ways in which the mainstream media consistently portrayed trade unionists in a 'bad' light. 'Bad' events such as disasters are part of the staple diet of news, yet much of the coverage subverts this 'negativity' by focusing on 'positive' angles – such as the 'heroic' activities of rescuers and the emergency services or on 'miracle escapes'.

What do the controversies over fake television programmes tell you about trends in journalistic standards?

During the late 1990s and into 2000, broadcasters became involved in a series of controversies over faking information which seriously damaged their reputations.

- In December 1998, the television watchdog, the ITC, fined Granada Television £2 million for breaches of its code in the 1996 documentary, *The Connection*. Made by Carlton for ITV's *Network First*, it focused on a supposedly new route for running heroin into Britain from Cali in Colombia. It was seen by 3.7 million viewers, won eight international awards and was broadcast on 14 stations around the world. But an exposé by the *Guardian* in May 1998 revealed that 'drug runners' were, in fact, actors playing the part and the 'heroin' shown was sweets. The company also had to pay £5,000 damages to a man it wrongly accused of supplying heroin.

- After a Channel 4 series debunking the green movement was screened in 1997, the Independent Television Commission required the channel to make an on-air apology in April 1998 to four environmentalists whose views had been misrepresented through selective editing.

- The 1997 BBC1 series *Driving School* made a celebrity of serial test failure Maureen Rees. But the BBC later admitted that certain scenes were staged, including the waking of husband Dave Rees at 4 a.m. to test her on the Highway Code.

- A *Cutting Edge* film, *Rogue Males*, about cowboy builders and petty criminals, was exposed in the *Mirror* in February 1998 as containing faked scenes including a violent row between two decorators and a customer and an incident in which a pair were shown stealing a pallet. Channel 4 apologised for 'several scenes that were effectively constructed for the camera'.

- On 9 June 1998, the *Guardian* revealed that another Carlton award winning documentary, which claimed it had secured an exclusive interview with Fidel Castro, Cuban President, was a fake. Shots of Castro talking to camera were actually unlabelled archive footage provided by the Cuban government.

- In June 1998, the Broadcasting Standards Commission criticised daytime confessional shows such as *Vanessa*, *Kilroy*, *Esther*, *Ricki Lake*, *Oprah Winfrey* and *Jerry Springer* for cultivating 'victim entertainment'. 'Exploitation of the misfortune of others is not an endearing human trait. A society which has long since abandoned the stocks as a form of public entertainment should think twice about the modern version designed to titillate rather than inform.' Then in February 1999, the *Mirror* revealed that, in a number of cases, guests on the *Vanessa Show* who laid bare their personal histories were actors and impersonators.

- Also in the same month, Matthew Parris, on Radio 5 Live's *Late Night Live*, revealed that stumped celebrities on Channel 4's quiz show *Countdown* were whispered suggestions through an earpiece.

- On 23 March 1999, the *Guardian* revealed that a Channel 4 documentary, *Guns on the Street*, that investigated how Manchester gangsters obtained illegal guns (and which led to the imprisonment of a man for seven years) was faked in key sections. One of the reporters who posed as a concerned citizen in the documentary withheld the fact that he had convictions for burglary and armed robbery.

- In April 1999, the BSC upheld a complaint of 'unfairness and unwarranted infringement of privacy' from a man portrayed as a criminal in the Channel 4 film *Stolen Goods* broadcast in May 1998. The commission concluded that broadcasters who did not seek to inform or use the police before screenings should take 'great care' before accusations of illegal behaviour are broadcast.

Most critics blame financial cutbacks for the drowning of investigative journalism under the floods of sensationalism. Significantly Alan Yentob, director of programmes at the BBC, admitted that the use of fake participants on the *Vanessa Show* was ultimately due to a lack of resources (*Press Gazette*, 25 February 2000). Others argue that reconstructions are an inevitable part of television. Roger Graef, a founding director of Channel 4, argues (2000) that the fuss over staging in documentaries 'misses the point' that most factual programmes have been staged since the heyday of great film-makers such as John Grierson and Humphrey Jennings. And Matthew Kieran (2000: 172–3) comments:

> Often people wish to remain anonymous and won't trust being filmed in shadow or having their voice synthesised, so someone is brought in to act out the part and utter the anonymous source's words for them. A sequence of events may be quite hard to describe, the relevant detail may be cumbersome or tricky and it may be much easier to convey the right kind of impression of what happened by dramatisation – not to mention making the documentary more telegenic. Or it may be that the actual filmed or tape recorded evidence is scratchy, fits badly together and is hard to discern.

He compares such practices to the reporter rewriting or making up quotes because they seem to express more clearly the interviewee's actual thoughts. 'As long as this is checked with the interviewee, to rule out misunderstandings on the part of the journalist, there seems to be nothing wrong.' But he stresses that reconstructions should be allowed only under strict conditions, namely:

1   The journalistic team can substantiate the dramatisation independently in a manner which shows they have sufficient grounds to claim that they either know this was or probably was the case.
2   Those independent grounds are made perfectly clear in the programme and the validity of the reconstruction is shown to rest on these grounds.
3   The reconstruction is labelled on screen as such to the audience and it is made clear whether the dramatisation is being presented in terms of what is known to be the

case, believed to be probable or merely a representation
of what might plausibly or possibly have happened.

Has investigative journalism gone out of fashion with comedians such as Mark Thomas taking over its role?

No, according to Hugo de Burgh, Professor of Journalism at the University of Westminster, former broadcaster and editor of a major study of
investigative journalism (2000). In fact, following the development
of investigative journalism during the 1960s and 1970s, by the 1990s,
he suggests, it was 'booming'. Among the documentary series he cites
were the BBC's *Inside Story*, *Public Eye*, *40 Minutes*, *Taking Liberties*,
Rough Justice, *Private Investigations*, *Timewatch* and *Here and Now*;
ITV's *Big Story*, *Network First*, *First Tuesday*, *The Cook Report* and Channel
4's *Cutting Edge*, *Street Legal*, *Countryside Undercover*, *Undercover Britain*,
Secret History and *Witness*. For 1995 alone, on UK terrestrial television
there were 300 discrete programmes that could be classified as investigative, excluding programmes with investigative elements. On BBC
radio there were *File on Four* and *Face the Facts* while other programmes
with a tradition of investigative work included *You and Yours*, the *Food
Programme*, *Farming Today*, the *Today Programme* and the *World This
Weekend*.

In print, Paul Foot's books *Who Framed Colin Wallace?* (1989) and
Murder at the Farm: Who Killed Carl Bridgwater? (1993) have examined
serious cases of injustice. John Pilger's print and screen journalism (much
of it collected in a special site: www.johnpilger.com) has consistently
examined injustices at both home and abroad: in East Timor, Australia,
South Africa and Iraq (see Hayward 2001; Pilger 2006). Don Hale, former
editor of the *Matlock Mercury*, investigated the case of Stephen Downing
(jailed for 27 years for a crime he did not commit) and defied massive
intimidation before seeing him finally cleared in February 2001. The
Guardian's investigations have exposed broadcast fakes and Parliamentary
corruption. Its exposure of Tory MP Neil Hamilton and the shady activities
of covert lobbyists such as Ian Greer are said to have played an important
role in the collapse of support for the Conservative Party in the 1997
general election. In early 1999 its exposure of ministerial corruption led
to the resignations of Geoffrey Robinson and Peter Mandelson. Over in
the Irish Republic, investigations by Frank Connolly, of the *Irish Mail*

on Sunday, revealed financial irregularities of the Irish Prime Minister Bertie Ahern which ultimately led to his enforced resignation in April 2008 (Glover 2007).

The special investigative role of Internet sites (free from the constraints of mainstream print and broadcast media) is being heralded by many. In the States, Matt Drudge's site was the first to reveal Monica Lewinsky's affair with President Clinton. And it was the tiny Internet e-zine, *TheSmoking-Gun*, founded by *Village Voice* investigative crime reporter William Bastone and freelance Daniel Green, and set up on a budget of $500, which revealed the hidden past of the groom on Rupert Murdoch's Fox Television's *Who Wants to Marry a Millionaire?* in February 2000. The revelation led to the sudden halting of the 'shockumentary' (Wittstock 2000). Moreover the global aspects of the Internet are seen as stimulating a new kind of investigative work. The Washington-based International Consortium of Investigative Journalists (www. publicintegrity.org/icij) has been formed, linking journalists from Moscow, Tel Aviv, Panama, Britain, Japan and the US to examine major global issues. Its first investigation provided the lead story in the *Guardian* of 31 January 2000 and exposed British American Tobacco condoning tax evasion and exploiting the smuggling of billions of cigarettes in a global effort to boost sales.

The Internet also provides easy access for British journalists to excellent investigative magazines such as the US-based *ZMag* (www.zmag.org), *Counterpunch* (www.counterpunch.org), *Covert Action Quarterly* (www. covertactionquarterly.org), the UK-based Corporate Watch (www. corporatewatch.org.uk) and UKWatch (www.ukwatch.net). Others argue that the media's growing commercialisation has marginalised expensive investigative journalism such as undertaken by the *Sunday Times* Insight team under Harold Evans in the 1970s (Knightley 1998). Its investigations on behalf of the thalidomide victims and into the DC-10 air crash of 1974 were among its most celebrated campaigns. In contrast, newspapers are now left 'exposing' human interest scandals or, paradoxically, the failings of broadcast investigations. According to David Northmore (1994: 319), the 'arms to Iraq' controversy exposed the weakness of investigative journalism in Britain:

> In fact, details of British arms exports to Iraq only surfaced at the trial of three executives of Matrix Churchill because of skilful legal manoeuvring by the defence lawyers. The role

of journalists and their respective media institutions in that case, as in the case of numerous fraud trials of the time, was to observe merely the proceedings from the sidelines and provide a detailed 'analysis by post mortem'.

Specific investigations have also drawn fierce criticisms from journalists. For instance, in March 1990, the *Daily Mirror* joined forces with Central Broadcasting's *Cook Report* to expose the National Union of Mineworkers as being in receipt of foreign funds during its strikes. Money donated by Soviet miners and Colonel Gaddafi, of Libya (dubbed a 'mad dog' by President Reagan), had also been siphoned off by leading NUM officials such as the widely demonised Arthur Scargill. But *Guardian* journalist Seamus Milne argued (1995), in a meticulously researched book, that the award-winning journalists had been duped by the secret services who had been seeking to smear the miners' leaders. Twelve years later, Roy Greenslade, editor of the *Mirror* in 1990, wrote a 1,840-word apology, headlined simply: 'Sorry, Arthur'. He said: 'We were all taken in. I can't undo what has been done, but I am pleased to offer the sincerest of apologies to Heathfield [NUM general secretary] and to Scargill, who is on the verge of retirement. I regret ever publishing that story. And that is the honest truth' (Greenslade 2002). Donal MacIntyre's investigations, into the international fashion industry and football hooligans, have drawn many plaudits – and many criticisms, as well. Some suggested that the style in which he carried out his investigations was given more prominence than the story he was delving into. According to Simon Hattenstone, his exposé of muggers on the streets of London 'seemed more like entrapment than investigative journalism' (2007). Tessa Mayes, investigative reporter on *Panorama*, the *Cook Report* and Carlton TV's the *Investigators*, says journalists 'work within the restrictions imposed by self-regulatory codes and laws which increasingly make it difficult to air stories'. She cites the Protection from Harassment Act and the 1994 amendment to the Video Recordings Act (which makes anyone showing an uncertified video in a public place liable to imprisonment) as new threats.

Some journalists argue that a new breed of satirist is taking a new, vital role in journalism. John Pilger, for instance, says of satirist Mark Thomas:

> He's essentially a satirist but he's helping to fill a vacuum in investigative journalism. Journalism has become obsessed with

lifestyle, gardening, trivia, celebrities and distractions. Mark has taken head-on the issues that touch our lives but in ways we may not immediately understand, then put them to us in a form we can engage with. So much journalism today doesn't do its basic job of keeping the record straight, peering under rocks, looking behind screens and telling people when they're being conned.

(*Press Gazette* 25 February 2000)

Thomas's stunts for his Channel 4 series have shown multiple sclerosis sufferers smoking cannabis in Home Secretary Jack Straw's constituency and a politician dressed as a giant bear being interviewed. Critics suggest he is reducing politics to entertainment. But this is precisely what Thomas hopes for and what he believes journalism requires. Drawing inspiration from Situationism, an anarchist/art student movement of the late 1960s which used comic spectacles to highlight political issues, Thomas argues that journalists, in general, are too close to their sources. Being a comedian frees him from such constraints. In one sketch he interviewed a representative of the Indonesian army posing as someone from a firm offering training to deal with tough questions from human rights activists. In the course of the questioning the man admitted torture was a necessary evil.

Another satirist/journalist, Chris Morris, specialises in exposing the crassness behind the shimmer of celebrity culture. But such routines have not gone uncriticised. An item in Chris Morris's *Brass Eye* series hoaxed MPs into condemning a new and dangerous drug called 'cake' which was said to be illegally flooding into the country from the Czech Republic. But in April 1997, the ITC ruled that that programme had breached its code by not making the MPs aware of its format or purpose. Channel 4 was also forced by the ITC in 2001 to broadcast an apology over its screening of a *Brass Eye* spoof documentary on paedophilia for causing 'exceptional and gratuitous offence'. The channel had received 2,000 protest calls while the ITC received 1,000 complaints about the programme.

Stephen Baker and Greg McLaughlin (2005) argue that the most probing political and social questions which should be asked by journalists are now being asked by 'media bards and jokers' such as Thomas and American film director Michael Moore. Vincent Campbell (2004: 185) traces the origins of this 'investigative satire' in such titles as *Private Eye* in Britain, *The Onion* (USA) and *Le Canard Enchaîné* (France). But Moore's brilliant films, such as *Roger and Me* (1989), the Oscar-winning *Bowling for Columbine* (2003), *Fahrenheit 9/11* (2004) and *Sicko* (2007) have brought the genre of 'investigative satire' into the mainstream. Campbell adds (ibid.: 186): 'Like the muckrakers, these contemporary satirists offer a much more impassioned and involved treatment of political and social issues than mainstream news media are perceived to offer.' And for Stephen Harrington (2008: 277), Michael Moore is important for breaking down the traditional hierarchy of news forms: 'through the media of film, television and best-selling books [he] has managed to make critiques of serious political issues perhaps because he is *not* a journalist'.

7
Race/anti-racism matters

Many journalists are concerned to remove discrimination on grounds of gender, sexual orientation, race, disability, age, mental health and so on. At the same time there is a dominant culture which tends to regard sceptically lobby groups interfering with journalistic professionalism and seeking to bend coverage to match their own biases. Such groups are often condemned as PC (political correctness) fanatics. Inevitably, in such emotionally charged contexts, argument, protest and defensiveness result – as well as lots of ideas for creative responses.

To what extent can the mainstream media's coverage of race/ethnic issues be described as racist?

The PCC's Code of Practice provides that the press:

- must avoid prejudicial or pejorative reference to an individual's race, colour or religion;
- and should not provide details of an individual's race, colour or religion unless genuinely relevant to the story.

And the NUJ's Code of Conduct stresses: 'A journalist shall mention a person's age, sex, race, colour, creed, illegitimacy, disability, marital status, or sexual orientation only if this information is strictly relevant. A journalist shall neither originate nor process material which encourages discrimination, ridicule, prejudice or hatred on any of the above-mentioned grounds.' Yet daily, ethnic minorities, refugees and asylums seekers face negative coverage in the media. Why? Many critics focus on the alleged institutional racism within the media industry. This racism is rooted in the country's imperial past, with feelings of racial superiority and crude nationalism now deeply embedded in the dominant culture. Columnist Polly Toynbee, in an article headed 'The West really is the best' (the *Observer*, 5 March 2000), argued: 'Deeply flawed maybe, but the best so far, Western liberal democracy is the only system yet devised that maximises freedom for the many.'

But how accurate is this? Some media workers have been identified as overtly racist. For instance, the *Sun*'s acting editor was recorded as saying: 'I'm not having pictures of darkies on the front page' (Hollingsworth 1990: 132). A small item in the diary of Lance Price (2005), serialised in the *Mail on Sunday*, intriguingly highlighted how this tradition continued. It read simply: 'Tuesday 16 March 1999: Blair and Alastair Campbell [his head of communications] went to lunch at the *Sun* – Alastair described it as like being at a BNP meeting.' And some of the headlines which appeared in the tabloids during the Euro 96 football tournament and again over stories about asylum seekers during the late 1990s up until the present day have been racist.

Significantly, the United Nations, on 19 November 1998, criticised the way in which Britain treated refugees. Yet, on 30 November 1998, the *Daily Mail* led its front page with the headline: 'Brutal crimes of asylum seekers'. In December of the same year the *Sun*, under the headline 'Inn-sane' condemned the decision of a Gravesend hotel to allow 21 Romanian women and children to spend a night in the hotel after being discovered among a group of 103 people packed into a goods container (Donovan 1999). Amnesty International even considered taking legal action over whether the *Mail*'s coverage could be considered to be inciting racial hatred. Local papers in Kent were accused of whipping up anti-immigrant sentiment in their coverage of asylum seekers (Platt 1998). 'Illegal immigrants, asylum seekers, bootleggers . . . and scum of the earth drug smugglers have targeted our beloved coastline,' raged the *Dover Express*. Concerns were also expressed after the *Sun*, *Daily Telegraph* and *Daily Mail* expressed 'ecstatic support' for William Hague, Conservative leader, after his 18 April 2000 speech recommending the detention of all new asylum seekers in secure units and the formation of a special removals agency to get rid of rejected asylum seekers.

In 2001, staff at the *Daily Express* went so far as to report their own newspaper to the PCC following a series of 'inflammatory' front-page headlines such as 'ASYLUM: WE'RE BEING INVADED'. Such assertions of editorial independence, according to Harcup (2007a: 125) are relatively few and far between.

> Far more common is the strategy adopted by individual journalists of using a variety of dodges – diversions, flattery, inertia, making sure they are useless at certain tasks, and so on – to avoid what they see as unethical or just plain bad 'suggestions' by their boss. Such everyday ducking and diving may not seem heroic, and it is rarely acknowledged in the academic literature about journalistic ethics, but it is one of the ways in which journalists strive to do the best they can, often in trying times.

However, the complaint by the *Express* journalists, alleging that the reports on asylum seekers breached the PCC Code of Practice on avoiding prejudicial references to race, was rejected. The NUJ then had to take the unusual step of reminding its members on Merseyside of the clause in its ethical code stressing that 'a journalist shall not originate nor process material which encourages discrimination, ridicule, prejudice or hatred'. This followed readers' complaints about a report headlined 'Refugees to get free IVF – but north west patients could still wait for 3 years' (Harcup 2002b).

Significantly in 2004 Britain was found to have adopted policies that discriminated against Gypsies trying to escape persecution in their own country. The Law Lords found that the Roma had good reason to flee persecution in the Czech Republic yet had been blocked from flying to Britain in the summer of 2001. But then, in the run-up to the 2004 enlargement of the European Union, the *Daily Express* ran a series of front-page reports attacking Gypsies, with headlines such as '1.6 MILLION GYPSIES READY TO FLOOD IN – BRITAIN HERE WE COME' and 'WE CAN'T COPE WITH HUGE GYPSY INVASION' (Ponsford 2004). A meeting of NUJ members went on to pass this motion:

> This chapel is concerned that *Express* journalists are coming under pressure to write anti-Gypsy articles. We call for a letter to be sent to the Press Complaints Commission reminding it of the need to protect journalists who are unwilling to write racist articles which are contrary to the National Union of Journalists' code of conduct.
>
> (ibid.)

They called on the PCC to insert a 'conscience clause' into its Code of Practice, to protect any journalist who refused unethical assignments from disciplinary action or dismissal. The NUJ had made a similar call when giving evidence to the Commons Select Committee on privacy and media intrusion in 2003. The request was rejected by the PCC, which claimed there was no evidence that journalists faced such pressures. If they did, it was a matter between employers and employees (Harcup 2005; 2007: 121–9). When the police made a series of dawn raids on houses in Slough in January 2008 against modern-day Fagins who were parting poor Roma children from their families and forcing them into a life of crime, all the stereotypes about Gypsies appeared confirmed. The media was invited to witness officers wearing body armour smash down doors to carry children away – apparently to safety. But within days of the raids, all but one of the children had been returned to their families and noe of the 24 adults arrested had been charged with child-trafficking offences (Pidd and Dodd 2008). Such is the power of stereotyping to distort coverage. And complaints against the *Express* continued into 2008 with demonstrations organised by Media Workers Against War in protest at inflammatory headlines such as 'Over 860 migrants flood in every day', 'Muslim laws must come to Britain' and 'Migrants send crime rate soaring'.

A study in 2003 by Article 19, the international organisation campaigning against censorship, of coverage of the closure of the Red Cross centre at Sangatte in France in six daily newspapers (the *Mail*, *Express*, *Sun*, *Telegraph*, *Mirror* and *Guardian* – though the last two were largely absolved from the criticism) found indiscrimate use of such labels as 'bogus asylum seekers', 'migrants', 'refugees' and 'inmates'. Insulting labels included 'illegal immigrants', 'asylum cheats', 'scroungers' and 'parasites'. In many of the reports the immigrants were dehumanised: the *Mail*, for instance, referred to a 'consignment of immigrants', the *Telegraph* to a 'batch of immigrants' (Greenslade 2005). Asylum seekers were often painted as criminals and threats to public health – as supposed importers of AIDS – as well as scroungers living off 'our' taxes and stealing 'our' jobs with words such as 'exodus', 'flood', 'swamp', 'deluge', 'mass influx' fuelling fears. Greenslade commented: 'In papers which pride themselves on their ability to tell human interest stories, human interest stories about people fleeing torture, oppression and gross poverty have been entirely absent' (ibid.). Analysis of television coverage by Cardiff University School of Journalism found similar stereotyping and lack of appropriate sourcing on statistics. Archive footage, often showing men climbing fences in Sangatte, was regularly shown whenever the topic of asylum seekers was dealt with, thus reinforcing a negative image of them.

In another analysis of press coverage of asylum seekers in the British press by Roy Greenslade for the Institute for Public Policy Research (2005), the popular tabloids were accused of pursuing a 'racist agenda'. Broadcasters are also failing to represent ethnic minorities, according to a YouGov poll commissioned by the Cultural Diversity Network in 2006. Some 30 per cent of those surveyed thought they reported on minority issues fairly badly while 21 per cent very badly. Channel 4 News was considered the best with 23 per cent of respondents naming it top (*Press Gazette*, 6 October 2006). Significantly, a survey in June 2007 by the broadcast regulator, Ofcom, found people from ethnic minorities preferring to watch non-terrestrial television, specialist channels (Holmwood 2007).

A report commissioned by the Lord Mayor of London, Ken Livingstone, into the coverage of asylum seekers and refugees in London's national, local and minority press in 2006 found clear evidence of 'poisonous racism' (Thomas 2006). The report, *Reflecting Asylum in London's Communities*, criticised the widespread negative, unbalanced and inaccurate reporting which, it said, was 'likely to promote fear and tension within communities across London'. The following year, another study commissioned by Ken Livingstone into the coverage of Muslims and Islam in the national media, also found ill-informed commentary, inaccurate reporting, distortion and the marginalisation of already marginalised voices (Petley 2007).

In 2007, the Campaign for Press and Broadcasting Freedom (www.cfpf. org.uk) complained to the PCC about a front page splash on 27 July – 'Bombers are spongeing asylum seekers' – which referred to four men alleged to have tried to detonate backpack suicide bombs in London six days earlier. As Tim Gopsill and Julian Petley commented (2007): 'It couldn't have been more inaccurate. At the time of the story the identity of only two of the suspected bombers was known and neither was an asylum seeker. Both were children of refugees, had grown up in Britain and had indefinite leave to remain.' Predictably, the PCC rejected the complaint.

Yet the PCC, in its guidance notes to editors, does stress that extreme caution should be taken when dealing with immigration reports. It provides the following definitions:

- an asylum seeker is a person currently seeking refugee status or humanitarian protection;
- a refugee is someone who has fled their country for fear of their life and been granted asylum under the 1951 Refugee Convention;
- an illegal immigrant is a person who has been refused such a status and failed to respond to a notice to quit the country.

Accordingly, the term illegal asylum seeker should be avoided – since it is inaccurate.

The policies of the British government effectively reinforce many of these anti-asylum seekers prejudices, according to critics. In June 2005, the United Nations went so far as to condemn Britain's policy of forcing failed asylum seekers to return to war-torn countries. As Yasmin Alibhai-Brown commented (2008): 'The government holds 2,000 asylum and migrant children in detention, some self-harming, others going psychotic . . . We deport adults to places we know to be brutal.' Britain had forcibly returned more Iraqis than any other European nation while more than 3,400 Iraqis whose asylum claims had been rejected were existing on a cashless system of vouchers pending their return, the human rights body, Amnesty International, reported in September 2007 (Norton-Taylor 2007). More than 8,800 people have died since 1993 trying to enter Europe, according to the organisation United Against Racism (see www. unitedagainstracism.org):

> Although media insist in naming them 'waiting zones', 'identification centres', 'accommodation centres', the centres where 'illegal' migrants and asylum seekers are held don't differ much from a common prison, except for the fact that, due to the overcrowding and the lack of a common policy of control, in most centres some of the basic human rights are daily violated . . . The whole management of detention is often military-based, and due to the lack of interpreters and social workers, conflicts and misunderstandings are solved with the use of violence. More and more frequent episodes of self-destruction practices take place in camps: from hunger strikes, eyes- and mouth-sewing to all manners of suicide, including putting oneself on fire. These episodes rarely catch the attention of the media, and are mostly witnessed by the medical staff allowed in the centres on rare occasions.

Few MPs were speaking out to protect the civil and human rights of migrants. And all the time, attacks on ethnic minorities throughout the country are soaring. Government figures released in October 2007 revealed that 41,000 attacks on people because of their race had been prosecuted in 2005–6, an increase of 12 per cent on the previous year. The figures also showed that black people were seven times more likely to be stopped and searched than white people and were much more likely to be caught up in the criminal system (Morris 2007). The final report of the Commission for Racial Equality (before being incorporated into the new Commission for Equality and Human Rights) in September 2007 described the UK as a 'place of inequality, exclusion and isolation'. If you were black, you were more likely to have left school early to go into either a low-paid job or no job at all, to have clashed with the law, to be ill, poor and cut off from the mainstream white community (McSmith 2007). This was confirmed in a study by the Joseph Rowntree Foundation which found that ethnic minorities were suffering from economic 'apartheid' in Britain: two-thirds of Pakistani and Bangladeshi children were living in poverty (compared to 25 per cent of white children). According to Kay Hampton, of the Commission for Racial Equality, 'It is a sad truth that a baby born today will have their future dictated by their race, not their abilities or efforts' (Dodd 2007).

How can you account for the discriminatory coverage of ethnic groups and asylum seekers?

The roots of racism are cultural, economic, political – and extremely complex. As Stuart Allan comments (2004: 168): 'The ways in which racist presuppositions are implicated in the routinised priorities of news production from the news values in operation to "gut instincts" about source credibility are often difficult to identify let alone reverse.' The dominant culture is white and tends to marginalise (or eliminate altogether) the experience of other ethnic groups. For instance, there are 12 million Roma Gypsies all over the world, eight million in Europe: 'They are the continent's largest ethnic minority group. Yet they are a forgotten people,' according to Martin Smith (*Socialist Worker* 3 June 2000). According to Roy Greenslade (2005: 11) most journalists who are responsible for racist material genuinely believe they are reflecting the views of society and therefore mirroring reality:

However, modern race relations legislation, the acknowledge-ment of the UK as a multicultural society and wider educational sensitivity to racial matters generally have made the current generation of journalists (as with the majority of British people) much more aware of overtly racist language, attitudes and actions. Yet this awareness has not necessarily changed an underlying bias against immigrants, whether or not they are 'people of colour'.

Only 1.8 per cent of NUJ membership is black. Asian, black and Arab journalists comprised just 2 per cent in the first industry-wide study by Anthony Delano and John Henningham (1995), a figure which was 'disproportionately low' compared to the national minority population of 5.26 per cent. In 2002, a survey by the Journalism Training Forum found that 96 per cent of journalists were white while the Sutton Trust, an educational charity, found that more than half of the country's top journalists had attended fee-charging schools while 45 per cent were Oxbridge graduates (Wilby 2008b).

A study by the Working Lives Research Institute in 2007, *Institutional Barriers to Recruitment and Employment in the Audio-Visual Industries*, found that 40 per cent of black and ethnic minority workers thought their ethnic background made it more difficult for them to secure work in the industry. Sonia McKay, of the Institute, said informal recruitment methods – the 'old boys networks' – were still widely used with nepotism a common means of gaining employment (*Journalist* 2007). Thus in 2008, newspaper staffs remained largely white. As Joseph Harker commented on Fleet Street (2008): 'One may find the occasional black or Asian journalist in a junior role on the commissioning desk but rarely, if ever, in a position where they can make a decision on what goes into the next day's paper, let alone have a major long-term impact.' White was the skin of most columnists too. As Harker added: 'Across the press there are literally hundreds of pundits with a regular space to air their views, yet the number from a minority background does not even reach double figures.' Yasmin Alibhai-Brown was the only non-white, female political commentator on Fleet Street. Very few journalists working in provincial papers were black. And according to critics, there is no industry-wide effort to improve on this. In response, editors often claim there is a shortage of suitable applicants from ethnic minorities and not a shortage of institutional will.

The BBC, under Director General John Birt, aimed to employ around 8 per cent of staff from black and minority ethnic groups, but by early 2000 only 2 per cent of managers were from ethnic minorities. On 7 April 2000 Greg Dyke, newly-appointed Director General, accused the corporation of being 'hideously white' and pledged to increase the number to 12.5 per cent of the total workforce. In the same month, the NUJ accused the BBC of institutional racism. Ethnic minority staff stood in for colleagues at higher grades but were rarely promoted. And according to the union, there was a bottleneck of ethnic minority staff at low levels in the World Service newsroom at Bush House in London (Wells 2000). And according to Yasmin Alibhai-Brown (2000), white, middle class Britons still hogged all the stories at the BBC. Professor Thom Blair, then editor of the *Chronicle* Internet magazine,[1] said: 'Clearly there is evidence of diversity fatigue in the upper echelons of the BBC. Managers are failing to keep up the momentum of their commitments to race equality practices.' In 2002, the BBC launched 1Xtra, the first national radio station aimed at a black audience, playing a mixture of hip-hop, raga, drum'n'bass and UK garage (Wells 2002). But by 2007, the corporation had still failed to achieve its diversity targets, with just 10.6 per cent of its workforce from ethnic backgrounds. Dr Robert Beckford, a reader in black theology and culture at Oxford Brookes University, went so far as to claim the BBC was practising apartheid on the airwaves. He said: 'If you were to bring Steve Biko [the murdered anti-apartheid campaigner] back from the dead and place him in any BBC office across Britain, he would think he was in South Africa in the 70s' (E. Taylor 2007).

And the BBC's 2008 series *White*, focusing on those allegedly marginalised in the mainstream media, was accused of treating bigotry with deep respect. As Alibhai-Brown (2008 op. cit.) argued:

> To flag up a BBC season on disgruntled white folk, a trailer shows a white face soiled with graffiti in 'wog' languages. Our public service broadcaster is surely inciting racial hatred when it privileges whiteness and seats Nick Griffin of the BNP at the high table of *Newsnight*? Our working classes include millions of black and Asian people too, ignored in this narrative.

But in response, Sarfraz Manzoor argued that the series did not so much celebrate racism as expose its 'thin crust' (2008): 'it is often not racism at all but rather bewilderment, ignorance and frustration'.

Minority employment in newsrooms of commercial broadcast companies is 'derisory', according to Jim Pines, author of the UK's contribution to a major trans-European study of media employment, *More Colour in the Media*. A survey by BECTU (Broadcasting, Entertainment, Cinematograph and Theatre Union) showed that, with the exception of LWT, most companies were falling short of reasonable targets for minority employment and, in some, the levels were going down (Trevor Phillips, the *Guardian* 20 September 1999). In 2000, GMTV's Deborah Bain was the only black female national television reporter. She commented in an interview with the author: 'Five or six years ago I was the only black person regularly on screen. Now I see more women and blacks and Asians on and off the screen. Blacks are being used as pundits and guest reporters. I believe a more diverse newsroom will create a more diverse agenda.' And according to Chambers, Steiner and Fleming (2004: 89) more than half of Britain's black journalists work in black print media, such as the *Caribbean Times*, the *Voice* and *New Nation*.

Data from UCAS and HESA suggest that minority students are under-represented on journalism courses and are less likely than white candidates to gain admission. There are mounting criticisms that, following the introduction of student fees, both undergraduate and postgraduate studies are becoming the privilege of the middle class, with black students increasingly excluded. Many jobs in the industry are not advertised but filled through 'old boy networks' from which blacks also tend to be excluded. Adding to the complexity of the issues, it is often claimed that greater racial diversity in the news organisation does not automatically translate into more diverse forms of news coverage.

According to the Runnymede Trust, the media's failure to represent the daily experience of fear, insecurity and intimidation cramps the lives of virtually all blacks and ethnic minorities in Britain (*Runnymede Bulletin* March 1996). Black stereotypes often associate them with crime. For instance, the *Bristol Evening Post* of 17 April 1996 under the headline 'FACES OF EVIL' showed 16 police 'mug shots' of convicted crack cocaine dealers: all were black. As Simon Cottle commented (1999: 192): 'For the *Post*'s 227,000 or so regular readers, the front page was unlikely to do other than confirm the prevalent views routinely fed by local news portrayal associating both the locality of St Paul's and its African–Caribbean population with crime and criminality.' In November 1998, a Channel 4 *Dispatches* documentary examined gang rapes in England and Wales. The programme identified 14 cases involving 79 youths,

80 per cent of them black. Did this not sensationalise the issue? Certainly the National Assembly Against Racism mounted a demonstration outside Channel 4's headquarters and called for it to be dropped from the schedules. In 2006, the Metropolitan Police Commissioner, Sir Ian Blair, accused the media of 'institutional racism' over its reporting of the murder of white, Cambridge-educated lawyer Tom ap Rhys Price. This had attracted massive coverage while the reporting of the murder of Asian manual worker Balbir Matharu had been largely ignored. Was Sir Ian right?

According to Valerie Alia and Simone Bull, coverage of ethnic minorities in the British media can be divided into two distinct categories: 'First immigration issues are formulated as a "problem". Second, minority people born in Britain are also perceived as "problems". In both cases, deviance underscores the "problem".' With people labelled 'deviant', then politicians and journalists are ideally positioned to demonise asylum seekers and refugees as 'bogus', 'economic migrants' and to instigate a moral panic over their alleged threat to British democratic values (Cohen 2002). 'Demonisation is important as it allows the problems of society to be blamed upon fictional Others who are already on the periphery of society. Asylum seekers have become the new "folk devils", the subjects of verbal and physical abuse fired by resentment and unreasoned hatred' (Alia and Bull op. cit.: 25). Criticism that television was failing to reflect the multi-cultural nature of the society, came in a report, *Include Me In*, published by Broadcasting Standards Commission in December 1999. Too often, programmes were guilty of presenting characters from ethnic minorities as two dimensional and without a role in society as a whole.

Should racist political parties be allowed to give election broadcasts and have a voice in the media?

You may feel it vital that in a democracy freedom of expression must always be respected and thus all voices should be given a platform. As the French Enlightenment philosopher Voltaire (1694–1778) famously declared: 'I disapprove of what you say, but I will defend to the death your right to say it.'[2] Sinn Fein, the political wing of the IRA, has a voice so why not the British National Party (BNP)? You may disagree with their policies but feel the public has a right to hear them and judge for themselves. If they are cranks then they will be exposed as such by their policies. In 2002, the former editor of BBC's *Today* programme, Rod Liddle, justified his interview with the controversial Muslim cleric Sheik Abu Hamza al-Masri with these words: 'The premise is that if we allow them to be reported, the people who are listening are more stupid than us and can't decide that these views are repellent. It's extremely presumptuous and arrogant to suggest that' (Tomlin 2002). The BBC took this approach again in June 2007 when it sought to interview BNP leader Nick Griffin (registering 11 per cent in a recent local poll) at a scene of earlier race rioting in Burnley, Lancashire. But after the police warned Radio 4's *Today* programme that the presence of the BNP leader could prove inflammatory, the interview went ahead over a telephone line.

An alternative view stresses that the NF's racism is, in effect, outlawed by race relations legislation. Freedom within democracy, it is argued, does have its limits and so voices that stir up race hate must be banned. A middle-view is promoted by the NUJ. In its *Guidelines on Race Reporting*, it suggests that when quoting representatives of racist organisations, journalists should carefully check all reports for accuracy and seek rebutting comments. The anti-social nature of such views should be exposed. Journalists should seek to publish or broadcast material which exposes the myths and lies of racist organisations while letters columns and phone-in programmes should not be allowed to be used to spread race hatred. Quinn (2007: 363) also recommends that when inflammatory racist comments are made, the reporter should paraphrase them rather than quoting directly 'so that the words you publish are not themselves "threatening, abusive or insulting"'.

Do you consider the marginalisation of African and Asian news to be part of the general 'dumbing down' of foreign news in the media?

In 1993, broadcaster Martyn Lewis said: 'I recently bumped into one well-known TV correspondent . . . who told me he had repeatedly proposed going to Africa specially to cover success stories . . . But he ran up against the stereotyped newsroom view of Africa as a continent racked by war, famine, corruption and AIDs.' Critics argue that such attitudes still prevail in newsrooms. For instance, *Guardian* writer John Vidal (28 February 2000) commented:

We almost certainly know less about what is happening in the world today than we did 10 years ago. TV hardly gives us a clue what is happening in most parts of the world, the social and economic forces shaping people's lives, how other cultures think or are responding on political or personal levels to some of the greatest scientific, ecological, cultural and social changes in world history. Even as business and politics has been globalised and as more people than ever are travelling abroad, so British TV – the prime source of information about the 5bn people living in the developing world – has become more insular, shallower, more opinionated, narrower, consumer-led, less intelligent and more self-obsessed. Our world map is massively diminishing as our ignorance is increasing.

Broadcast freelance Lara Pawson (2007) suggests that modern news-gathering routines encourage superficial coverage of African wars:

It was amazing the number of times the BBC would call me after seeing my report on Reuters and ask me to file exactly the same story I had offered hours earlier and they had rejected. Simply because the producers had seen the piece on the wires, they believed it (mattered). This proved a useful way for me to increase my meagre freelancer income – I could simply play the BBC off my agency work – but it never ceased to depress me.

(ibid.: 47)

Virtually all the major recent African wars – in the Ivory Coast, the Democratic Republic of the Congo, Burundi, Algeria, Somalia, Chad – had been ignored. 'When conflicts are reported, the attention comes in brief spurts, produced by non-specialist reporters and focuses primarily on the humanitarian aspects of the war, thus confirming the partial and paternalistic view that most Africans are helpless victims and their leaders unusually cruel and greedy' (ibid. 42–3).

A survey by Professor Steve Barnett and Emily Seymour, of the University of Westminster, in 2006, found substantial reductions in factual international programming on television. Since 2000–1 output fell 2 per cent on ITV1, 32 per cent on Channel Four and 14 per cent on Five. But over the same period coverage increased by 18 per cent on BBC1 and 39 per cent on BBC2 (Redding 2006). *Channel 4 News* presenter Jon Snow has criticised the 'scandalously low profile that foreign affairs have in broadcasting'. Virtually all the media over recent decades have made substantial cutbacks on their foreign reporting. 'Firemen' (and they are usually male) tend to fly out to foreign locations when major stories break and become instant experts – but how large is their knowledge of the country, its history, customs and language? A study entitled *Losing Perspective* by Jennie Stone, of the International Broadcasting Trust,[3] shows that the vast majority of factual programmes about poorer countries at peak times are celebrity-led and about travel or wildlife.

At the same time, foreign news coverage relies to an increasing extent on reporting disaster and conflict. Why is this? Stone suggests it is the result of diminishing budgets, the advent of new technology allowing images to be transmitted cheaply and quickly but which results in less in-depth coverage and a changing production culture, with staff more likely to move across programme genres with less overall commitment. Increasingly, resources are being diverted to online services and away from mainstream foreign coverage. Figures show that over the last decade factual programming on developing countries has declined on television by 50 per cent; ITV by 74 per cent, BBC by more than a third, Channel 4 by 56 per cent. Channel 5 has commissioned almost nothing from non-Western countries since it was set up. *Observer* investigative journalist Greg Palast (2000) highlighted the way in which the media failed to cover the fight against water privatisation in Bolivia when a general strike forced the government to retreat:

> It showed globalisation could be stopped in its tracks. Yet it was barely reported in the press. This is not because of direct pressure from institutions like the World Bank (although the leader of the bank did rush to condemn what he called 'rioters'). Rather it is because of the strange and horrid consensus which has emerged that there is no alternative to the New World Order that the people of Bolivia – and Third World peoples everywhere – simply don't understand.

And a report from the Glasgow Media Group in July 2000 for the Department of International Development found that most television coverage of the developing world concentrated on conflict, war or terrorism, often with little explanation and only rare follow-ups. Out of 137 developing countries, there was no coverage of 67 of them. Of the 72 countries covered, 16 were mentioned only in the context of reporting visits by westerners, wildlife events, sport – or the fact that a round-the-world balloon had flown over them.

Concern is also expressed over the influence of relief agencies in setting the agenda for foreign coverage. Bridget Harrison (1997) comments:

> In crisis situations, the British element to a story is further perpetuated by aid agencies and charities who work in the Third World. Relief agencies actively court western media to publicise their activities and generate donations from the public. As a result, not only do we equate the Third World with disasters but imagine that these are rarely resolved without our help.

Some critics also point to the anglocentrism and inherently racist assumptions underlying the media's portrayal of death. John Taylor describes the 'hierarchy of death' (1998: 90–1):

> In general, dead bodies in Britain are treated with more respect or restraint than corpses of foreigners. The simple explanation for this may be that editors choose pictures on the basis of good taste and decency or at least they realise it may be counterproductive to upset readers with horrifying pictures of identifiable British people. They also seem to assume that the audience's stomach for pictures of dead foreigners is stronger and guess that such images are unlikely to provoke complaints from relatives. A rider to the general rule would be that the dead are accorded more respect if they are white, or if they are from Western liberal democracies.

Critics also suggest that the coverage of African wars is crucially influenced by the level of the West's political and military involvement. For instance, as US/UK military ambitions focused on Somalia in 1992/3, coverage of that country increased; as the soldiers withdrew (humiliated) so did the press, and reporting disappeared altogether. Significantly, by December 2007 Somalia was suffering the continent's biggest humanitarian disaster yet it was largely ignored by the Western media.[4]

The extraordinary events in Chad (a former French colony) over the last 25 years have also been largely ignored by the UK media. Following one of the most remarkable human rights campaigns in recent years, Chad's former dictator, Hissène Habré, in 2007 was facing charges of crimes against humanity. Installed as head of state in Chad following a CIA-backed coup in 1982, Habré was responsible for appalling human rights abuses before being ousted in another coup in 1990. In a rare instance of coverage, on 21 May 1992 the *Guardian* carried four short paragraphs reporting how 40,000 people were estimated to have died in detention or been executed during the tyranny of Habré. A justice ministry report concluded that he had committed genocide against the Chadian people.

Habré's victims first looked to Belgium where its historic 'universal human rights' 1993 law allowed victims to file complaints in the country for atrocities committed abroad. Following threats from the United States in June 2003 that Belgium risked losing its status as host to NATO's headquarters, the law was repealed. Yet a new law, adopted in August 2003, allowed for the continuation of the case against Habré – much to the delight of human rights campaigners. Then Senegal, where Habré was living in exile, finally responded to an appeal by the African Union (AU) to try the former Chadian dictator. The AU mandated Senegal to prosecute Habré 'on behalf of Africa' while President Abdoulaye Wade of Senegal asked the EU and AU for technical and financial support to carry out the trial. The EU, in principle, agreed to this request and the AU named an envoy to the case. But media consumers in the UK were told little about these events in a 'far-away country'.[5]

Yet many mainstream journalists maintain they are still committed to campaigning on Third World issues and raising awareness about distant conflicts. In 2000, for instance, the *Mirror* campaigned to highlight the plight of child victims of war. Mike Moore, whose powerful photographs (of child soldiers in Sierra Leone, for instance) were used prominently in the campaign, commented: 'If my pictures raise awareness then my job is done.' Robert Fisk, of the *Independent*, has won many awards for his outstanding and brave reporting, often against the dominant consensus, from trouble-spots around the globe. And John Pilger's films on East Timor, Diego Garcia and Iraq have been used by campaigning bodies to inspire action. Ken Metzler (1997: 139) stresses the potential of the Internet to globalise the news: 'The sources represent a worldwide selection so that even the most local of media can achieve a worldly feel by quoting people from far-away places.'

To what extent have Arabs/fundamentalists/terrorists replaced communists as the new 'enemies' of Western civilisation in dominant media representations?

Representations of the 'enemy' pose many political/ethical dilemmas for journalists. Following the collapse of the Berlin Wall in 1989 many elite commentators in the West, such as Samuel P. Huntingdon (1997), saw the major threat shift from communists to Islamic fundamentalists and terrorists. The rise to power of the Ayatollahs in Iran, of the Taliban in Afghanistan, of President Gaddafi in Libya, of the radical Hizbollah guerrillas in southern Lebanon and of the Saudi Arabian terrorist 'warlord' Osama bin Laden (blamed for masterminding the bombings of US embassies in Africa) were all seen as part of the growing global threat to Western interests. Moreover, in a series of Hollywood blockbusters in the years leading up to the Gulf crisis of 1990–1 (and later shown on British television), Middle Eastern characters served as symbols for greed, primitive behaviour and violence (Kellner 1995: 75–88). As Stephen Prince (1993: 240) argues:

> Films like *Top Gun* and *Rambo* dramatised the heroic ideals of empire and the aggressive heroes of these narratives functioned as personifications of a national will and warrior spirit encoded by the foreign policy rhetoric of the Reagan period.

Concerns over the threat to Western interests posed by 'rogue' dictators focused on Iraq's Saddam Hussein after the invasion of Kuwait in August 1990. All Fleet Street editors were united in backing the military attacks to eject Iraqi forces from Kuwait. The invasion posed an unacceptable threat to the New World Order as proclaimed by US President George Bush. But many critics, such as Edward Said (1981) and Rana Kabani (1994) have argued that the demonisation of the Iraqi leader as 'the evil, barbarous, mad, megalomaniac Butcher of Baghdad' and the 'new Hitler' fed on orientalist myths and anti-Islamic clichés so embedded in dominant Western perceptions. Stuart Hall (1995: 21) argued that representations of the 'savage barbarian' lie at the root of racist ideology. Significantly, Roy Greenslade who edited the *Daily Mirror* at the time of the Gulf conflict, later commented: 'I can now see that our coverage in the *Mirror* was built on a lot of anti-Iraqi bias, an anti-Moslem bias and an anti-Arab bias' (Keeble 1997: 71). He said it never occurred to him at the time to question the dominant Fleet Street consensus.

Since the 9/11 atrocities in the United States and the launching of the 'war on terror' (with the attack on Afghanistan in 2001 and the illegal US/UK invasion of Iraq in 2003) Muslims have suffered appalling demonisation in large sections of the UK mainstream media. Only two bombing incidents followed in the UK (in London and Glasgow). Yet, according to Simon Jenkins (2007): 'while being freed of bombs, we have not been freed of fear. Scaremongering by ministers, police and security officials has bordered on the hysterical.' Jenkins could have added the media to his list since regular scare stories focusing on 'Islamic fundamentalists' or 'jihadists' have fuelled the demonisation of Muslims in general. Significantly, an international Harris poll in August 2007 found striking levels of Islamophobia with 30 per cent of British people believing it's impossible to be both a Muslim and a Briton (compared with 14 per cent who think you can't be French and a Muslim); 38 per cent thought Muslims posed a threat to national security (compared with 21 per cent in the US) while 46 per cent believed Muslims had too much political power (Milne 2007).

The Gordon Brown government continued to indulge in dubious scare tactics over the alleged 'terrorist' threats – even creating in March 2008 four new regional counter-terrorism units and four new regional intelligence centres to help the police. Extra resources were to be directed at MI5, MI6, GCHQ and anti-terrorist police while a new national security forum bringing together 30 private sector experts and academics was to advise the current ministerial National Security Committee. Yet significantly, figures from Europol, the European police agency, in May 2007 revealed that Islamist terror attacks in Europe constituted just 0.2 per cent of all the 'terrorism' on the continent in 2006. The *European Terrorism Situation Report 2007* listed 424 'ethno-nationalist and separatist' attacks (mostly in France and Spain), 55 'left-wing and anarchist' attacks (mainly in Greece, Italy, Spain and Germany), one failed Islamist terrorist attack (in Germany plus two allegedly foiled attempts in Denmark and the UK) and one right wing attack (in Poland). But the report also notes that half the 706 arrests of suspected terrorists in Europe were Muslims. David Miller, of www.spinwatch.org, comments:

> The UK itself has seen hundreds of arrests on trumped up charges which are later shown to be false and often propagandist. Indeed, one of the two alleged 'foiled' attacks in the

figures is the much heralded transatlantic bomb plot in the UK which has certainly adversely affected millions of air passengers. However, it does appear that this plot existed much more in the minds of the security establishment than in reality.

Miller also conducted a database search on national press coverage in 2006. Some 26,277 reports mentioned the word 'terrorist' or 'terrorism'. Of these 7, 620 referred to 'Islam', 'Islamist' or 'Muslim'. He concludes: 'In other words, the media reported Islamist violence out of all proportion to the number of attacks' (2007).

According to Alia and Bull (op. cit.: 29), Islamophobia (directed at the roughly one million Muslims living in Britain) is not a new phenomenon so much as a redirection of old phobias about African-Caribbean and other ethnic minority communities. In 2007, the portrayal of women wearing the veil was used by some British newspapers to generate an atmosphere of suspicion. When three young mothers wearing the niqab were photographed in Birmingham one made a two-fingered gesture which encouraged menacing comments. The *Daily Express* called it 'an image of veiled defiance'. The *Daily Mail* said it was 'a chilling insight into the minds of many young Muslims . . . hungry for the harshness of Sharia law'. But according to Nicholas Jones (2007): 'Needless to say neither newspaper acknowledged that it was probably the provocation of being photographed in the street without their permission which prompted the women's defiant attitude.' Moreover, many critics argued that alarmist news stories about women wearing headscarves illustrated a wider failure to understand the Muslim world: mainstream media often portrayed the hijab as an Islamic symbol when, in fact, it was often a reflection of socio-economic factors and had nothing to do with religion as such. Intriguingly, an Edinburgh student newspaper, *The Journal*, reported that the owners of the *Daily Mail*, which we have seen is not averse to criticising ethnic minorities – and the large number of foreign nationals studying in the UK – is the sole owner of the student recruitment service, Hobsons, which specialises in attracting international students to the country. Are there not some serious contradictions here?

Another row exploded in February 2008 after the Archbishop of Canterbury, Rowan Williams, suggested that British law recognise some role for Islamic arbitration. Modelling his proposal on the existing practice of orthodox Jewish courts, he stressed that acknowledgement of sharia law should never override equal rights for all, especially women. According to Seamus Milne (2008), the response of the media was largely 'hysterical and ugly', 'from the *Sun*'s declaration that Williams had "handed al Qaida a victory" to the *Express* claim that he had "surrendered to fanatics", to the endless replays of floggings in Western-backed states like Saudi Arabia.'

Are there any particular language issues to consider when covering race issues?

Criticisms of journalists who focus on language issues come from both the political left and right. The first group claims that terminology matters are of minor importance in a largely visual culture and in comparison with the campaign for equal opportunities. From the right come allegations that such obsessions are the preserve of the laughable Politically Correct and 'loony left' who seek to impose their Stalinist rules on society. Others argue that journalistic writing/'journalese' (which is poorly regarded in academic circles) has many positive qualities: it's direct, accessible and able to present complex issues in straightforward, non-abstract ways. Cliché, over-simplification, distortion and stereotyping inevitably result. But the essential routines of journalism are honourable.

All the same, most style books follow the line of Reuters, which says (MacDowall 1992: 125): 'Mention a person's race, colour or ethnic or religious affiliation only if relevant to the story.' But John Wilson (1996: 253) argues that the media tend to ignore this principle when covering urban deprivation and race:

> A deprived estate that is nearly all white will be referred to simply as a deprived estate. A deprived area that has a majority of black people is likely to be referred to as a deprived black area regardless of whether its black majority is relevant. If it is a mixed area it will be referred to as racially mixed whether the racial mix matters or not.

The NUJ *Guidelines on Race Reporting* suggest a range of useful strategies in this area. It reminds journalists that words which were once in common usage are now considered offensive. Thus instead of 'half-caste' and 'coloured' use 'mixed-race' and 'black', though it is always best to ask people how they define themselves. 'Immigrant', it says, is often used as a term of abuse and should only be used when a person is strictly an immigrant. Most black people in Britain were born here and most immigrants are white. On the reporting of Gypsies, it says journalists should only mention the word 'Gypsy' or 'traveller' if strictly relevant and accurate. Is not care also needed when using the word 'riot'? Simon Cottle (1993: 164) argues that it can serve to de-politicise an event, with the media failing to identify the deeper structural causes of the conflict, namely social deprivation and acute levels of inner-city unemployment.

In 2006, the global charity, Survival International, launched a campaign to stop journalists using easy but inaccurate and offensive epithets to describe tribal people. During the coverage of the Asian tsunami of 2004 and its aftermath, hundreds of reports described the tribes of Andaman as 'primitive' or 'stone-age'. For instance, a report in the *Daily Telegraph* in November 2005 was titled 'Guardian of the Stone Age tribes'; a report in *Marie Claire* of a woman growing up with the Fayu people of West Papua was headed 'Growing up with cannibals'. According to SI's director, Stephen Corry, such language is often used to justify persecution and forced 'development' by governments. 'It conveys that they are somehow not as intelligent as we are; that they haven't progressed as far as we have. It is fundamentally a colonial mentality' (Brown 2006). Do you agree?

Milica Pesic, director of the Media Diversity Institute (www.media-diversity.org), who has particular concerns over the reporting of 'ethnic cleansing' and the Balkans crisis, advises journalists:

> Try to describe events accurately and cite the sources of your information instead of relying on inflammatory adjectives like 'brutal', 'inhuman' and 'barbaric'. Journalists often fall back on such expression as a way of demonising one side and, whether intentionally or not, goading the other side to perpetuate the cycle of violence. In doing so, they are generally fulfilling the goals and disseminating the views of just one party to the conflict.
>
> (Pesic 2008)

How can journalists improve coverage of people from ethnic minorities?

The *Daily Mail*'s campaign over Stephen Lawrence is often cited as an example of brave, anti-racist coverage. With the famous 'Murderers' headline of 14 February 1997, the newspaper dared to accuse five men of the April 1993 murder of the 18-year-old black student in south London – and challenged them to sue the paper. Significantly they chose not to. But the campaign for justice, led by the parents of Stephen Lawrence and backed by the *Mail* (though many years after the black ethnic press had focused on the murder), ultimately led to the Macpherson report which identified serious institutional racism within the police force and throughout society.

The *Mail* is not normally identified with anti-racism campaigning. Some commentators suggested the u-turn occurred because Stephen's father had once worked as a plasterer and decorator for Paul Dacre, the paper's editor. Others suggested it was all part of the *Mail*'s strategy to extend its appeal to middle-class ethnic minority audiences. It certainly had little impact on its campaign against asylum seekers. Is positive discrimination an answer? No: it's illegal, as is the setting up of specific race- or gender-specific quotas. But positive action could be the answer.

Asylum seekers, refugees and people from ethic minorities are often, understandably, afraid to speak to the mainstream media. Thus there is a need for mainstream journalists to extend the range of their contacts to incorporate more ethnic minority voices while, at the same time, groups representing them need to form strong contacts with sympathetic reporters – and members of the NUJ who, as we have seen, have in some instances been prepared to take industrial action in their defence. The *Washington Post* has shown a commitment to improving coverage by setting up a diversity committee which reviews the ethnic and racial composition of staff; it has appointed a correspondent dedicated to race relations issues. And it arranges a series of informal lunches where staff and ombudsman meet to discuss the way the paper reported race issues. A call by the American Society of Newspaper Editors 20 years ago to have newsrooms reflect the country's ethnic diversity resulted in a 270 per cent rise in journalists of black and Hispanic origin.

In Britain, the *Guardian* has scholarships reserved for minority journalists at City University, London; the National Council for the Training of Journalists has had a diversity fund since 2005 to complement the NUJ's

George Viner Fund while Johnston Press, which owns around 300 local newspapers, has a bursary scheme to encourage entrants from minority backgrounds and poor homes. Small-scale schemes to help ethnic minorities are also offered by Trinity Mirror and the Scott Trust, owners of the *Manchester Evening News* (Aldridge 2007: 150). All Channel 4 proposals now have to indicate what contribution they make to the channel's new remit which demands three and a half hours of identifiably multicultural programmes a week. And the BBC, along with other broadcasting institutions, has set up the Broadcasting Cultural Diversity Network (www.cdnetwork.org.uk) to promote diversity and track the progress of ethnic minority staff. Some call for a more 'anti-racist' focus, arguing that 'diversity' projects are politically naïve and aim primarily at promoting the career interests of the ethnic middle class.

Investigative journalists also have a responsibility to expose the plight of immigrants in this country. A BBC documentary in 2005, *Detention Undercover – the Real Story*, did just this after an undercover reporter filmed asylum seekers and immigrants being assaulted, racially abused and sexually humiliated by private security guards. At the local level, in 2007, the Nottingham *Evening Post* produced an in-depth multi-media series exploring issues affecting Nottingham's Muslim community – in their own words. The package included six double-page spreads, together with a picture special and online coverage with a number of four-minute picture slideshows narrated by the interviewees themselves. The paper said it 'wanted to raise awareness and create debate on the city's 15,000 Muslim community'. And in the following year the *Aldershot Mail* launched a bilingual edition in Nepali and English as a way to connect with the largest ethnic minority group in its circulation area. *Mail* editor Elaine Cole told *Press Gazette* (P. Smith 2008a):

> This paper has always striven to serve everyone. This has traditionally included people who struggle to make their voices heard – such as young people, the homeless and those with disabilities. With this edition we hope to do the same for our significant Nepalese population. There are concerns about friction between the Nepalese and white communities including reports of gangs of young people fighting and bullying in schools. Hopefully this will go some way to help heal those rifts and build greater understanding.

Do not fashion magazines need to be more aware of representing ethnic diversity in their choice of models? According to Carole White, co-founder of Premier Model Agency, editors keep on telling her that white faces sell at news stands (Akbar 2008). 'If fashion editors were a bit braver and tried out black, Asian and Chinese models, our eyes would be easier on that look. They don't give the opportunities to these girls.' Moreover, do not journalists need to challenge the myths surrounding 'compassion fatigue' which serve largely to excuse the media from covering the Third World systematically? Fergal Keane, BBC news special correspondent, agrees that most of what is shown of Africa is negative. The media, he stresses, need to show 'the numerous small miracles of African life' placing the imagery of despair in its proper political and economic context. Is there not also a need for more ethnic minority students in journalism training schools? A BT survey published in May 2000 showed the number of such students enrolling on journalism courses had risen by 94 per cent over the previous four years: but still just 208 non-white students enrolled in 1999 compared with 107 in 1995.

Should not all journalists be more aware of religions such as Catholicism, Islam, Buddhism, Hinduism and Judaism, their customs, principal festivals and titles of their leaders? Journalists also need to be made aware of alternative ethnic media, their different ethical standpoints, their creation of important counter-public spheres (Fraser 1993) and the opportunities they offer for alternative careers away from mainstream stereotyping. *Muslim News*, *Q News*, *Eastern Eye*, *Asian Times*, *New Nation*, *Jewish Chronicle* should all be closely watched, along with black Internet sites such as *Blacknet* (www.blacknet.co.uk) and *Voice-online*, radio stations such as Colourful Radio (www.iamcolourful.com) – and anti-racist journals such as *Searchlight* and *Race and Class*, *Socialist Worker*, *Fight Racism Fight Imperialism*, *Campaign Against Racism and Fascism*, *Peace News* and the *New Left Review*. Sunny Hundal's Pickled Politics blog (www.pickledpolitics.com) also presents an interesting perspective on Asian politics in Britain.

Notes

1   www.chronicleworld.org though now transformed into a blog at http://chronicleworld. wordpress.com/.

2   See www.ourcivilisation.com/cooray/btof/chap211.htm, accessed 1 May 2008.

3   See www.ibt.org.uk, accessed 1 May 2008.

4   See www.medialens.org/alerts/index.php and www.medialens.org/blogs/richard-keeble-blog.php.

5   See www.medialens.org/blogs/richard-keeble-blog.php.

8

Getting the representation right

Tackling issues over gender, mental health, suicide, disability, HIV/AIDS and gays/lesbians

How serious a threat do you consider institutional sexism to be to media standards?

Critics tend to focus on the alleged institutional sexism within the media industries as a crucial factor behind the coverage of women. A survey by Liz Curtis (1994) found serious cases of sexual harassment of women within the BBC and other broadcasting organisations, while research by Margareta Melin-Higgins (1997) found women alienated by the dominant male newsroom culture. According to media commentator Peter Wilby, newspaper managements will only give women 'a fair wind provided they behave like good chaps and adapt their lifestyles to a masculine pattern' (2008c). Significantly, in November 2003, MP Clive Solely revealed under Parliamentary privilege that Rupert Murdoch's company, News International, had paid £5000,000 to silence allegations of serious sexual harassment against Stuart Higgins, a former editor of the *Sun*. Soley told Parliament that *Sun* staff had suffered 'sexual harassment and bullying'. 'As far as I am aware no proper disciplinary hearings took place and other senior staff appear to have colluded with what was by any standard extremely offensive and destructive behaviour' (Hencke 2003).

Former managing director at the *Independent* Amanda Platell (1999: 144) talks of institutional sexism as being 'endemic' in newspapers:

it's about pigeonholing women journalists, denying equality of pay and conditions and opportunities, demeaning them and making assumptions about them. It is about a widespread and inherent belief by some men that women can't quite cut it, that newspapers are a man's world, that women are good for only one thing – 'features' – and that ritual humiliation is a way of keeping girls in their place.

Take a look at any panel in a magazine, newspaper or television programme and see if the organisers have demonstrated any gender sensitivity. So often they fail. Take the 'leftist' *New Statesman* magazine: its edition for 12 November 2007 carried a supplement (intriguingly sponsored by Macdonald's) looking at standards in catering and hospitality. Out of a 14-person roundtable discussion panel chosen by *NS* only two were women – and only one was black. David Randall's colourful celebration of outstanding, brave journalism, in *The Great Reporters* (2005), managed to highlight the careers of just three women (Nelly Bly, Edna Buchanan and Ann Leslie) out of a total of 13 reporters. According to Chambers, Steiner and Fleming (2004: 1) women journalists present a paradox: while their presence is now commonplace in the media, they continue to be marked as 'other' from their male colleagues.

> In print news, official rhetoric proclaims that a journalist's gender is irrelevant. However, while maleness is rendered neutral and male journalists are treated largely as professionals, women journalists are signified as *gendered* their work is routinely defined and judged by their femininity . . . Women are still concentrated in sectors to be considered 'soft' news such as those with an emphasis on 'human interest' stories, features and the delivery of magazine-style journalism. In television – where spectacle counts – emphasis on the decorative value and even sexualisation of women journalists is overt.

The percentage of women on national dailies remains low at 22. But magazines often employ more women than men. Women also comprise 44 per cent of journalists in independent television, 38 per cent in independent radio and 37 per cent at the BBC (Franklin 1997: 61). The numbers of women trainees are rising all the time: by 2000, half the entrants to newspapers were female.

And the 1990s also witnessed a few advances for women in the mainstream press. In May 1991, Eve Pollard became the first woman editor of the *Sunday Express* while Rosie Boycott, in April 1998, became the first woman editor of a broadsheet (the struggling *Independent on Sunday*) before moving on, first to edit the *Independent* and then – in April 1998 – the struggling *Express*. At the *Sunday Mirror*, editorial control in November 1996 was in the hands of three women: managing director Bridget Rowe, deputy managing director Pat Moore and acting editor Amanda Platell. This was the first time in Fleet Street history that an all female executive triumvirate had held power on a national newspaper. In May 2000, Rebekah Wade, at 31, became editor of the *News of the World*. Then in January 2003 she moved to become the first woman editor of the *Sun* (though in December 2007 its circulation dipped to below three million for the first time since 1974). Significantly, Wade was one of only three women listed in the *Guardian*'s top twenty media movers and shakers on 18 July 2005. Also in May 2000 Rebecca Hardy, at 34, became the first woman editor of the *Scotsman*. At the management level, Dame Marjorie Scardino became the first woman chief executive of a top FTSE 100 company when she was appointed chief of media giant Pearson (its stable including the *Economist*, *Financial Times* and Penguin Books) in 1997 (Burrell 2008b).

At the local level, the *Diss Express* was staffed entirely by women. On 8 March 2000, to mark International Women's Day, the *Western Mail* changed its name to the *Western Femail* and was edited by Pat English with Michelle Bower as head of content. But Linda Christmas (1997), journalism lecturer and co-founder of Women in Journalism, questions whether the media are becoming as women friendly as it may seem: 'It's about who controls the purse strings. Yes, women edit magazines but hardly any are magazine publishers which is where the real power is.'

Women in similar jobs are often paid less: in 1997 it was revealed that while John Humphrys and James Naughtie were paid £120,000 a year, Sue McGregor, also a presenter on Radio 4's *Today* programme, received £100,000. A MORI survey of 537 national newspaper and magazine journalists by telephone in the autumn of 1997 suggested that women earned significantly less than men (Allan 2004: 124). According to Chambers, Steiner and Fleming (2004: 88) women earned on average 83 per cent of men's salaries. Award-winning interviewer Ginny Dougary, author of *Executive Tarts and Other Myths* (1994) objected after she was criticised for being an 'ambitious girl reporter' (she was 38) following her profile of Chancellor Norman Lamont in *The Times* magazine in September 1994. Dawn Alford (2000), the *Mirror* reporter who duped Jack Straw's son into selling her cannabis, claimed she was victimised afterwards: 'Columnists used up hundreds of inches inferring I was a cross between Mata Hari and a black widow spider and my family and friends were doorstepped by agency reporters hoping I had a murky past.'

Women are also significant for their absence in the reporting of science. A study commissioned by the UK Resource Centre for Women in Science Engineering and Technology found that five male scientists were quoted for every female scientist. The researchers, who examined 1,500 articles in the areas of science, engineering and technology over a six-month period, also found that journalists were more likely to comment on appearance when focusing on women. For instance, the *Sunday Times* reported: 'The 55-year-old academic's mane of blonde hair, her short, navy, voluminous skirt teamed with a Vivienne Westwood jacket and knee-length boots sets a high benchmark' (Levenson 2008).

A report from the Fawcett Society in April 1997 showed that in BBC, ITV and Channel 4 news bulletins, 80 per cent of election coverage was carried out by male journalists. Female politicians appeared on screen only eight times compared with 127 by men. Of 17 academics asked opinion, not one was female. Such figures merely reinforce research which suggests that journalists' conventional sourcing routines tend to prioritise male sources above females. Other research by the Fawcett Society, published in August 2000, showed that TV news reporters tended to seek women's views on 'soft' news items, leaving politics and business to the men. The historic role of feminism is often marginalised by the media. A report from the campaigning group, Women in Journalism, *Real Women – The Hidden Sex*, in November 1999, expressed concern over the constant sexist use of images of women to 'lift' pages.

- The NUJ has published a document on sexual harassment, including a section of 'How to prevent it' and a model clause for house agreements.

Do you feel the employment of more women will improve news values?

Just 22 per cent of Fleet Street journalists are women, though research by the Journalism Training Forum in 2002 found that of the 60,000 print journalists in the country half were women. Some 24 per cent of women reported discrimination at work while, overall, women's pay lags men's by £5,000 a year.

Research by Linda Christmas (1997), suggested that the employment of more women in newspapers had a dramatic impact on 'humanising' news values:

> Women have already made a difference, particularly on the magazine and feature side of newspapers . . . the features content of all national daily and Sunday newspapers has increased in the last 15 years. There has been a huge increase in human interest stories, tales of triumph over tragedy and advice on handling relationships.

Women had also helped change the content of news pages with material of interest to women spread throughout national newspapers. She argued that women wrote differently from men. They tended to put readers' needs above those of policy makers, were more 'people' than 'issue' oriented, placed more importance on seeing news in context and preferred to examine the consequences of events. *Sunday Times* columnist A.A. Gill has also highlighted the 'feminisation' of television, but sees it as a worrying development. TV boardrooms may still be occupied by men but mostly women are making the important day-to-day decisions: 'They are middle-ranking commissioning editors and producers who see themselves as role model women in a traditionally male-oriented business. Television is deeply concerned with women's issues, desperate not to offend women, not to get it wrong' (Ellis 1998).

But many challenge these views. Women journalists often claim they do not have a news agenda distinct from their male colleagues and that it is patronising to suggest they are more interested in 'softer', featurish stories. Lindsey Hilsum, diplomatic correspondent of *Channel 4 News*, accused Christmas of promoting 'old fashioned, clichéd notions of gender'. Jaci Stephen (1997) questioned women's role in 'humanising' journalism: 'My experience has been that executive female journalists are a terrifying bunch of unscrupulous, spiteful, cruel, manipulative and often grossly unprofessional cows.' Others claim that the economic, ideological factors behind the growth of 'human interest' stories are more important than the rise in the numbers of prominent women journalists. Women editors often reproduce the same values as men. Bridget Rowe, for instance, led her 52 staff at the *People* in 1996 at a time when the paper was packed with stories about royals, Pamela Anderson, Hugh Grant's prostitute Divine Brown (shown naked except for a strategically placed star marked 'censored') and more sex. In any case, numbers in themselves don't count: more important is the need to have women (and ethnic minority) journalists employed with a political understanding of the ways in which their subordination is reproduced – and with a will to change it.

Clearly, not enough men (and particularly those in positions of power in the media) perceive gender issues to be a 'problem'. At the same time, others express concern over mounting anti-male rhetoric – dubbed 'womanism' by journalist Ros Coward – in the media. Coward commented (1999):

> Womanism came out of feminism's attack on male pomposities but now has a much wider constituency. Womanism is feminism's vulgate, found everywhere, from the humorous disparagement of men by stand-up comedians and novelists through to more savage criticisms of men in the context of fears of social disintegration. It unites unlikely allies. The ubiquitous New Age philosophies promote the idea of woman as caring, in touch with natural, healing forces, while men are men, responsible for destructive technology and science.

Intriguingly, the focus turned during 2008 on to abuse suffered by men at the hands of women. Erin Pizzey, who set up Britain's first refuge for victims of domestic violence in the 1970, launched an online campaign and research project (see www.feminezone.com) into what she described as 'one of the last great taboos' with as many as one in six men believed to suffer physical and mental abuse from women (Dugan 2008). Are these concerns merely obscuring the reality of the patriarchal oppression of women in society – both nationally and globally (with the UN reporting, for instance, that one in three women on the planet will be raped or beaten in her lifetime)?

Certainly, one of the many paradoxes in this area is that women often promote sexism as much as men. For instance, a profile of Barbara Amiel, wife of the disgraced Lord Black, former owner of the *Telegraphs*, in the *Guardian* of 3 September 2004 by Sandra Laville, headlined on her being 'drop-dead gorgeous', 'fiercely attractive' and 'sexy as hell'. And the copy went on to mention her 'beauty' and 'sex appeal' no less than seven times. Elected editor of the *Toronto Sun* in 1983, the paper publicised her as 'beauteous and brainy, rightwing and right on', Laville reported. Significantly too, no assault on sexist news and picture values at the *Sun* and *News of the World* was at all evident after Rebekah Wade became editor of those papers. But while women reproduce sexist attitudes, this does not legitimise such attitudes: according to David Roberts (2008), it merely highlights the fact that both men and women are equally deeply socialised into 'punishing' women for social 'deviation'.

Should Page Three-type images be banned?

In 1970, the *Sun*, acquired a few months earlier by Australian Rupert Murdoch, carried its first Page Three picture – of Stephanie Rahn. Over the following year, the paper doubled its circulation – and thus began Fleet Street's descent in sexploitation and trashy titillation. Or at least, so its critics argue. Others claim Page Three's undoubted success (becoming a national institution by the 1990s) proves its popularity with both men and women readers. Isn't the model exploiting her sexuality for financial gain? What's wrong with that? A lot, claim some feminist critics who see the Page Three-type image (which quickly spread to other tabloids) as legitimising the crude sexist stereotyping of women.

These criticisms came to a head in 1986 when Labour MP Clare Short, backed by the anti-porn crusader Lord Longford, tried, unsuccessfully, to introduce legislation to outlaw such images. Under the editorship of the abrasive Kelvin MacKenzie, the *Sun* hit back at Short, with Samantha Fox, the most famous Page Three 'lovely', denouncing her as a 'killjoy'. The *News of the World*, then edited by Patsy Chapman, set out to find a picture of the MP in her nightdress (Holland 1998: 27). And when a council in Sowerby Bridge, West Yorkshire, banned the paper from its library, the *Sun* dubbed them the 'Barmy Burghers of Sowerby Bridge' and pictured three local 'lovelies' posing in mini-skirts. All the same, the controversy raises a number of issues: can an issue as complex as the representation of women be tackled through legislation, to what extent do Page Three-type images contribute to a culture in which women are routinely exploited and suffer intolerable levels of physical harassment and violence, and, if legislation is not the answer, how can such sexist attitudes and images be challenged?

In 2006, a new campaign, Object, shifted the campaigning focus from Page Three to the sexist lads' mags such as *Zoo*, *Nuts*, *Loaded* and *FHM*. And it gained its first success when Marks & Spencer agreed to drop the sale of all lads' mags. M&S said it was keen to promote its ethical policies and refused to invest in businesses involved in the pornography industry. A detailed, critical analysis of lads' mags by Object concluded: 'Their constant denigration, trivialization and sexualization of women is further bolstered by their promotion of voyeurism; the blurring of fantasy and reality; the message that women are to be judged, rated, scored and found wanting; that women are commodities to be owned' (see www.object.org.uk). A spokesperson for Object said that many women and men were feeling insulted, if not harassed, by the 'wall to wall' pornography on display in most sweet shops, petrol stations and supermarkets. 'There are an increasing number of members of the public challenging the "normalising of pornography" across the country – either as individuals or groups – as an issue of sexual discrimination and indeed harassment' (Crummy 2006).

Many argue that such campaigns are direct attacks on freedom of expression. And Decca Aitkenhead argues that the feminist critique of the lads' mags culture fails to account for women's own complicity in the genre (2007). The *Nuts* website, for instance, invites men to study photographs of naked breasts and rank them. 'Without these willing armies of female volunteers, there would be no breast for any reader of *Nuts* to assess.'

Is the media coverage of sport particularly sexist?

Male sport dominates the media. Women cricketers, footballers and golfers hardly get a look-in. In September 2007, China hosted the women's football World Cup – but apart from the BBC it was largely ignored. When women do feature their presence is usually heavily sexualised. From the early 1980s to the present day, the coverage of sportswomen – such as the late Florence Griffith-Joyner, Katarina Witt, Gabriela

Sabatini, Mary Pearce, Anna Kournikova, Maria Sharapova, Venus and Serena Williams – has tended to focus on their sexuality.

For instance, in the lead-up to Wimbledon 2000, and before her quick exit, Fleet Street carried 52 pictures of 19-year-old Kournikova (ranked 14 in the world at the time and dubbed Cor!-nikova by the red-tops) compared to 46 of all the other top female players combined. Kournikova was also caught in a typical, manufactured row with Elizabeth Hurley, the representation of women competing for the attention of males being a prominent sexist stereotype. The Russian tennis star had apparently described Ms Hurley to Russian *Vogue* as 'so ugly' but, in response to journalists' probing, Ms Hurley had merely described Kournikova as 'looking smashing'. There was no stopping the media frenzy. The *Sun*, *Mirror* and *Scottish Daily Record* ran polls asking readers who was the prettier; columnists such as Dominic Mohan, Lynda Lee-Potter and Melanie McDonagh all waded in with their words of wisdom on the matter. David Rowe (2005: 128) argued that Kournikova was a mega-celebrity because her image had been deliberately sexualised by her management (Octogan) and by the news, sport and entertainment media. But he went on: 'Is it the role of sports journalists to be complicit in the selling of Anna, or should they ask the awkward questions that are central to the professional duties of the Fourth Estate?'

Or take Lyndsay Clydesdale, in the *Mirror* of 9 July 2004. Sharapova, the Wimbledon 2004 winner, was described as a 'sexy smasher' who has both beauty and talent (as if they were mutually exclusive) and later on as a 'tennis babe' (thus predictably infantilising one of the world's top players). A LexisNexis search on 'Sharapova and babe' for just two weeks in 2004 produced 80 Fleet Street references. In a similar way, 34-year-old Kelly Holmes, double gold winner at the Athens Olympics in 2004, was constantly described throughout the national press as 'our golden girl'. And in typical sexist mode, on 1 March 2008, the *Sun* used its punning powers to the full as England Under-21 women's international football star Natasha Hughes was pictured pouting in a skimpy bikini. 'What a striker!' the caption warbled about the 'sexy footie ace' who had 'more than enough up front as well'. You might even compare the number of images of women with those of men in sports magazines. The *Observer Sport Monthly* of March 2008 was typical: more than 100 pictures of men and just five of women and one of these, the 'petite, feminine' cyclist Victoria Pendleton was shown entirely starkers (on the cover and in a double page spread inside). To what extent do such prevalent images of women foster the illusion that all women are sexually available in a culture in which a rape is recorded every 34 minutes and 26 per cent of people consider that 'inappropriately' dressed women are 'asking for it' (Bell 2008)?

In a damning report in 2006, the Women's Sport Foundation found that most media coverage was condescending, focusing on physique, personal life and personality rather than physical prowess.[1] Typically on 3 November 2004, the *Sun* described former Wimbledon champion Serena Williams as a 'smasher' and 'looking stunning' in a two million dollar necklace! And in a similar, unimaginative sexist style, Martin Johnson, in the *Daily Telegraph*, commented on 19 January 2006: 'Bottom line for media is size of Serena's bloomers.'

Yet the issue becomes complicated when some of these women happily capitalise on the commercial advantages of such representations. Academic David Rowe comments (1999: 128): 'Such debates are especially intense when sportswomen explicitly play the role of soft pornographic subjects on the covers of sports magazines, in calendars, posters and publicity shots.' Katarina Witt, for instance, posed for *Playboy* while top UK athlete Denise Lewis stripped for *Total Sport*. And Kournikova has never shirked publicising her good looks. Just take a look at her current official website (www.kournikova.com) where, for instance, her appearance in the fortieth Swimsuit Anniversary edition of *Sports Illustrated* is prominently advertised.

Overall, women's sport receives not only just 5 per cent of media coverage but a tiny fraction of the total sponsorship money. In other words, women often have to uncover to get covered – and keep those drooling sports reporters happy (Gatton 2000).

Significantly, in response to these pressures the Women's Sports Foundation has issued guidelines on how 'women athletes can create a positive image without losing their dignity'. In a new campaign for more coverage, WSF is calling for people to email editors to demand change. A spokeswoman commented: 'At the moment, the most vocal consumers of sports coverage are those who want more of the same – that is, more professional football, more (men's) professional rugby and cricket. If we are to achieve a more balanced approach, we have to make our voices heard.' And at the local level, important changes *are* being made. The *Lincolnshire Echo* is one of many local newspapers which gives prominence to women's sport.

What other strategies can journalists adopt for improving coverage of women?

A number of issues arise:

- Are separate women's sections and programmes the answer – or do they tend to perpetuate sexist stereotyping with the focus on sex, health, beauty, domestic issues, personal advice columns and lifestyles? Should men be allowed to contribute to special women's sections?

- Should we all not have a firmer grasp of the writings and journalism of the leading feminist theorists such as Mary Wollstonecraft, Emma Goldman, Germaine Greer, Ros Coward, Sheila Rowbotham, Andrea Dworkin, Dale Spender, Susan Faludi, Camilla Paglia and Kate Millett? Significantly, the centenary of the birth of French icon of feminism, Simone de Beauvoir (author of the seminal *The Second Sex*, of 1949), in January 2008 went largely unreported in Britain. Even in France, the 'Leftist' *Le Nouvel Observateur* magazine featured de Beauvoir completely starkers on its front cover – and even carried the same photograph inside while commentary throughout the national media focused more on her controversial sex life than on her radical ideas.

- Should not journalists be 'gender sensitive' in their sourcing routines? It's often all too easy to find willing male commentators.

How important is the use of non-sexist language in countering stereotypes? For instance, was not the widespread use of 'Blair's Babes' to describe new women MPs in the Labour-dominated House of Commons post-1997 sexist? Similarly, *The Sunday Times* on 23 March 2008 resorted to tired, sexist clichés in its reporting of the visit of French President Nicolas Sarkozy to London with his 'chic' female ministers. According to reporter Matthew Campbell (2008), the 'Sarkozy babes' included 31-year-old Rama Yade, Secretary of State for human rights, with her 'model good looks'; Rachida Dati, the 42-year-old Justice Minister, 'who has raised eyebrows by posing in designer outfits in her office for glossy magazines'; Christine Lagarde, the 'elegant', 52-year-old Minister of Finance; and Michèle Alliot-Marie, 61, the Interior Minister, 'of whom the previous president, Jacques Chirac, once said: "She has the best legs in the party"'. Earlier on 5 March, *Sunday Times* Paris correspondent Charles Bremner (2008) had started the sexist ball rolling by describing the 42-year-old new Justice Minister Rachida Dati as a 'Sarko babe'. A competition for the best-looking topless 'girlfriend' in the *Daily Star* in April 2008 was dubbed all too predictably a 'babe search' while special features included 'celeb babes' and 'bikini babes'.

Challenging this widespread bias is no easy task. Some style books avoid all mention of sexist language issues except in relation to the use of 'Ms', 'Miss' and 'Mrs'. Most now accept the use of 'Ms' where appropriate and avoid using 'he' when 'he or she' or 'they' (as a singular bisexual pronoun) is more accurate. Phrases such as 'the common man' and the 'man in the street' are also widely avoided. Discussions over style book changes can provide opportunities to raise language issues. But style book revisions can often be dominated by an editorial elite so it might be appropriate to work with colleagues in the NUJ to confront sexist stereotyping in language. To assist such campaigns, the union has drawn up an *Equality Style Guide* suggesting words to be avoided and alternatives. For example, there is:

businessman	business manager, executive, boss, business chief, head of firm
cameraman	photographer, camera operator
newsman	journalist or reporter
fireman/men	firefighter/fire services staff/fire crews
forefathers	ancestors
dustman	refuse collector
workmen	workers/workforce
mankind	humanity/people
gentleman's agreement	verbal agreement
foreman	supervisor
ice cream man	ice cream seller
manpower	employees/workforce
old masters	classic art
policeman/men	police officer or just police
salesman	shop worker/shop staff/representative/ sales staff
spaceman	astronaut
stewardess/air hostess	airline staff/flight attendant
nightwatchman	caretaker/security guard
rights of man	citizens'/people's rights

Even where editors fail to acknowledge these issues, there is often a certain degree of stylistic freedom available to the reporter to use such language. Special attention also needs to be given to the reporting of murders and serial killers (often with women as their victims). Too often tabloids emphasise the abnormality of the killer (with words such as 'evil', 'monster', 'beast', 'sick', vicious', 'brute', 'fiend' and 'bizarre') and the randomness of the attack. And yet, as Peter Wilby commented (2008d): 'The majority of murders are still domestic, committed by people known to their victims. The motives are perfectly comprehensible: lust, love, jealousy and greed.'

What issues should journalists be aware of when covering mental health matters?

First some facts as presented by the MHF (Mental Health Foundation, www.mentalhealth.org.uk): mental health problems occur when feelings such as depression, anxiety and stress become more extreme or long lasting that they affect a person's ability to carry on their everyday life. Mental illness, on the other hand, is a term used by doctors and other health professionals to describe clinically recognisable psychological symptoms and patterns of behaviour. Mental illness is not a single condition and mentally-ill people are not a homogeneous group. Like mental health problems, mental illness can be regarded as a continuum, ranging from minor distress to severe, long-term disorders.

- One in four of the UK's adult population will experience some kind of mental health problem in any year.
- Over any year, 12 million adults attending GP surgeries have symptoms of mental illness.
- Some two million children are estimated to have some form of mental health problem and evidence suggests the figure is rising.
- Mental health remains one of the least popular causes for charity despite being one of the most universal issues.

Do the media not have a responsibility to make people aware of the scale of the mental health problem? Yet headlines containing words like 'psycho', 'madman', 'loonies', 'nutters' and 'maniac' are very common and only fuel negative myths and stereotypes about mental illness. A controversy erupted in September 2003 after the *Sun* headlined a report on former heavyweight boxing champion Frank Bruno being admitted into a psychiatric hospital 'Bonkers Bruno locked up' (though it was rapidly to changed to 'Sad Bruno in mental home'). Moreover, people with mental health problems are not normally deemed newsworthy, unless attached to a spectacularly negative event or are celebrities – such as Bruno. As pop superstar Britney Spears went through some kind of mental crisis in January 2008, the media pack pursued her relentlessly and mercilessly. A leading Hollywood gossip site reported more than 10,000,000 Spears page impressions in 24 hours: an all-time record (Preston 2008). Mental illness was being transformed into a spectator sport.

Given the number of people suffering mental illness of some kind, if you are not personally affected then someone close to you is likely to be. The Health Education Authority and the mental health charity, Mind, are also concerned over the media emphasis on crime and violence when covering mentally-ill people. The Press Complaints Commission also criticised the *Daily Star* for describing (in November 1995) a patient at Broadoak hospital who cycled up to Princess Diana and asked for a kiss as a 'raving nutter' and a loony.

A survey the two organisations published in 1997 showed half of total press coverage in 1996 dealt with crime, harm to others and self harm, while more than 40 per cent of tabloid articles used pejorative terms such as 'nutter' and 'loony'. Articles providing advice and guidance on mental health subjects accounted for less than 8 per cent of the coverage. Reports of Home Office homicide figures tend to focus on the mentally ill – even though their numbers have not increased while those committed by others have more than doubled. Yet the suicide rate among the mentally ill runs at two a day: in other words, they are more likely to harm themselves than other people.

A survey of mental health sufferers published by Mind in February 2000 showed that half believed their condition was made worse by the way they were covered in the media. A quarter of the respondents to the survey, *Counting the Cost*, said they had experienced hostility from local communities as a result of the coverage. Sue Baker, of Mind, said:

> Nobody can deny that when something goes tragically wrong with the care of a person with a diagnosed mental health problem that this is of valid public concern. What equally

cannot be denied is that often news reporting of these rare and tragic events has stated or suggested that all mentally ill people are a danger to others and are 'time bombs waiting to explode'.

Local journalists were considered better than national counterparts, though radio was felt to be the fairest medium. David Brindle, of the *Guardian*, suggested that the focus on violence and crime was not all the fault of the journalists: 'Part of the problem is the system of having an independent inquiry every time there is a homicide involving a mentally ill person. The news agenda is set that way and that is an issue both the press and the government need to think about' (Johnson 1997a). Other journalists are keen to defend their coverage as being in tune with public sentiments and editorial lines.

Reporters are advised by the MHF not to use diagnostic labels such as 'schizophrenic' or 'manic depressive' but less stigmatising phrases such as 'someone who has a diagnosis of schizophrenia' or 'someone who has bouts of depression'. At the same time, reporters should not understate or trivialise the pain and damage mental health problems can cause. Significantly, the PCC code states that the media must avoid 'prejudicial reference to an individual's race, colour, religion, gender, sexual orientation or to any physical or mental illness or disability' while the *Guardian*'s stylebook bans 'offensive and unacceptable' terms such as 'loony', 'maniac', 'nutter', 'psycho' and 'schizo'. A media handbook, *What's the Story: Reporting Mental Health and Suicide*, published by the Department of Health in 2008 (see www.shift.org.uk/mediahandbook), suggests journalists avoid references to the 'mentally ill' preferring terms such as 'people with mental health problems' and 'mental health patients'. According to former readers' editor of the *Guardian*, Ian Mayes, quoted in the handbook, journalists 'stand in relation to some aspects of mental health – particularly the way we refer to mental illness – roughly where we stood in relation to race 20 or 30 years ago'. Or are these language concerns the unnecessary obsessions of PC fanatics? In a booklet, *Shock Treatment*, the National Union of Journalists advises reporters to 'take a fresh look at their mental health coverage' and see 'people with mental health problems as an untapped source of stories and comment'. The National Institute for Mental Health in England (see www.shift.org.uk) also published a report in January 2006 examining media coverage of mental health and suggesting improvements (Eaton 2006).

What issues arise when reporting suicides?

The question of suicide lies at the heart of the human predicament – drawing in a vast range of philosophical, ethical, social and cultural issues. Indeed, according to the French journalist, novelist and philosopher Albert Camus, at the start of *The Myth of Sisyphus* (1942): 'There is but one truly serious philosophical problem and that is suicide. Judging whether life is or is not worth living amounts to answering the fundamental question of philosophy. All the rest – whether or not the world has three dimensions, whether the mind has nine or twelve categories – comes afterwards.'

Moreover there are around a million suicides around the world each year, according to the World Health Organisation (Williams 2007: 180). It is now the third biggest cause of death among people aged 15 to 34 across the globe, killing more people than all the world's wars. Some 30 per cent of the world's population suffer some form of mental illness yet two thirds receive inadequate or no treatment – even in countries with the best resources. In Britain, almost 6,000 people kill themselves every year, most of them men. Indeed, since 1950 suicide rates for English and Welsh males under 45 have doubled (ibid.: 181). A 2002 study found that nearly one adult Briton in six considers attempting suicide at some point in their lives. Williams also stresses the class dimension to the suicide crisis: people living in deprived industrial areas (with their soaring divorce rates and unemployment) are most likely to suffer from depression while those least likely come from middle class, comfortable, suburban areas (ibid.: 182).

Clearly, given the current national and global crisis in mental illness, the media bear an enormous responsibility to cover the fundamental issues surrounding suicide and depression with appropriate sensitivity. Inevitably, coverage of a suicide is likely to cause deep distress to close family and friends. How can it, then, be justified? According to Englehardt and Barney (2002: 84):

> Reporters and editors, while fully aware of the anguish they will cause with the publication of such information, need to identify the greater goods that may result from such publication, that is, identify the benefits that may more than offset the harm. The basic good, of course, is that to gather and distribute information is good – the journalist's basic function.

And, as the title of a study by the MediaWise Trust (www.mediawise. org.uk) of the media's portrayal of suicide stresses: *Sensitive Coverage Saves Lives*. Suicide was decriminalised in 1961 and the *Guardian* style guide, for instance, advises that the phrase 'committed suicide' should not be used. Sensational headlines, dramatic photographs and attributing the suicide to a single cause are also to be avoided. The Samaritans, a charity providing phone call assistance to those contemplating suicide, recommend suicide notes should not be disclosed.

MediaWise's review of coverage of suicides in the UK media concluded that the 'shock' and 'celebrity' factors appeared to count higher in rating the newsworthiness of a suicidal event than broader, more relevant issues (such as debt, depression and despair). 'The provision of helpline details is not commonplace and there is some evidence throughout that even the most basic guidance on responsible reporting has been ignored or at least not taken into full account.'

In Britain, a massive controversy erupted in January 2006 after three newspapers (*The Times*, the *Sun* and London's *Evening Standard*) published pictures taken by Jonathan Bushell, a photographer from the Matrix agency, of a woman leaping to her death from the ledge of a London hotel.[2] A series of complaints were made to the Press Complaints Commission, yet the PCC first ruled that the existing Code of Conduct had not been breached since the decision to publish was one of 'taste and decency' over which it had no jurisdiction.

Then on 29 June 2006, following the submission of compelling evidence from the Samaritans and others that media reporting of suicide often prompted copycat cases, the PCC added a new Clause 5 ii to the Code: 'When reporting suicide, care should be taken to avoid excessive detail about the method used.' Whether this amendment to the Code actually changes journalistic practice remains to be seen. A cynic might argue that journalists operating in the capitalist market-place often see the Code's clauses as hurdles to be jumped rather than as clear ethical guidelines to be respected. All the same, in October 2007, the *Wigan Evening Post*, the *Wigan Observer* and their shared website became the first newspapers to be criticised by the PCC over their suicide coverage. The Commission ruled that their reporting of the death of a teacher who had electrocuted himself carried 'too much detail' and there was a 'danger that sufficient information was included to spell out to others how to carry out a suicide'.

Concerns were also expressed after Northcliffe media thisisgloucestershire. co.uk website, on 1 February 2008, carried such detailed reports they appeared to go against the PCC's new code. One headline read 'Hairdresser set timer for suicide' while another said: 'Dad wired fingers to the mains'.

Significantly, the MediaWise survey found that there was 'some reluctance' among journalists to engage in self criticism, with suicide rarely considered a 'compelling topic for discussion'. Such a reluctance to engage in self criticism may characterise many other journalistic cultures around the world. The survey added:

> Journalists themselves are not immune to the pressures that drive people to suicide or bring on depression, and they too have personal experience of the distress caused by sudden death. The pity is that media professionals seem to isolate themselves from their audiences, as if unwilling to acknowledge a correlation between their life experiences and their work.

Both the MediaWise report and media academic Antonia Carding (2007) highlight the need for better education of journalists on the issues surrounding suicide and mental illness if the stigma surrounding the issues are to be removed. As Carding argues:

> stereotypical and sensational media representation of mental health issues in the popular press is one of the major contributors to the public's poor understanding of such issues, including suicide. Since the media and the popular press play such an important role in determining dominant attitudes and agendas, it is more crucial than ever that journalism teaching and practice acknowledges the importance of the responsible handling of suicide.

Much of the debate over media coverage of suicide has focused on the danger of encouraging copycat behaviour (known as the Werther effect after Goethe's 1774 novel, *The Sorrows of Young Werther*, which was believed to have triggered a series of suicides across Europe). The BBC *Producers' Guidelines* suggests that the factual reporting of suicides may encourage others and thus reports should avoid graphic details of suicide methods. Special care should be taken when the method is unusual. According to Mike Jempson, director of MediaWise, international research from countries as diverse as Taiwan, Japan, the United States and Sri Lanka suggests that copycat suicides are undeniable facts (Jempson 2008). Oxford University's Centre for Suicide Research examined 90 studies from around the world and found that more than half identifed evidence that suicides reported in the media were followed by a rise in the number of cases. None had identified a drop (Wilby 2008e). The Oxford research also found that imitation was more likely when people could identify with the suicide victim in some way – for example, age, gender or nationality.

In January 2004, the Prison Service blamed the media's sensational coverage of the death in prison of serial killer Harold Shipman for a spate of hangings by inmates. In the five days after Shipman was found dead at Wakefield Prison, five prisoners – including three on remand – were found hanged in their cells. The Service was particularly annoyed over the graphic instructions given by the *Sun* to Rod Whiting, the killer of schoolgirl Sarah Payne, on how to take his life. In 2003, 94 people in custody killed themselves and there were an estimated 15,000 cases of inmates self-harming, a 30 per cent increase on the previous year. Critics claimed over-crowding was a crucial factor (Morris 2004).

Suicides appeared to rise when photographs of the victim or location were used or when the report was sensationalised, prominent and repeated (Butterworth 2008c). A US study found that the suicide rate among teenagers rose by 7 per cent during the month after any high-profile suicide. After Marilyn Monroe's death in August 1962, the increase was 12 per cent (Rayner and Savill 2008). A Department of Health handbook, produced as part of the Shift Stigma project, similarly highlights newspaper reports of an unusual suicide involving an easily available household toxin – which were followed by nine cases which used the same method in the following month alone. Another reported suicide in Hong Kong using a barbecue was followed by what was believed to be the first use of this method in the UK. But the copycat theory was challenged by media academic Simon Cross (2007: 20):

> It would appear then that there is a good deal of certainty that sensitive reporting deters 'copycat' suicides. Or is there? Let me ask a straightforward question: how do we know that some who commit suicide may have been influenced by either the suicide of someone else or the depiction of suicide, factual

or fictional? Unfortunately, I have no hope of furnishing you with a conclusive answer to this question since (as I see it) we can never know because the only people who can confirm that they have been influenced by a depiction of suicide are *dead*. It may appear as though I am being pithy with a sensitive issue. This is not my intention since it remains an inconvenient truth that 'copycat suicides' are *by definition* dead and unable to shed light into how 'insensitive' reporting led to their suicide. This simple but decisive point pulls the rug from under the common sense view that some suicides *must* be copycats because they have chosen to kill themselves in a manner akin to someone whose suicide has been reported. However, correlation does not equal causality i.e. because events occur in near time does not mean that one *causes* the other. To surmise that a depiction of suicide influenced someone to take their own life obfuscates the myriad psychological and social complexities engulfing individuals, and which contribute to their decision to end their life.

The copycat issue erupted in 2008 after the South Wales Assistant Chief Constable, Dave Morris, joined the many critics of the allegedly sensational media coverage of 20 apparent suicides by young people in the Bridgend county borough (and not simply the town of that name) of Wales. On 24 January, a news feature in the *Daily Telegraph* depicted Bridgend as a town of utter hopelessness with an unnamed girl saying: 'Suicide is just what people do here because there is nothing else to do.' On the same day the *Daily Express* (dubbing itself the 'greatest newspaper in the world'!) carried the headline: '"Suicide is cool" says friend of death gang' while on 6 February, it headlined: 'Another girl hangs herself in death town' and reported 'fears of an Internet death cult' (Bonnici and Dixon 2008). A mother added fuel to the controversy by claiming the media had put the idea of suicide into her son's head. Other mothers claimed they had been aggressively 'doorstepped' by journalists anxious for scoops. The local MP, Madeleine Moon, joined the fray, accusing the media of exploiting desperate youngsters and encouraging copycats. And Sir Christopher Meyer, chair of the PCC, called on the public to report articles 'which in their view are either insensitive or which provide such excessive detail'. Papyrus, the charity for the prevention of young suicides, also criticised the Bridgend reporting for carrying 'sensationalist headlines and big pictures of an attractive girl that glamourised their suicide' and called for an end to the coverage (Laurance 2008). But Stephen Glover (2008) questioned this approach:

> My suspicion is that young people in Bridgend were as aware of the suicides before the national media took an interest as subsequently. They probably depend more for information on their social networks, many Internet-based, than on 'traditional' media such as newspapers and television.

In the end, is there not a case to restrict suicide coverage only to those when there is a clear 'public interest' involved? In his study of the Canadian mainstream media's reporting of suicide, Raphael Cohen-Almagor (2001: 105–23) found many top media companies had adopted the policy of refraining from publishing individual stories (because of fear of copycat cases) – but did cover suicides when some wider issues were involved. For instance, Mr Gord Sinclair, director of News and Public Affairs of CJD, the leading English radio station in Quebec, told Cohen-Almagor that murder and crimes were covered – but suicide was not a crime and generally of no public interest. But if the suicide caused a traffic accident or involved a public figure, then that would be covered because it had 'public interest' aspects (ibid.: 109). However, Alan Rusbridger, editor of the *Guardian*, in a follow-up interview (ibid.: 119) said journalists must be careful not to sanitize the news. Copycat was not a good enough reason to have a general policy of refraining from reporting suicides.

Concerns also emerged in March 2007 after 100 Internet chatroom users witnessed a British man kill himself online – with some of them allegedly inciting him to hang himself. According to one charity working to prevent suicides, there have been 17 deaths in the UK since 2001 which involved chatroom or sites giving advice on suicide methods. Many search engines, such as Google, already ensure that 'suicide' searches always have prominent links to organisations such as the Samaritans. But, as Jon Ungoed-Thomas reported (2007): 'There are concerns that there is no UK organisation which monitors suicide websites and collates complaints.'

The coverage of suicide bombers, say in Israel, Palestine, Pakistan, Iraq, Afghanistan, Lebanon, Sri Lanka, Turkey and London, also raises further complex ethical issues (Cook and Allison 2007; Chehab 2007). Generally they are represented as lunatic fanatics, inhuman and beyond understanding. But is that the right approach? How can we distinguish them from governments that launch illegal attacks on defenceless countries leading to the countless deaths, poverty, insecurity and trauma? How can the West hope to deal with suicidal warfare unless its complex religious, economic, political, psychological and cultural origins are properly understood? Alex Thomson (2005), chief reporter on *Channel 4 News*, argues that it is wrong to have different terms for suicide bombers in different countries: for instance, in Israel they are known as 'militants', in Iraq 'insurgents' and in London as 'terrorists'. 'The terms "insurgent", "militant" and "terrorist" carry different meanings and gradations of objectivity, even morality.' As a solution, he suggests cutting altogether the words 'terrorist' and 'terrorism' – loaded terms of political abuse used, debased and discredited by governments the world over. 'Just call them suicide bombers . . . And let's leave the "t" words to governments and confine ourselves to the uppercase version when referring to acts of parliament.' Do you agree?

- **Samaritans 08457 90 90 90: www.samaritans.org;**
- **www.papyrus-uk.org;**
- *What's the story? Reporting mental health and suicide.* Available online at **www.shift.org.uk/mediahandbook** or order from 0845 223 5447

How can coverage of disabled people be improved?

A survey by Peter White (2000), BBC's disability affairs correspondent, found up to 30 stories a day in national and local papers on disability. But he concluded: 'A close reading of the press leads me to believe that the disabled person as "newsworthy victim" is still alive and satisfyingly unwell.' Do not the media tend to assume their audiences are able-bodied? If people with disabilities are covered, the focus tends to be on the disability even when it is irrelevant. White expresses concern that in almost every newspaper story about 'Superman' actor Christopher Reeve (who had a freak riding accident and died in October 2004 aged just 52) and 'pornographer' Larry Flynt (who was shot by a stranger) their disabilities would feature large. Yet he stresses that 'disability is a very minor factor in the way people behave compared with all the other quirks and oddities that are driving them'.

A survey of NUJ members in 2007 found 10 per cent were disabled yet a 'worrying' 31 per cent were unemployed. Further evidence of discrimination appeared in a 2008 media report by Colin Barnes for the British Council of Organisations of Disabled Persons which found that, while government figures suggested at least 12 per cent of the population had a disability, in television films and dramas they represented less than 1.5 per cent of all characters. Those shown usually fell into stereotypes such as the Disabled Person as Super-Cripple or the Disabled Person as Pitiable and Pathetic (Barton 2008).

News about disability is usually represented by able-bodied 'experts'. As a booklet produced by the NUJ, People First, stresses: 'People with disabilities are the real experts on their own lives. The organised collective voice of people with disabilities is rarely consulted.' Damaging stereotypes often distort coverage. People with disabilities are presented as courageous, pathetic, helpless, victims, recipients of charity, eternally cheerful, grateful, constantly searching for miracle cures, asexual.[3] How often is it acknowledged that they may be black, lesbian or gay? White also finds distinct advantages in being disabled. Of the war correspondent John Hockenberry, he says:

> We have both found that people talk to us more readily, trust us more quickly, identify with us more strongly. Both of us would admit to having used, and on occasion abused, the trust and identification to get a story. We are not necessarily proud of it but journalism is about publishing things some people don't want to be known. This is never going to be a clean business and eliciting information is what it's about.
>
> (op. cit.)

Looking for a positive example of disability coverage? Well, Ouch! . . . it's a disability (www.bbc.co.uk/ouch/tvradio/) is an extremely imaginative BBC website targeted at people with disabilities. Its publicity takes a suitably light-hearted, irreverent approach:

> Ouch is a website from the BBC that reflects the lives and experiences of disabled people. It has regular columns, features, quizzes, a monthly near-cult podcast, a blog or two and a community messageboard among other stuff. All contributors, well, 99 per cent of them, are disabled – and Ouch's editorial team is rather wonky and deserve big fat special diversity badges too . . . Often media doesn't report how rich and varied the

lives of us disableds are, and so, here we are, putting our necks on the line for BBC bosses telling them that you lot are more fascinating than just a DSS form, a ramp or a massive drugs prescription list.

The *Guardian* also carries a column by Cathy Heffernan, who is deaf. In a piece on 24 January 2008, she wrote on her travels abroad (2008): 'One advantage of being deaf is that it can set you apart from the zillions of backpackers passing through tourist-weary countries, and locals take an interest in you. No common spoken language? *Pas de problème*. Dear travellers use gesture and body language.' Should not the media do more to incorporate the experiences of people with disabilities (such as Cathy Heffernan) as part of their everyday routines? And should not the media do more to promote the interests of people with disabilities? In January 2006, the Disability Rights Commission (later merged into the Commission for Equality and Human Rights) called for new measures to increase representation of people with disability including a requirement for political parties to have a disabled candidate on their shortlists for every Parliamentary seat as well as a target of 20 per cent for the number of disabled people on public bodies (Milmo 2006). Are these not great campaigning issues for the media to pick up?

Style books also often highlight other language issues relating to the coverage of disability: for instance, it is better to refer to 'disabled people' than 'the disabled' which depersonalises them and focuses entirely on their disability; words such as 'cripple', 'deaf and dumb' and 'abnormal' should be avoided. Negative words and phrases should not be linked with disabilities as in 'lame duck', 'blind stupidity' and 'deaf to reason'. And 'wheelchair user' should be used rather than 'wheelchair bound'.

How can coverage of people with HIV/AIDS be improved?

One in 100 people became infected with HIV in the decade between 1987 and 1997 and it killed 11 million people (compared to eight million people killed in World War One). In June 2000, the United Nations reported that 23.3 million Africans living south of the Sahara were infected with HIV – 70 per cent of the global total. By 2008, there were 40 million cases worldwide; 25 million had died (Weeks 2007: 17). In Africa it has become the leading cause of death and the fourth leading cause of death worldwide, according to the Global Fund to Fight AIDS, Tuberculosis and Malaria (see www.theglobalfund.org). By 2050, the disease may have claimed up to 280 million lives (Williams 2007: 171). These are some of the stark facts.

As Jeffrey Weeks stresses (ibid.: 14):

> The pandemic reveals as nothing else the impossibility of separating the sexual and the intimate from other social forces, and the inevitable flows, in an increasingly globalised world, of sexual experiences and tragedies from nation to nation, continent to continent. AIDS has become the symbol, if not the only example, of the risks of rapid sexual change in a world uncertain of its values and responses.

In the UK, by 2008, 89,000 cases of HIV had been reported since the early 1980s making it the fastest growing serious health risk in the country (see the Terrence Higgins Trust at www.tht.org.uk). Men living with HIV outnumbered women who had HIV by 2:1. But the majority of people diagnosed with HIV had been infected through heterosexual sex. Some 43 per cent were living in London. Campaigners warned of growing complacency among UK politicians, the media and the public about the risks of HIV and sexually transmitted infections (STIs).

Originally during the early 1980s AIDS was dubbed the 'gay plague'. For instance, *The Times* leader commented: 'AIDS horrifies not only because of the prognosis for its victims. The infection's origins and means of propagation excites repugnance, moral and physical, at promiscuous male homosexuality.' But since the over-sensationalised coverage in the mid-1980s, when a moral panic exploited and perpetuated fears of the fatal condition – and of sexuality in general – the issue has largely gone off the agenda in Britain (though Princess Diana constantly campaigned over AIDS and the *Sunday Times* ran a prominent and controversial campaign claiming HIV was not the principal cause). The AIDS 2000 conference in Durban gained substantial coverage with sensational comments and statistics emerging. For instance, the President of Botswana claimed his country faced extinction while scientists stated that AIDS represented the biggest infectious disease to befall humanity. But how much did this coverage reinforce negative stereotypes of Africa as a doom-laden continent? How dedicated were the media to campaign consistently for the revolution in spending priorities essentially needed to tackle the crisis?

Some style books highlight areas where special care is needed while covering AIDS-related stories. For instance, the Reuters style book says on reporting claims for an AIDS cure:

> If a story making dramatic claims for a cure for AIDS or cancer does not come from a reputable named source it must be checked with recognised medical experts before being issued (or spiked). If such a story is issued it should include whatever balancing or interpretative material is available from such authorities.

According to a leaflet produced by the Health Education Authority and the NUJ, confidentiality about infection by either a child or adult should always be respected. When names and addresses have been supplied by the police, these should only be revealed with the consent of those concerned.

Some stories perpetuate myths that AIDS can be spread through casual contact such as kissing. It can only be spread through intimate sexual contact, by the sharing of needles by drug addicts, by blood transfusion or from mother-to-infant in pregnancy (though the use of anti-HIV treatment, having a caesarian delivery and not breastfeeding can reduce the risk of mother passing on HIV to baby to less than 1 per cent). On the question of language, the NUJ suggests that instead of 'carrying AIDS', 'AIDS carrier' or 'AIDS positive' (which confuses the two phases of being infected with HIV and having AIDS) it suggests 'people with HIV'. Also, avoid using the term 'high-risk groups' since there is risk behaviour rather than risk groups. 'The fact of being classified a member of any particular group does not put anyone at greater risk, but what he or she does, regardless of groups, may do.' People with HIV often express concern over being represented as 'sufferers' and 'victims': many continue working after diagnosis. It is better to say 'person with AIDS'. In its 2006 report, the PCC, following meetings with the National AIDS Trust, reminded editors of the differences between the offence of 'recklessly' infecting someone and 'deliberately' infecting someone. The former involves individuals who are aware they are HIV positive but still have unprotected sex. The latter must involve evidence that someone consciously wanted to infect their partner. The Trust expressed its concerns after the reporting of a number of court cases involving people who had unprotected sex though knowing about their HIV status.

- The online site at www.aidsmap.com, in French, Spanish, Russian and Portuguese and backed by substantial funds from the government, pharmaceutical and biotech companies, charities and individuals, carries a great deal of useful information. For instance, it lists 3,300 AIDS organisations in 175 countries.

Do the media discriminate against gays/lesbians?

The coverage of gays has improved significantly since 1990 when the PCC ruled against the use of the word 'poofters' to describe gays, at least according to activist Peter Tatchell (2000). He comments:

> Now gay people are more visible than ever before and public attitudes are moving towards greater acceptance. Positive gay images and characters abound on television. Politicians and entertainers are openly gay. The police are serious, at last, about tackling homophobic hate crimes. Gayness is no longer a sickness.

The passing of the Civil Partnership Act in 2005 (and the largely positive response to it in the mainstream media), allowing same-sex unions, and the Employment Equality (Sexual Orientation) Regulations of 2003, outlawing anti-gay or lesbian harassment at work, appeared to symbolise the 'normalisation' of homosexuality. The automatic link between marriage and heterosexuality had been severed.

Other critics point to the underlying macho, aggressive heterosexuality of the mainstream media's culture which automatically marginalises other sexual orientations. Significantly, more than half of the NUJ's gay, lesbian and trans-sexual members had suffered discrimination at work, according to a survey in 2004. Research by academics at the University of Leeds in 2006 found that, during 168 hours of programming, only 0.4 per cent focused on gay and lesbian issues while 80 per cent of that coverage was considered negative. Focus groups singled out the BBC, which they dubbed as 'almost endemically homophobic', as the worst broadcaster in terms of its coverage of gay men and women (Frith 2006). And anti-gay broadsides can still appear prominently in the mainstream media. For instance, Boris Johnson MP, elected Mayor of London in May 2008, commented in the *Daily Telegraph* in 2005: 'Gay marriage can only ever be a ludicrous parody of the real thing' (Williams 2008).

Larry Gross (2003) suggests that gays are always portrayed as controversial by the mass media:

> Being defined as controversial invariably limits the ways in which lesbians and gay men are depicted on the rare occasions that they appear, thereby shaping the effects of such depictions on the images held by society at large and by members of these minority groups.

Most of the sleaze coverage of the 1990s was premised on the reactionary notion of the 'normality' of heterosexual, family life and the consequent 'sinfulness' of variants, though right-wing commentators criticised it for highlighting a new permissiveness in media priorities and intrusiveness. Media commentator Roy Greenslade suggests that 'lots of people, including many of those who proclaim a lack of prejudice towards gays, find the actual acts involved in gay sex, especially between men, deeply repugnant'. And editors are quick to exploit those ambivalent feelings. The most overt manifestations of discrimination can still appear in the redtop tabloids. For instance, the *Sun* has constantly vilified lesbians and gay men. Rupert Murdoch, its owner, is a born-again Christian, vocal in his denunciations of gays. So predictably, it attacked President Clinton's alleged obsession with hiring lesbians and gays and described Janet Reno, the US Attorney General, in this way: 'Her name is Janet Reno and she smokes a pipe. She is six foot tall, with a short shapeless hairdo and has never married.' The innuendo was clear (Page 1998: 134).

A notorious example of anti-gay hysteria followed the hounding of Ron Davies MP after he claimed to have been mugged while on Clapham Common in November 1998. On the same day, *Times* columnist Matthew Parris mentioned on a TV programme that minister Peter Mandelson was gay. Soon afterwards the *News of the World* 'outed' Nick Brown, Agriculture Minister, and when the *Sun* followed it up with the headline: 'Tell us the truth Tony – is gay mafia running Britain?' the country appeared to be in the midst of an anti-gay 'moral panic'. The *Guardian* responded by publishing a poll which suggested a majority of voters regarded being gay as morally acceptable. And on 12 November, responding to the outrage its coverage had sparked, the *Sun* pledged it would no longer 'out' ministers.

But many Christians and politicians on the right argue that media toleration of gays is unacceptable. Significantly, the Pope condemned homosexuality in July 2000 as a 'moral disorder and an offence to Christian values'. The leader of Scotland's Catholics, Cardinal Thomas Welling, gave full support to the campaign against the repeal of the anti-gay Section 28 of the 1988 Local Government Act (which banned the 'promotion' of homosexuality by local authorities), describing homosexuality as a 'perversion'. And Scotland's biggest-selling newspaper, the *Daily Record*, launched a petition to keep Section 28, as Brian Souter, the multi-millionaire chief of the Stagecoach transport empire and member of the Christian fundamentalist sect, the Church of Nazarene, launched his own campaign against repeal and financed a private referendum on the legislation.

Thus, despite the growing acknowledgement of sexual diversity, homosexuality still remains shrouded in mystery and fear. According to Weeks (op. cit.: 12), the result is a terror that makes homosexuality as a way of life impossible. He continues:

> Homosexuality may have come out into the open, it may have made institutionalised heterosexuality porous, but even in the advanced cultures of the West, it is still subjected to the minoritising forces that excluded it in the first place. It remains the Other, even if its Otherness now for many has a warm and friendly face.

Notes

1   See www.wsff.org.uk/media/professionals.php?param=PR_20070202_87, accessed 27 February 2008.

2   Bushell afterwards said he had had flashbacks every day since witnessing the suicide. He told *Press Gazette*: 'In some ways I wish I hadn't taken the picture. I just thought she was going to back off the ledge.' (see 'Papers face PCC probe for printing images of suicide leap', *PG*, 13 January 2006).

3   But not always: see 'Sex on wheels' by Julie Fernandez, *Guardian*, 27 November 2007.

9
Battling for news

The dilemmas of war and peace reporting (and not just on the frontlines)

When a government wages war should journalists automatically give it their support?

Journalists tend to be more courageous in criticising the government when British forces are not engaged; when 'our boys' (and a few of 'our girls') are in action, most of the media tend to back it. But is this right? William Howard Russell's famous despatches for *The Times* from the Crimea chronicled the failings of the army and supposedly led to the resignation of Aberdeen's cabinet. But was he justified in sending his reports? Many commentators who stress the 'inevitable' adversarial relationship between the media and the military focus on Russell's reporting (see Snoddy 1993; de Burgh 2000: 33–4). Yet how much is this myth? Phillip Knightley (2000: 16), in his seminal history of war reporting, *The First Casualty*, says that while Russell exposed military failures he failed to understand their causes. And while he criticised the lot of the ordinary soldier, he never attacked the officers 'to whose class he belonged himself'. 'Above all, Russell made the mistake, common to many a war correspondent, of considering himself part of the military establishment.' Moreover, *The Times* played only a small role in the fall of the government. An important section of the elite was determined on Aberdeen's fall, irrespective of any views expressed in the press.

Were American journalists too outspoken in their coverage of US actions in Vietnam? For the US elite the defeat in Vietnam against a far less technologically sophisticated enemy – accompanied by assassinations, race and student upheavals at home – was a trauma of unprecedented proportions. Many blamed the media. Long after the end of the conflict, it is argued, television images still dominate perceptions of it: a US Marine

Zippo lighting a Vietnamese village, the execution of a Vietcong suspect in a Saigon street, a Vietnamese girl running naked and terrified down a road after a napalm attack. Images such as these, along with press criticism of the conduct of the war, are said to have eroded public support.

Yet how much of this is myth? Surveys showed that media consumption, in fact, promoted support for the war (Williams op. cit.: 305–28). And virtually every Vietnam reporter backed the war effort. A Gannett Foundation report commented (1991: 15): 'Throughout the war, in fact, journalists who criticised the military's performance did so out of a sense of frustration that military strategy and tactics were failing to accomplish the goal of decisively defeating the North Vietnamese forces.' Most commentators have seen a shift to more 'advocacy' reporting following the Vietcong Tet offensive of 1968. But such a shift occurred among the American elite with significant sections beginning to question the costs, effectiveness and overall moral/political justification for the war. The media followed the shift in the elite consensus rather than created it (Hallin 1986: 21; Williams 1987: 250–4; Cummings 1992: 84; Cohen 2001). Susan Carruthers comments (2000: 148): 'As elite dissatisfaction with US involvement deepened, journalists (both print and television) began reporting as "atrocities" American actions which had previously received minimal, or no, attention.' Also, after 1968, many in the US military were concerned to show the difficulties and daily frustrations of the war to the American public and welcomed the press as potential allies in conveying this message. Philip Taylor (2003: 73) also suggests the power of the media in promoting opposition to the Vietnam war has been widely exaggerated: 'It is too easily forgotten that American troops were not withdrawn from Vietnam until 1973. This was five years after Tet, a period just as long and as significant as US involvement in Vietnam before it – and a period longer than American involvement in the Second World War!'

The patriotic imperative lies at the heart of British journalists' culture (Norton-Taylor 1991). Not surprisingly this patriotic loyalty appears strongest during times of war. Both the BBC and ITN have identified themselves as guardians of national morale and national interest during wars. Significantly ITN's submission to a Commons select committee inquiry into handling of information during the Falklands War of 1982, opposed battlefield restrictions on journalists on these grounds: 'Great opportunities were missed for the positive projection of the single-minded energy and determination of the British people in their support of the task force.' Max Hastings, editor of the *London Evening Standard* but most famous for being the first journalist to march into Port Stanley at the end of the Falklands War, commented:

> I felt my function was simply to identify totally with the interests and feelings of that force [the task force] . . . when one was writing one's copy one thought: beyond telling everybody what the men around me were doing, what can one say that is likely to be most helpful in winning the war?
>
> (Williams 1992: 156–7)

Other journalists argue that they have a permanent responsibility for bringing the authorities to account and that their dissident role is all the more important when lives are at stake. Censorship, they claim, is too often used to hide military incompetence and inefficiency resulting in the loss of service people's lives. During the Gulf War of 1991, all Fleet Street significantly backed the 'allied' attacks on Iraq, though the *Guardian* maintained a certain scepticism throughout. Ron Spark, chief *Sun* leader writer, said journalists had a responsibility to support the cause uncritically: 'Newspapers are in the business of telling news and freedom of information is a precious part of our democracy. Yet when we are fighting men and women are in peril and we have no choice but to accept some limitations.' Max Hastings, in the *Telegraph* of 5 February 1991, remained 'unconvinced of the case for objectivity as between the US-led coalition forces and Saddam when even the most moral assessment . . . suggests he is an exceptionally evil man'. Robert Fisk, of the *Independent*, came in for particular criticism when on 23 January 1991, under the headline 'Bogged down in the desert', he described the complete breakdown of convoy discipline on the supply route and revealed details about medical preparations for casualties. Miles Hudson and John Stainer (1997: 235) comment: 'Such reporting was scarcely helpful to the families of those about to be launched into battle.' Should Fisk have exercised more self censorship in this case?

In 1999, the Fleet Street consensus again backed the US/UK attacks – this time on Yugoslavia (with the *Guardian* proving to be one of the most jingoistic) and called for a ground assault. Only the *Independent on Sunday* opposed the war, and its editor (Kim Fletcher) was sacked just days after the bombings ended. Some journalists, however, argue that while an editorial line may back a war, balance can be achieved in the coverage by presenting both sides. For instance, while the *Guardian* backed the Kosovo attacks, some of its prominent columnists opposed them and a large proportion of the letters took a similar 'balancing' line. Similarly, while the *Mail* backed the bombings, some of its most prominent columnists were given considerable space to express opposition.

Governments traditionally criticise media performances as being 'unpatriotic' during wars. During World War Two, Clem Attlee warned the Newspaper Proprietors' Association that if its editors were not restrained, the government would bring in compulsory censorship. The *Daily Mirror* was close to being closed down after a cartoon by Donald Zec showed an exhausted sailor clinging to a life raft with the caption: 'The price of petrol has been increased by one penny.' In 1986, Norman Tebbit criticised the BBC's eminent war correspondent Kate Adie after the US/UK bombing of Libya. Similarly Tony Blair's director of communications, Alastair Campbell, accused the media of being taken in by 'Serb lie machine' during the Kosovo War. The Government's attacks were specifically aimed at John Simpson, the BBC's man in Belgrade after he claimed in his *Daily Telegraph* column that the war 'wasn't working', and at John Humphrys who had said on Radio 4's *Today* programme that the war was 'a mess'. Minister Clare Short even attacked investigative reporter John Pilger in the Commons as a 'traitor' for using his columns in the *New Statesman* and *Guardian* to oppose the Kosovo War.

But how much of this 'flak' is ritual serving to reinforce democratic myths of the adversarial media? Some journalists argue that, given the broadcasters' independence from government, conflict is inevitable during wars. John Simpson, the BBC's world affairs editor, for instance, criticised CNN during the Kosovo crisis for getting 'too close' to the US Government since senior journalists there knew about NATO's plans to bomb the Serb television station but had not warned them. 'The BBC has a difference of philosophy from CNN because we prefer not to get too close to the governments we are reporting on,' he said. He would have passed on the information: 'We're not just scribblers and recorders. We're human beings with consciences and souls' (Hodgson 1999).

Campbell also criticised Yugoslavia-based reporters for not taking risks to witness events with their own eyes. Not surprisingly, such views were swiftly condemned. Michael Williams, foreign correspondent for Radio 4's *Today* programme, commented (1999):

Every day we ran the risk of falling victim to NATO bombs or to the violent reaction of angry soldiers, policemen or ordinary Serbs. Two days after being expelled from Belgrade I returned to the country only to spend nine hours in the hands of enraged military policemen, screaming as they searched my bags and checked my notebooks, holding their guns to my head and threatening to shoot every time I failed to answer a question satisfactorily.

And Alex Thomson, chief correspondent of *Channel 4 News*, stressed (1999): 'Like many, many others, I have been shot at, arrested, roughed up, shelled, abused and robbed by the Serb army through Vukovar, Srebrenica, Dubrovnik and sundry other war crime venues through the 90s. And yes, Alastair, we were telling the public about Serb fascism long before you were losing sleep over it.'

Many rank-and-file journalists certainly remain critical during wars, though their perspectives often differ and their activities gain little publicity. Some are concerned over media stereotyping and demonising of the enemy; some stress the journalist's constant need to challenge government/military propaganda and misinformation; others are concerned to highlight the ruthlessness of American capital's imperial ambitions (as, for instance, in the Middle East and in eastern Europe). Others are motivated by straight pacifist instincts. During the Cold War, Journalists Against Nuclear Extermination was formed by members of the NUJ to campaign for nuclear disarmament; during the two Gulf Wars of 1991 and 2003, Media Workers Against War was one of their most vociferous opponents, while during the Kosovo crisis journalists again came together at a packed London meeting I organised to oppose the bombings. Significantly, no broadcasters or Fleet Street newspaper covered the event.

Did mainstream journalists succumb too easily to government media agenda-setting and manipulation during the Gulf conflict of 1991?

Some journalists argued that government censorship ground-rules were inevitable and necessary during the Gulf conflict. The BBC's Kate Adie, who happily wore a military uniform, commented: 'I'm not just a reporter reporting independently, I'm actually with the army.' Yet many criticisms in 1991 focused on the use of the pools for US/UK journalists in Saudi Arabia to manipulate coverage. Journalists were the real prisoners of war, trapped behind the barbed wire of reporting curbs, according to William Boot (1991: 24). Alex Thomson, ITN *Channel 4 News* reporter during the conflict (1992: 82), used the same image: 'The pools were a prison.' Very few journalists were allowed to travel with the troops and very little actual combat was observed; most journalists were confined to hotels in Saudi Arabia. Those journalists who tried to evade these constraints were harassed by the authorities – and sometimes even by their colleagues.

Robert Fox, with the Seventh Armoured Corps for the *Daily Telegraph*, summed up the situation: 'Too few journalists were locked into the British armoured division for weeks on end with little to do.' David Beresford of the *Guardian* suggests that journalists were supposed to be eye-witnesses to history but added: 'Recent US Defense Department estimates that as many as 200,000 Iraqis may have died suggests that much witnessing was left undone.' The attacks were conducted from the air primarily but only one journalist, ABC's Forrest Sawyer, flew with a fighter jet. Pool reporters confined to ships saw virtually nothing. The pooling system was also used by the military to enforce delays in the transmission of news. Five of the six pool journalists in a 1991 International Press Institute survey complained of delays. Paul Majendie of Reuters, with the Americans, commented: 'At best the copy took 72 hours to get back to the pool. At worst it just vanished.'

Almost 80 per cent of pool reports filed during the 'ground offensive' took more than 12 hours to reach Dhahran, by which time the news was often out of date. Given these controls and constraints should journalists have co-operated with the pools? Some American journalists quit in protest at the manipulation; other journalists such as Peter Sharp, of ITN, and Robert Fisk, of the *Independent*, decided to work outside the official arrangements, being dubbed 'unilaterals', 'mavericks' or 'rovers'. They shared a mixed fate. They were tolerated (they clearly could have been kicked out at any time) but they were also closely watched and heavily intimidated. Many commentators have agreed with the conclusion of Phillip Knightley (1991: 5): 'The Gulf War is an important one in the history of censorship. It marks a deliberate attempt by the authorities to alter public perception of the nature of war itself, particularly the fact that civilians die in war.'

During the US/UK invasion of Iraq in 2003, the mainstream media's pro-war consensus appeared to fracture: why was this and how significant was it?

In 2003, with significant opposition to the rush to war being expressed by politicians, lawyers, intelligence agents, celebrities, religious leaders, charities and human rights campaigners – together with massive street protests – both nationally and internationally, the breakdown in Fleet Street's consensus was inevitable. Significantly, an International Gallup poll in December 2002, barely noted in the United States, found virtually no support for Washington's announced plans for war in Iraq carried out 'unilaterally by America and its allies' (see Ismael and Ismael 2004). And on 15 February 2003, just days before the launch of the US/UK attacks on Iraq, an estimated 2 million people protested in London in the largest demonstration ever seen in Britain. Here was clearly a market that Fleet Street could not ignore. Yet still for the invasion of Iraq, the vast bulk of Fleet Street backed the action (though columnists and letter writers were divided). Rupert Murdoch's mass-selling *Sun*, *News of the World*, *Times* and *Sunday Times* (along with virtually all his other global media outlets) were gung-ho backers of the military action. The *Independents*, carrying prominently the critical views of foreign correspondent Robert Fisk, were the most hostile. Following the massive global street protests on 15 February, the *Independent on Sunday* editorialised: 'Millions show this is a war that mustn't happen' (see Keeble 2007: 208–9).

The *Guardian* did not criticise military action on principle but opposed the US/UK rush to war and promoted a wide range of critical opinions. Yet significantly, its sister paper, the *Observer* (generally regarded as a 'liberal', left-of-centre newspaper famous for its brave opposition to Britain's invasion of Suez in 1956) was one of the most vociferous supporters of the military action. As Nick Davies comments (2008a: 331) in his wide-ranging critique of the *Observer*'s pro-war shift under editor Roger Alton: 'this flagship of the left was towed along in the wake of a determinedly right-wing American government: on this crucial, long-running story, the essential role of journalism to tell the truth, was compromised.'

The *Mirrors* were also 'anti' in the run up to the conflict (perhaps more for marketing reasons since the Murdoch press was always going to be firmly for the invasion) with the veteran dissident campaigning journalists

John Pilger and Paul Foot given prominent coverage. But then, after editor in chief Piers Morgan claimed his paper's stance attracted thousands of protesting letters from readers, their opposition softened. And the *Mail's* managed to stand on the fence mixing both criticism of the rush to military action with fervent patriotic support for the troops during the conflict.

The pro-war bias was not limited to the mainstream press. A major survey by researchers at the universities of Manchester, Liverpool and Leeds, published in December 2006, found that in considering the 'humanitarian' rationale for the invasion, more than 80 per cent of mainstream media coverage (both print and broadcast) mirrored the government position while less than 12 per cent challenged it (Robinson *et al.* 2006). 'Most reports (54 per cent TV and 61 per cent press) making substantial reference to the WMD rationale for war reflected and reinforced the coalition argument by, for example, relaying the coalition's claims in unproblematic terms.'

What impact did the embedding of journalists with 'frontline' troops have on the coverage of the 2003 invasion of Iraq?

Most of US/UK imperialism advances essentially in secret. Both countries have deployed forces virtually every year since 1945 – most of them away from the glare of the media (Peak 1982). But at various moments the US/UK chooses to fight overt, manufactured 'wars'. We, the viewers and readers, have to see the spectacle. It has to appear 'real'. During the first Gulf 'war', the pooling system was used to keep correspondents away from the action (Keeble 1997: 109–26; McLaughlin 2002: 88–93). And since most of the action was conducted over the 42 days from the air, with journalists denied access to planes, the reality of the horror was kept secret.

In contrast, during the 2003 conflict, journalists were given remarkable access to the 'frontlines'. And those frontline images and reports from journalists who were clearly risking their lives, aimed to seduce the viewer/reader with their facticity; the correspondents were amazed at their 'objectivity'. Yet beyond the view of the camera and the journalist's eye-witness, with the war unproblematised, the essential simulated, mythical nature of the conflict lay all the more subtly and effectively hidden (see Keeble 2004b; Hammond 2007). Moreover, military censorship regimes always serve essentially symbolic purposes – expressing the arbitrary power of the army over the conduct and representation of 'war'. Significantly Defence Minister Geoff Hoon claimed: 'I think the coverage . . . is more graphic, more real than any other coverage we have ever seen of a conflict.' Most of the critical mainstream coverage highlighted the information overload. But, as David Miller (2003) commented: 'It is certainly true to say that it is new to see footage of war so up-close but it is a key part of the propaganda war to claim that this makes it "real".'

Some 775 journalists were embedded with military units, including 128 from UK media (such as the *Western Daily Press, Scotsman, Manchester Evening News, Ipswich Evening Star* and *Eastern Daily Press*). Some 70 per cent of embeds were from US national media, 10 per cent from US local media while 85 were women (11 per cent). In all, 352 slots were with the army; 214 with the marines; 124 with the navy; 71 with the air force and 15 with Special Operations 15 (Seib 2004: 53). Vietnam reporter for the Forth Worth *Star-Telegram* (and later CBS news correspondent), Ron Schieffer, welcomed the system: 'I think putting reporters with the military gave the reporters a better chance of coming to know the military and I dare say it gave the military a chance to have a better understanding of what the press does. So I think it was good for both sides' (see Sylvester and Huffman 2005: 20). According to Phillip Knightley (2003):

> The idea was copied from the British system in World War 1 when six correspondents embedded with the army on the Western front produced the worst reporting of just about any war and were all knighted for their services. One of them, Sir Phillip Gibbs, had the honesty, when the war was over, to write: 'We identified ourselves absolutely with the armies in the field.' The modern embeds, too, soon lost all distinction between warrior and correspondent and wrote and talked about 'we' with boring repetition.

As *The Times* media commentator, Brian MacArthur, reported (2003): 'Embeds inevitably became adjuncts to the forces.' An analysis commissioned by the Ministry of Defence of newspaper content produced by embeds found that 90 per cent of their reports were 'either positive or neutral' (Miller 2004). Audrey Gillan, with the Household Cavalry for the *Guardian*, was one of the few to accuse the military of censorship. She reported that soldiers complained of being like mushrooms – kept in the dark with you know what shovelled on top of them – but she could not use this phrase for fear of upsetting the brigade HQ.

Some 5,000 journalists were in the Gulf region to cover the hostilities. Two thousand were in Kuwait and on ships with the US and UK naval task forces in the Arabian Gulf; 290 were in Baghdad; 900 in Northern Iraq with Kurdish fighters: the rest were in Jordan, Iran, Bahrain and at the Allied Central Command in Doha, Qatar (Milmo 2003). Here there was little consistent challenge to the dominant military agenda. On one occasion *New York* magazine writer Michael Wolff (2003) dared to break ranks and ask the provocative question: 'Why are we here? Why should we stay? What's the value of what we're learning at this million-dollar press center.' He was soon to pay the price for his daring. Fox TV attacked him for lacking patriotism and after right-wing commentator Rush Limbaugh gave out his email address, one day Wolff received 3,000 hate messages.

Unprecedented access to the 'front lines' was the carrot, but the stick was always on hand. Fifteen non-Iraqi journalists were killed, two went missing and many unilateral non-embeds were intimidated by the military. Had there been the same death rate for journalists during the Vietnam war, there would have been 3,000 killed. As John Donvan (2003) argued, 'coalition forces saw unilaterals as having no business on their battlefield'. Unilateral Terry Lloyd, of ITN, was killed by marines who fired at his car; Reuters camera operator Tara Protsyuk and Jose Couso, a cameraman for the Spanish TV channel Telecino, died after an American tank fired at the fifteenth floor of the Palestine hotel in Baghdad while Tayek Ayyoub, a cameraman for Al-Jazeera, died after a US jet bombed the channel's Baghdad office. In all, seven journalists were killed in US attacks. A major report by Committee to Protect Journalists, *Permission to Fire*, blamed the US army for a breakdown in communication with the media and claimed the attack on the Palestine Hotel could have been avoided. Yet an investigation by the US military, released in November 2004, failed to explain why troops were not made aware the hotel was widely used by journalists (Tomlin 2008). The killings of journalists by US forces in Iraq continued relentlessly, even after the official ending of hostilities by President Bush on 1 May 2003. Of the 127 journalists and media workers killed in Iraq since 20 March 2003 and up until April 2008, at least 16 journalists and six media-support staffers were killed by US forces (ibid.).

According to BBC correspondent John Simpson (2004: 359), a cameraman from Al-Jazeera television channel, Akil Abdul-Amir, came under fire from British artillery while they were filming the shelling of food warehouses west of Basra. Simpson added: 'This is, however, the only incident I have come across where British forces attacked journalists.' Two journalists working for RTP Portuguese television, Luis Castro and Victor Silva, were held for four days, had their equipment, vehicle and video tapes confiscated and were then escorted out of Iraq by the 101st Airborne Division. How many Iraqi journalists perished in the slaughters we will never know. For the most of the Western mainstream media they are non-people.

While the threats to war correspondents are clearly growing all the time, one small victory was gained by *Washington Post* reporter Jonathan Randall in December 2002 when his refusal to testify in The Hague against former Yugoslav prime minister Radoslav Brdjanin was accepted by an appeals court. It was felt that testifying would endanger war correspondents (*Index on Censorship* 2003: 169). In 2002, the decision by the BBC's Belgrade correspondent Jacky Rowland to testify against former Serbian president Slobadan Milosevic at the war crimes tribunal in the Hague, had drawn contrasting responses. Some journalists admired her courage; others claimed that by being seen to collude with authority, the BBC risked losing its hard-won reputation for impartiality and could even put correspondents' lives in danger. What do you think?

Should journalists accept restrictions and report from 'enemy' countries?

Journalists reporting from Berlin would have been unthinkable during World War Two. Yet during the undeclared Falklands, Gulf and Kosovo wars, British journalists sent despatches from 'enemy' territory, though not without sparking some major controversies. A number of prominent journalists (such as Peregrine Worsthorne in the *Sunday Telegraph*) and politicians argued in 1991 that journalists based in Baghdad would inevitably become pawns of the Iraqi dictatorship. Alexander Cockburn reported that the US attaché in Baghdad instructed all Americans to leave the capital just before the bombings began, while John Simpson revealed in his history of the conflict (1991: 277): 'President Bush himself telephoned various American editors to urge them to evacuate their teams. That frightened a lot of people.' CNN's Peter Arnett came in for particularly severe criticisms in the United States for his reporting. In Britain, anger at the BBC's presence in Baghdad boiled over after US jets attacked the al Ameriyya shelter, killing hundreds of women and children. Reporter Jeremy Bowen looked distinctly distressed as he consistently refused to be drawn by anchorman Michael Buerk to say the shelter appeared to have a dual military purpose, as the military and most of Fleet Street claimed the following day. *Today* said the broadcasters were 'a disgrace to their country'; the *Mail on Sunday* said the coverage, not the bombing, was 'truly disgusting' and 'deplorable'. As Steve Platt observed, the only occasion on which Fleet Street expressed 'outrage' during the war was over the BBC's coverage of the shelter disaster. 'Outrage over BBC bias' headlined an edition of the *Express* (see Keeble 1997: 166–72).

Just before the Iraq invasion of 2003, a number of British and American media organisations withdrew their correspondents from Baghdad, citing anxieties over safety or the usefulness and reliability of their copy. Home Secretary David Blunkett complained on 2 April that journalists reporting behind 'enemy lines' were treating US and British soldiers and the Iraqi regime as moral equivalents while Foreign Secretary Jack Straw claimed the media pressure over the conflict would have made World War One more difficult to win. Tory MP Christopher Chope joined in claiming the BBC's reporting of Iraqi statements meant taxpayers were being 'forced to subsidise Saddam Hussein's propaganda campaign'. But Alan Rusbridger, editor of the *Guardian*, was convinced he was right to keep a number of reporters in the Iraqi capital. He commented (2003):

> Yes, they were – initially at least – working under restrictions. But none of those I've spoken to seems to think that they were unduly compromised by this. And it may or may not be significant that most of the obvious examples of misleading reporting came, not from the reporters actually inside Baghdad, but from journalists elsewhere, some of them travelling with the coalition forces.

Suzanne Goldenberg had spent 89 days in Baghdad and her reporting 'humanised the people who were, in conventional news reporting terms, supposed to be the enemy'.

Central to the controversy over the presence of reporters in 'enemy' countries is the belief that the 'enemy' issue propaganda (which goes on to 'infect' British journalists based in their capitals) while 'our side' reports the truth. But how true is this? Moreover, the controversy, in focusing on the role of frontline reporters, tends to downplay the significance of journalists based 'at home'. In fact, some of the greatest war reporting has been done far from the battle zones. For instance, the exposure of the My Lai atrocity (in which men, women and children were massacred on 16 March 1968) raised profound questions about the conduct of US soldiers in Vietnam. But it was exposed by freelance reporter Seymour Hersh, of the small, alternative Despatch News Service, based in Washington after all of the US top media outlets rejected the story. According to John Pilger (2003), there were 649 reporters in Vietnam at the time of the massacre: none reported it. 'The unspoken task of the reporter in Vietnam, as it was in Korea, was to normalise the unthinkable – to quote Edward Herman's memorable phrase.' And Phillip Knightley commented (2000: 428):

> It was the racist nature of the fighting, the treating of the Vietnamese 'like animals' that led inevitably to My Lai and it was the reluctance of correspondents to report this racist and atrocious nature of the war that caused the My Lai story to be revealed, not by a war correspondent, but by an alert newspaper reporter back in the United States – a major indictment of the coverage of the war.

However, maverick US intellectual and journalist Noam Chomsky argued that, in the context of the mass slaughter of civilians by US troops, My Lai represented merely 'a tiny footnote to one of these operations, insignificant in context' (Chomsky 2000: 167–8).

> It gained a lot of prominence later after a lot of suppression and I think the reason is clear: it could be blamed on half-crazed uneducated GIs in the field who didn't know who was going to shoot at them next, and it deflected attention away from the commanders who were directing atrocities far from the scene – for example, the ones plotting the B52 raids on villages.

Were the media right to agree to the news blackout over Prince Harry's deployment to Afghanistan in 2008?

During the Falklands conflict of 1982 Prince Andrew, the Duke of York, served on the aircraft carrier HMS Invincible. No media blackout was necessary. There were no suggestions that his presence on the frontline was putting the lives of other soldiers at risk. It was very different in 2008. Then, the media – following an agreement between the Ministry of Defence and the Society of Editors – simply went mum over Prince Harry's deployment to Helmand province, Afghanistan in December 2007. And amazingly, in this age of transparency, tabloid hysteria and surveillance when it appears hardly any secrets can be held for any length of time, the global embargo lasted ten weeks! On 26 December, eight days after Harry had been deployed, the Ministry of Defence received a call from US broadcast channel, CNN, saying they were planning to run the story. After a short discussion they quickly fell into line (Green 2008). A soldier also approached the *Sun* with photographs of Harry witnessing the beheading of a live goat during Christmas Day celebrations – but this, of course, never saw the light of day. Thus, while an Australian women's magazine, *New Idea*, first leaked the story on 7 January, the global embargo was not lifted until Matt Drudge's notorious US gossip website, the Drudge Report (www.drudgereport.com), spilled the beans on 28 February.

So poor Harry had to quit the front – and the international media went immediately bananas. The BBC Ten O'Clock News devoted its first 15 minutes to the story; the *Sun* carried nine pages of coverage (plus a big poster pull-out of the handsome 'hero'); the *Mirror* 14 pages, the *Daily Mail* ten. Harry appeared to have found the whole war thing 'fun'. It had helped him feel 'normal' (yet killing Taliban in an unnecessary and outrageously expensive conflict was a somewhat strange way of achieving 'normality'). A clearly delighted Bob Satchwell, executive director of the Society of Editors, commented: 'There were some editors who thought it was a great idea and some who didn't think it was such a great idea. But the consensus was that because [Harry] is going we have got to do this for his safety and more importantly for the safety of the soldiers around him' (Crummy and Smith 2008).

What do we learn from the Warrior Prince saga? Perhaps more than anything else, does it not illustrate the extent to which over the decades since the Falklands War the global media (despite all the dire warnings about Internet freedoms) have been seduced into embarrassing levels of complicity by the military and political elite? In 2005, the British media had similarly exposed themselves to international ridicule when they respected a Downing Street request not to reveal Prime Minister Tony Blair's holiday location for 'security reasons' – even though a US-based agency was regularly filing exclusive pictures from the location and a Google search could easily identify it.

And did not the media chiefs who backed the Harry embargo expose themselves to allegations that they had signed up to nothing more than a sophisticated PR stunt that ultimately served to lend legitimacy to a conflict and a royal family – both of which should be subject to rigorous, radical critique? In short, the Hero Harry story was deflecting attention away from the real Afghan news – that this was an unnecessary, expensive war (leading to massive civilian casualties) which Britain should quit immediately. According to John Tulloch (2008), the coverage provided crucial 'good news' to the media from an essentially 'bad news' conflict:

> Something quite ancient is being celebrated. But of course the modern function of this coverage is to dissociate the royals from the despised political class who have got our troops stuck there, provide a positive story from Afghanistan and restore the image of the army. Afghanistan becomes an adventure. Instead of the mirror of our limitations and society's decadence, the army becomes again the mystical mirror of society in which a warrior elite redeems us and 'Britishness'. Harry, like Shakespeare's Prince Hal, is groomed to be the author of our redemption. One of the founding myths of Britishness is Shakespeare's Hal renouncing Falstaff and becoming a military leader. What does all this really mean? It means nothing. Or rather, it represents a quest for meaning. 'Contemporary war is both a pragmatic exercise in risk management and an attempt to recover a sense of historical purpose' observes Philip Hammond (2007: 122). One doesn't have to be a mad post-modernist to see that meaning has somehow to be injected into a meaningless war.

Ultimately the Hero Harry coverage could only further damage the public's trust in the media – since they would be left thinking: 'If the media can shroud Harry's frontline fun and games in secrecy, what other more important secrets are they hiding away?'

Do mainstream media reports sanitise war?

On the one hand, journalists argue that the public simply has not the stomach for seeing horrific images of warfare: their self censorship is responding to these perceptions. As John Simpson commented: 'Television viewers no doubt want to be informed about the world but they do not enjoy being shocked.' On the other hand, the media are criticised for presenting a sanitised view of war. Anti-war campaigners argue that showing the 'brutal, horrific realities' will jolt people out of their apathy; others argue that journalists have a professional responsibility to show the 'truth', however unsettling it may be. And according to Miles Hudson and John Stainer (op. cit.: 315) modern mass media coverage of war has proved an 'enormous bonus to mankind': 'Could the carnage on the Somme, Passchendale or Verdun possibly have continued if it had been witnessed nightly in millions of European sitting rooms? The answer must be that it could not.'

Martin Bell, the white-suited BBC war correspondent turned Independent MP, has called for the 'journalism of attachment' arguing forcefully (1998: 21) that the media are increasingly failing in their representation of 'realworld violence'. Broadcasters were becoming more concerned with ratings than the truth:

> Some images of violence – as for instance most of the pictures of both the market place massacres in Sarajevo – are almost literally unviewable and cannot be inflicted on the public. But people have to be left with some sense of what happened, if only through the inclusion of pictures sufficiently powerful at least to hint at the horror of those excluded. To do otherwise is to present war as a relatively cost-free enterprise and an acceptable way of settling differences, a one-sided game that soldiers play in which they are seen shooting but never suffering. The camera shows the outgoing ordnance but seldom the incoming.

Veteran war correspondent and Middle East specialist Robert Fisk agrees. 'Pain, death, massacre are now all of "potential use to the enemy",' he comments. 'But war is not primarily about cynicism or defeat or victory or danger or blood. It is about pain and, ultimately, about death. Death, death, death. It's a word you don't often hear on CNN or Sky TV or BBC or even RTE. Having persuaded ourselves that we can go to war without casualties we don't believe in death any more.' Paradoxically, as media coverage portrays 'bloodless' wars, Hollywood recreates violence with ever increasing graphic 'realism'. Fisk adds:

Saving Private Ryan was the final touch in this recreation. Why bother to visit wars when you can act them out in virtual reality? Why bother to smell the shit and blood – and those smells, unhappily, are exactly what you find in frontline hospitals – when you can watch wars without such distractions?

Criticisms of the media's sanitising of wars have tended to focus on the coverage of the Gulf conflict. This was largely represented as a Nintendo-style, bloodless conflict fought by the 'heroic' allies with 'surgical', 'precise', super-modern weaponry. Shots from video cameras on missiles heading towards their targets (shown on television and reproduced in the press) meant viewers actually 'became' the weapons. These images, constantly repeated, came to dominate the representation of the Gulf conflict (and later the Kosovo War). As Kevin Robins and Les Levidow comment (1991: 325):

> It was the ultimate voyeurism: to see the target hit from the vantage point of the weapon. An inhumane perspective. Yet this remote-intimate kind of watching could sustain the moral detachment of earlier military technologies. Seeing was split off from feeling: the visible was separated from the sense of pain. Through the long lens the enemy remained the faceless alien.

Also during the Kosovo War, many critics argued that the media failed to convey its real horror. According to Phillip Knightley (2000: 505), between 10,000 and 15,000 civilians were killed, thousands were traumatised and left jobless and in terrible poverty (see Chomsky 1999; Hammond 2000; Hammond and Herman 2000). But these figures were rarely reported. When refugee convoys were bombed by NATO jets they were 'mistakes' (rather than moral outrages) or blamed on 'Milosevic'. Kate Adie, however, prefers to stress the importance of the journalist's self censorship when covering scenes of appalling violence. 'I've seen things I would never put on the screen. It is immensely upsetting to see humans dead on-screen or alive being mistreated. A corpse is OK if it is not being interfered with. If it is kicked or bits are being removed, that is not acceptable.' She had once witnessed an infant crucifixion but would never screen it (Methven 1996).

The issues are still further complicated since complex historical, political and ethical factors so often collide in the coverage of wars. The significance and power of images together with attitudes towards taste can change over time. For instance, John Taylor (1998: 22) highlights the way in which Eddie Adams' now famous picture of General Loan summarily executing a Vietcong suspect in a Saigon Street on 1 February 1968 appeared when its moral and political dimension was acceptable to journalists: Harold Evans, a former editor of *The Times*, reports how in 1962 Dickey Chapelle photographed a Vietcong prisoner about to be executed by his captor, a South Vietnamese soldier with a drawn gun. But this picture was 'universally rejected and published only in an obscure little magazine', probably because in 1962 the war in Vietnam was too small or viewed too favourably for hostile coverage.

The decisions facing journalists are clearly never easy. To complicate the issue further for broadcasters, different criteria apply to programmes throughout the day's schedule. For instance, images following the horrific massacre in Bosnia at Amici were not shown during the day but later, following the 9 p.m. threshold, on *Channel 4 News* and *News at Ten*.

During the US/UK invasion of Iraq in 2003, critics also argued that the mainstream media still failed to show the real horror of warfare with the press constantly reaffirming the propaganda stress on 'precision', 'clean' and 'humanitarian' conflict. Yet this appeared to reach new heights of exaggeration. As John Pilger (2004) reported, according to the non-governmental organisation Medact, between 21,700 and 55,000 Iraqis died between 20 March and 20 October 2003. Deaths and injury from unexploded cluster bombs were put at 1,000 a month. Pilger added: 'These are conservative estimates: the ripples of trauma throughout the society cannot be imagined.' But the *Sun*, of 20 March 2003, reported beneath the headline: 'The first "clean" war': 'A senior defence source said last night: "Great attention to precision-guided weapons means we could have a war with zero casualties. We are a lot closer towards that ideal. We may be entering an era where it is possible to prosecute a humanitarian war."' In effect, could not the military's rhetoric about precision and smart weapons have betrayed its ultimate ambition – to destroy war itself? Postmodernist iconoclast Jean Baudrillard (2003: 16) highlights the contradictions of a hyper-militarised society which still 'operates on the basis of the exclusion of death, a system whose ideal is an ideal of zero deaths'. Even the *Guardian*, one of the most critical of the US/UK rush to invade Iraq, reported on 19 March: 'The last Gulf war may have marked the introduction of space age weapons – from laser-guided bombs to cruise missiles smart enough to know which set of Baghdad traffic lights to turn left at – but as collateral damage figures later proved, the technologies were still largely in their infancy' (see Keeble 2005b).

Following the Ameriyya shelter bombing by an American Stealth jet during the Gulf massacres of 1991 (when hundreds of Iraqi women and children perished) most of Fleet Street blamed "Saddam", described it as a propaganda coup for the Iraqi leader or claimed it was inevitable (Keeble 1997: 166–72). All of this was part of a strategy to deflect blame for the atrocity away from its perpetrators. Similar strategies appeared during the 2003 invasion. For instance, after a bomb fell on a Baghdad market on 26 March most of Fleet Street followed the military agenda and questioned whether the Iraqis (incredibly) had fired the missile. In the *Mail* of 27 March, the headline focused on 'the propaganda coup Saddam had hoped for' while correspondent Ross Benton reported: 'It was the first major incident of "collateral damage" since the war began but allied officials said they could not confirm that the bombs were dropped by US or British warplanes.' The *Sun* on the same day headlined 'Who's to blame?' and reported: 'if the market blasts were caused by off-target Allied bombs, it will be a propaganda gift to Saddam.' The *Guardian*, alongside a moving eye-witness account by Suzanne Goldenberg of the aftermath of the bombings, highlighted US 'confusion over blame for raid'. But the *Mirror*, fiercely anti-war at the time, discounted US denials and condemned it as 'the worst civilian outrage since the war began a week ago'. No paper listed nor profiled the 14 Iraqis reported killed: they were the nameless victims of the carnage.

Even in those newspapers critical of the US/UK invasion, the dominant images reflected the military agenda of marginalising the reality of the slaughter. For instance, a special issue of the *Independent Review* of 9 April 2003 was devoted to images from the conflict. But out of 14 photographs, just three focused on Iraqi casualties while another showed blurred images of bodies on a road after a 'friendly fire' attack on a convoy of US and Kurdish forces. The pro-Blair *Times*' Section 2 issue of 10 April carried 49 images: out of these just five showed casualties (but pictures of 24 British soldiers killed and the coffins of another six were also carried). Similarly the *Sun*'s '24 page souvenir' of 15 April displayed 43 images – all of them predictably celebrating US/UK military heroics, with no casualties shown and Iraqis almost invisible. Again pictures of 'the brave men who died for freedom' were carried. The *Observer* of 13 April carried an eight page 'war in pictures' supplement:

out of 50 images, just six focused on casualties. The dead unnamed are always Iraqi (see Keeble 2004b: 54).

Does not media coverage of wars alert public opinion and politicians to human rights abuses and help stop them?

Here again, views among journalists are strikingly different. You may agree with Mark Lattimer, then communications director of Amnesty International, who argued that media coverage of brutal rebel attacks in Freetown in April 2000 helped inspire British intervention in Sierra Leone. Or you may side with the *Independent*'s Robert Fisk who is more sceptical of the media's powers in halting the torturers: 'I have to question whether journalists really have the effect – long-term – of breaking open those prison doors, of tearing down the scaffolds and dismantling the torture equipment.'

One of the most famous instances of the media inspiring humanitarian intervention by the West occurred after images of fleeing Kurdish refugees filled our television screens soon after the end of the Gulf War in 1991. ITN's Nik Gowing wrote (1991: 9):

> [Six weeks after the end of the war] television further forced the hands of Western politicians. Governments could not ignore the horror of the Kurdish catastrophe which unfolded on their TV screens. The pictures were politically uncom-fortable and strategically inconvenient. But no government dare avoid them. Led by John Major, the British government had to jettison policy papers drawn up in the bureaucratic comfort of Whitehall. On an RAF jet flying to Luxembourg Britain's Prime Minister was forced to sketch out – on the back of an envelope – a concept for 'humanitarian' enclaves. As television showed the deepening catastrophe, George Bush had no option but to follow the British initiative. The US troops which he promised would never send back into Iraq's civil war, were sent back.

The media were representing the views of the compassionate, global community. As Martin Woollacott reported in the *Guardian*, the creation of the Kurdish safe haven was a job 'of which the whole world approved'.

Similar conclusions were drawn in the States. Daniel Schorr commented in the *Columbia Journalism Review*: 'Within a two week period the president had been forced, under the impact of what Americans were seeing on television, to reconsider his hasty withdrawal of troops from Iraq.' How much of this was a myth? While the media represented Premier John Major (rather quaintly) as dreaming up the enclave idea on the spur of the moment, different political pressures probably had far more significance. In particular the Turkish leadership feared the mass of Kurds fleeing over their borders would aid support to the growing revolt of the Turkish Kurds spearheaded by the Marxist-oriented Partia Karkaris Kurdistan (PKK). Given their support during the allied attacks on Iraq, the Turks probably felt they had reason to expect some favours from the US. In fact, Turkish President Turgut Ozal first suggested the haven on 7 April; Major's proposal came the following day. It was also argued that the West's intervention was far from altruistic. Bill Frelick commented: (1992: 27):

> Far from being a breakthrough for human rights and humanitarian assistance to displaced persons, the allied intervention on behalf of the Kurds of Iraq instead affirmed the power politics and hypocrisies that have long characterised the actions of states with respect to refugees and other victims of official torture.

The creation of the enclave in northern Iraq also served as a significant precedent for intervention by the US and UK elites into the affairs of foreign enemy states. Significantly Gowing later modified his views about the power of the media to influence politicians. Commenting on the coverage of the Bosnian conflict, he wrote (1994):

> Certainly news pictures can shock policy-makers just as they do the rest of us ... But television's new power should not be misread. It can highlight problems and help to put them on the agenda but when governments are determined to keep to minimalist, low-risk, low-cost strategies, television reporting does not force them to become more engaged.

You may also consider the saturation coverage of the terrible plight of the Kosovo refugees fleeing the Serb terror helped inspire and legitimise NATO's 'humanitarian' bombing in 1991. Ethnic cleansing on such a mammoth scale (with accompanying stories of massacres and mass rapes) was totally unprecedented in Europe and demanded massive global coverage, according to those who backed the bombing. When NATO forces entered Kosovo at the end of the bombing campaign they were accompanied by 2,700 media personnel (compared to just 500 war correspondents in Vietnam at its peak).

But you may join those critics who accused the mainstream media of meekly following the agenda of the US/UK elites who were determined to draw Yugoslavia into the capitalist bloc alongside other east European countries. Significantly, the worst human rights crisis throughout the 1990s occurred in Colombia where thousands of lawyers, teachers, journalists, trade unionists and teachers have been assassinated. In addition, as Noam Chomsky stresses (1999: 49) the civil war between the government and left-wing guerrillas had created well over one million internal refugees, far more than in Kosovo. In Turkey, as a result of the civil war between government forces and Kurdish rebels, up to three million refugees have been created. In both these cases, the media have remained silent over the refugees' plight. Is not the fact that the US/UK support the appallingly repressive governments of Colombia and Turkey with massive military aid packages significant?

Because it's so hard to define precisely what is war today aren't the ethical issues even more difficult to define?

Most discussions about the media and conflict fail to problematise adequately the notion of 'warfare' or place it with a wider social, economic, political and cultural contexts (see Shaw 1991: 4–5). Historians and journalists conventionally focus on a few major, post-1945 wars. So the main spotlight tends to fall on Vietnam, the Falklands, the Gulf Wars of 1991 and 2003, the NATO attacks on Yugoslavia of 1999 and the US-led assaults on Afghanistan following the 9/11 'terrorist' attacks in 2001. Yet these conflicts constitute only a tiny fraction of US/UK military activities. Some critics point to the fact that the focus on the few major wars serves to represent Britain as primarily at peace, only turning to war in defence against unforeseen threats (from the 'Argies' in 1982; 'mad monster, new Hitler Saddam Hussein' in 1991 and 2003 and 'evil Milosevic' in 1999). Most significantly, the dominant perspective obscures the offensive elements of US/UK military strategies. In fact, Britain and the US have deployed military forces every year since 1945 – on many occasions in secret and away from the gaze of the prying media (Prades 1986; Risen 2006). Do not ethical and political issues become even more problematic in the face of this growth of secret warfare (known in the jargon as Low Intensity Conflict)? (Collins 1991).

Moreover, the ending of the Cold War – with the collapse of the Berlin Wall and the old Soviet Union – has meant that the massively resourced military/industrial complex has had to look elsewhere for 'enemies'. Some critics have suggested that major overt wars today are essentially 'manufactured'. The threats posed by the 'enemy' are grossly exaggerated; in the end US/UK jets are left (as in Libya in 1986, Panama in 1989, Iraq from 1991 to the present and Yugoslavia in 1999) attacking defenceless 'targets'. As *Daily Telegraph* defence correspondent John Keegan reported on the 2003 Iraq invasion (2005: 2):

> Against the advance of an invading force only half its size, the Iraqi army faded away. It did not fight at the frontier, it did not fight at the obvious geographical obstacles, it scarcely fought in the cities, it did not mount a last-ditch defence of the capital where much of the world media predicted Saddam would stage his Stalingrad.

This is certainly not warfare as generally understood. In this new era of manufactured, 'humanitarian', short wars, when Britain's national security is hardly at stake (but when weapons are 'clean' and 'precise' and soldiers are all pacifists at heart) propaganda becomes an even more crucial arm of the military.

As Tony Blair's press secretary Alastair Campbell said on *Panorama*'s 'Moral Combat' on 12 March 2000 (looking back on the Kosovo War): 'It wasn't just a military campaign it was also a propaganda campaign and we had to take our public opinion with us.' James Combs identifies the emergence of a distinctly new kind of warfare with the UK's Falklands campaign and the US invasion of Grenada in 1983. He argues (1993: 277):

> It is a new kind of war, war as performance. It is a war in which the attention of its *auteurs* is not only the conduct of the war but also the communication of the war. With their political and military power to command, coerce and co-opt

the mass media the national security elite can make the military event go according to script, omit bad scenes and discouraging words and bring about a military performance that is both spectacular and satisfying.

The shift to volunteer forces and nuclear 'deterrent' signalled in both the US and UK a growing separation of the state and military establishment from the public. According to some critics, the populist press, closely allied to the state, serves to create the illusion of participatory citizenship. As *The Times* editorial trumpeted during the Falklands crisis: 'We are all Falklanders now.' How justified are these criticisms?

How important is peace journalism as a critique of mainstream coverage of wars?

Too much mainstream journalism is clearly 'war journalism', being violence and victory-oriented, dehumanising the enemy and prioritising official sources. I have always been committed to peace journalism. In the early 1980s, for instance, I launched the group, Journalists Against Nuclear Extermination (JANE), to campaign for peace through the National Union of Journalists. And similar preoccupations have been ever-present in my journalism and academic writing and practice since then. My PhD (published as *Secret State, Silent Press: New Militarism, The Gulf and the Modern Image of Warfare* by John Libbey in 1997) examined the press coverage of the 1991 Gulf conflict. But it was essentially a protest (in appropriate academic prose) at the unnecessary massacres inflicted on defenceless Iraqis by the US-led coalition – and the way the mainstream media hid the reality of that horror behind the myth of heroic, precise warfare.

For me, it has always been clear that some of the most important responsibilities of the journalist are to promote peace, dialogue and understanding; to confront militarism in all its forms – and the stereotypes and lies on which it is based. And yet, while the mainstream media are awash in debates over citizen journalism and the impact of the Internet on traditional routines and professional values little is heard beyond a select group of activist reporters and academics about peace journalism.

One of the most original contributions to the debate over its practical and theoretical aspects appears in *Peace Journalism* by Jake Lynch and

Annabel McGoldrick (2005; see also Lynch 2002 and 2003). Every journalist should be aware of it; every journalism education programme should include it in their reading lists. Most academic analysis of conflict reporting is quick to condemn. But this text is far more ambitious. It both highlights the media's many failings and also offers convincing alternative strategies. Lynch and McGoldrick, drawing on 30 years' experience reporting for the BBC, ITV, Sky News, the London *Independent* and ABC Australia as well as teaching peace journalism at four universities, rightly call for a 'journalistic revolution'. Drawing particularly on the peace research theories of Professor Johan Galtung, they argue that most conflict coverage, thinking itself neutral and 'objective', is actually war journalism. It is violence and victory orientated, dehumanising the 'enemy', focusing on 'our' suffering, prioritising official sources and highlighting only the visible effects of violence (those killed and wounded and the material damage).

In contrast, peace journalism is solution-orientated, giving voice to the voiceless, humanising the 'enemy', exposing lies on all sides, highlighting peace initiatives and focusing on the invisible effects of violence (such as psychological trauma). Dotted throughout the text are comments from practising journalists and advice from the authors. For instance, to resist war propaganda they advise journalists:

* to be on the look out for shifting war aims;
* to avoid repeating claims which have not been independently verified;
* to avoid demonising a person or group; and
* to remind their audience of when war propaganda turned out to be misleading.

In its handbook on reporting crises, the Institute for War and Peace Reporting (2004: 202–4) stresses six core duties for responsible peace journalism: to understand conflict, to report fairly, to present the human side, to cover the background and the causes of conflict, to report on peace efforts and to recognise the media's influence. Journalists also have a responsibilty to know international humanitarian law. As IWRP comment (ibid.: 179):

> seeing an army shell a church or other historic site which is
> sheltering civilians is bad enough; but understanding that

such an attack represents a violation of the Geneva Conventions raises it to another level of importance – elevating what may seem a routine article into a breakthrough report on a major shift in the tactics and implications of the conflict.

Lynch and McGoldrick focus their study almost entirely on the mainstream media and thus fail to acknowledge the contribution of campaigning, alternative media (such as those linked to radical left, feminist, environmental, human rights causes) to the promotion of peace journalism. For instance, *Peace News* (edited by Milan Rai and Emily Johns) is an outstanding publication worth highlighting. Its international coverage is particularly impressive (see www.peacenews.info). So too websites such as www.medialens.org (media monitoring), www.Indymedia.org.uk (grassroots anti-war, environmental campaigns in the UK and globally), www.counterpunch.org (investigative journalism site run by Alexander Cockburn and Jeffrey St Clair) Inter Press Service at http://ipsnews.net (an alternative, Rome-based agency 'giving a voice to the voiceless' and backed by a network of journalists in more than 100 countries), www.warandmedia.org (a group bringing together academics, military and journalists to debate issues relating to war strategy and its coverage) and www.Dahrjamailiraq.com (showcasing the work of an outstanding freelance reporter in Iraq: see Moss 2008).

Lynch and McGoldrick lavish praise on the London *Independent* which they argue 'more than any other newspaper' fulfils the criteria of peace journalism. While the excellence of much of its reporting of the 2003 Iraq invasion (particularly by Robert Fisk and Patrick Cockburn) cannot be denied, critical research suggests that, in many respects, the newspaper reproduces many of the dominant news values of Fleet Street (Zollmann 2007). Nor do Lynch and McGoldrick highlight the many creative ways in which media companies can promote peace – even through their employment strategies. For instance, Belfast's Catholic *Irish News* (the only morning newspaper to put on sales in the May 2007 figures from the Audit Bureau of Circulation) employs both Catholic and Protestant journalists in a city largely divided on religious lines. As editor Noel Doran commented (Lagan 2007a): 'Communities are still divided in where people live, work and study although the *News* has a mixed workforce. And if journalists can work together then there is some hope there.'

What implications do the recent anti-terrorism Acts in the UK have for investigative journalism?

Recent Labour governments have passed a series of anti-terrorism Acts which have profound implications for journalists. Critics argue that the legislation appears directed not only at the perpetrators and supporters of terrorist acts but even those reporting them.

Since the passing of the 2000 Terrorism Act journalists should be cautious of paying suspected terrorists for an interview since it is an offence if money is provided that will be used 'for the purposes of terrorism'. It is also an offence if a journalist finds out that someone has been funding terrorism and does not inform the police immediately. This must be done 'as soon as reasonably practicable'. Journalists could also face five years in gaol if they have information that could secure the apprehension of someone involved in terrorism and they do not give it to the police 'as soon as reasonably practicable'.

The case of four Muslim students at Bradford University (and a schoolboy) who were convicted in 2007 under Section 57 of the Act for simply downloading material from jihadi sites for research highlighted the threats to investigative reporting. The five were finally freed by the Court of Appeal in February 2008. The men always denied having extremist views. The material they downloaded from Internet sites was not intended to encourage terrorism or martyrdom but simply to research ideology. And yet they were originally convicted for being in possession of articles for a purpose connected with the commission, preparation or instigation of an act of terrorism under section 57 of the Terrorism Act 2000 (Judd 2008).

The Terrorism Act 2006 Section 8 makes it an offence for a person to attend any place in the UK or abroad that is being used to train terrorists. As media legal expert Barry Turner comments (2007: 11–12):

> There is no requirement under this section for the person to be actually receiving any training and, therefore, any journalist being present at such a place would effectively be committing the offence. It is clear that a journalist who was perhaps invited to interview any person connected with terrorism would need to be especially careful about where this interview took place. To conduct such an interview at a location used for

training or instructing terrorists could lead to the charge of encouragement and glorification as well as the separate charge of attending the place. These laws undoubtedly threaten effective investigative journalism. Before embarking on any such investigation now the journalist has not only to consider the direct threat to their safety but the other insidious threats posed by such legislation.

In 2008 journalist Shiv Malik faced unprecedented legal action by the police under the Terrorism Act 2000 following a series of investigative articles in the *Sunday Times*, *New Statesman* and *Prospect* on 'terrorist' groups in the UK. Greater Manchester Police raided his home demanding to see the notes from his interview with Hassan Butt, a former member of an Al-Qaeda-linked organisation. The NUJ general secretary warned that the police were now regarding journalists as 'simply another tool of intelligence gathering' (*Free Press* 2008). As Brian Cathcart commented in the *New Statesman* (2008): 'This case also undermines the ability of the news media to report on extremism at all, as talking to journalists will become identical to talking to the police. That in turn leads us to the position where the government can decide virtually alone what the public is told about the terror threat.' And further concerns emerged in 2008 over the new planned counter terrorism legislation that could see journalists arrested for securing information on, or reporting on, the armed forces (White 2008). Police are given powers to arrest anyone for 'eliciting, publishing or communicating information about a person who is, or has been, a member of HM forces which is likely to be useful to a person committing a terrorism offence'. There is no public interest defence, though prosecutions are 'subject to a reasonable excuse'. Clause 65 of the Bill could ban journalists from inquests which could reveal information relating to Britain's relationship with another state – or if considered in the public interest by the Secretary of State.

- The Campaign Against Criminalising Communities (www.campacc. org.uk), drawing together progressive journalists, academics and lawyers, was launched in 2001 to oppose the Terrorism Act 2000 which allowed the Home Secretary to ban any organisation he deemed 'terrorist'.

10

Constraints on journalists – and how to challenge them

Given the many constraints on journalists, how can we talk of the free media?

Murder

The ultimate constraint on journalists is said to be imposed through murder. The killing of Veronica Guerin, crime reporter of the *Sunday Independent*, in Dublin on 26 June 1996, highlighted starkly the dangers posed to intrepid investigative journalists. Yet her reporting style and death (the subject of a 2003 Hollywood blockbuster starring Cate Blanchett) raised serious questions about journalists' training for dangerous assignments and newspapers' cultivation of their star reporters' personalities as a deliberate marketing ploy. In her biography of Guerin, Emily O'Reilly (1998) quotes Ben Bradlee, editor of the *Washington Post*: 'Although it has become increasingly difficult for this newspaper and for the press generally to do since Watergate, reporters should make every effort to remain in the audience, to stay off the stage, to report history, not to make history.' According to O'Reilly, the *Sunday Independent* broke the Bradlee rule – and Guerin paid a terrible price.

In September 2001, Martin O'Hagan, an investigative reporter for the *Sunday World* was shot in front of his wife near his home in Lurgan. He was the first working journalist to be killed in Northern Ireland since the start of the civil war in 1969 (see McKay 2001). Twenty years previously he had been jailed for gun-running for the IRA. Becoming a journalist late in life, he was a key source for the material used in Channel 4's 1991 *Dispatches* documentary, 'The Committee', about the so-called Ulster Central Co-ordinating Committee, a group of loyalists and security forces members who allegedly conspired to carry out sectarian assassinations. Seven years after his murder his killers had not been found. But just before his death, O'Hagan expressed fears he was under surveillance by members of the splinter loyalist group, the Loyalist Volunteer Force (LVF). His death barely registered on the British or international news agenda. But the *Sunday World* bravely faced regular threats and intimidation after O'Hagan's death as it broadened its investigation to take in the activities of all the paramilitary groups. As McLaughlin and Baker commented (2005): 'The refusal of the *Sunday World* to back down despite paramilitary intimidation was a fitting tribute to Martin O'Hagan and the hundreds of other unsung local journalists and media workers who have been killed doing similar work around the world.' And in September 2007, Robin Livingstone, editor of *Andersonstown News* in Belfast, received death threats following a series of reports about Loyalist gangs and drugs dealers.[1]

Fortunately, in Britain and Ireland murder remains an extremely rare threat to journalists though correspondents on foreign assignments and particularly in war zones can be killed and beaten up. Journalists in Northern Ireland, however, regularly face intimidation: the NUJ revealed at its meeting with Northern Ireland's security minister in May 2002 that seven of its members were under threat from paramilitaries. Four BBC journalists arrested at gunpoint (under section 30 of the Offences Against the State Act) while researching a programme to mark the tenth anniversary of the Good Friday Agreement in 2008 were questioned and then released by police but afterwards received death threats from dissident republicans. Left-wing, anti-racist journalists such as Peter Lazenby, of the *Yorkshire Evening Post*, are regularly targeted by Redwatch website and threatened with physical violence. Progressive journalists in Leeds, Liverpool, Sheffield, Sunderland, Birmingham and Cardiff have also been intimidated (M. Taylor 2006). And in many other countries reporting is a profoundly dangerous job. In May 2003, for instance, James Miller, of Channel Four, was killed while filming in the Gaza Strip. Each year the Paris-based group, Reporters Without Borders (www.rsf.org), the US-based Committee to Protect Journalists (www.cpj.org) and the Brussels-based International Federation of Journalists (www.ifj.org) issue reports documenting the numbers of journalists killed in action or jailed. They make for grim reading. In 2007, according to the IFJ, 171 journalists and media workers were killed, 65 in Iraq alone. In fact, since the launch of US/UK invasion of Iraq in March 2003 until early 2008 more than 250 journalists had been killed in Iraq – the vast majority of them Iraqis (such as Khalid Hassan, Salih Saif Aldin and the former President of the Iraqi Union of Journalists in Baghdad, Shihab Al-Timimi) so largely ignored by the Western media (see www.fromthefrontline.co.uk; and Lagan 2007b). As Kim Sengupta reported (2007):

> There is a feeling among Iraqi journalists that the reason their plight receives so little attention is because the majority of those affected are not members of the Western media. On the occasions when the victims were, in fact, foreigners, the scope of the coverage was glaringly different.

In April 2008, Bilal Hussein, a Pulitzer prize-winning photographer for the Associated Press news agency, was released without charge after being held for two years by US forces on suspicion of aiding insurgents. According to the general secretary of the NUJ, Jeremy Dear: 'A media worker is killed every 48 hours and less than 2 per cent of those who attack them are brought to justice, There is a culture of impunity that has to be fought' (*Free Press* 2008b: 4). Iraq had become the most dangerous assignment for journalists in history. Compare previous conflicts: two were killed during the First World War, 68 in the Second; 77 in Vietnam and 36 in the Balkans during the 1990s (ibid.). In all, since the D-Day landing in Normandy in 1944, 2,000 journalists have been killed on duty around the world – all of them remembered in a dedicated park in Bayeux, com- missioned by Reporters Without Borders and the local mayor (Stafford 2008). And throughout the world, journalists, writers and intellectuals are persecuted, jailed and harassed simply for speaking out (see www.indexoncensorship.org). For instance, the Al-Jazeera camera operator, Sami al-Haj (known as 'prisoner 345'), was imprisoned without charge for almost six years and tortured at Guantanamo Bay, the notorious US detention centre on Cuba, until being suddenly released in May 2008 and flown to his native Sudan (Black 2007; Norton-Taylor 2008a). So why was the UK mainstream media so silent about his plight? (see www.reprieve.org.uk, www.prisoner345.net and www.cpj.org/Briefings/2006/DA_fall_06/prisoner/prisoner.html). He was one of an estimated

23,000 detainees in US military custody in Iraq who have never been charged – but deemed a security risk. In 2006, Anna Politkovskaya, a journalist who was fearless in exposing Russian atrocities in Chechnya, was shot dead. She joined over a dozen investigative journalists who have been murdered in Russia in contract-style killings since 2000.

Robert Fisk, of the *Independent*, (and probably the greatest war correspondent of his generation) suggested that journalists themselves bore a certain responsibility for becoming targets in conflict zones (2002). He cited the examples of journalists wearing Pashtun hats in Peshawar or a US Marine costume outside Kandahar. Geraldo Rivera, of Rupert Murdoch's *Fox News*, even came to Afghanistan with a gun proclaiming his intention to kill Osama bin Laden, the Al-Qaeda leader.

> We are all of us – dressing up in combatants' clothes or adopting the national dress of people – helping to erode the shield of neutrality and decency which saved our lives in the past. If we don't stop now, how can we protest when next our colleagues are seized by ruthless men who claim we are spies?

Even in Britain, journalists are coming under increasing threats covering demonstrations, while investigative journalists constantly face intimidation. For instance, after writing a story about a Brazilian illegal immigrant for the London *Evening Standard* in 1997, Jo-Ann Goodwin faced death threats, anonymous phone calls and open hostility. In 2005, freelance photographer Ben Leamy was assaulted by the police while covering a demonstration: he was pushed against a wall, handcuffed and jailed for 11 hours even though he showed his press card and continually told the police he was not part of the protest. His camera was confiscated and held by the police for a month. Two years later he received £4,000 compensation from the City of London Police. In 2008, *Milton Keynes Citizen* reporter Sally Murrer was bugged by police and locked up twice – once for 30 hours – after being accused of receiving leaks from an officer about the police bugging of MP Sadiq Khan while he was interviewing in Woodhill prison a suspected terrorist. Clearly managements have a responsibility to invest more in the training in risk awareness for all their staff, while journalists on dangerous assignments should always be encouraged to work in pairs or threes.

Legal constraints

Many laws exist in Britain restraining the media. In 1992, the White Paper, *Open Government*, identified 251 laws outlawing information disclosure. Two years later the Guild of Editors listed 46 directly relating to journalists. They included the Children and Young Persons Act 1993 and the Trade Union Reform and Employment Rights Act 1993 which imposed reporting restrictions on industrial tribunals involving sexual harassment. The Criminal Procedures and Investigations Act 1998 gave the courts further powers to impose reporting restrictions. Reporters have found restrictions imposed under Section 39 of the Children Act – even in cases where the identity of minors is known. Andrew Johnson (1997b) comments: 'In many cases the knee-jerk response is to impose restrictions and overturn them only when challenged.' In addition, the laws of libel, contempt, defamation, obscenity and 'gagging' injunctions to stop alleged breaches of confidence all act as restraints on the media. In January 2008, for instance, the Ministry of Defence secured a gagging order preventing the media repeating allegations (first reported in the *Guardian*) of abuse by British soldiers of Iraqis. But did this not appear more the act of a government desperate to protect itself from embarrassment than one concerned with national security?

Other controversies have focused on the police's attempts to use the 1997 Protection from Harassment Act against photographers such as Chris Eades of Kent News and Pictures after he tried to take shots of John Major's son James and partner Emma Noble at their new house in Kent in April 1999. By 2007, the NUJ was highlighting the use of injunctions under the Protection from Harassment Act as a 'worry trend'. For instance, freelance photographer Adrian Arbib was originally banned under the Act by npower from taking pictures at a site where protestors were opposing plans of the energy giant to create an ash dump. But after the intervention of the NUJ, the company agreed to amend the injunction to allow journalists to operate. Concerns also grew that the Youth Justice and Criminal Evidence Act 1999 would ban identification of child witnesses. But then after a government compromise, only the naming of alleged perpetrators of crime was banned if they were under 18.

The Public Record Office officially operates a 30-year rule before releasing official documents. But most papers relating to secret events or other sensitive matters are exempt from this and 'closed' to public access for much longer – sometimes for as much as 100 years. This is allowed under the 1958 Public Records Act with the permission of the Lord Chancellor, who does not appear to object very often. In the case of the secret services, nothing ever enters the PRO. As a result of the US Freedom of Information Act, a researcher in Britain can usually find out more about the UK secret services in the US because of their links with the CIA.

The numerous anti-Terrorism Acts passed since the late 1980s are, in reality, used for intelligence gathering rather than securing prosecutions, since only a very small percentage of those held are charged with terrorist offences. They have also been used by the state in an attempt to intimidate journalists into revealing confidential sources. Thus, in 1988, the BBC was forced to hand over footage of the mobbing of two soldiers who ran into a funeral procession in Belfast. Following a *Dispatches* programme by the independent company, Box Productions, in 1991, alleging collusion between Loyalist death squads and members of the security forces in Northern Ireland, Channel 4 was committed for contempt for refusing to reveal its source and fined £75,000.

The Terrorism Acts have other serious implications for journalists. For instance, following the passing of the Terrorism Act 2000,[2] journalists should be cautious of paying suspected terrorists for an interview since it is an offence if money is provided that will be used 'for the purposes of terrorism'. It is also an offence if a journalist finds out that someone has been funding terrorism and does not inform the police immediately. This must be done 'as soon as reasonably practicable'. Journalists could also face five years in gaol if they have information that could secure the apprehension of someone involved in terrorism and they do not give it to the police 'as soon as reasonably practicable'. The police have extensive investigatory powers in relation to terrorism: for instance, they can apply to a circuit judge for an order giving them access to journalistic material. As Frances Quinn outlines (2007: 267):

> The order can require a person to hand over, or give the police access to such material within seven days (or the judge can decide on a different period). If the person is not in possession of the material, they can be required to disclose, to the best of their knowledge, its location, again within seven days.

Other legislation providing powers to order the disclosure of information includes the Financial Service Act 1986, the Criminal Justice Act 1987 and the Police Act, the Serious Organised Crime and Police Act 2005.

Under the Terrorism Act 2006 Section 8 it is an offence for a person to attend any place in the UK or abroad that is being used to train terrorists. The person does not have to be actually receiving any training and, thus, any reporter being present at such a place would effectively be committing the offence. According to legal expert Barry Turner (2007: 11–12): 'It is clear that a journalist who was perhaps invited to interview any person connected with terrorism would need to be especially careful about where this interview took place. To conduct such an interview at a location used for training or instructing terrorists could lead to the charge of encouragement and glorification as well as the separate charge of attending the place.' Turner adds (ibid.: 12):

> These laws undoubtedly threaten effective investigative journalism. Before embarking on any such investigation now the journalist has not only to consider the direct threat to their safety but the other insidious threats posed by such legislation. The press and broadcasters have always been forced to accept the dangers of reporting on terrorism. Their physical well-being has been at risk when approaching fanatical and violent subjects. They are now clearly threatened by laws ostensibly designed to fight the threat they are reporting on. And they are now at an increasing risk of being caught in the crossfire – not only of the terrorist bomb and bullet but in that of the anti-terror laws.

In 2000, concerns also mounted that the Regulation of Investigatory Powers Act (RIPA) would provide a 'Big Brother's charter' (Naughton 2000), since it would allow the police, Revenue and Customs and security services wide-ranging powers to intercept e-mail and other electronic communications. The Act also gives local councils the power to carry out undercover surveillance work if they suspect a crime. Thus, they can follow an individual and record what they do (though they are not authorised to use a recording device) and they can obtain data from a phone provider outlining who owns a number and the calls made (Schlesinger 2008). Scary? The RIPA can also lead to people facing criminal charges if they can not decode files on their computers, even if they did not create them. As Quinn explains (op. cit.: 269): 'If you encrypt your email messages, you can be ordered to reveal the encryption code and if you are ordered to reveal the code, it is an offence to tell anyone that you have done so.' In response, Home Secretary Jack Straw stressed that intrusive surveillance was to be used only in accordance with human rights principles.

Advertisers: the hidden persuaders?

Certainly the media depend enormously on the advertising industry for their survival. For instance, according to Peter Preston, former editor of the *Guardian*, three of Britain's quality nationals, the *Independent*, *Observer* and *Guardian*, are dependent on advertisements for '75 per cent or more of their total take' (2001). Many journalists argue that advertisers exert no influence on reporters' copy. Guy Keleny, of the *Independent*, for instance, argued (2006):

> A free press run commercially has to set a firewall between the journalistic writing and the advertising that pays the bills . . . The journalists do not allow their reporting to be muffled by the interests of advertisers, and the advertisers are free to say what they like in the space they have bought (subject to the law and industry codes) without regard to the newspaper's editorial opinions.[3]

But others argue against this view. The BBC's Andrew Marr, no less, comments (2004: 112): 'The biggest question is whether advertising limits and reshapes the news agenda. It does, of course. It's hard to make the sums add up when you are kicking the people who write the cheques.'

Sometimes pressures from advertisers can be overt as when they seek to influence editorial policy or withdraw support after critical coverage. Edwards and Cromwell (2006: 7) report on how financial giants BP and Morgan Stanley, in 2005, informed major publications of new guidelines requiring their ads to be removed if negative stories about the companies were published. But some critics suggest that more often the pressure operates more subtly: Curran and Seaton (1991: 38) argue that the emergence of an advertisement-based, mass-selling newspaper industry in the latter half of the nineteenth century helped stifle the development of a radical, trade union-based press. 'The crucial element of the new control system was the strategic role acquired by advertisers after the repeal of the advertisement duty in 1853.' Newspapers' focus shifted from overt political propaganda to a more subtle, entertainment-based propaganda. Significantly, the radical, leftist *Daily Herald*, which during the 1930s became the biggest selling newspaper in the world with two million readers, was eventually closed down largely because its working class audience could not attract advertisers (Campbell 2004: 60–1).

According to Anthony Sampson (2004: 243) the power exerted by advertisers over newspapers is 'insidious':

> Today, as newspapers have become fatter and supplements have multiplied, the advertisers have imposed their own choice of subject matter, requiring features about what readers can buy – on shopping, travel, fashion and lifestyles – rather than about social problems or pleasures which are free.

Advertisers are, then, best seen as promoting the values of materialism and consumerism as well as a conservative respect for the status quo. While advertisements encourage us all the time to consume more, the media insist they are serious about promoting respect for the environment. Are there not serious contradictions here? Facts and issues which conflict with the interests of big business end up being marginalised or omitted entirely. Or you may consider ads as the bulwark of the free press, freeing it from any dependency on the state for funding.

The influence of Press Relations, a branch of the advertising industry, on the media industry certainly appears to have grown during recent years. A study by media academics at Cardiff University of four 'qualities' (*The Times, Guardian, Independent* and *Daily Telegraph*) and the *Daily Mail* found that 60 per cent of their reports consisted wholly or mainly of copy from news agencies (such as the Press Association and Agence France Press) and/or PR material. In only 12 per cent of stories could the researchers say that all the material was generated by the reporters themselves (Davies 2008a: 52). Yet this PR influence remains largely hidden from the readership. 'PR professionals generally aim specifically to make their own role in a story invisible, and journalists are happy to go along with that. As the Cardiff report put it: "We found many stories apparently written by one of the newspaper's own reporters that seem to have been cut and pasted from elsewhere"' (ibid.: 53).

According to Karen Sanders (2003: 126): 'Advertising and marketing departments have often been seen as the Great Satan by reporters, besmirching their journalistic purity in the search for filthy lucre.' But other critics claim journalists are too quick to demonise PR and are eager to challenge the 'journalist-as-victim-of-spin' culture. Julia Hobsbawm (2003), for instance, argues that journalists and PR folk should drop their antagonisms:

> Journalism loves to hate PR. It has become the norm in the media to knock us, whether for spinning, controlling access, approving copy or protecting clients at the expense of the truth. Yet journalism has never needed public relations more and PR has never done a better job for the media.

Pressure from proprietors: is this inevitable or a serious threat to democracy?

Over the years, newspaper journalists have also faced considerable pressures from their proprietors. Men like Northcliffe, Beaverbrook, Rothermere, Rowland, Murdoch, Maxwell and most recently Desmond[4] have all gained reputations of being eccentric, egocentric, super-powerful, super-rich – and constantly interfering in the operations of their newspapers. Editorials have been re-written, layouts have been changed; editors have been sacked and favoured hacks have been promoted. Robert Maxwell, owner of the Mirror until his mysterious drowning in 1991, even paid £40,000 to have his offices bugged so that he could keep a close watch on critical journalists. Roy Greenslade, editor of the Mirror 1990–1, said Maxwell 'tried to interfere as often he could' (2003: 513). And as Andrew Marr (2004: 240) observes:

> Proprietors are rich. Journalists, particularly editors, depend on their whims. They are the creatures of the proprietors and that defines the relationship before everything else. Because these are democratic times, in general both sides, proprietor and journalist, make a pretence of some equality. Any decent editor will stand up to the proprietor at times, for the sake of self-respect if nothing else, and to convince the proprietor that he has chosen wisely in having someone who will speak

back. Yet no editor who survives speaks back very often or ignores little errands and favours the proprietor requires.

In May 2001, Michael Pilgrim, editor of the *Sunday Express*, quit after criticising his proprietor, Richard Desmond (with a personal wealth of £1.9 billion, according to the 2008 *Sunday Times* Rich List), for interfering in editorial decisions and suppressing legitimate stories for commercial reasons and to settle scores. Then in January 2002, five senior staff members of *OK!* were sacked allegedly because their proprietor Desmond was 'livid' over the coverage of his fiftieth birthday since it did not contain photographs of certain celebrities and business contacts. Most recently News Corp boss Rupert Murdoch, owner of vast media interests world-wide and with a personal wealth estimated at $8.3 billion, has been described as 'a highly politicised proprietor who perceives himself to be fighting a global battle on behalf of capitalism, the free market and Christian values' (McNair 2000: 20).

Certainly the backing of the Murdoch stable, including the *News of the World* and the *Sun*, *The Times* and *Sunday Times*, was of enormous benefit to Tony Blair and the New Labour project. As Lance Price (2003), former director of communications for the Labour Party, commented: 'Not for nothing did he make a 22-hour journey to address Mr Murdoch's executives at their private resort off Australia in 1995 or to keep in regular contact ever since.' A Freedom of Information request by the *Independent* revealed that Murdoch enjoyed a hotline to Prime Minister Tony Blair at crucial times during his premiership: for instance, the pair spoke three times in the run-up to the 2003 invasion of Iraq (Foley 2008). While News Corp's UK media includes its Fleet Street publications, Sky Television and the publishers HarperCollins, it is best seen as American: almost 70 per cent of the company is generated by its US operation. This includes 20th Century Fox, MySpace and the *Wall Street Journal*, which sells more than two million copies a day and boasts millions more online readers (Robinson 2007a).

Despite being a stout defender of media freedoms, Murdoch shows little hesitation in censoring writers who cross his path. For instance, Doug Gay's religious *Credo* column in *The Times*, was abruptly ended after he criticised the proprietor in 1998. A row erupted after Murdoch, owner of the publishing company, HarperCollins, intervened to ban a book by former governor Chris Patten about Hong Kong and critical of China (where he holds significant media interests).[5] In July 2000 an unauthorised biography of Murdoch by Michael Crick, due to be published by Fourth Estate, was suddenly dropped after the company was purchased by HarperCollins. And in August 2001, Sam Kiley resigned as *Times* Middle East correspondent claiming reports were regularly censored by editors living in terror of irritating Mr Murdoch.

Andrew Neil, former editor of the Murdoch-owned *Sunday Times*, gave the House of Lords communication committee investigating media ownership in 2008, a graphic insight into the proprietor's influence on the newspaper (Rose 2008): 'There's no major political position the *Sun* will take – whether it is its attitude to the euro, to the current EU treaty, or to whom the paper will support in the general election – none of that can be decided without Rupert Murdoch's major input.' Similarly Roy Greenslade, former assistant editor on the *Sun*, said that during the 1980s' clash between socialism and Thatcherism, Murdoch was engaged in an 'ideological war and used the *Sun* to do so' (ibid.). Martin Dunn, editor-in-chief and deputy publisher of *New York Daily News* and a former editor of Murdoch's *Today*, was frank when he said (2007):

> Content, layout, display: he has a view on all of them all and doesn't hesitate to express it . . . Understanding that Murdoch favours a certain politician does not always guarantee that he or she will receive positive editorial treatment, but does make it almost certain that there will be no negative or hostile coverage.

Significantly, in the run up to the Iraq invasion of 2003, all but one of Murdoch's 175 editors across the world echoed his support for the US/UK action (Sampson 2004: 234). And in the United States, all of his television channels overtly propagandise on behalf of the Republican Party. His ties with Saudi Arabia were further tightened in 2005 when Saudi billionaire Prince Alwaleed bi Talal (the world's fifth richest man) increased his stake in News Corporation (Teather 2005). Roy Greenslade (2003b: 673–4) also highlights the power of Murdoch to eliminate embarrassing news from branches of his media empire. In 1997, for instance, it was revealed that News Corporation paid just 7.8 per cent tax on operating profits of £800 million.

> This tax avoidance was totally legal but it said a great deal about the difficulties national governments were facing in dealing with global capital. What was so fascinating was that the revelation was published in the *Independent*. No word appeared

in *The Times*, the paper of record. The power of the propagandist in deciding what should and should not be published reminds us all how precious diversity of ownership remains.

The reclusive David and Frederick Barclay (better known as the Barclay Brothers), owners of the right-wing *Daily Telegraph*, are also known to interfere in the running of their newspaper. In March 2008, for instance, the *DT* failed to report the embarrassing climb-down by the *Daily Express* over its reporting of the Madeleine McCann saga – probably as a favour to Barclays' friend, Richard Desmond, owner of the *Express*. Later, a review by the eminent Fleet Street interviewer, Lynn Barber, was dropped – because it included criticism of the brothers.

In particular, the integration of the proprietors' empires into the world of global finance has given rise to concerns that a vast range of no-go areas has been created for the media. Not surprisingly, proprietors are not keen to have reporters probing into their more murky activities. Maxwell managed to keep the scandal of his pension fund rip-off secret during his lifetime through a merciless use of the libel laws, intimidation and a clever exploitation of journalists' desire for the quiet life (Greenslade 1992). The moguls have also tended to promote their own financial interests through their own media. Tiny Rowland campaigned in the *Observer* against the Al Fayeds following their purchase of Harrods (Bower 1993), Maxwell constantly publicised his many 'charities' and political activities, while Murdoch's media interests take every opportunity to attack the BBC and ITV and promote his own Sky channels.

Investigative reporter John Pilger puts special blame for the *Sun*'s trashy tabloid style on its proprietor, Murdoch. He writes (1998: 449):

> Labour politician Tony Benn is not a hyprocrite, but his principles are anathema to Murdoch. Benn was declared 'insane' in a malicious *Sun* story whose 'authority', an American psychologist, described the false quotations attributed to him as 'absurd'. The Thatcher government's campaign against 'loony' London councils, which probably helped turn the Labour Party in on itself and away from progressive policies, was based substantially on a long-running series of inventions and distortions in the *Sun*. The person ultimately responsible for this is Rupert Murdoch.

But Reiner Luyken, of the German newspaper *Die Zeit*, stresses: 'The most striking effect of Murdoch is self-censorship. Self-censorship is now so commonplace in the British media that journalists admit to it without blushing.' Nick Cohen (1999: 128–9) comments on the role of press magnates:

> Freedom of the press means the freedom for these gentlemen to do what they want. They, and their counterparts in television, have changed journalism from a trade that encouraged reporters to develop specialist knowledge to a kind of feudal system with a few over-paid managers, columnists and newscasters at the top and a mass of casual, pressured and often ignorant serfs underneath.

Perhaps more inspiration should be drawn from countries such as Sweden, France, Norway, Finland and the Netherlands where selective subsidy systems have countered monopolising trends and helped preserve vigorous minority political media (Curran 2000: 46). The *Guardian* also escapes proprietorial pressures since it is run on the principles promoted by its long-time editor C.P. Scott (1872–1929) with editors appointed by a Trust and then left to run the paper as they see fit. As Campbell (2004: 67) argues, the *Guardian* 'remains a benchmark for many journalists of the right way to run a newspaper'.

Many journalists, however, argue that the overall monopoly ownership structures in the mainstream media are an inevitable product of a profit-based economic system within an advanced capitalist society. The media may have their many faults, but at least there is no Orwellian thought control like that which strangled free expression in the old Soviet Union. Simon Jenkins, former editor of the London *Evening Standard* and *Guardian* columnist, argues that 'left wing bias' leads some journalists to exaggerate the influence of the proprietors (Jenkins 2008b):

> Did Lord Rothermere's corporate interest impede the *Daily Mail*'s bold decision to reveal Stephen Lawrence's killers? Did Murdoch's supposed corporatism interfere with *The Times* devoting resources to investigating the money affairs of the Tory treasurer or the *Sunday Times* to exposing cash for honours?

Even at the local level, monopolies dominate. Here, the top four companies, Johnston Press, Newsquest, Northcliffe and Trinity Mirror, account for 64 per cent of the total circulation.As Charlie Burgess comments: 'One by one the locally owned groups are selling out. The corporate owners, however, counter this by saying they allow their papers to be locally managed and that they benefit from sharing back office costs and big investment in state-of-the-art regional printing centres' (2003). And pressures from local proprietors can still be significant. For instance, in 2003, Sir Ray Tindle, owner of more than 120 local newspapers (with a personal wealth of £225 million, according to the *Sunday Times* 2008 Rich List), ruled that his editors refuse the publication of letters or articles protesting against the Iraq invasion. 'I do this, not just as a proprietors to the newspapers, but as someone who served as a British soldier from 1944 to 1947 in the Far East,' said Sir Ray (Bell and Alden 2003: 29). In any case, in an age of media convergence, are not new forms of ownership emerging which require new kinds of analysis? Increasingly the power over the selection, organisation and flow of information is held by the new information providers such as search engine companies, telecoms, Internet service providers. Granville Williams argues (2008: 5): 'Growing consolidation will undermine diversity of both content and ownership and transform the Internet from an open, global means of communication into one designed primarily to serve the interests of corporate brands and commercialism.'

New pressures from the police?

Concerns were mounting in 2000 that police interpretation of data protection legislation had seriously restricted the reporting of crimes over the previous two years. Nearly two-thirds of regional journalists surveyed by *Press Gazette* (14 July 2000) believed it had become more difficult to report crimes accurately as a result of media policies adopted by police forces around the country. Many journalists commented that it was not just details of road traffic accident victims or victims of crime which were being withheld but information about serious crimes – including rape, murder and assault. Harry Blackwood, editor of the *Hartlepool Mail*, commented:

> Many police officers don't want newspapers to report crime
> as they say it increases the fear of crime. Maybe they'd like
> to consider how the victims feel when their house is burgled

and they feel their whole world has collapsed. The victims then discover that the crime wasn't serious enough to merit a couple of paragraphs in the local paper.

In response to journalists' pressure, the Association of Chief Police Officers, in July 2000, said it would advise its members to encourage people to allow their names and other details to be given to the press.

Does the secret state impinge on the work of journalists?

Richard Thurlow (1994: 399) talks of the 'insidious growth of the secret state throughout the 20th century' creating another vast no-go area for journalists. And *Independent* journalist Paul Vallely commented: 'That power corrupts is now a truism. But it does not just apply to the dictators of Africa. It applies to the elective dictatorship which has taken root in Britain since the war whereby governments exercise power largely unchecked by parliament.' According to Clive Ponting (1990: 16): 'In Britain, absolute secrecy has been the policy of all post-war governments.' Today an estimated £750 million is spent annually on MI5 (domestic security), MI6 (overseas intelligence) and GCHQ (surveillance headquarters). Yet some argue that the growth of the secret services is an inevitable and necessary process in an era of political extremism, global terrorism and drug-running – and in the face of threats from such unpredictable 'rogue' states as Iraq, Libya and North Korea. Journalists must simply accept the consequences. What do you think?

The secret state is protected from probing media by a series of laws. The 1989 Security Service Act (actually drafted by MI5 lawyers) placed the service on a statutory basis for the first time and provided it with legal powers to tap phones, bug and burgle houses and intercept mail. The *UK Press Gazette* commented (6 September 1993): 'The greatest invasion of privacy is carried out every day by the security services, with no control, no democratic authorisation and the most horrifying consequences for people's employment and lives. By comparison with them the press is a poodle' (see Urban 1996: 53). The Intelligence Services Act of 1993 created the Intelligence and Security Committee which meets in secret to overview services' activities, reporting to the Prime Minister and not Parliament. Following the 1996 Security Service Act, MI5's functions were extended to 'act in support of the prevention and detection of crime'. The in-coming Labour government then moved to extend the powers allowing the intelligence services and other government agencies to conduct covert surveillance including bugging phones and property.

In 1989, a new Official Secrets Act (OSA) replaced the 1911 OSA which had proved notoriously cumbersome, particularly after civil servant Sarah Tisdall was jailed in 1983 for leaking to the *Guardian* government plans for the timing of the arrival of cruise missiles in England. Then followed the acquittal of top civil servant Clive Ponting charged under Section 2 (1) of the OSA after he leaked information showing the government had misled the House of Commons over the sinking of the Argentinian ship, the *Belgrano*, during the Falklands conflict of 1982. The 1989 Act covered five main areas: law enforcement, information supplied in confidence by foreign governments, international relations, defence, and security and intelligence. The publishing of leaks on any of these subjects was banned. Journalists were also denied a public interest defence. Nor could they claim in defence no harm had resulted to national security through their disclosures.

The system of Defence Advisory Notices (better known as D Notices) also serves to restrain the media in their coverage of sensitive security issues (Liberty and Article 19 2000: 22–4). Once a notice is issued by the Secretary of the Defence, Press and Broadcasting Advisory Committee, editors are asked to censor reporting. The system, introduced in 1912 to prevent breaches in security by German spies, is entirely voluntary (see its website at www.dnotice.org.uk). There are five notices in all: covering the operations, plans and capabilities of the UK armed forces, the nuclear industry, emergency underground oil reserves, and so on (Sheldon 1999). Around 800 media professionals have a copy of the official list (though it is available on the web at www.btinternet.com/~d.a.notices). In July 2000, the new D Notices secretary, Rear Admiral Nick Wilkinson, said the sytem was 'not allowed to stifle debate about politically sensitive matters'. And in November 2007, Simon Bucks, associate editor of Sky News Online and vice-chair of the Defence, Press and Broadcasting Advisory Committee, commented (2007):

> Some people, mainly from civil liberty groups, have been critical of the system in the past – accusing it of indulging in cosy self-censorship. But the media members of the current

committee are no pussycats and demand firm evidence that national security is threatened before agreeing to government requests . . . The current secretary, Air Vice-Marshal Andrew Valliance (whose contact details are also on the website) takes an independent line sometimes to the chagrin of the MoD.

Yet should journalists always co-operate? Some critics argued in 1999 that the harassment of former *Sunday Times* defence correspondent Tony Geraghty after he refused to submit his book, *The Irish War*, for clearance exposed the myth of the 'voluntary' system. Geraghty became the first journalist charged under the new Official Secrets Act after he revealed the extent of the army's surveillance operations and MI5 dirty tricks in Northern Ireland. In the sections the army particularly did not like, *The Irish War* mentioned their Caister/Crucible computers, which contain intelligence data on most people living in Northern Ireland; the Vengeful computer, which tracks vehicle movements around the province; and the Glutton TV camera system, which scans and automatically reads number plates of vehicles at locations as far apart as Derry, Dover and Gretna Green (see Campbell 2000b). The charges were eventually dropped against Geraghty – and later, in November 2000, against one of his alleged contacts, Col. Nigel Wylde. The *Sunday Times* Northern Ireland editor, Liam Clarke, was also summoned by the police special squad after his newspaper was prevented by an injunction from publishing allegations of further dirty tricks by the army's force research unit – a clandestine cell set up to handle informants in the IRA and Loyalist paramilitary groups (Norton-Taylor 2000).

Even at the European level, sweeping new controls on information were agreed by EU governments in August 2000. Drawn up in secret by Javier Solana, the EU security supremo, the blanket secrecy rules will cover plans to set up a 5,000 strong EU paramilitary police force and a rapid reaction force as well as all EU discussions on criminal justice, border controls and trade policy. Moreover, as Anthony Sampson highlighted, MI5 and MI6 are only part of a much wider intelligence community (2004: 151): 'This includes private companies, often employing ex-MI6 officers, which have their own interests in cultivating mystery and which rapidly expanded in the 1980s and 1990s, benefitting from the global market-place.'

How should journalists respond if their services are sought by the secret services?

According to Ann Rogers (1997: 64):

> Journalists, critics and scholars have focused on the legal–rational processes mandated by the OSA and by doing so have amplified a liberal model of adversarial state–media relations. However, an examination of the record of official secrecy cases involving the press suggests that this focus obscures the extent to which the media have actually supported and colluded with the secret state. The media have been more likely to contribute to, rather than mitigate, secrecy in Britain.

Indeed, David Leigh (2000) records a series of instances in which the secret services manipulated prominent journalists. He says reporters are routinely approached by intelligence agents: 'I think the cause of honest journalism is best served by candour. We all ought to come clean about these approaches and devise some ethics to deal with them. In our vanity, we imagine that we control these sources. But the truth is that they are very deliberately seeking to control us.' Leigh identifies three ways in which the secret intelligence service manipulates journalists:

- They attempt to recruit journalists to spy on other people or to go themselves under journalistic 'cover'.
- Intelligence officers are allowed to pose as journalists 'to write tendentious articles under false names'.
- And 'the most malicious form: – when intelligence agency propaganda stories are planted on willing journalists who disguise their origin from readers'.

John Simpson, BBC world affairs editor (1999: 296–7), describes in his autobiography how he was once approached by a 'man from MI5'. 'At some point they might make me broadcast something favourable to them. Or they might just ask me to carry a message to someone. You never knew,' he said. But Simpson adds: 'It doesn't do journalists any good to play footsie with MI5 or the Secret Intelligence Service; they get a bad reputation.' *Observer* foreign correspondent Mark Frankland talks in his autobiography of his time in SIS in the late 1950s and comments (1999: 92): 'Journalists working abroad were natural candidates for agents and particularly useful in places such as Africa where British intelligence was hurrying to establish itself.' Similarly, many journalists have admitted wanting actually to become spies: Taki, the *Spectator*'s 'High Life' correspondent, has confessed he tried to become a CIA agent after he found out that his father had been one. The BBC *Newsnight* presenter Jeremy Paxman approached an SIS recruiter at university but was turned down (Knightley 2006).

The hard evidence of journalists' links with the secret services is inevitably limited, but it can be striking. Going as far back as 1945, George Orwell no less became a war correspondent for the *Observer* – probably as a cover for intelligence work. Significantly most of the men he met in Paris on his assignment, Freddie Ayer, Malcolm Muggeridge, Ernest Hemingway were either working for the intelligence services or had close links to them (Keeble 2001). Stephen Dorril (2000: 456–7), in his seminal history of MI6, reports that Orwell attended a meeting in Paris of resistance fighters on behalf of David Astor, his editor at the *Observer* and leader of the intelligence service's unit liaising with the French resistance.

Significantly, the spy novelist John le Carré, who worked for MI6 between 1960 and 1964, has stated that the British secret service then controlled large parts of the press – just as they may do today (Dorril 1993: 281). David Leigh (1989: 113), in his seminal study of the way in which the secret service smeared and destabilised the government of Harold Wilson before his sudden resignation in 1976, quotes an MI5 officer: 'We have somebody in every office in Fleet Street.' Investigative reporter Phillip Knightley, author of a seminal study of the secret services, *The Second Oldest Profession* (1987), argues that today not only do they have representatives in all the major publishing houses but also at their printing works. In particular, Knightley has highlighted the activities, immediately after the Second World War, of the Kemsley Imperial and Foreign Service, better known by its cable address, Mercury. It was part of the Kemsley and then the Thomson chain of newspapers, which provided foreign news and features to papers like *The Sunday Times* and the *Empire News*. The head of Mercury was Ian Fleming, celebrated author of the James Bond spy novels. Fleming, who had served in British naval intelligence during the war, controlled as head of Mercury a worldwide network of journalists many of whom had wartime intelligence backgrounds (Knightley 2006).

In 1975, following Senate hearings on the CIA which highlighted the extent of agency recruitment of both American and British journalists, sources revealed that half the foreign staff of a British daily were on the MI6 payroll. Jonathan Bloch and Patrick Fitzgerald (1983: 134–41), in their study of British intelligence and covert action, report the 'editor of one of Britain's most distinguished journals' as believing that more than half its foreign correspondents were on the MI6 payroll. And Roy Greenslade, former editor of the *Mirror*, has commented: 'Most tabloid newspapers – or even newspapers in general – are playthings of MI5. You are recipients of the sting' (Milne 1994: 262). Also, in 1991, Richard Norton-Taylor revealed in the *Guardian* that 500 prominent Britons had been paid by the CIA and now defunct Bank of Commerce and Credit International, including 90 journalists (Pilger 1998: 496). Just before his mysterious death in 1991, *Mirror* proprietor Robert Maxwell was accused by the American investigative journalist Seymour Hersh (1991) of acting for Mossad, the Israeli secret service, though Dorril (2000: 141) suggests his links with MI6 were equally strong.

Following the resignation from the *Guardian* of Richard Gott, its literary editor, in December 1994 in the wake of allegations that he was a 'paid agent' of the KGB, the role of journalists as spies suddenly came under the media spotlight – and many of the leaks were fascinating. For instance, according to *The Times* editorial of 16 December 1994: 'Many British journalists benefited from CIA or MI6 largesse during the Cold War.' The release of Public Record Office documents on 17 August 1995 about some of the operations of the MI6-financed propaganda unit, the Information Research Department of the Foreign Office, threw new light on this secret body which even George Orwell aided by sending them a list of 'crypto-communists' (Saunders 1999: 298–301). Set up by the Labour government in 1948, it 'ran' dozens of Fleet Street journalists until it was closed down by Foreign Secretary David Owen in 1977. According to John Pilger (1998: 495), 'in the anti-colonial struggles in Kenya, Malaya and Cyprus, IRD was so successful that the journalism served up as a record of those episodes was a cocktail of the distorted and false in which the real aims and often atrocious behaviour of the British were suppressed'. Dorril later claimed that, despite IRD's closure, some of its elements 'lingered on'. Some journalists work for foreign secret services. Kim Philby, for instance, worked as foreign correspondent for the *Observer* as a cover for his work as a Soviet spy.

And the most famous whistleblower of all, Peter (Spycatcher) Wright, revealed that MI5 had agents in newspapers and publishing companies whose main role was to warn them of any forthcoming 'embarrassing publications' (1987). Wright also disclosed that the *Daily Mirror* tycoon, Cecil King, 'was a longstanding agent of ours' who 'made it clear he would publish anything MI5 might care to leak in his direction'. Selective details about Prime Minister Harold Wilson and his secretary, Marcia Falkender, were leaked by the intelligence services to sympathetic Fleet Street journalists. Wright comments: 'No wonder Wilson was later to claim that he was the victim of a plot' (ibid.). King was also closely involved in a scheme in 1968 to oust Prime Minister Harold Wilson and replace him with a coalition headed by Lord Mountbatten.

Hugh Cudlipp, editorial director of the *Mirror* from 1952 to 1974, was also closely linked to intelligence, according to Chris Horrie, in his history of the newspaper (2004: 237). David Walker, the *Mirror*'s foreign correspondent in the 1950s, was named as an MI6 agent following a security scandal while another *Mirror* journalist, Stanley Bonnet, admitted working for MI5 in the 1980s investigating the Campaign for Nuclear Disarmament. According to Stephen Dorril (1993), intelligence gathering during the miners' strike of 1984–5 was helped by the fact that during the 1970s MI5's F Branch had made a special effort to recruit industrial correspondents – with great success. *Guardian* journalist Seumas Milne (1994) claimed that three quarters of Fleet Street's industrial correspondents were at that time agents for MI5 or for Scotland Yard's Special Branch.

In December 1998, Labour MP Brian Sedgemore named Dominic Lawson, editor of the *Sunday Telegraph*, in Parliament as an MI6 agent after receiving information from former MI6 officer Richard Tomlinson (Machon 2005: 135). The *Guardian* also reported that Lawson had published articles in *The Spectator* while he was editor by a 'Ken Roberts', who was actually an MI6 officer, and by Alan Judd aka Alan Petty, another MI6 officer. Machon adds (ibid.: 136): 'Although Lawson has denied the claims that he was a paid agent of MI6, we do know that he regularly and uncritically reproduced stories from MI6 sources in the *Sunday Telegraph*.'

Similarly in the reporting of Northern Ireland, there have been longstanding concerns over security service disinformation. Susan McKay, Northern editor of the Dublin-based *Sunday Tribune*, has criticised the reckless reporting of material from 'dodgy security services'. She told a conference in Belfast in January 2003 organised by the NUJ and the Northern Ireland Human Rights Commission: 'We need to be suspicious when people are so ready to provide information and that we are, in fact, not being used' (www.nuj.org.uk/inner.php?docid=635). Phillip Knightley offers clear advice to anyone approached by the intelligence services (2006: 11):

1   It is not ethical for a journalist to work for an intelligence service because you are hiding an important fact about yourself from your readers.
2   It is not safe to get too close to any intelligence service. It may use you to plant disinformation or blackmail you into working for it.
3   It can be physically dangerous to have anything to do with an intelligence service – not only dangerous for you but for your colleagues. Foreign security services argue that if only one British journalist can be shown to have worked for British intelligence, then they are perfectly entitled to assume that all British journalists are spies and react accordingly.

How might journalists respond to these challenges, temptations and threats?

Backing the whistleblowers

Journalists have adopted a variety of strategies for evading these constraints. For instance, after dissident MI5 officer David Shayler alleged MI6 had been involved in an unsuccessful plot to assassinate Colonel Gaddafi, of Libya, the *Guardian* published details, claiming they had entered the public domain through publication in the *New York Times* (see Machon 2005). When Shayler and the *Mail on Sunday* were sued by the government for breaches of confidence and of contract in February 2000, and he sent names to the media of two intelligence officers involved in the Gaddafi plot, newspapers obeyed instructions not to publish. But later when the Labour government threatened to send reporters on the *Observer* and *Guardian* to jail over their contacts with Shayler, 150 fellow journalists signed up to a half-page advertisement in *The Times* on 3 May 2000 protesting at the threat to press freedom.

Then, on 23 July, Lord Justice Igor Judge ruled that the newspapers were right to resist police pressure to hand over documents. Lawyers for the newspapers claimed the police action was clearly in breach of Article 10 of the European Convention on Human Rights (due to become part of British law on 2 October 2000) and of Article 6 which guarantees the rights of suspects not to incriminate themselves. The ruling was said to be 'the most ringing defence of freedom of expression heard in Britain for years' by the *Guardian*. All this did not save David Shayler from jail. In November 2002 he was found guilty of three charges under the Official Secrets Act 1989 and sentenced to six months in prison (though he was released after seven weeks under licence). Shayler's lawyers later argued in the Court of Appeal that his trial had been conducted in breach of his right to a fair hearing under common law and under Article Six of the European Convention on Human Rights (www.hri.org/docs/ECHR50.html). But in July 2003, his appeal was rejected.

The media sometimes campaign against specific constraints. For instance, the *Guardian's* campaign against EU secrecy gained a major success in October 1995 after the European Court in Luxembourg upheld a claim that it was unlawfully denied the minutes of ministers' private debates. Moreover, following the *Guardian's* 'Open Up' campaign for freedom of information, on 15 March 2000 it was reported that the minutes of the Welsh Assembly Cabinet were to be put on the Internet within six weeks of the meeting. In Britain, in contrast, the Home Secretary was insisting that much government information would remain a state secret for 30 years.

Whistleblowers are often used by the media to expose corruption in high places and break through the constraints on coverage. For instance, Cathy Massiter, an MI5 F Branch officer, bravely revealed to Channel 4's *20/20* how surveillance of Campaign for Nuclear Disarmament activists had been stepped up in the early 1980s. Peter Wright, a retired MI5 officer, is the whistle-blower *par excellence*. After he revealed a series of security service dirty tricks in his largely unreadable memoirs, *Spycatcher*, the Thatcher government began a long, drawn-out and ultimately futile attempt to prevent publication. In June 1986, the *Observer* and *Guardian*, which had published some of Wright's allegations ahead of publication, were served with injunctions. Then the short-lived *News on Sunday*, the *Sunday Times* and the *Independent* were each fined £50,000 for having intended to prejudice legal proceedings in the original case through publishing extracts from the book. Eventually these fines were set aside on appeal, as were the injunctions, after the Law Lords ruled that, in view of the world-wide publicity, national security could not be damaged by publication in the UK.

In February 2004, charges were surprisingly dropped against whistle-blower Katherine Gun, a translator at the Cheltenham-based GCHQ (Government Communication Headquarters) who had leaked to the *Observer* details of moves by the US National Security Agency to bug the UN delegations of countries likely to oppose an invasion of Iraq. The government feared its legal case for the Iraqi invasion would be challenged in court – and so abruptly halted the prosecution. Gun (2004) went on to help form the US-based Truth-Telling Coalition to support those engaged in public-spirited whistleblowing (www.truth tellingproject.org).

A Cabinet Office communications officer David Keogh suffered a much harsher fate after he leaked a memo to Leo O'Connor, a researcher for an anti-war Labour MP, which appeared to indicate that President Bush favoured bombing the offices of the progressive Arabic television station, Al-Jazeera. In May 2007, Keogh was jailed for six months after the memo was published in the *Daily Mirror* – while O'Connor was jailed for three months. But the collapse of the case against Foreign Office official Derek Pasquill in January 2008 threw the government's handling of OSA cases into severe disrepute. Pasquill leaked documents to Martin Bright (then an *Observer* investigative reporter) relating to government policies on 'extraordinary rendition' (the seizure and eventual torturing of terrorist suspects by the CIA) and radical Islam (Bright 2007). Yet the government had to admit that the disclosures in no way threatened national security.

After Brazilian Jean Charles de Menezes was shot dead by police who suspected him of being a terrorist in a London tube on 22 July 2005, Independent Police Complaints Commission employee Lana Vandenberghe bravely leaked to ITN the lies told to cover up the tragedy. And in July 2005, whistleblower former police officer Neil Putnam revealed in a BBC programme that John Davidson, a senior detective in the first inquiry into the notorious death of black student Stephen Lawrence in 1993 had a corrupt relationship with Clifford Norris, one of the alleged killers.[6]

By 2008 some whistleblowers in non-politically sensitive areas were often able to make hefty financial gains – thanks to the generosity of newspapers. For instance, Channel 4 office worker Ms X received £20,000 after revealing to the *Mail on Sunday* that the Richard and Judy programme was conning premium-rate callers entering a competition at £1 a time – since the winners had already been selected. The broadcasting regulator, Ofcom, later fined the channel £1.5 million.

Employment law in the UK currently partially protects whistleblowers – many of them assisted by the www.cash4yourstory.co.uk website – from reprisals from their employer. Significantly, the Public Interest Disclosure Act, of July 1998, displayed New Labour's intention to protect whistle-blowers. It covers a wide range of issues from the mistreatment of patients and financial malpractice to miscarriages of justice and dangers to health and safety, but the army, police, intelligence services, volunteers and self-employed are exempted from its clauses.

Leaks by brave whistle-blowers can be used to expose corruption – as Paul Van Buitenen found at the European Commission. They can also be used to discredit opponents. David Leigh (1989) and Stephen Dorril and Robin Ramsay (1991) have shown the extent to which secret service leaks to sympathetic journalists in national newspapers were used systematically to smear Harold Wilson and his close associates during his premiership before he unexpectedly resigned in 1976.

In the United States a unique *qui tam* lawsuit allows employers to bring cases on behalf of the federal government and receive up to 30 per cent of any damages paid out (Hollis 2008). Since 1986, an amazing £11 billion (£5.5 billion) has been awarded in judgments to company whistleblowers. In the UK, some campaigners were urging the government to legislate in favour of cash incentives; others wanted the current legislation to be given greater prominence, claiming the alternative 'uses greed to combat greed'.

In 2008, another international website, www.wikileaks.org, that aims to expose corporate and government fraud, was closed down by a US court after the Julius Baer Bank sought to prevent claims being posted online that it was involved in money laundering and tax evasion in the Cayman Islands. Information on the site exposing money laundering by former President Daniel Arap Moi in Kenya was picked up by the *Guardian* in August 2007 and a confidential note from the troubled UK bank Northern Rock was picked by the *Guardian*, *Financial Times* and BBC (Zetter 2008). Even after the Wikileaks site hosted in the US was closed down, mirror sites were hosted in India and Belgium while the Cryptome website (cryptome.org) provided the controversial Julius Baer documents in a convenient download. The Internet is clearly providing investigative journalists with a vast range of new resources and possibilities to expose fraud and wrong-doing by the powerful. But are mainstream journalists being slow to exploit the Internet's full potential?

Backing freedom of information

Protests by the media (in particular by the trade weekly, *Press Gazette*: www.pressgazette.co.uk) also halted government plans in 2007 to make it harder to use the Freedom of Information Act to extract information from public bodies. Under the Freedom of Information Act 2000, which came into force on 1 January 2005, anyone may request information from more than 100,000 public authorities in England, Wales and Northern Ireland. The Act confers two statutory rights on applicants:

- to be told whether or not the public authority holds the information and if so;
- to have that information communicated to them.

As a result thousands of stories have come to light via the FoI Act – from councillors' junkets and dodgy business dealings to EU farm subsidies and guests visting Chequers (Brooke 2005). Disclosures under FoI in January 2008 revealed the annual salary of novelist Martin Amis as visiting professor of creative writing at Manchester University: a cool £80,000 a year for just 28 hours of work. In April 2008, an FoI request made public the expense claims of politicians such as former Prime Minister Tony Blair, PM Gordon Brown, Opposition leader David Cameron and Shadow Chancellor George Osborne. And how embarrassing the revelations proved! For instance, Blair had claimed £116 for a TV licence, Brown had claimed for a Sky Sports subscriptions while former Labour deputy leader John Prescott had claimed £4,000 for groceries in 2003–4. In Northern Ireland, FoI requests by the *Belfast Telegraph* (along with tips-offs and leaks, official comments, Google searches, blog gossip and further reporting by a range of other media, including the BBC, the *Irish News* and the *News Letter*) forced the resignation of Minister Ian Paisley Jnr over his links to property developer Seymour Sweeney.

Local newspapers' FoI requests have led to reports about cracks at a local nuclear power station, MRSA infections in hospitals and schools' failure to meet health and safety requirements. The *Derby Evening Telegraph* discovered that murderers were on the run from a local prison; the *Welwyn and Hatfield Times* found that convicted sexual offenders were working as licensed taxi drivers; while the *Yorkshire Post* found that North Yorkshire Police had spent £28,400 on a new shower for the Chief Constable. In April 2007, an FoI request by the *Worcester News* revealed that West Mercia police had released 93 people who admitted sexual offences – including eight rapists – without charge over the previous five years. The FoI Act even claimed its first head: David McLetchie, leader of the Scottish Conservative Party, who resigned in November 2005 after details of his improper taxi claims were released under the legislation (see www.foicentre.com). In April 2008, a Freedom of Information request by the satirical magazine, *Private Eye*, revealed officials at the Ministry of Justice, the department responsible for the Act, were trying to cover up details of their own junketing. As the *Eye* reported (No 1208: 18 April to 1 May): 'Junketeer-in-chief is finance director Barbara Moorhouse, entertained on 47 occasions since taking the job in 2005 to the end of 2006. For some reason her generous hosts tended to be the firms to whom she would be writing generous cheques.'

But a survey by the think tank, the Constitution Unit, in April 2007, found that both tabloid and broadsheet newspapers had experienced 'significant disappointment' with the process of getting answers to and appealing against requests. Most journalists said the Act had made little difference to their reporting. (see 'FoI requests leave journos "disappointed"', *Press Gazette*, 24 April 2007). Undeterred, campaigners sought to extend the remit of the Act to bodies strangely omitted from the list of those accountable to the public under FoI. These included Network Rail, City Academies, harbour authorities, regional development agencies, the Association of Chief Police Officers, water companies and the London Organising Committee of the Olympic Games. As freelance journalist Heather Brooke, author of *Your Right to Know*, commented (2008): 'Many of these bodies receive the majority of their funding from taxpayers (either directly or via other public bodies) and perform a public function, yet remain unaccountable under FoI.'

Indeed, the BBC avoided having to release its internal review of Middle East reporting (known as the Balen report) in January 2008 after a ruling by the Court of Appeal. In the same month, the government was accused by human rights groups of a cover-up after it refused a Freedom of Information appeal over its policy on 'extraordinary rendition' (in which terrorist suspects are flown by the CIA and other intelligence services to secret prisons around the world for torture) and the use of British bases to hold suspects without charge (Verkaik 2008). According to the human rights group, Reprieve (www.reprieve.org), the British territory in the Indian Ocean, Diego Garcia, could well have played a major role in the US system of rendition and secret detention. Days later, the government shifted its position and admitted that two US planes carrying 'rendition' suspects landed twice on the island in 2002. But then soon afterwards, Manfred Novak, the United Nations special rapporteur on torture, claimed he had credible evidence suggesting detainees *were* held on Diego Garcia between 2002–4.

Protests have also grown over Labour's local government legislation allowing councils to set up secret cabinet-style meetings. A campaign by the *Evening Chronicle*, Newcastle, forced the city council to back down in April 2000. In November 1999 the *Evening Echo*, covering Southend and Basildon, forced its local authority to back down while the *Uxbridge Gazette* in 1999 ran a hard-hitting campaign against the introduction of cabinet-style government to the London borough of Hillingdon. The *Evening Echo*, covering Southend and Basildon, and the *Nottingham Evening Post* also ran campaigns for open local government. And in 2005, freelance journalist and university lecturer Richard Orange demonstrated the power of the individual to challenge local government secrecy when he successfully challenged Lincolnshire County Council in the High Court to hand over its accounts. Orange found it imposs-ible to access the council's 2003/4 accounts within the 20 working days allowed by law because of the difficulties in accessing information held in more than 100 locations across the county (Ponsford 2005). Orange commented: 'If people don't go and look at their council's finances, there is no way the public can hold local authorities and councillors to account.'

Right to visit prisoners

A campaign by two resourceful journalists over journalists' right to visit prisoners and write about their cases also ended in a notable victory. Bob Woffinden, an investigative journalist, and Karen Voisey, a BBC Wales producer, had earlier refused to sign undertakings not to publish material obtained during visits to two prisoners whose life sentences for murder they were investigating as possible cases of miscarriages of justice. On 20 December 1996, the High Court ruled that a blanket ban by the government a year earlier on journalists interviewing prison inmates was illegal and an unjustified restriction of freedom of speech. The appeal court renewed the ban. But this decision was finally over-ruled by the Law Lords on 8 July 1999.

Campaigning against censorship

The magazine *Index on Censorship* and the campaigning body Article 19 have consistently fought for the rights of writers and journalists worldwide. *Lobster* magazine takes a close, critical watch on the activities of the security services in Britain while *Covert Action Quarterly* does the same in the United States. Both are invaluable resources for journalists. *State Research, Socialist Worker*, monitored and infiltrated by MI5 F7 section, according to Stephen Dorril (1993: 8), and the US *Z Magazine* and the investigative *Mother Jones* are all worth watching. *Project Censored* published each year by Sonoma University highlights major stories censored by the mainstream media in the US.

One of the most notorious examples of government censorship in the UK followed the Thatcher government's introduction of the Broadcasting Ban in 1988 – to deny terrorists 'the oxygen of publicity'. But this was not an isolated incidence of censorship: John Pilger noted that between 1959 and 1989 *forty eight* television programmes on Ireland had been banned, censored or delayed (1989: 517). The ban followed the massive controversy in 1985 which erupted when the BBC scheduled a programme in its *Real Lives* series contrasting the lives of Martin McGuinness, believed to be the commander in chief of the IRA, and Gregory Campbell, of Ian Paisley's Democratic Unionist Party. Though the Home Office called on the BBC governors to ban it, the programme finally went ahead – with images of IRA violence included (McLaughlin and Baker 2005). In a remarkable stand against the government's interference in broadcasting, some 4,000 NUJ members staged a one-day strike (Gopsill and Neale 2007: 264). The ban prohibited the broadcast of voices of the 'terrorists' and their supporters or anyone expressing sympathy or understanding of terrorism. As a result interviews were dubbed by actors or subtitled.

According to broadcast historian Jean Seaton (2003: 30) the ban was a 'terrible humiliation' for the BBC that undoubtedly damaged its authority in the world'. But a number of producers exploited various loopholes in the ban. For instance, in the BBC documentary *Inside the Maze* (1991), Peter Taylor interviewed prisoners as private individuals – and so circumvented the ban. 'However, he did have to dub the voice of any prisoner speaking in an official capacity, including that of the IRA "food spokesperson" as he was filmed discussing with prison officers the size and quality of the prison sausage rolls' (ibid.; see also Miller 1994).

Challenging MoD secrecy

In January 2008, the *Guardian*, BBC and *The Times* successfully challenged a gagging order which aimed to prevent it from reporting allegations of serious abuse of Iraqis by British soldiers. The High Court dismissed attempts by the Ministry of Defence to stop the reporting of allegations about the detention, torture, abuse, mutilation and execution of Iraqi civilians in May 2004. Of the 31 originally held, more than 20 were allegedly returned in body bags (Norton-Taylor 2008b).

Challenging media accreditation plans

In 2007, the government introduced controversial plans to 'accredit' journalists covering family courts. The Department of Constitutional Affairs feared that opening family courts to the press could lead to unnecessary disruptions with members of groups such as Fathers4Justice gaining access by claiming to be writing for their organisation's newsletter. In response, media organisations stressed their opposition to the move as a serious threat to press freedom. They also opposed the idea of introducing a new criminal offence for breaching a reporting restriction since courts already had enough of an armoury through the contempt laws and other legislation (*Media Lawyer* 2007b).

How do you think journalists should respond when the police demand camera footage of riots and demonstrations?

Following the Police and Criminal Evidence Act (PACE) 1984, police investigating a 'serious offence' can obtain an order requiring the journalist to hand over evidence considered useful to the court. This can include unpublished notes and photographs. Very few other countries provide the police with such powers. In France, *juges d'instruction* have powers to search and seize reporters' notebooks and film rushes but they must go in person to examine the material. No interference in the free flow of information is allowed. They must leave copies of material seized so that the broadcast or publication can go ahead. In the US, the First Amendment guarantees freedom of speech. Police and prosecutors can apply for access to notebooks and rushes but the presumption is that press freedom is paramount. Press freedom is enshrined in German law, being protected from state interference ever since *Der Speigel* was raided on the order of Defence Minister Franz-Joseph Strauss (Graef 1993).

In Britain, then, journalists are faced with a difficult dilemma: on the one hand, they may consider their first responsibility is to uphold the law; on the other hand, they may feel their independence is best preserved by rejecting the dictate of the state. The first major controversy emerged just eight months after PACE passed into law. The *Bristol Evening News* refused to hand over film following a drug bust, lost the case and had the police take away 264 pictures and negatives. After violent demonstrations at Rupert Murdoch's News International offices in Wapping, east London, in early 1987, the *Independent*, *Mail on Sunday* and *Observer*, two television companies and four freelance photographers appealed against an order requiring them to hand over pictures. On 23 May 1988, Mr Justice Alliot ruled that the pictures should be surrendered since this would not undermine the freedom and independence of the press. All complied except the four freelance photographers who had earlier taken the unprecedented step of sending their materials, via the NUJ, to the International Federation of Journalists in Brussels. In October 1988, the contempt charges against the freelances were thrown out because they were considered to be no longer owners of the material or to possess it.

Following the poll tax riots of 31 March 1990, the police applied under PACE for access to 'all transmitted, published and/or unpublished cine film, video tape, still photographs and negatives of the demonstration and subsequent disturbances which was obtained with a view to being of a newsworthy interest'. Some national newspapers complied. Again, the NUJ moved fast, sending prints and negatives out of the country. An attempt by the police to force the media to hand over photographs and journalists' notes taken during the riots in the City of London in June 1999 was thrown out by a judge on 2 July 1999. But then in July

2001, BBC Leeds, ITN, Sky and Yorkshire Television were forced to
hand over footage of the June riots in Leeds after police overturned an
earlier court ruling against the seizure. And in September 2005, BBC
Scotland, Scottish television and Sky television all handed over tapes
of G8 summit protestors in Edinburgh on 4 July after police used court
warrants to force the companies to comply. The NUJ in Scotland condemned the move claiming it could expose journalists to attack by militant
anarchists at future events.

With complaints of police harassment growing, the NUJ and the
Association of Chief Police Officers agreed in 2007 a set of guidelines
on media handling. But the union continued to complain of heavy-
handed policing at demonstrations. In particular, the Metropolitan Police
were accused of over-zealous media restrictions at the April 2008 Olympic
torch run in London (Crummy 2008). How do you explain the increasing
intimidation of journalists by the police?

Notes

1   See www.ifex.org/es/content/view/full/86612, accessed 1 May 2008.

2   See www.opsi.gov.uk/acts/acts2000/ukpga_20000011_en_1, accessed 12 April 2008.

3   See The Fictititous Firewall, by David Cromwell. Available at www.coldtype.net/
    Assets.06/Essays.06/1106. Reader9.pdf, accessed 24 May 2007.

4   An excellent, witty, brief overview of the history of British press proprietors and
    their eccentricities appears in Marr, Andrew (2004) pp. 236–45.

5   Intriguingly, Murdoch later admitted his spiking of Patten's memoir was a mistake.
    'It's been a long career and I've made some mistakes along the way. We're not all
    virgins.' (See 'Why does he want to buy the Wall Street Journal?' by Eric Pooley,
    Time, 9 July 2007 pp. 43–8).

6   See http://news.bbc.co.uk/1/hi/uk/5214644.stm, accessed 27 February 2008.

11

And finally: some useful websites

www.ajr.org – site of *American Journalism Review*

www.alternet.org – an excellent, US-based project of the Independent Media Institute

www.arabmediawatch.com – important critiques of UK mainstream media

www.chomsky.info – website of radical US intellectual and political activist Noam Chomsky

www.cjr.org – *Columbia Journalism Review*: bi-monthly publication of Columbia University Graduate School of Journalism

www.communication-ethics.net – site of Institute of Communication Ethics which publishes quarterly *Ethical Space*

www.concernedjournalists.org – site of US-based Committee of Concerned Journalists

www.consortiumnews.com – US-based investigative journalism site

www.cpbf.org.uk – Campaign for Press and Broadcasting Freedom

www.ejo.ch – Lugano-based media monitoring organisation, the European Journalism Observatory

http://empower-sport.com/ – promoting anti-racism in sport, founded by investigative reporter Satish Sekar

www.fair.org – Fairness and Accuracy in Reporting: US-based campaign for higher standards in journalism

www.freemedia.at/cms/ipi/ – International Press Institute

www.glasgowmediagroup.org – site of Glasgow University Media Group

www.holdthefrontpage.co.uk – site covering local newspapers in the UK

www.indexonline.org – site of the campaigning journal Index on Censorship www.indymedia.org – an excellent collective of independent, alternative media organisations

www.ire.org – site of US-based Investigative Reporters and Editors

www.ifex.org – International Freedom of Expression Exchange

www.journalism.org – site of the US-based Project for Excellence in Journalism

www.media-accountability.org – site, founded by Claude-Jean Bertrand, of the Donald W. Reynolds Journalism Institute at the Missouri School of Journalism: contains codes of practice from around the world

www.media-diversity.org – site of Media Diversity Institute: promotes conflict resolution and non-partisan journalism

www.merip.org – excellent site of the US-based Middle East Research and Information Project which also publishes the journal, *Middle East Report*

www.newsombudsmen.org – site of the Organisation of News Ombudsmen, including the *Guardian*, *Le Monde*, *Kansas City Star* and *El Nacional*

www.newspapersoc.org.uk – UK regional newspaper trade association, the Newspaper Society

www.nicar.org – National Institute for Computer Assisted Reporting, backed by the Missouri School of Journalism

www.nuj.org.uk – National Union of Journalists

www.ojr.org – Online Journalism Review of Annenberg School for Communication

www.ourmedianet.org – global network of media activists

www.pcc.org.uk – Press Complaints Commission

www.poynter.org – excellent site of US-based Poynter Institute with massive database of ethics related reports

www.pressgazette.co.uk – *Press Gazette*, weekly trade magazine for UK journalists

www.projectcensored.org – highlighting the news that doesn't make the news plus lots of excellent comment and analysis

www.robert-fisk.com – useful database of articles by award-winning, extraordinary war correspondent of the *Independent*

www.rsf.org – Reporters Without Borders, campaigning for press freedom globally

www.savekidstv.org.uk – campaigning for higher standards in children's television

www.spinwatch.org – radical critique of spin and PR

www.spj.org – American Society of Professional Journalists

www.statewatch.org – monitoring the state and civil liberties in Europe

www.thefword.org.uk – feminist site campaigning against sexist media

www.ukwatch.net – daily review of radical comment and analysis

www.vlv.org – Voice of the Listener and Viewer campaign – concerned to promote higher standards in broadcasting

www.wifp.org – Washington-based Women's Institute for Freedom of the Press

www.womeninjournalism.co.uk – networking and campaigning organisation

Blogs

http://adrianmonck.blogspot.com/ –Adrian Monck, director of journalism at City University, London

http://journalism.nyu.edu/pubzone/weblogs/pressthink/ – American journalism professor and ethicist Jay Rosen

http://kristinelowe.blogs.com/kristine_lowe/ – media commentator Kristine Lowe

http://www.psr.keele.ac.uk/blogindex.htm – useful index of political blogs

http://blogs.guardian.co.uk/greenslade/ – *Guardian* media commentator Roy Greenslade: a must read!

www.tomdispatch.com – the excellent blog of American historian Tom Engelhardt

Bibliography

Abdullah, Rasha A. (2007) *The Internet in the Arab World: Egypt and Beyond*, New York: Peter Lang.

Aitchison, James (1988) *Writing for the Press*, London: Hutchinson.

Aitkenhead, Decca (2007) 'No wonder men treat us as sex objects if we act like this', *Guardian*, 13 September. Available online at www.guardian.co.uk/commentis free/2007/sep/13/comment.pressandpublishing, accessed 1 May 2008.

Akbar, Arifa (2008) 'White on black: the racism in women's glossies', *Independent*, 14 April.

Albert, M. (1997) 'What makes alternative media alternative?', *Z Magazine*, October. Available online at www.zmag.org/whatmakesalti.htm, accessed 1 May 2008.

Aldridge, Meryl (2007) *Understanding the Local Media*, Maidenhead: Open University Press.

Alford, Dawn (2000) 'Would you care if I had a beard?', *Guardian*, 31 May.

Alia, Valerie and Bull, Simone (2005) *Media and Ethnic Minorities*, Edinburgh: Edinburgh University Press.

Alibhai-Brown, Yasmin (2000) 'Goodness gracious me! The BBC is still a white, middle class ghetto', *Independent*, 25 July.

—— (2008) 'Powell's Rivers of Blood are back again', *Independent*, 10 March.

Allan, Stuart (2004) *News Culture*, 2nd edn, Maidenhead: Open University Press.

Allen, Katie (2007) 'Numbers rise for stations that count locally', *Guardian*, 10 September.

Allison, Eric (2007) 'Drugs, bribe offers, staff in fear . . . life at Rye Hill jail', *Guardian*, 16 April.

Alterman, Eric (2008) 'Wall Street to daily papers: "Drop dead"', *The Nation*, 11 February.

Armstrong, Stephen (2008) 'Everyone's a winner', *Guardian*, 3 March.

Atkins, Joseph B. and Nezmah, Bernard (2002) 'Ryszard Kapuscinski: the empathetic existentialist', in Joseph B. Atkins, (ed.), *The Mission: Journalism, Ethics and the World*, Iowa: Iowa State University Press, pp. 217–26.

Atton, Chris (2002) *Alternative Media*, London: Sage.

—— (2003) 'Ethical issues in alternative journalism', *Ethical Space: The International Journal of Communication Ethics*, Vol. 1 No. 1, pp. 26–31.

—— (2004) *An Alternative Internet: Radical Media, Politics and Creativity*, Edinburgh: Edinburgh University Press.

Bagdikian, Ben H. (1992; originally 1983) *The Media Monopoly*, Boston, MA: Beacon Press.

Baistow, Tom (1985) *Fourth-Rate Estate*, London: Comedia.

Baker, Stephen and McLaughlin, Greg (2005) 'News: what is it good for?', available online at www.variant.randomstate.org/22texts/News.html, accessed 2 November 2007.

Bakir, Vian and Barlow, David M. (2007) *Communication in an Age of Suspicion: Trust and the Media*, Basingstoke: Palgrave Macmillan.

Barker, Dennis (2007) 'Friend or faux', *Press Gazette*, 11 May.

Barnett, Steve (2002) 'Will a crisis in journalism provoke a crisis in democracy?', *The Political Quarterly*, Vol. 73, No. 4, pp. 400–8.

—— (2005) 'The way we watched', *Guardian*, 21 March.

Barton, Laura (2008) 'From hero to hate figure: how perceptions of disability can change', *Guardian*, 20 March.

Baudrillard, Jean (2003) *The Spirit of Terrorism*, London/New York: Verso (trans. Chris Turner).

BBC (2004) 'Net blamed for child porn', available online at http://news.bbc. co.uk/1/hi/technology/3387377.stm, accessed 22 February 2008.

—— (2007) *From Seesaw to Wagon Wheel: Safeguarding Impartiality in the 21st Century*, London: BBC Trust.

Beaman, Jim (2000) *Interviewing for Radio*, London: Routledge.

Beaumont, Peter and Sweeney, John (2000) 'The price of telling the awful truth', *Observer*, 28 May.

Bell, Emily and Alden, Chris (eds) (2003) *Media Directory 2004*, London: Guardian Books.

Bell, Martin (1998) 'The journalism of attachment', in Matthew Kieran (ed.), *Media Ethics*, London: Routledge, pp. 15–22.

Bell, Rachel (2008) 'I was seen as an object, not a person', *Guardian*, 19 March.

Belsey, Andrew and Chadwick, Ruth (1992) *Ethical Issues in Journalism and the Media*, London: Routledge.

Bernstein, Carl (1992) 'The idiot culture', *New Republic*, 8 June, pp. 22–8 (also appeared in the *Guardian*, 3 June 1992, under the title 'Idiot culture of the intellectual masses').

Berry, Oliver (2008) 'Sex, sunshine and sangria? You must be joking!', *Guardian*, 1 May.

Bertrand, Claude-Jean (1999) *La Déontologies des Médias*, Paris: PUF.

—— (2000) *Media Ethics and Accountability Systems*, Piccataway, NJ, and London: Transaction.

—— (2001) *Arsenal for Democracy*, Creeskill, NJ: Hampton Books.

Bevins, Anthony (1990) 'The crippling of the scribes', *British Journalism Review*, Vol. 1, No. 2, pp. 13–17.

Black, Ian (2007) 'What about prisoner 345?', *Guardian*, 30 April.

Bloch, Jonathan and Fitzgerald, Patrick (1983) *British Intelligence and Covert Action*, London: Junction Books.

Bonnici, Tony and Dixon, Sarah (2008) 'Another girl hangs herself in death town', *Daily Express*, 6 February.

Boorstin, Daniel (1962) *The Image*, New York: Basic Books.

Boot, William (1991) 'The press stands alone', *Columbia Journalism Review*, March/ April, pp. 23–4.

Borg, Joseph (2008) 'Extracting the privacy issues in reporting party leader's surgery', *Ethical Space: The International Journal of Communication Ethics*, Vol. 5, Nos 1 and 2, pp. 25–9.

Boundy, Charles (2003) 'A tale of two liberties', *Guardian*, 6 January.

Bourdieu, Pierre (1998) *On Television and Journalism*, London: Pluto Press.

Bousfield, Andrew (2008) 'Could Cole win kill "kiss-and-tell"?', *Independent*, 12 May.

Bower, Tom (1993) *Tiny Rowland: Rebel Tycoon*, London: Heinemann.

Bradshaw, Paul (2008) 'Ten changes in 10 years for journalists', *Press Gazette*, 15 February.

Bright, Martin (2007) 'Secrets and sources', *Index on Censorship*, available online at www.indexoncensorship.org/?p=67, accessed 2 January 2008.

Brighton, Paul and Foy, Dennis (2007) *News Values*, London: Sage.

Bremner, Charles (2008) '"Sarko babe" Rachida Dati shakes up chic streets with outsider glamour', *Sunday Times*, 5 March.

Bromley, Michael (1994) *Teach Yourself Journalism*, London: Hodder & Stoughton.

—— (1998) 'The "tabloiding" of Britain: "quality" newspapers in the 1990s', *Sex, Lies and Democracy: The Press and the Public*, in Hugh Stephenson and Michael Bromley (eds), *Sex, Lies and Democracy: The Press and the Public*, Harlow: Addison Wesley Longman, pp. 25–38.

—— (2000) 'The manufacture of news: fast moving consumer goods production or public service?', in David Berry (ed.), *Ethics and Media Culture: Practices and Representations*, Oxford: Focal Press, pp. 111–31.

Bromley, Michael and O'Malley, Tom (1997) *A Journalism Reader*, London: Routledge.

Brooke, Heather (2005) 'FOI: turning the tide of secrecy', *British Journalism Review*, Vol. 16, No. 4, pp. 39–45.

—— (2006) *Your Right to Know: A Citizen's Guide to the Freedom of Information Act*, 2nd edn, London: Pluto Press.

—— (2008) 'Time is running out to vote on future of FoI', *Press Gazette*, 18 January.

Brown, Colin (2008) 'Increase childcare funding to tackle poverty, Brown told', *Independent*, 3 March.

Brown, Gerry (1995) *Exposed! Sensational True Story of Fleet St Reporter*, London: Virgin Books.

Brown, Jonathan (2005) 'Abuse of immigrants at detention centre exposed by TV film', *Independent*, 2 March.

—— (2006) 'Journalists need to leave the Stone Age', *Independent*, 23 January.

Brown, Maggie and Martinson, Jane (2008) 'When can you use "off the record" quotes?', *Guardian*, 17 March.

Browne, Christopher (1996) *The Prying Game: The Sex, Sleaze and Scandals of Fleet Street and the Media Mafia*, London: Robson Books.

Bucks, Simon (2007) 'DA-notice voluntary code under threat from Net', *Press Gazette*, 16 November.

Burgess, Charlie (2003) 'Keeping it local', in Emily Bell and Chris Alden (eds), *Media Directory 2004*, London: Guardian Books, p. 30.

Burgh, Hugo de (ed.) (2000) *Investigative Journalism: Context and Practice*, London: Routledge.

Burke, P. (1988) *Popular Culture in Early Modern Europe*, Hants: Wildwood.

Burrell, Ian (2008a) 'Bear of the *Standard*', *Independent*, 3 March.

—— (2008b) 'Will the good times last at Pearson?', *Independent*, 4 March.

Butterworth, Siobhain (2008a) 'The reader's editor on . . . journalists and online etiquette', *Guardian*, 10 March.

—— (2008b) 'The readers' editor on . . . Russian dolls and tangled webs', *Guardian*, 14 April.

—— (2008c) 'The readers' editor on . . . reporting suicides in south Wales', *Guardian*, 25 February.

Byrne, Ciar (2008) 'Holy Moly! Even a celebrity website has pity on Britney', *Independent*, 13 February.

Cameron, James (2006) *Points of Departure*, London: Granta Books (first published in 1967 by Arthur Barker).

Campbell, Alastair (2008) 'A crisis of credibility', *Guardian*, 29 January.

Campbell, Duncan (2000a) 'I spy an ally', *Guardian*, 15 March.

—— (2000b) 'Led by the nose', *Guardian*, 2 November. Available online at www.guardian.co.uk/politics/2000/nov/02/freedomofinformation.uk, accessed 7 March 2008.

Campbell, Matthew (2008) 'C'est chic: Nicolas Sarkozy's "babes" sashay into town', *Sunday Times*, 23 March.

Campbell, Vincent (2004) *Information Age Journalism: Journalism in an International Context*, London: Arnold.

Carding, Antonia (2007) 'Handling suicide coverage: the importance of the ethical approach', *Ethical Space: The Internal Journal of Communication Ethics*, Vol. 4, No. 3, pp. 22–4.

Carruthers, Susan (2000) *The Media at War*, London: Macmillan.

Carter, Helen (2001) '£500,000 media deal for conjoined twins story', *Guardian*, 15 June.

Carter, Meg (1999) 'Hey, good looking', *Guardian*, 29 November.

Carter, Cynthia and Allan, Stuart (2000) ' "If it bleeds, it leads": ethical questions about popular journalism', in David Berry (ed.), *Ethics and Media Culture: Practices and Representations*, Oxford: Focal Press, pp. 132–53.

Cathcart, Brian (2008) 'An unprecedented focus on the wounded', *New Statesman*, 28 April, p. 21.

Chalaby, Jean (1998) *The Invention of Journalism*, London: Macmillan.

Chambers, Deborah, Steiner, Linda and Fleming, Carole (eds) (2005) *Women and Journalism*, London: Routledge. Available online at http://books.google.co.uk/books?id=olAJxqGZ6VkC&printsec=frontcover&dq=Women+in+Journalism&sig=be3T8eLZZxkq1-tXjOcNGQtjrBo.

Chehab, Zaki (2007) *Inside Hamas: The Untold Story of Militants, Martyrs and Spies*, London: I.B. Tauris.

Chilton, Paul (ed.) (1985) *Language and the Nuclear Arms Debate: Nukespeak Today*, London: Frances Pinter.

Chippendale, Peter and Horrie, Chris (1988) *Disaster*, London: Sphere.

—— (1999) *Stick It Up Your Punter! The Uncut Story of the Sun Newspaper*, London: Simon & Schuster.

Chomsky, Noam (1999) *The New Military Humanism: Lessons from Kosovo*, London: Pluto Press.

—— (2000) *Rogue States: The Rule of Force in World Affairs*, London: Pluto Press.
—— (2004) *Hegemony or Survival: America's Quest for Global Dominance*, London: Penguin Books.

Christmas, Linda (1997) *Chaps of Both Sexes? Women Decision-Makers in Newspapers: Do They Make a Difference?*, Wiltshire: Women in Journalism in association with the BT Forum.

Clark, Andrew (2008) 'Throughout the 90s Yahoo was King of the Net. Then came Google', *Guardian*, 2 February.

Cockerell, Michael, Hennessy, Peter and Walker, David (1984) *Sources Close to the Prime Minister: Inside the Hidden World of the News Manipulators*, London: Macmillan.

Cohen, Jeff (2001) 'The myth of the media's role in Vietnam', available online at www.fair.org/index.php?page=2526, accessed 13 December 2006.

Cohen, Nick (1999) *Cruel Britannia*, London/New York: Verso.
—— (2002) 'Of course it's true. After all, it was MI5 who told us', *Observer*, 21 July.

Cohen, Stanley (2002) *Folk Devils and Moral Panics*, 3rd edn, London/New York: Routledge.

Cohen-Almagor, Raphael (2001) *Speech, Media, and Ethics: The Limits of Free Expression*, Basingstoke: Palgrave.

Cohn, David (2007) 'Time citizen journalism pulled its acts together', *Press Gazette*, 16 November.

Collins, John M. (1991) *America's Small Wars*, Washington, DC: Brassey's.

Combs, James (1993) 'From the Great War to the Gulf War: popular entertainment and the legitimation of warfare', in Robert Denton (ed.), *The Media and the Persian Gulf War*, Westport, CT: Praeger, pp. 257–84.

Cook, David and Allison, Olivia (2007) *Understanding and Addressing Suicide Attacks*, Westport, CT: Praeger.

Cottle, Simon (1993) *TV News, Urban Conflict and the Inner City*, Leicester: Leicester University Press.
—— (1999) 'Ethnic minorities and the British news media: explaining (mis)-representation', in Jane Stokes and Anna Reading (eds), *The Media in Britain: Current Debates and Developments*, Basingstoke: Macmillan, pp. 191–200.

Coward, Ros (1999) 'Women are the new men', *Guardian*, 1 July.

Cox, David (2002) 'The men and women who control broadcasting believe that television is an idiot's lantern', *New Statesman*, 9 December.

Coxall, Bill and Robins, Lynton (1998) *Contemporary British Politics*, 3rd edn, London: Macmillan.

Cross, Simon (2007) 'Why the copycat theory on suicide coverage is a conceptual red herring', *Ethical Space: The International Journal of Communication Ethics*, Vol. 4, No. 4, pp. 19–21.

Crummy, Colin (2006) 'Feminist campaigners stage protest as lads' mags bill reaches Parliament', *Press Gazette*, 23 June.
—— (2008) 'Photographers lobby met after Olympic protest clash', *Press Gazette*, 18 April.
—— and Smith, Patrick (2008) 'News blackout "was justified"', *Press Gazette*, 7 March.

Cummings, Bruce (1992) *War and Television*, London: Verso.

Curran, James (2000) 'Press reformism 1918–98: a study in failure', in Howard Tumber (ed.), *Media Power, Professionals and Policies*, London: Routledge, pp. 35–55.
—— and Seaton, Jean (1991) *Power Without Responsibility: The Press and Broadcasting in Britain*, 4th edn, London: Routledge.
Curtis, Liz (1994) 'Hands off!', *Journalist*, February/March.
Daly, Mark (2003) 'My life as a secret policeman', available online at http://news.bbc.co.uk/1/hi/magazine/3210614.stm, accessed 1 January 2008.
Davies, Caroline (2008) 'Army probes tabloid leak over Harry', *Observer*, 9 March.
Davies, Nick (2008a) *Flat Earth News*, London: Chatto & Windus.
—— (2008b) 'Churnalism has taken the place of what we should be doing: telling the truth', *Press Gazette*, 1 February.
Day, Julia (2005) 'We had 50 images within an hour', *Guardian*, 11 July.
Delano, Anthony and Henningham, John (1995) *The News Breed: British Journalism in the 1990s*, London: London Institute.
Deuze, Mark (2007) *Mediawork*, Cambridge: Polity Press.
Devenport, Mark (2000) *Flash Frames: Twelve Years Reporting Belfast*, Belfast: Blackstaff Press.
Dick, Jill (1998) *Freelance Writing for Newspapers*, 2nd edn, London: A. & C. Black.
Dodd, Vikram (2007) 'Report finds "economic apartheid"', *Guardian*, 30 April.
Donovan, Paul (1999) 'Are we being too reckless with the issue of race?', *Press Gazette*, 15 January.
Donvan, John (2003) 'For the unilaterals, no neutral ground', *Columbia Journalism Review*, May/June. Available online at www.cjr.org/year/03/3/donvan.asp, accessed 12 July 2003.
Dorril, Stephen (1993) *The Silent Conspiracy: Inside the Intelligence Services in the 1990s*, London: Heinemann.
—— (2000) *MI6: Fifty Years of Special Operations*, London: Fourth Estate.
—— and Ramsay, Robin (1991) *Smear! Wilson and the Secret State*, London: Fourth Estate.
Dougary, Ginny (1994) *Executive Tarts and Other Myths*, London: Virago.
Dugan, Emily (2008) 'Defender of abused women finds a new cause: male victims', *Independent*, 17 January.
Dunn, Martin (2007) 'How to survive Rupert Murdoch', *Guardian*, 3 December.
Dunnett, Sinclair (1996) 'Advice to a young journalist', *The Journalists' Handbook*, October, No. 17, pp. 38–9.
Dyer, Clare (2006) 'Landmark ruling could spell end of "kiss and tell"', *Guardian*, 15 December.
Eaton, Lynn (2006) 'Mind your language', *Guardian*, 23 January.
Edwards, David and Cromwell, David (2006) *Guardians of Power: The Myth of the Liberal Media*, London: Pluto Press.
Ellis, Carolyne (1998) 'Out go the suits, in come the skirts', *Guardian*, 24 August.
Engel, Matthew (1996) *Tickle the Public: One Hundred Years of the Popular Press*, London: Victor Gollanz.
Engelhardt, Elaine E. and Barney, Ralph D. (2002) *Media and Ethics: Principles for Moral Decisions*, London: Wadsworth.
Evans, Harold (1999) 'Freedom of information: why Britain must learn from America', *Guardian*, 31 May.

Fisk, Robert (2000) 'War is not primarily about cynicism or defeat . . .', *Press Gazette*, 21 April.
—— (2002) 'Journalists are now the targets – but who is to blame?' *Independent*, 23 February.
Fiske, John (1989) *Understanding Popular Culture*, London: Unwin.
Fixter, Alyson (2005) 'Lancet hits out at its publisher over Docklands arms exhibition', *Press Gazette*, 16 September.
Fletcher, Kim (2006) 'A fine line between journalism and PR', *Guardian*, 31 July.
Foley, Michael (2000) 'Press regulation', *Administration*, Vol. 48, No. 1, pp. 40–51.
—— (2004) 'Absolutism and the confidential controversy', *Ethical Space: The International Journal of Communication Ethics*, Vol. 1, No. 2, pp. 18–19.
Foley, Stephen (2008) 'Is there no limit to the expansion of Rupert Murdoch's media empire', *Independent*, 24 April.
Foot, Paul (1991) 'Strenuous liberty . . . a nervous revival', *British Journalism Review*, Vol. 2, No. 4, pp. 5–8.
—— (1999): 'The slow death of investigative journalism', in Stephen Glover (ed.), *Secrets of the Press: Journalists on Journalism*, London: Allen Lane/Penguin Press, pp. 79–89.
Frankland, Mark (1999) *Child of My Time*, London: Chatto & Windus.
Franklin, Bob (1997) *Newszak and New Media*, London: Arnold.
—— (2004) *Packaging Politics: Political Communications in Britain's Media Democracy*, 2nd edn, London: Arnold.
—— (2005a) 'McJournalism: the local press and the McDonaldization thesis', in Stuart Allan (ed.), *Journalism: Critical Issues*, Maidenhead: Open University Press, pp. 137–50.
—— (2005b) 'Amateurs or adversaries? Local journalists and reporting the UK non-general election in 2005', paper presented to autumn conference of the Association for Journalism Education, 9 September.
—— and Murphy, David (1991) *What News? The Market, Politics and the Local Press*, London: Routledge.
—— and —— (eds) (1998) *Local Journalism in Context*, London: Routledge.
Fraser, Nancy (1993) 'Rethinking the public sphere: a contribution to the critique of actually existing democracy', in Bruce Robins (ed.) *The Phantom Public Sphere*, Minneapolis: University of Minnesota Press, pp. 1–32.
Free Press (2008a) 'NUJ promises support for terror investigator', *Free Press*, March–April, p. 3.
—— (2008b) 'Our work may be harder, but it is still worth doing', *Free Press*, January–February.
Freedman, Des (2003) 'Witnessing whose truth?', available online at www.open democracy.net/debates/artice-8-92-1007.jsp, accessed 5 April 2004.
Frelick, Bill (1992) 'The false promise of operation provide comfort: protecting refugees or protecting state power', *Merip*, May/June, pp. 22–7.
Frith, Maxine (2006) 'BBC accused of "institutionalised homophobia"', *Independent*, 1 March.
Frost, Chris (2000) *Media Ethics and Self-Regulation*, Harlow: Longman Education.
—— (2007) *Journalism Ethics and Regulation*, Harlow: Pearson Education.
Gall, Gregor (1993) 'The employers' offensive in the provincial newspaper industry', *British Journal of Industrial Relations*, Vol. 31, No. 4, pp. 615–24.

—— (2005a) 'Back from the brink or still on the margins? The National Union of Journalists in the provincial newspaper industry in Britain', *Journalism*, Vol. 6, No. 4, pp. 421–41.

—— (2005b) *Journalists' Collective Representation and Editorial Content in British Newspapers: Never the Twain Shall Meet?*, University of Hertfordshire Business School Working Paper Series, 2005, No. 7.

Gallagher, Rachel (2008) 'Secrets of the fake sheik', *Press Gazette*, 9 May.

Galtung, Johan and Ruge, Mari (1965) 'Structuring and selecting news', in Stanley Cohen and Jock Young (eds) (1973), *The Manufacture of News: Deviance, Social Problems and the Mass Media*, London: Constable, pp. 52–63.

Gannett Foundation (1991) *The Media at War: The Press and the Persian Gulf Conflict*, Columbia University, NY: Freedom Forum.

Gatton, Adrian (2000) 'Get your kit off', *Big Issue*, 4–10 September.

Gibson, Owen (2005a) 'No win no fee costs "are a threat to free speech"', *Guardian*, 21 October.

—— (2005b) 'Birt attacks "easy cruelty" of tabloid Britain', *Guardian*, 27 August.

—— (2007a) 'Broadcasters woo "lost generation" in deal with social networking site Bebo', *Guardian*, 14 November.

—— (2007b) '*Daily Mail* editor accuses BBC of indulging in cultural Marxism', *Guardian*, 23 January.

—— (2007c) 'Model's complaint over beach photos upheld', *Guardian*, 8 February.

Glasgow University Media Group (1976) *Bad News*, London: Routledge & Kegan Paul.

—— (1980) *More Bad News*, London: Routledge & Kegan Paul.

—— (1982) *Really Bad News*, London: Writers & Readers.

—— (1985) *War and Peace News*, Milton Keynes/Philadelphia: Open University Press.

—— (1993) in John Eldridge (ed.), *Getting the Message*, London: Routledge.

Glasser, Theodore (1992) 'Objectivity and news bias', in Elliot D. Cohen, *Philosophical Issues in Journalism*, Oxford: Oxford University Press, pp. 176–83.

Glover, Stephen (1999) 'What columnists are good for', in Stephen Glover (ed.), *Secrets of the Press: Journalists on Journalism*, London: Allen Lane/Penguin Press, pp. 289–98.

—— (2007) 'Troubles over? Not in the Irish Republic's newspaper offices', *Independent*, 25 June.

—— (2008) 'Why the Bridgend suicides can't be blamed on the messenger', *Independent*, 25 February.

Goodman, Geoffrey (2008) 'Why ethics matters to journalists', Talk at the School of Journalism, University of Lincoln, 11 February.

Goodwin, Eugene (1994) *Groping for Ethics*, Iowa: Iowa State University Press.

Gopsill, Tim (2008) 'Life on flat Earth', *Free Press*, March–April, pp. 4–5.

—— Tim and Neale, Greg (2007) *Journalists: A Hundred Years of the National Union of Journalists*, London: Profile.

—— Tim and Petley, Julian (2007) 'Express defiant on asylum splash', *Free Press: Journal of the Campaign for Press and Broadcasting Freedom*, January/February.

Gowing, Nik (1991) 'Dictating the global agenda', *Spectrum*, Independent Television Commission, summer.

—— (1994) 'Instant pictures, instant policies?' *Independent on Sunday*, 8 July.

Graef, Roger (1993) 'Can justice be seen to be done?', The Times, 27 October.
—— (1998) 'Friend of the family', Guardian, 6 April.
—— (2000) 'Garbage in, garbage out', New Statesman, 28 August.
Gramsci, Antonio (1971) Prison Notebooks: Selections, London: Lawrence & Wishart.
Green, Chris (2007) 'Riding the tube', Independent, 19 November.
—— (2008) 'The warrior prince and the reporters', Independent, 10 March.
Greenslade, Roy (1992) Maxwell's Fall, London: Simon & Schuster.
—— (2000) 'Reaping the whirlwind', Guardian, 6 March.
—— (2002) 'Sorry Arthur', Guardian, 27 May. Available online at www.guardian.
  co.uk/media/2002/may/27/mondaymediasection.politicsandthemedia, accessed
  1 May 2008.
—— (2003a) 'Lexicon of lies', Guardian, 19 May.
—— (2003b) Press Gang: How Newspapers Make Profit from Propaganda, London:
  Macmillan.
—— (2004) 'Do these people have a right to privacy?', Guardian, 26 January.
—— 2005) Seeking Scapegoats: The Coverage of Asylum in the UK Press, London:
  Institute of Public Policy Research.
—— (2008) 'The digital challenge', Media Guardian, 7 January.
Grevisse, Benoit (1999) 'Chartres et codes de déontologie journalistique: une approche
  internationale comparée', in Claude-Jean Bertrand (ed.), L'Arsenal de la Democratie:
  Media, deontologie et MARS, Paris: Economica, pp. 54–70.
Gripsrud, Jostein (1992) 'The aesthetics and politics of melodrama', in Peter Dahlgren
  and Colin Sparks (eds), Journalism and Popular Culture, London: Sage, pp. 84–95.
Gross, Larry (2003) 'Privacy and spectacle: the reversible panopticon and media-
  saturated society', in Larry Gross, John Stuart Katz and Jay Ruby (eds), Image
  Ethics in the Digital Age, Minneapolis: University of Minnesota Press, pp. 95–113.
Grundy, Bruce (2007) So You Want to be a Journalist, Cambridge/Melbourne:
  Cambridge University Press.
Guha, Krishna (2002) 'CCTV "is not as effective as street lighting in cutting
  crime"', Financial Times, 15 August.
Gun, Katharine (2004) 'The truth must out', Observer, 19 September.
Hall, Phil (2000) 'You couldn't make it up!', The Times, 20 July.
Hall, Stuart (1995) 'The whites of their eyes: racist ideologies and the media', in
  Gail Dines and Jean M. Humez (eds), Gender, Race and Class: A Text Reader,
  Thousand Oaks/London/New Delhi: Sage, pp. 18–22.
—— et al. (1978) Policing the Crisis, London: Macmillan.
Hallin, Daniel (1986) The 'Uncensored' War, Oxford: Oxford University Press.
Hammond, Philip (2000) 'Reporting "humanitarian" warfare: propaganda, moralism
  and Nato's Kosovo war', Journalism Studies, Vol. 1, No. 3, pp. 365–86.
—— (2007) Media, War and Postmodernity, London: Routledge.
—— and Herman, Edward S. (eds) (2000) Degraded Capability: The Media and the
  Kosovo Crisis, London: Pluto Press.
Hanlin, Bruce (1992) 'Owners, editors and journalists', in Andrew Belsey and Ruth
  Chadwick (eds), Ethical Issues in Journalism and the Media, London: Routledge,
  pp. 33–48.
Hanna, Mark and Epworth, Jennifer (1998) 'Media payments to witnesses: the press
  faces the first breach of its post-Calcutt defences', Self Regulation and the Media,
  papers for annual conference of the Association for Journalism Education, London:
  pp. 5–18.

Harcup, Tony (2002a) 'Journalists and ethics: the quest for a collective voice', *Journalism Studies*, Vol. 3, No. 1, pp. 101–14.

—— (2002b) 'Conduct unbecoming?', *Press Gazette*, 1 March.

—— (2004) *Journalism: Principles and Practice*, London, Thousand Oaks, CA, New Delhi: Sage.

—— (2005) 'Citizens in the newsroom: democracy, ethics and journalism', *Ethical Space: The International Journal of Communication Ethics*, Vol. 2, No. 3, pp. 25–31.

—— (2007a) *The Ethical Journalist*, London: Sage.

—— (2007b) 'Journalists could borrow skills from librarians', *Press Gazette*, 16 November.

—— and O'Neill, Diedre (2001) 'What is news? Galtung and Ruge revisited', *Journalism Studies*, Vol. 2, No. 2, pp. 261–80.

Harding, Phil (2008) 'A spiral of mistrust', *Guardian*, 31 January.

Hargreaves, Ian (2003) *Journalism: Truth or Dare?*, Oxford: Oxford University Press.

Harker, Joseph (2008) 'Too much Purley and not enough Peckham', *Guardian*, 3 March.

Harrington, Stephen (2008) 'Popular news in the 21st century: time for a new critical approach?', *Journalism: Theory, Practice and Criticism*, Vol. 9, No. 3, pp. 266–84.

Harris, John (2008) 'The John Harris files', *Guardian*, 5 April.

Harris, Nigel (1992) 'Codes of conduct for journalists', in Andrew Belsey and Ruth Chadwick (eds), *Ethical Issues in Journalism and the Media*, London: Routledge, pp. 62–76.

Harris, Robert (1990) *Good and Faithful Servant*, London: Faber.

Harrison, Bridget (1997) 'Thousands die, but is Diana flying out?', *Independent*, 15 January.

Harrison, Jackie (2006) *News*, London: Routledge.

Hattenstone, Simon (2005) 'Looking for trouble', *Guardian Weekend* magazine, 5 March.

—— (2007) 'Undercover and overexposed?', *Guardian*, 5 December.

Hayward, Anthony (2001) *In the Name of Justice: The Television Reporting of John Pilger*, London: Bloomsbury.

Heffernan, Cathy (2008) 'Being deaf has one big advantage when you're travelling abroad – it breaks down all the barriers', *Guardian*, 24 January.

Heller, Zoë (1999) 'Girl columns', in Stephen Glover (ed.), *Secrets of the Press: Journalists on Journalism*, London: Allen Lane/Penguin Press, pp. 10–17.

Hellinger, Daniel and Judd, Dennis (1991) *The Democratic Façade*, Belmont, CA: Wadsworth.

Hencke, David (2000) 'A little mole told me – honest', *Guardian*, 24 July.

—— (2003) 'The case of the *Sun* editor, sexual harassment and a £5000,000 payoff', *Guardian*, 12 November.

Herman, Edward (1996) 'The propaganda model revisited', *Monthly Review*, July. Available online at http://ics.leeds.ac.uk/papers/vp01.cfm?outfit=pmt&folder=715&paper=1073, accessed 6 April 2008.

—— and Chomsky, Noam (1988) *Manufacturing Consent: The Political Economy of Mass Media*, New York: Pantheon Books (reissued 1994, London: Vintage Books).

Hersh, Seymour (1991) *The Samson Option: Israel, America and the Bomb*, London: Faber & Faber.

Hill, Amelia (2008) 'Working lives "intolerable" for millions in UK', *Observer*, 4 May.

Hill, Annette (2005) *Reality TV: Audience and Popular Factual Television*, London: Routledge.

Hipwood, John (2008) 'When journalists decide to get political', *Press Gazette*, 15 February.

Hobsbawm, Julia (2003) 'Why journalism needs PR', *Guardian*, 17 November.

Hodgson, Jessica (1999) 'CNN get "too close" to US government', *Press Gazette*, 12 November.

Hogan, Dan (1998) 'Sobriety in the last chance saloon', *Self Regulation and the Media*, papers for the annual conference of the Association of Journalism Education, pp. 26–9.

Hogshire, Neil (1997) *Grossed-out Surgeon Vomits inside Patient! An Insider's Look at Supermarket Tabloids*, Venice, CA: Feral House.

Holland, Patricia (1998) 'The politics of the smile: "soft news" and the sexualisation of the press', in Cynthia Carter, Gill Branson and Stuart Allan (eds), *News, Gender and Power*, London: Routledge, pp. 17–32.

Hollingsworth, Mark (1990) *The Press and Political Dissent*, London: Pluto Press.

—— (2000) 'Secrets, lies and David Shayler', *Guardian*, 17 March.

—— and Fielding, Nick (1999) *Defending the Realm: MI5 and the Shayler Affair*, London: Deutsch.

Hollis, Liz (2008) 'Money talks', *Guardian*, 2 February.

Holmwood, Leigh (2007) 'Ethnic minority viewers turn to non-terrestrial TV', *Guardian*, 22 June.

Horrie, Chris (2004) *Tabloid Nation: From the Birth of the Daily Mirror to the Death of the Tabloid*, London: Deutsch.

Hudson, Gary and Rowlands, Sarah (2007) *The Broadcast Journalism Handbook*, London: Pearson Education.

Hudson, Miles and Stanier, John (1997) *War and the Media*, Stroud: Sutton Publishing.

Huntingdon, Samuel P. (1997) *The Clash of Civilisations and the Remaking of World Order*, London: Touchstone Books.

Hyde, Marina (2007) 'The fame generation needs to learn the value of privacy', *Guardian*, 10 November.

Illich, Ivan (1973) 'The professions as a form of imperialism', *New Society*, 13 September.

Index on Censorship (2003) 'Index: United States', Vol. 2.

Institute for War and Peace Reporting (2004) *Reporting for Change: A Handbook for Local Journalists in Crisis Areas*, London/Washington, Johannesburg: IWPR.

Ismael, Tareq Y. and Ismael, Jacqueline S. (2004) *The Iraqi Predicament: People in the Quagmire of Power and Politics*, London: Pluto Press.

Jack, Ian (1999) 'Gandhi's luck to miss the spiteful press', *Independent*, 6 February.

Jaehnig, Walter (1998): 'Kith and sin: press accountability in the USA', in Hugh Stephenson and Michael Bromley (eds), *Sex, Lies and Democracy: The Press and the Public*, Harlow: Addison Wesley Longman, pp. 97–110.

James, Oliver (2000) 'Playing on parents' fears', *Guardian*, 20 July.

Jeffries, Stuart (1997) 'Tune in, turn on, freak out', *Guardian*, 4 January.

Jempson, Mike (2003) 'Bad decision – welcome precedent', *PressWise Bulletin*, No. 89, 14 July.

—— (2004) *MediaWise Bulletin* No. 100, 23 March.

—— (2007) 'The ethics of journalism', *Journalist*, April, pp. 22–3.

Jenkins, Simon (2007) 'These fear factory speeches are utterly self-defeating', *Guardian*, 7 November.

—— (2008a) 'Britain is slithering down the road towards a police state', *Guardian*, 6 February.

—— (2008b) 'No topic is so surrounded by myth as the golden age of the press', *Guardian*, 8 February.

Johnson, Andrew (1997a) 'Taking more care over mental health coverage', *Press Gazette*, 8 August.

—— (1997b) 'The rising tide of shutdown culture', *Press Gazette*, 15 November.

Jones, Nicholas (1996) *Soundbites and Spin Doctors: How Politicians Manipulate the Media – and Vice Versa*, London: Indigo.

—— (2007) 'Islamist extremists "are using media to promote hatred"', *Free Press*, March–April.

—— (2008) 'Media intrusion: sharing the blame', *Free Press*, Journal of the Campaign for Press and Broadcasting Freedom, available online at www.cpbf.org.uk/body. phtml?doctype=news&id=1996, accessed 2 January 2008.

Joseph, Manu (2007) 'The British media rush to make a mark in Indian ink', *Independent*, 3 December.

Journalist (2002) 'PCC snubs an NUJ complaint', *Journalist*, January/February.

—— (2007) 'Old boy network bars black people from media jobs', *Journalist*, April.

Judd, Terri (2008) 'Freed: the students who downloaded extremist material', *Independent*, 14 February.

Julyan, Ann-Marie (2008) 'Be careful where you keep your contact', *Guardian*, 10 March.

Kabani, Rana (1994) *Imperial Fictions: Europe's Myths of the Orient*, London: Pandora.

Karpf, Anne (2000) 'Net stations? We've got thousands of 'em', *Guardian*, 27 May.

Katz, Jon (1997) *Media Rants: Postpolitics in the Digital Nation*, San Francisco, CA: Hardwired.

Keeble, R. (1997) *Secret State, Silent Press: New Militarism, the Gulf and the Modern Image of Warfare*, Luton: John Libbey Media.

—— (1998) 'The politics of sleaze reporting', *Recherches en Communication*, Louvain: Catholic University of Louvain, pp. 71–81.

—— (2000) 'New militarism and the manufacture of warfare', in Philip Hammond and Edward S. Herman (eds), *Degraded Capability: The Media and the Kosovo Crisis*, London: Pluto Press, pp. 59–69.

—— (2001) 'Orwell as war correspondent: a reassessment', *Journalism Studies* Vol. 2, No. 3, pp. 393–406.

—— (2003) 'Spooks are represented on every newspaper', *Press Gazette*, 9 October.

—— (2004a) 'The unknown quantity', *Press Gazette*, 6 August.

—— (2004b) 'Information warfare in an age of hyper-militarism', in Stuart Allan and Barbie Zelizer (eds), *Reporting War*, London: Routledge, pp. 43–58.

—— (2005a) *The Newspapers Handbook*, 4th edn, London: Routledge.

—— (2005b) 'New militarism, massacrespeak and the language of silence', *Ethical Space: The International Journal of Communication Ethics*, Vol. 2, No. 1, pp. 39–45.

—— (2005c) 'Journalism ethics: an Orwellian critique?', in Stuart Allan (ed.), *Journalism: Critical Issues*, Maidenhead: Open University Press, pp. 54–66.

—— (2005d) 'Is virtuous journalism possible? A critical overview of ethical dilemmas', in Richard Keeble (ed.), *Print Journalism: A Critical Introduction*, London: Routledge, pp. 267–78.

—— (ed.) (2006) *Communication Ethics Today*, Leicester, Troubador

—— and Wheeler, Sharon (2007) *The Journalistic Imagination: Literary Journalists from Defoe to Capote and Carter*, London: Routledge.

—— (2007) 'The necessary spectacular "victories": new militarism, the mainstream press and the manufacture of the two Gulf conflicts 1991 and 2003', in Sarah Maltby and Richard Keeble (eds), *Communicating War: Memory, Media and Military*, Bury St Edmunds: Arima, pp. 200–12.

Keegan, John (2005) *The Iraq War: The 21-Day Conflict and its Aftermath*, London: Pimlico.

Keleny, Guy (2006) 'Error and omissions', *Independent*, 7 October.

Kellner, Douglas (1990) *Television and the Crisis of Democracy*, Boulder, CO, San Francisco, CA, and Oxford: Westview Press.

—— (1995) *Media Culture: Cultural Studies, Identity and Politics Between the Modern and the Postmodern*, London: Routledge.

Kerbel, Matthew Robert (1995) *Media Politics in a Cynical Age*, Boulder, CO: Westview.

Kieran, Matthew (1998) 'Objectivity, impartiality and good journalism', in Matthew Kieran (ed.) *Media Ethics*, London: Routledge, pp. 23–36.

—— (2000) 'The regulatory and ethical framework', in Hugo de Burgh (ed.) *Investigative Journalism: Context and Practice*, London: Routledge, pp. 156–76.

Kiley, Robert (1999) 'Easy as falling off a log', *Guardian*, 12 January.

Killick, Mark (1994) *The Sultan of Sleaze: The Story of David Sullivan's Sex and Media Empire*, London: Penguin.

Kiss, Jemima (2008) 'Soaring online user figures offer solace – and challenges', *Guardian*, 25 February.

Klaidman, Stephen and Beauchamp, Tom L. (1987) *The Virtuous Journalist*, Oxford: Oxford University Press.

Knightley, Phillip (1987) *The Second Oldest Profession: The Spy as Patriot, Bureaucrat, Fantasist and Whore*, London: Pan.

—— (1991) 'Here is the patriotically censored news', *Index on Censorship*, London.

—— (1998) *A Hack's Progress*, London: Vintage.

—— (2000) *The First Casualty: The War Correspondent as Hero and Myth Maker from the Crimea to Kosovo*, 2nd edn, London: Prion.

—— (2003) 'Turning the tanks on the reporters', *Observer*, 15 June.

—— (2006) 'Journalists and spies: an unhealthy relationship', *Ethical Space: The International Journal of Communication Ethics*, Vol. 3, Nos 2/3, pp. 7–11.

Kovach, Bill and Rosenstiel, Tom (2003) *The Elements of Journalism*, London: Guardian/Atlantic Books.

Kuhn, Raymond (2007) *Politics and the Media in Britain*, Basingstoke: Palgrave Macmillan.

Kurtz, Howard (1993) *Media Circus: The Trouble with America's Newspapers*, New York: Random House.

Lagan, Sarah (2005) 'Coventry Telegraph to deliver more good news', Press Gazette, 16 September.
—— (2007a) 'Bucking the trend', Press Gazette, 11 May.
—— (2007b) 'Forgotten victims', Press Gazette, 20 July.
Laitila, Tiina (1995) 'Codes of ethics in Europe', in Kaarle Nordenstreng (ed.), Reports on Media Ethics in Europe, Tampere, Finland: University of Tampere, Department of Journalism and Mass Communication, pp. 23–79.
Lamont, Duncan (2004) 'Is libel back in fashion', Guardian, 12 January.
Langdon-Davies, John (2007) Behind the Spanish Barricades, London: Reportage Press (first published in 1936 by Martin Secker & Warburg).
Lashmar, Paul (2000) 'Character assassination by committee', Independent, 6 June.
—— (2008a) 'Source protection – it's "the one immutable rule"', Press Gazette, 8 February.
—— (2008b) 'Minimising evidence and protecting your source', Press Gazette, 15 February.
—— and Oliver, James (1998) Britain's Secret Propaganda War 1948–1977, Stroud: Sutton Publishing.
Laurance, Jeremy (2008) 'Should the media stop reporting the suicides in and around Bridgend?', Independent, 22 February.
Lawrence, Felicity (2007) 'Underpaid, easy to sack: UK's second class workforce', Guardian, 24 September.
Lawson, Mark (2008) 'A formula for morality', Guardian, 5 April.
Leadbetter, Charles (2008a) We-Think, London: Profile.
—— (2008b) 'People power transforms the web in the next online revolution', Observer, 9 March.
Leigh, David (1989) The Wilson Plot: The Intelligence Services and the Discrediting of a Prime Minister, 2nd edn, London: Heinemann.
—— (2000) Britain's security services and journalists – the secret story', British Journalism Review, Vol. 11, No. 2, pp. 21–6. Available online at www.bjr.org.uk/data/2000/no2_leigh.htm. (It also appeared in the Guardian of 12 June 2000 under the title 'Tinker, tailor, soldier, journalist'.)
—— (2008) 'Licence to steal', Guardian, 7 April.
—— and Vulliamy, Ed (1997) Sleaze: The Corruption of Parliament, London: Arnold.
Levenson, Ellie (2008) 'Women, science and representation', Guardian, 25 February.
Lezard, Tim (2007) 'Amnesty launches net campaign', Free Press, November–December.
Liberty and Article 19 (2000) Secrets, Spies and Whistleblowers: Freedom of Expression and National Security in the United Kingdom, London: Liberty and Article 19.
Liebes, Tamar (1998) 'Television's disaster marathons', in Tamar Liebes and James Curran (eds), Media, Ritual and Identity, London: Routledge, pp. 71–84.
Linklater, Magnus (2000) 'A bunfight in Scotland', The Times, 17 March.
Lloyd, John (2004) What the Media Are Doing to Our Politics, London: Constable.
Lodge, David (2000) 'Public property', The Times, 7 July.
Lowe, Kristine (2007) 'Facing up to the privacy risk of using Facebook', Press Gazette, 6 July.
—— (2008) 'Why blog?', Talk at the University of Lincoln School of Journalism, 25 February.
Lynch, Jake (2002) Reporting the World, Taplow: Conflict and Peace Forums.

—— (2003) 'Reporting the world and peace journalism', *Peace News*, December–February 2004, p. 27.

—— and McGoldrick, Annabel (2005) *Peace Journalism*, Stroud: Hawthorn Press.

Lyon, David (2007) *Surveillance Studies: An Overview*, Cambridge: Polity Press.

MacArthur, Brian (2003) 'Changing pace of war', *The Times*, 27 June.

McCue, Andy (2000) 'Is it cos i is black?', *xcity*, City University Journalism Department, pp. 20–1.

Macdonald, Myra (2000) 'Rethinking personalization', in Colin Sparks and John Tulloch (eds), *Tabloid Tales: Global Debates over Media Standards*, Oxford, and Lanham, MD: Rowman & Littlefield, pp. 251–66.

—— (2003) *Exploring Media Discourse*, London: Arnold.

MacDowall, Ian (ed.) (1992) *Reuters Handbook for Journalists*, Oxford: Butterworth-Heinemann.

McGowan, Eve (2000) 'Let's talk about sex baby', *xcity*, City University Journalism Department, pp. 26–7.

Machon, Annie (2005) *Spies, Lies and Whistleblowers*, Lewes: The Book Guild.

MacIntyre, Donal (1999) *MacIntyre: One Man. Four Lives: Undercover*, London: BBC Worldwide.

McKay, Susan (2001) 'Faith, hate and murder', *Guardian*, 17 November.

McLachlan, Shelley and Golding, Peter (2000) 'Tabloidisation in the British press: a quantitative investigation into changes in British newspapers, 1952–1997', in Colin Sparks and John Tulloch (eds), *Tabloid Tales: Global Debates over Media Standards*, Oxford, and Lanham, MD: Rowman & Littlefield, pp. 75–89.

McLaughlin, Greg (2002) *The War Correspondent*, London: Pluto Press.

—— and Baker, Stephen (2005) 'The media, terrorism and Northern Ireland: changing frameworks, changing images', available online at www.ccrj.org/13207/13901.html, accessed 1 May 2008.

McNab, Geoffrey (2007) 'Fears of a clown', *Independent*, 28 August.

McNair, Brian (1996) *News and Journalism in the UK*, 2nd edn, London: Routledge.

—— (1998) *The Sociology of Journalism*, London: Routledge.

—— (2000) *Journalism and Democracy: An Evaluation of the Political Public Sphere*, London: Routledge.

McQuail, Denis (1987) *Mass Communication Theory: An Introduction*, 2nd edn, London/Newbury Park, CA: Sage.

—— (1992) *Media Performance: Mass Communications and the Public Interest*, London: Sage.

McSmith, Andy (2007) 'The search for racial equality', *Independent*, 20 September.

Mair, John (2008) 'The McCanns and the media: a morality tale for our times?', *Ethical Space: The International Journal of Communication Ethics*, Vol. 5, Nos 1 and 2, pp. 30–2.

Malcolm, Janet (2004) *The Journalist and the Murderer*, London: Granta (originally published, London: Bloomsbury, 1991).

Maltby, Sarah and Keeble, Richard (2007) *Communicating War: Memory, Media and Military*, Bury St Edmunds: Arima.

Manzoor, Sarfraz (2008) 'The forgotten people', *Guardian*, 3 March.

Marks, Naomi (2000) 'Money can boost your circulation', *Independent*, 14 March.

Marr, Andrew (1999) 'The lying game', *Observer*, 24 October.

—— (2004) *My Trade: A Short History of British Journalism*, London: Macmillan.

Martin-Clark, Nick (2003) 'When a journalist must tell', British Journalism Review, Vol. 14, No. 2, pp. 35–9.

Martinson, Jane (2000) 'Spider in the web', Guardian, 3 May.

Mayes, Ian (2000) 'My word', Guardian, 1 July.

Mayes, Tessa (ed.) (1998) Disclosure: Media Freedom and the Privacy Debate after Diana, London: London International Research Exchange Media Group.

—— (2000) 'Submerging in "therapy news"', British Journalism Review, Vol. 11, No. 4, pp. 30–6. Available online at www.bjr.org.uk/data/2000/no4_mayes.htm, accessed 22 February 2007.

—— (2001) 'Personal services', Guardian, 6 December.

—— (2002) 'Restraint or revelation: free speech and privacy in a confessional age', London: spiked-online. Available online at www.spiked-online.com/articles/00000006DAC6.htm, accessed 27 March 2004.

—— (2007) 'When children become TV sleuths', Ethical Space: The International Journal of Communication Ethics, Vol. 4, No. 3, pp. 13–14.

—— and Hollingsworth, Mark (2007) 'The case is notable for one thing – he got caught', Guardian, 19 March.

Media Lawyer (2007a) 'BP chief steps down over lie', Media Lawyer, July, p. 1.

—— (2007b) 'Media oppose "accreditation" plan', Media Lawyer, January, p. 17.

Melin-Higgins, Margareta (1997) The Social Construction of Journalist Ideals: Gender in Journalism Education, paper presented at Journalists for the New Century Conference, London College of Printing, 24 April.

Mercer, Derrik (ed.) (1987) The Fog of War, London: Heinemann.

Merrill, John C. (1996; originally published 1977) Existential Journalism, Iowa: Iowa University Press.

Merritt, Davis 'Buzz' (1995) Public Journalism and Public Life, Hillsdale, NJ: Lawrence Erlbaum.

Methven, Nicola (1996) 'Gruesome TV news reports should be cut, says Kate Adie', Press Gazette, 11 October.

Metzler, Ken (1997) Creative Interviewing, Boston, MA: Allyn & Bacon.

Meyer, Philip (1987) Ethical Journalism: A Guide for Students, Practitioners and Consumers, Lanham, MD: University Press of America.

Millar, Stuart, Norton-Taylor, Richard and Black, Ian (2001) 'Worldwide spying network is revealed', Guardian, 26 May.

Miller, David (1993) 'Official sources and "primary definition": the case of Northern Ireland', Media, Culture and Society, Vol. 15, pp. 385–406.

—— (1994) Don't Mention the War: Northern Ireland, Propaganda and the Media, London: Pluto Press.

—— (2003) 'Embedding propaganda', Free Press, special issue, June.

—— (2004) 'The domination effect', Guardian, January 8.

—— (2007) 'The statistical invisibility of Islamist "terrorism"', spinwatch.org, 23 May, available online at www.spinwatch.org/index.php?option=com_content&task=view&id=4236&Itemid=29, accessed 16 December 2007.

—— and Dinan, William (2008) 'The dark history of spin and its threat to genuine news values', Independent, 14 April.

Milmo, Cahil (2003) 'One death a minute: toll of the booming arms trade', Independent, October 10.

—— (2006) 'Disabled campaign seeks end to "daily humiliation"', *Independent*, 30 January.

Milne, Seamus (1995) *The Enemy Within: The Secret War Against the Miners*, London: Pan.

—— (2007) 'This onslaught risks turning into a racist witch-hunt', *Guardian*, 20 September.

—— (2008) 'We need to listen to the man from Special Branch', *Guardian*, 14 February.

Monck, Adrian (2008) 'Why should we trust storytellers', *Guardian*, 28 April.

Moore, Alison (1999) 'Articles of faith', *Press Gazette*, 5 February.

Moore, Charles (1997) 'The right way to tell it', *Guardian*, 14 April.

Morgan, Jean (1999) 'Reporter who refused to death-knock loses job fight', *Press Gazette*, 17 December.

Morgan, Peter (2000) 'Can we stop global capital?', *Socialist Review*, July/August.

Morris, Nigel (2004) 'Shipman coverage blamed for suicide rise', *Independent*, 22 January.

—— (2007) 'Number of attacks on ethnic minorities soar', *Independent*, 30 October.

Morris, Steven (2004) 'Fleet Street editors and media law experts give their verdict', *Guardian*, 7 May.

Mosley, Ivo (2000) *Dumbing Down: Culture, Politics and the Mass Media*, London: Imprint Academic.

Moss, Stephen (2008) 'I wanted to report on where the silence was', *Guardian*, 8 May.

Mosynski, Peter (2000) 'Mumbo gumbo', *Index on Censorship*, No. 5, p. 24.

Murdoch, Rupert (2005) 'Speech by Rupert Murdoch to the American Society of Newspaper Editor', News Corporation, 13 April. Available online at www.news corp.com/news/news_247.html, accessed 2 January 2008.

Naughton, John (2000) 'Your privacy ends here', *Observer*, 4 June.

Neil, Andrew (2008) 'The slide to extinction', *Guardian*, 11 February.

Newman, Jay (1992) 'Some reservations about multiperspectival news', in Elliot D. Cohen (ed.), *Philosophical Issues in Journalism*, Oxford/New York: Oxford University Press, pp. 205–17.

Nordenstreng, Kaarle (ed.) (1997) *Reports on Media Ethics in Europe*, Tampere, Finland: University of Tampere, Department of Journalism and Mass Communication.

Norman, M. E. (1999) 'A shotgun wedding', *Press Gazette*, 12 December.

Norris, Bob (2000) 'Media ethics at the sharp end', in David Berry (ed.), *Ethics and Media Culture: Practices and Representations*, Oxford: Focal Press, pp. 325–38.

Northmore, David (1990) *Freedom of Information Handbook*, London: Bloomsbury.

—— (1994) 'Probe shock: investigative journalism', in Richard Keeble (ed.), *The Newspapers Handbook*, London: Routledge, pp. 319–36.

Norton-Taylor, Richard (1991) 'Pressure behind the scenes', *Index on Censorship*, 4/5, p. 14.

—— (2000) 'Secrets and spies', *Guardian*, 18 May.

—— (2007) 'Amnesty criticises Britain over forced returns of Iraqi refugees', *Guardian*, 25 September.

—— (2008a) 'The other Alan Johnson', *Guardian*, 5 May.

—— (2008b) 'Gag on allegations of army abuse lifted', *Guardian*, 2 February.

Oborne, Peter (1999) *Alastair Campbell: New Labour and the Rise of the Media Class*, London: Aurum Press.

O'Hara, Kieron and Shadbolt, Nigel (2008) *The Spy in the Coffee Machine: The End of Privacy as we Know It*, London: Oneworld.

O'Malley, Tom and Soley, Clive (2000) *Regulating the Press*, London: Pluto Press.

O'Neill, John (1992) 'Journalism in the market place', in Andrew Belsey and Ruth Chadwick (eds), *Ethical Issues in Journalism and the Media*, London: Routledge, pp. 15–32.

O'Neill, Onora (2002) 'The Reith lectures', available online at www.bbc.co.uk/radio4/reith2002/, accessed 14 October 2007.

O'Reilly, Emily (1998) *Veronica Guerin: The Life and Death of a Crime Reporter*, London: Vintage.

Ostrovsky, Simon (2008) 'I went undercover to expose fashion's dark secret . . .', *Press Gazette*, 22 February.

O'Sullivan, Sally (1999) 'Change is good for your figures', *Independent*, 16 February.

Page, Adrian (1998) 'Interpreting codes of conduct', in Hugh Stephenson and Michael Bromley (eds), *Sex, Lies and Democracy: The Press and the Public*, Harlow: Addison Wesley Longman pp. 127–35.

Palast, Greg (2000) 'Corporate criminals', *Socialist Review*, July/August (recorded by Pete Ainsley and Sonia Carroll).

Paterson, Chris (2007) 'International news on the Internet: why more is less', *Ethical Space: The International Journal of Communication Ethics*, Vol. 4, Nos 1 and 2, pp. 57–63.

Paterson, Ronald (1971) *The Nihilistic Egoist: Max Stirner*, Oxford: Oxford University Press.

Pawson, Lara (2007) 'Reporting Africa's unknown wars', in Sarah Maltby and Richard Keeble (eds), *Communicating War: Memory, Media and Military*, Bury St Edmunds: Arima, pp. 42–54.

PCC (2007) *PCC Annual Report 2006*, London: Press Complaints Commission, available online at www.pcc.org.uk/assets/80/Annual_Review2006_mid_res.pdf.

Peak, Steve (1982) 'Britain's military adventures', *Pacifist*, Vol. 20, No. 10.

—— and Fisher, Paul (eds) (2000) *The Media Guide, 2000*, London: Fourth Estate.

Pesic, Milica (2008) 'General tips on reporting diversity', pamphlet available online at Media Diversity Institute, www.media-diversity.org.

Petley, Julian (1999) 'The regulation of media content', in Jane Stokes and Anna Reading (eds), *The Media in Britain: Current Debates and Developments*, Basingstoke: Macmillan, pp. 143–57.

—— (2007) 'Ken's Islam study', *Free Press*, November–December.

Pidd, Helen and Dodd, Vikram (2008) 'From brilliant coup to cock-up. How the story of Fagin's urchins fell apart', *Guardian*, 2 February.

Pierce, Andrew (2000) 'Whispers in the corridors of power', *The Times*, 7 July.

Pilger, John (1989) *Heroes*, London: Pan.

—— (1996) 'The hidden power of the media', *Socialist Review*, September.

—— (1998) *Hidden Agendas*, London: Vintage.

—— (2003) 'War by media', Coldtype, available online at www.coldtype.net/Assets.07/Essays/0307.Pilger.War.pdf, accessed 3 March 2007.

—— (2004) 'American terrorist', *New Statesman*, 12 January. Available online at www.newstatesman.co.uk, accessed 15 May 2004.

—— (2006) *Freedom Next Time*, London: Transworld.

Pilkington, Ed (2007) 'Howls of protest as web gurus attempt to banish bad behaviour from blogosphere', *Guardian*, 10 April.

Pinker, Robert (2006) 'Regulation the local press', in Bob Franklin (ed.), *Local Journalism, Local Media: Making the Local News*, London: Routledge, pp. 115–26.

Platell, Amanda (1999) 'Institutionalised sexism', in Stephen Glover (ed.), *Secrets of the Press: Journalists on Journalism*, London: Allen Lane/Penguin Press, pp. 140–7.

Platt, Steve (1998) 'The barbarous coast', *Independent*, 15 December.

Ponsford, Dominic (2004) 'Express staff call in PCC over anti-gypsy articles', *Press Gazette*, 30 January.

—— (2005) 'A force for good: poll shows positive impact of journalism', *Press Gazette*, 21 January.

—— (2008) 'It could end up with the death of Britney Spears or someone else', *Press Gazette*, 11 February.

—— and Farge, Emma (2005) 'DoH spend £40k rating health hacks', *Press Gazette*, 26 August.

—— and Slattery, Jon (2004) 'European privacy protection grows', *Press Gazette*, 3 December.

Ponting, Clive (1990) *Secrecy in Britain*, Oxford: Basil Blackwell.

Porter, Bernard (1991) 'How difficult is it for today's historians to uncover secret histories?', *History Today*, November, pp. 33–5.

Porter, Henry (2007) 'Our sex lives are our own business', *Observer*, 16 September.

Postman, Neil (1985) *Amusing Ourselves to Death*, London: William Heinemann.

Prades, John (1986) *President's Secret Wars: CIA and Pentagon Covert Operations from World War II through Iranscan*, New York: William Morrow.

Preston, Peter (2001) 'War, what is it good for?', *Observer*, 7 October.

—— (2002) 'Scandal fans read and run', *Observer*, 10 November.

—— (2006) 'More things that we're not allowed to tell you', *Observer*, 17 December.

—— (2008) 'Blame us all for Britney', *Guardian*, 7 January.

Price, Lance (2003) 'Rupert Murdoch: the man who would be kingmaker', *Independent on Sunday*, 16 November.

—— (2005) 'What Blair really thinks: a spin-doctor's diary', *Mail on Sunday*, 18 September.

Prince, Stephen (1993) 'Celluloid heroes and smart bombs: Hollywood at war in the Middle East', in Robert Denton (ed.), *The Media and the Persian Gulf War*, Westport, CT: Praeger, pp. 235–56.

Privacy International (2003) 'Silenced: censorship and control of the Internet', available online at www.privacyinternational.org/article.shtml?cmd[347]=x-347-61390&als[theme]=Silenced%20Report, accessed 22 February 2007.

Randall, David (1996) *The Universal Journalist*, London: Pluto Press.

—— (2005) *The Great Reporters*, London: Pluto Press.

Quinn, Frances (2007) *Law for Journalists*, Harlow: Pearson Education.

Rayner, Gordon and Savill, Richard (2008) 'Suicides spread like a contagion . . . If one death happens in a community, it's as if permission has been granted', *Daily Telegraph*, 23 February.

Reading, Anna (1999) 'Campaigns to change the media', in Jane Stokes and Anna Reading (eds), *The Media in Britain: Current Debates and Developments*, Basingstoke: Macmillan, pp. 170–83.

Reddick, Randy and King, Elliot (1997) *The Online Journalist: Using the Internet and Other Online Resources*, 2nd edn, Fort Worth, TX: Harcourt Brace College Publishers.

Redding, Don (2006) 'New research: 3WE bringing the world to the UK', available online at www.warandmedia.org/commentary/comment/3W_report.htm, accessed 25 January 2008.

Reeves, Ian (2000) 'We have been watching . . .', *Press Gazette*, 2 June.

Richstad, Jim (1999) 'Le droit de communiquer a l'age de l'Internet', in Claude-Jean Bertrand (ed.), *L'Arsenal de la Démocratie: Médias, Deontologie et MARS*, Paris: Economica, pp. 31–41.

Richards, Ian (2005) *Quagmires and Quandaries: Exploring Journalism Ethics*, Sydney: University of New South Wales Press.

Richards, Jonathan (2008) 'CIA enlists Google's help for spy work', *San Francisco Chronicle*, 8 March. Available online at http://rinf.com/alt-news/sicence-technology/cia-enlists-googles-help-for-spy-work/2843/, accessed 6 April 2008.

Risen, James (2006) *State of War: The Secret History of the CIA and the Bush Administration*, London/NewYork: Pocket Books.

Ritzer, George (1993) *The McDonaldisation of Society*, London: Sage.

—— (1998) *The McDonaldisation Thesis*, London: Sage.

Roberts, David (2008) 'We must rout the residual prime evil of our primevil world', *Times Higher Education*, 3 April.

Robertson, Geoffrey (1993) *Freedom, the Individual and the Law*, London: Penguin.

Robins, Kevin and Levidow, Les (1991) 'The eye of the storm', *Screen*, Vol. 32, No. 3, autumn, pp. 324–8.

Robinson, James (2007a) 'Despite the net, Brits drop £10 a month on mags', *Observer*, 16 September.

—— (2007b) 'News Corp shake-up prompts a global chain reaction', *Observer*, 9 December.

Robinson, Piers *et al.* (2006) 'Media wars: news performance and media management during the 2003 Iraq war', available online at www.esrcsocietytoday.ac.uk, accessed 26 January 2007.

Rogers, Ann (1997) *Secrecy and Power in the British State: A History of the Official Secrets Act*, London: Pluto Press.

Rose, David (2007) 'News gathering "needs to be done ethically"', *Press Gazette*, 19 October.

—— (2008) 'Neil: Murdoch too busy with "new toy" to meddle at *Sun*', *Press Gazette*, 1 February.

Rosen, Nick (2007) 'Ten ways to thwart Big Brother', *Observer*, 28 October.

Rowe, David (1999) *Sport, Culture and the Media*, Buckingham: Open University Press.

—— (2005) 'Fourth Estate or fan club? Sports journalism engages the popular', in Stuart Allan (ed.), *Journalism: Critical Issues*, Maidenhead: Open University Press, pp. 125–36.

Rowland, Jacky (2002) 'Grilled by the butcher', *Guardian*, 29 August. Available online at www.guardian.co.uk/media/2002/aug/29/bbc.yugoslavia, accessed 1 May 2008.

Rozenberg, Joshua (2004) *Privacy and the Press*, Oxford: Oxford University Press.

Rusbridger, Alan (2003) 'Reporting the war', in Emily Bell and Chris Alden (eds), *Media Directory 2004*, London: Guardian Books, p. 5.

——— (2007) 'Editors for a digital era', *Press Gazette*, 6 June.

Said, Edward (1981) *Covering Islam: How the Media and Experts Determine How We See the Rest of the World*, London: Routledge.

Sampson, Anthony (2004) *Who Runs This Place? An Anatomy of Britain in the 21st Century*, London: John Murray.

Sanders, Karen (2003) *Ethics & Journalism*, London: Sage.

Saunders, Frances Stonor (1999) *Who Paid the Piper? The CIA and the Cultural Cold War*, London: Granta Books.

Schiller, Dan (1981) *Objectivity in the News*, Philadephia: University of Pennsylvania Press.

Schlesinger, Fay (2008) 'Is my local council allowed to spy on me?' *Guardian*, 12 April.

Schlesinger, Philip (1978) *Putting Reality Together*, London: Methuen.

Schmidt, Jeff (2000) *Disciplined Minds*, Lanham, MD: Rowman & Littlefield.

Schudson, Michael (1978) *Discovering News*, New York: Basic Books.

——— (1992) 'Watergate: A study in mythology', *Columbia Journalism Review*, May/June.

Seaton, Jean (2003) 'Rows and consequences', *British Journalism Review*, Vol. 14, No. 4, pp. 26–31.

Sebba, Anne (1994) *Battling for News: The Rise of the Woman Reporter*, London: Hodder & Stoughton.

Seib, Philip (2004) *Beyond the Front Lines: How the News Media Cover a World Shaped by War*, New York: Palgrave Macmillan.

Sengupta, Kim (2007) 'The most dangerous war in the history of journalism', *Independent*, 19 November.

Shannon, Richard (2001) *A Press Free and Responsible*, London: John Murray.

Shaw, Martin (1991) *Post-Military Society*, Cambridge: Polity Press.

Sheldon, Ed (1999) 'Public Exposure', *Press Gazette*, 5 May.

Shepard, Alicia C. (2007) 'For news media, transparency is a matter of trust', *Chicago Tribune* (with the *Yomiuri Shimbun*), 31 July.

Shirky, Clay (2008) *Here Comes Everybody: The Power of Organizing Without Organizations*, London: Allen Lane.

Siebert, Fred, Peterson, Theodore and Schramm, Wilbur (1963) *Four Theories of the Press*, Urbana: University of Illinois Press.

Silvester, Judith and Huffman, Suzanne (2005) *Reporting from the Front: The Media and the Military*, Oxford: Rowman & Littlefield.

Simpson, John (1991) *From the House of War*, London: Arrow.

——— (1999) *Strange Places, Questionable People*, London: Pan.

——— (2004) *The Wars Against Saddam: Taking the Hard Road to Baghdad*, London: Pan.

Smith, David (2008a) 'Web video surge brings broadband overload', *Observer*, 6 April.

——— (2008b) 'Your 10 o'clock meeting is being held in second life', *Observer*, 4 May.

——— (2008b) 'Internet addiction recognized as an "illness"', *Japan Times*, 5 April.

Smith, Patrick (2007) 'A chequered history of chequebook journalism', *Press Gazette*, 13 April.

―― 2008) 'Aldershot mail in bilingual edition', *Press Gazette*, 18 April.

―― and Gallagher, Rachael (2008) 'Unpaid interns: "It's exploitation"', *Press Gazette*, 18 April.

Smithers, Rebecca (2004) 'Girls' teen glossies avoid age limits', *Guardian*, 29 May.

Snoddy, Raymond (1993) *The Good, the Bad and the Unacceptable*, 2nd edn, London: Faber & Faber.

Spark, David (2000) *Investigative Reporting: A Study in Technique*, Oxford: Focal Press.

Sparks, Colin (1999) 'The press', in Jane Stokes and Anna Reading (eds), *The Media in Britain: Current Debates and Developments*, Basingstoke: Macmillan, pp. 41–60.

―― and Tulloch, John (2000) *Tabloid Tales: Global Debates over Media Standards*, Oxford, and Lanham, MD: Rowman & Littlefield.

Stabe, Martin (2007) 'Lords refuse NHS trust's appeal in Robin Ackroyd source protection case', *Press Gazette*. Available online at www.pressgazette.co.uk/story. asp?storycode=38367, accessed 1 March 2008.

―― Smith, Patrick and McNally, Paul (2007) 'New media, integration and you', *Press Gazette*, 7 December.

Stafford, Robin (2008) 'Bayeux Memorial: some corner of a foreign field', *Independent*, 10 March.

Starr, Sany (2004) '"Communication ethics" and the new censorship', 2 July, available online at www.spiked-online.com/Printable/0000000CA5C4.htm, accessed 14 May 2005.

Stephen, Jaci (1997) 'The trouble with women', *Guardian*, 7 July.

Stephenson, Hugh (1998) 'Tickle the public: consumerism rules', in Hugh Stephenson and Michael Bromley (eds), *Sex, Lies and Democracy: The Press and the Public*, Harlow: Addison Wesley Longman, pp. 13–24.

Stevens, Mary (2001) 'The new doorstep challenge', *Press Gazette*, 16 June.

Steyn, Mark (1998) 'All Venusians now: sentimentality in the media', *Faking It: The Sentimentalisation of Modern Society*, London: Penguin Books, pp. 163–79.

Stone, Elizabeth (1999) 'Using children as sources', *Columbia Journalism Review*, September/October, pp. 32–4.

Sutherland, John (2007) 'War of words', *New Statesman*, 12 November.

Swain, Gill (2000) 'I can't just choose to walk away', *Independent*, 6 June.

Sylvester, Judith and Huffman, Suzanne (2005) *Reporting from the Front: The Media and the Military*, Oxford, New York: Rowman & Littlefield.

Tait, Richard (1999) 'This man is about to be murdered', *Guardian*, 20 December.

Tatchell, Peter (2000) 'It's now OK to be gay but what's next?', *Observer*, 2 July.

Taylor, Ernest (2007) 'Smashing the mould', *Independent*, 10 December.

Taylor, John (1998) *Body Horror: Photojournalism, Catastrophe and War*, Manchester: Manchester University Press.

Taylor, Matthew (2006) 'Web of hate', *Guardian*, 4 October.

Taylor, Philip (2003) 'Journalism under fire', in Simon Cottle (ed.), *News and Public Relations and Power*, London: Sage, pp. 63–79.

Teather, David (2005) 'Prince pledges support for Murdoch', *Guardian*, 7 September.

Thain, Manny (2008) 'Big Brother Britain', *Socialism Today*, No. 116, March, pp. 7–10.

Thomas, Lou (2006) 'Ken says Mail newspapers are broadly racist', *Press Gazette*, 22 June.

Thomas, Richard (2005) 'Individuals value their privacy – institutions do not', *Independent*, 22 November.

Thomas, Rosamund M. (1991) *Espionage and Secrecy: The Official Secrets Acts 1911–1989*, London: Routledge.

Thomson, Alex (1992) *Smokescreen: The Media, Censors and the Gulf*, Tunbridge Wells: Laburnham Books.

—— (1999) 'Truth and Lies', *Guardian*, 12 July. Available online at www.guardian. co.uk/media/1999/jul/12/mondaymediasection.kosovo, accessed 22 April 2008.

—— (2005) 'Time to stop using the word "terrorist"', *Press Gazette*, 9 September.

Thurlow, Richard (1994) *The Secret State: British Internal Security in the Twentieth Century*, Oxford: Blackwell.

Tiffen, Rodney (1989) *News and Power*, London: Unwin Hyman.

Tinic, Serra (2006) '(En)visioning the television: revisiting questions of power in an age of interactive television', in Kevin, D. Haggerty and Richard Ericson (eds), *The New Politics of Surveillance and Visibility*, Toronto: University of Toronto Press.

Tomlin, Julie (2002) 'Liddle defends the right to broadcast extremist views', *Press Gazette*, 18 October.

—— (2008) 'US short on answers', *Press Gazette*, 18 April.

Toynbee, Polly (2007) 'Our press, the worst in the West, demoralises us all', *Guardian*, 13 April.

Tracey, Michael (2000) 'Death of a dream', *New Statesman*, 24 July.

Travis, Alan (1999) 'One in three Britons online, but the Net shows big gaps', *Guardian*, 20 December.

—— (2004) 'Public supports private law for stars in backlash against Beckham story', *Guardian*, 21 April.

Tulloch, John (1998) 'Managing the press in a medium-sized European power', in Hugh Stephenson and Michael Bromley (eds), *Sex, Lies and Democracy: The Press and the Public*, Harlow: Addison Wesley Longman, pp. 63–83.

—— (2008) 'Soldiers and citizens: the press, the military and the breaking of the "military covenant" in the Iraq/Afghan conflicts', Talk at University of Lincoln, 2 April.

Turner, Barry (2007) 'Reporting extremism: why do we still want to shoot the messenger?', *Ethical Space: The International Journal of Communication Ethics*, Vol. 4, No. 3, pp. 11–12.

Tusa, John (2000) 'Miserable small-mindedness', *New Statesman*, 24 July.

Ungoed-Thomas, Jon (2007) 'Police hunt chatroom users over web suicide "goading"', *Sunday Times*, 25 March.

Urban, Mark (1996) *UK Eyes Alpha: The Inside Story of British Intelligence*, London: Faber.

Verkaik, Robert (2008) 'Government blocks access to secret military papers on Diego Garcia', *Independent*, 1 February.

—— and Taylor, Jerome (2007) 'Facebook backlash over sale of personal data', *Independent*, 24 November.

Wachman, Richard (2005) 'Trinity Mirror swoops for net jobs firm', *Observer*, 21 August.

Wade, Alex (2008) 'All the news that's not fit to print', *Guardian*, 10 March 2008.

Walsey, Andrew (2000) 'Peace offerings', *Press Gazette*, 31 March.

Waltz, Mitzi (2005) *Alternative and activist media*, Edinburgh: Edinburgh University Press.

Watts, Jonathan (2008) 'Behind the great firewall', *Guardian*, 9 February.

Watts, Mark (2005) *The Fleet Street Sewer Rat: Exclusive – The Muckraker Who Got Rich Scavenging Celebrities' Binbags*, London: Artnik.

—— (2007) 'Why Britain's newspapers have to return to real journalism', available online at www.foiacentre.com/news-press-data-crime-060817.html, accessed 1 and 16 March 2008.

Weeks, Jeffrey (2007) *The World We Have Won*, London: Routledge.

Wells, Matt (2000) 'BBC "tries to bury" inquiry on equality', *Guardian*, 28 April.

—— (2002) 'BBC enlists raw talent for radio station to woo black audience', *Guardian*, 19 August.

Welsh, Tom (2007) 'Getting to grips with the online legal minefield', *Press Gazette*, 29 June.

Whale, John (1972) *Journalism and Government*, London: Macmillan.

—— (1977) *The Politics of the Media*, London: Fontana.

White, Barry (2007) 'A fresh threat to the BBC', *Free Press*, January/February.

—— (2008) 'New terror bill is threat to journalists', *Free Press*, March–April, p. 8.

White, Dominic (2007) 'Ofcom report suggests digital revolution could spell the end of advertising as we know it', *Daily Telegraph*, 24 August.

White, Peter (1999) 'A blind bit of difference', *Press Gazette*, 5 February.

—— (2000) 'Different . . . but equal', *Press Gazette*, 10 March.

White, Richard and Case, Philip (2008) 'Chelsea's Cole is a love cheat', *Sun*, 25 January.

Wilby, Peter (2007) 'Would Goodman be in such trouble if he'd found a decent story?', *Guardian*, 29 January.

—— (2008a) 'Campbell's media critique is only half the story', *Guardian*, 4 February.

—— (2008b) 'A job for the wealthy and connected', *Guardian*, 7 April.

—— (2008c) 'Where are the female high-flyers?', *Guardian*, 12 May.

—— (2008d) 'Portraits of a killer', *Guardian*, 10 March.

—— (2008e) 'More consideration, less volume', *Guardian*, 25 February.

—— and Conroy, Andy (1994) *The Radio Handbook*, London: Routledge.

Wilkins, Lee and Coleman, Renita (2005) *The Moral Media: How Journalists Reason About Ethics*, Mahwah, NJ: Lawrence Erlbaum Associates.

Williams, Andrew and Franklin, Bob (2007) 'Turning around the tanker: implementing Trinity Mirror's online strategy', available online at www.nuj.org.uk, accessed 27 February 2008.

Williams, Granville (2008) 'Our target is £10,000', *Free Press*, January–February.

Williams, Hywel (2000) 'Politics: showbusiness for ugly people', *Observer*, 28 May.

Williams, Jessica (2007) *50 Facts That Should Change the World*, 2nd edn, Cambridge: Icon Books.

Williams, Kevin (1987) 'Vietnam: the first living room war', in Derrik Mercer (ed.), *The Fog of War*, London: Heinemann, pp. 213–60.

—— (1992) 'Something more important than truth: ethical issues in war reporting', in Andrew Belsey and Ruth Chadwick (eds), *Ethical Issues in Journalism and the Media*, London: Routledge, pp. 154–70.

—— (1998) *Get Me a Murder a Day! A History of Mass Communication in Britain*, London: Routledge.

Williams, Michael (1999) 'Check your facts', *Guardian*, 12 July. Available online at www.guardian.co.uk/media/1999/jul/12/mondaymediasection.kosovo1, accessed 22 April 2008.

Williams, Zoe (2008) 'Be afraid. Be very afraid', *Guardian*, 1 May.

Wilson, John (1996) *Understanding Journalism*, London: Routledge.

Winston, Brian (1998) '8 v 10: the British press and the ECHR', *Self Regulation in the Media*, papers from the Annual Conference of the Association for Journalism Education, pp. 43–7.

—— (2005) *Messages: Free Express, Media and the West from Gutenberg to Google*, London: Routledge.

Wittstock, Melinda (2000) 'How TV crossed the taste barrier', *Observer*, 5 March.

Wolff, Michael (2003) 'I was only asking', *Guardian*, 14 April.

Woods, Richard and Nathan, Adam (2004) 'Virtual murder', *Sunday Times*, 30 May.

Worsthorne, Peregrine (1999) 'Dumbing up', in Stephen Glover (ed.), *Secrets of the Press: Journalists on Journalism*, London: Allen Lane/Penguin Press, pp. 115–24.

Wright, Peter (with Paul Greengrass) (1987) *Spycatcher*, Melbourne: Heinemann.

Yorke, Ivor (1987) *The Techniques of Television News*, 2nd edn, London: Focal Press.

Zadeh, Somaye (2000) 'Double standards for bosses', *Socialist Review*, July/August.

Zetter, Kim (2008) 'Cayman Islands bank gets Wikileaks taken offline in US', available online at http://blog.wired.com/27bstroke6/2008/02/cayman-island-b.html, accessed 24 February 2008.

Zobel, Gibby (2000) 'Rights mess', *Guardian*, 3 May.

Zollmann, Florian (2007) 'Fighting fanatics, killing people: the limits of corporate journalism during the US assault on Fallujah', *Ethical Space: The International Journal of Communication Ethics*, Vol. 4, No. 4, pp. 24–9.

Index

428601

Lightning Source UK Ltd.
Milton Keynes UK
UKOW04f1027061014

239645UK00005B/40/P